A Tolerance for Inequality

CHICAGO STUDIES IN AMERICAN POLITICS

A series edited by Susan Herbst, Lawrence R. Jacobs,
Adam J. Berinsky, and Frances Lee; Benjamin I. Page, editor emeritus

Also in the series:

Additional series titles follow index.

A Tolerance for Inequality

American Public Opinion and Economic Policy

ANDREW J. TAYLOR

The University of Chicago Press
Chicago and London

The University of Chicago Press, Chicago 60637
The University of Chicago Press, Ltd., London
© 2025 by The University of Chicago
Published 2025

34 33 32 31 30 29 28 27 26 25   1 2 3 4 5

ISBN-13: 978-0-226-84363-6 (cloth)
ISBN-13: 978-0-226-84364-3 (paper)
ISBN-13: 978-0-226-84365-0 (ebook)
DOI: https://doi.org/10.7208/chicago/9780226843650.001.0001

Library of Congress Cataloging-in-Publication Data

Names: Taylor, Andrew J., 1966– author.
Title: A tolerance for inequality : American public opinion and economic policy / Andrew J. Taylor.
Other titles: Chicago studies in American politics.
Description: Chicago : The University of Chicago Press, 2025. | Series: Chicago studies in American politics | Includes bibliographical references and index.
Identifiers: LCCN 2025011307 | ISBN 9780226843636 (cloth) | ISBN 9780226843643 (paperback) | ISBN 9780226843650 (ebook)
Subjects: LCSH: Equality—Economic aspects—United States—Public opinion. | Public opinion—United States. | Equality—Economic aspects—United States. | Attitude (Psychology)—Political aspects—United States. | United States— Economic policy—2009—Public opinion.
Classification: LCC HC106.84.T397 2025 | DDC 330.973—dc23/eng/20250423
LC record available at https://lccn.loc.gov/2025011307

Contents

Figures

Tables

Preface and Acknowledgments

American political scientists have become fascinated with the country's comparatively wide and enduring economic inequality. They are puzzled by its existence in a robust mass democracy where responsive government should act like a stabilizer, countering the concentration of wealth and bringing the economy back to more egalitarian times. Their investigations and resultant diagnoses have focused on institutional reform. Since public policy appears to contribute to inequality, a system where the poor are alienated and the rich vote, mobilize, contribute financially to campaigns, and dominate elected office requires rehabilitation. Overhauling campaigns and elections and the operations of the federal government will provide us with the redistribution required to narrow an unfair and destructive wealth gap.

I have thought this reaction was off the mark for some time. Examination of survey and election data and numerous conversations with academics, practitioners, journalists, and friends and acquaintances motivated a more thorough inquiry, and this book was born. It takes the position that economic inequality is not something Americans think or care especially about. They may sometimes feel uncomfortable, but they view it as natural and, even at the elevated levels this country has familiarity with, largely legitimate. They may not condemn policymakers who address it, but those who do should not expect the public's adoration either. If progressives yearn for more equal outcomes, they would be advised to persuade the man and woman in the street to buy into policies such as higher taxes on the well-off and increased transfer payments to the poor and not invest heavily in efforts to transform our political system and government.

Along the way, I have naturally incurred many debts. I recognize them here. An army of NC State students assisted with data collection over the past seven years. They are, in an order determined strictly by the alphabet, Madison Alligood, Cole Beck, Phillip Black, Grey Davis, Sam Hart, Seeby Jarvis-Earle, Michael Kolor, Anna Manning, Jamie McCall, Val Mera, Mary Stuart Sloan, Chris Spencer, Jacob Trubey, and Michael Walton. Academic colleagues Sean Trende, Jeff Essic, and Zack Dean helped me with the visual presentation of data.

A large number of political scientists offered suggestions and read parts of the manuscript, often as discussants for panels I sat on at academic conferences. They are Joe Aistrup, Adam Cayton, Chris Donnelly, Eric Hansen, Tom Holyoke, Justin Kirkland, Ruoxi Li, Irwin Morris, Jason Roberts, Mike Rocca, Jacob Straus, and Ann Whitesell. Conversations with Chris Ellis, Kris Miler, Peter Enns, and Matt Grossmann were particularly helpful. Susan Herbst has been an enthusiastic champion of the book, and I am deeply grateful for her advocacy. Sara Doskow, my acquisitions editor at the University of Chicago Press, was terrific, too. The John William Pope Foundation provided financial support for other projects that permitted me to spend more time on this one.

I deeply appreciate Gary Jacobson, Tracy Sulkin, and Sarah Treul for sending their data directly to me, and Nicholas Carnes (occupation and net worth of members of Congress), Craig Volden and Alan Wiseman (legislative effectiveness scores), Adam Dynes and Gregory Huber (federal government spending), Stephen Pettigrew (primary candidates), Matt Grossmann (IPPSR's Congress data), Chris Tausanovitch and Christopher Warshaw (public opinion at the congressional district level), Martin Gilens (public opinion by income group), Jim Stimson (public mood), Charles Hunt (background of members of Congress), Erika Franklin Fowler, Michael Franz, Travis Ridout (Wesleyan Media Project), Scott Adler and John Wilkerson (Congressional Bills Project), Bryan Jones and his colleagues (Policy Agendas Project), and Colton Heffington, Brandon Beomseob Park, and Laron Williams (most important problem) for making their datasets publicly available to researchers. Stephen Ansolabehere and Brian Schaffner at the Cooperative Election Study and the numerous principal investigators at the American National Election Studies deserve the gratitude of hundreds of political scientists, including me. I appreciate the Pew Research Center and the Roper Center at Cornell University for publishing reams of survey data. Of course, there are a number of anonymous reviewers I should also thank, whomever they are.

My work—and these people's contributions to it—I hope will have some impact. The book, I believe, will influence the debate within social science about the political roots of our economic inequality. That debate will be better for such alternative voices.

1

Political Science and Economic Inequality

As we entered the 2010s, President Barack Obama identified economic inequality—not immigration, gun violence, racial tension, or the wars in Iraq and Afghanistan—as "the defining issue of our time."[1] It appears he was right. A widening gulf between rich and poor was at the center of the two fierce presidential campaigns of the self-described democratic socialist Senator Bernie Sanders. In 2016, it contributed to the rise of Donald Trump, a new kind of Republican who talked of protecting blue-collar jobs and entitlement programs in a way few leaders of his party ever had. Joe Biden, who ultimately defeated both Sanders and Trump in 2020, nevertheless announced that an effort to combat inequality would be a focus of his administration. As testament to his commitment, he delivered three "big bills"—the American Rescue Plan Act, the Bipartisan Infrastructure Act, and the Inflation Reduction Act—designed to meet the nation's biggest challenges, including the alleviation of economic hardships felt by the working and middle classes.

Academics rushed to explain the causes of our era's deep inequality. Economists assert that the polarization of wealth in the "New Gilded Age" is an inevitable consequence of liberal capitalism's application to the era of globalization and the internet. The rewards it now metes out are fantastic, the punishments especially brutal. Sociologists see the erosion of public education, health, and housing as vital to both inequality's determinants and effects. They tag race, ethnicity, and gender as prominent causal factors as well.

Political science naturally sees the roots of economic inequality in politics.[2] Its case is perhaps made most forcefully by Larry Bartels (2008, 2016), whose seminal book *Unequal Democracy: The Political Economy of the New Gilded Age* found its way onto Obama's nightstand. In short, Bartels argues, political inequality leads to economic inequality. Having finagled their way into government, the wealthy make policy to satisfy their own narrow economic interests at the expense of the other classes and broader common good.[3] Bill Clinton's secretary of labor, Robert Reich, calls this governance by the affluent a "corporate oligarchy" (Reich 2020). Hacker and Pierson (2020) describe the current situation as a "tyranny of the wealthy and extreme minority." As Skocpol and Hertel-Fernandez (2016, 695–6) write, a right-wing alliance of the well-off pushes for "government cutbacks, upward-tilted tax reductions, and anti-union measures" in opposition to "what most Americans say they prefer." It steers "American democracy away from the wants and needs of most citizens." Inequality may not be the intended result. But it is the product of a vicious cycle, one in which the rich get richer, maintain their hold on political power, and consign everyone else, against their will and national sentiment, to a stagnant, in real terms even reduced, standard of living.

This political-science model of the causes of inequality has various parts. Their resources grant the wealthy the wherewithal to vote in greater numbers. They are informed and capable of paying the opportunity costs of going to the polls.[4] They donate more money to campaigns.[5] They also participate energetically in interest-group and other political activities, including contacting their elected officials more frequently than do fellow citizens.[6] With their disproportionate influence over politics, economic policy reflects the interests and conservative preferences of America's well-to-do. In a parsimonious but elegant analysis, Gilens and Page (2014) find that a model assuming that economic elites dominate policymaking better explains American reality than do competing models constructed from broad measures of public participation and opinion.[7]

The political science of economic inequality now forms a large and impressive corpus. In their more recent book, Page and Gilens (2017) pull much of the work together into a cohesive argument. They assert that bias—in favor of the interests and preferences of the wealthy and of large corporations—pervades American politics. Economic policy outcomes, entrenched because of gridlock in Washington, are consequently conservative and accentuate inequality. In different work with a similar thesis, Kelly (2019, 3) calls this system a "self-perpetuating plutocracy," and a 2013 Dēmos report concludes that "political and economic inequality are mutually reinforcing."[8] To the extent that poorer Americans get their way, their success is therefore purely coincidental and limited to the few issues on which the public has homogeneous opinions. Our democracy is unfair and, by extension, not really a democracy at all.

This book pushes back against that understanding. It is not a direct refutation of many of this model's components. It is clear, for example, that when it comes to American politics the well-off vote more, participate more, and contribute more in the way of money. It is undeniable that labor unions are feeble and that this weakness must have some effect on the capacity of progressives to influence economic policy. It seems obvious that inequality is, at least to some degree, a function of government action. There are legitimate reasons why we consider much of the political science I refer to above as canonical.

Indeed, my findings often qualify, as opposed to contradict, existing thinking. For example, the policy preferences of poorer Americans can appear distinct, but they are difficult to discern and largely agnostic on important economic matters like redistribution. Politics are increasingly partisan and ideologically polarized, but this polarization has not been much to the benefit of the affluent and their policy interests. It is true that there are few working-class policymakers at the federal level, but less affluent Americans seem to care little, and material change would have marginal effects on government outputs and any concomitant alleviation of inequality.

I offer the book, then, as a corrective—albeit perhaps modest—to the political-science literature on inequality and a defense—albeit perhaps partial—of American democracy. There have been others, which I refer to throughout (Branham et al. 2017; Enns 2015; Grossmann et al. 2021; Soroka and Wlezien 2008; Ura and Ellis 2008, 2012). Mine, however, is an integrated effort at rehabilitation of our system's reputation. I will argue that economic-policy outcomes are more reflective of public opinion, including that of low-income citizens, than is commonly believed. I will report that less affluent Americans are not necessarily apathetic but conflicted. I will demonstrate that their policy preferences are, on many important matters, largely indistinguishable from those of their wealthier compatriots and that, where meaningful differences exist, those differences do not concern issues policymakers care much about. I will show that the federal government is more facilitative of the views of low-income people than we give it credit for. The substantive and descriptive representation of blue-collar and poorer Americans in Congress is more complicated than portrayed. Economic-policy output is reasonably reflective of public input. I believe we essentially have the kind of economy that we, as a nation, say we want.

I do not claim to understand how government action brings about unequal outcomes, although I do not dispute the assumption that conservative policy is more likely to do so than the kinds of policy generally advocated by liberals or progressives. I do not attempt to explain why American inequality accelerated so perceptibly in the 1980s and 1990s—the Gini coefficient often used to measure economic disparities within societies has increased by about 20 percent in the past forty years, from roughly 0.4 to 0.48. I focus on federal policy and the national economy, not on state and local government and politics, where scholars increasingly see unwarranted inequality (Franko and Witko 2018; Grossmann 2019; Grumbach 2022; Grumbach et al. 2022; Hertel-Fernandez 2019; Schaffner et al. 2022; Wager 2024). I hope, however, to convince the reader that the outcomes we experience are neither gross distortions of Americans' views nor actions of rogue or unresponsive policymakers. Political science appears to give American democracy's economic performance a resounding "F." It surely deserves some form of passing grade.

Many analyses of American inequality place institutions at the center. Scholars propound partisan polarization and procedures like the Senate filibuster protect status quo policy, resulting in drift as programs go underfunded and regulatory regimes lag behind economic developments. This state of affairs only enriches the already well-off (Enns et al. 2014; Kelly and Morgan 2022). Elkjaer and Iversen (2023) suggest that the American system does not redistribute because of its counter-majoritarian institutions and racial conservatism. McCarty, Poole, and Rosenthal (2006) claim there exists a "dance" between inequality and ideological polarization in Washington. The two move together, facilitated by electoral procedures and even immigration policy. A large right-of-center think-tank, media, and cyberspace ecosystem enhances the conservative advantage (Martin and Yurukoglu 2017; Schradie 2019). Kelly (2019) argues that wealthy Americans' grip on political power generates conservative economic-policy outcomes that, in turn, create an "inequality trap" from which the country cannot seem to escape. Inequality means lower turnout from the poor and Republican victories. The inevitable result is a feedback loop and continuing, possibly worsening, inequality.

The most extensive institutional model of the twenty-first-century economy is the incipient American Political Economy, or APE. As described by the authors of an edited volume on the subject, APE explains the country's unrivaled inequality as a product of institutional design, political and economic fragmentation, and social division (Hacker et al. 2022a, 2022b). Here, powerful financial groups—such as the Koch organization, a favorite target of progressive ire (Skocpol and Tervo 2020)—exploit a decentralized and counter-majoritarian political system and a history of racial conflict to perpetuate their economic interests. They try to push reluctant public opinion rightward.[9] They purposely block redistribution and the just provision of important public goods. Labor unions, which generally help move policy to the left, not least by providing financing and human capital for the Democrats, are frail, especially in the private sector (Becher and Stegmueller 2021; Engstrom and Huckfeldt 2020, 145–50; Franko and Witko 2023a; Hertel-Fernandez 2022). They, and other movements representing the interests of less affluent

Americans, are unable to resist. APE's remedy is comprehensive institutional reform, including the empowerment of racial minorities and numerical majorities, invigoration of labor unions, and breaking up of corporations.

Institutions are not central to my approach. I focus on public opinion and its reflection in the behavior of policymakers and the decisions they make, both individually and collectively, considerably more than I do subjects such as constitutional design and market structures, two central features of APE's institutionalism. This focus is intentional. If mass attitudes and economic policy align reasonably with each other, then democracy appears to be functioning satisfactorily, regardless of the performance of its component institutions and their tendency to thwart majorities and amplify the influence of certain privileged groups. I suggest that political science, with its focus on the distortive nature of institutions, has constructed an incomplete account of the relationship between politics and policy on one hand and inequality on the other.

That is not to say I ignore institutions. In various places throughout the book, for example, I find that the ideological divergence of the major parties has affected public opinion and economic policymaking, especially since the 1990s. Political leaders and status quo policy shape national debate about the economy. I also show how legislators use congressional procedures to meet the policy goals of those they represent.

For the most part, I steer clear of two other literatures that touch upon politics and economic inequality. The first is what Marxists call "false consciousness." It asserts that the poor vote "values" rather than the economy or, as Obama put it rather inelegantly during his 2008 campaign, "they cling to guns or religion or antipathy to people who aren't like them" (Zeleny 2008). Thomas Frank (2004) made this argument famous in his book *What's the Matter with Kansas?* It is an argument not of expressed preferences but implied interests, something responsive policymakers cannot reasonably be expected to act upon.

The other literature is about race and ethnicity. It asserts that biased institutions, policies, and public sentiment explain much of our inequality. The economic disadvantages that Blacks and Latinos experience are then entrenched in the dynastic transmission of wealth and opportunity. I do examine minorities' policy attitudes in places, but I largely account for their views as contributions to national public opinion. My focus is aggregated policy views and outputs.

The book begins with an analysis of the relationship between mass attitudes and public policy in the postwar era, with particular emphasis on the period since the 1960s. I reveal that, for the most part, Washington has been responsive and attentive to the economic-policy views of Americans. I take several approaches. In chapter 2, there is a broad evaluation of economic policy and public opinion at the aggregate and individual-issue levels. I argue, among other things, that the conservative economic policies of the 1980s were as close to national public opinion as the progressive policies of the 1960s and 1970s. I present evidence revealing that Americans have held consistently conservative positions on government management of the macro-economy and redistributive issues like social welfare, but they have held more liberal attitudes regarding regulatory matters such as the environment and public goods like education and transportation. In chapter 3, I examine certain important individual policies and episodes of economic policymaking since the 1980s—the period of elevated inequality according to most measures. Specific findings include the alignment between popular attitudes and economic policy outcomes during the Reagan, Clinton, and early Obama years, and on issues such as domestic-spending priorities, taxing the rich, and requiring welfare recipients to work for benefits. I also show that Americans may want the minimum wage increased, but it is of little interest to them.

In chapter 4, I proceed to divide the public into groups based on income. Leaning on the work of others, I show that at the aggregate level there is little difference in the opinions of various groups on economic policy across time. I also examine attitudes on fundamental economic concepts and reveal Americans' general ambivalence toward inequality and their support for markets and human agency to govern economic behavior and outcomes. I conclude by directly addressing the question, explored by Gilens (2012), of whether the wealthy tend to "win" and get the economic policies they want. I show, using his data, that this is not the case.

In chapter 5, I investigate the clarity and homogeneity of the economic policy views of individuals and various income cohorts. I look at self-identified ideology and party identification and links to the act of voting and attitudes toward issues. I show repeatedly that lower-income Americans have undeveloped, unclear, and incoherent views. I argue that lower-income citizens do not present themselves as a unified group in the way that those with higher incomes do. To the extent that they have cohesive preferences, they do not convey those preferences to policymakers as strongly.

Chapter 6 explores lower-income Americans' preferences for distributive policy. I examine survey data to demonstrate mass views about policy outcomes and policymaker behavior by income cohort. I also use surveys to understand the reasons why there is a difference in views across people of varying financial means. The results suggest that the less affluent do not view politics as "zero-sum" and have a greater sense of geographic identity—a concept that is less abstract than identities wealthier compatriots often hold. I also examine Congress members' "legislative style," assignment of staff to the district, and committee assignments, and the grants and contracts directed to their constituents. The findings reveal significant differences in legislator behavior driven appreciably by district income.

In the next four chapters, I investigate arguments—now well established—that Congress does not adequately represent the interests and preferences of low-income Americans, either substantively or descriptively. Chapter 7 examines whether House districting and Senate malapportionment disadvantage the working class. Observers often claim that these features of congressional life benefit conservative economic policies because they advantage Republicans, but the geographic distribution of lower-income Americans is beneficial to the advancement of their interests. I also evaluate the effectiveness of the legislators who represent low-income districts and find them to be no less capable than colleagues. Chapter 8 provides further dyadic analysis of congressional representation. Here, I look at whether the relationship between constituent and member ideology attenuates as jurisdictions' residents become poorer. I am also interested in the effect of economic inequality on lawmakers' responsiveness. I find that lower-income blue-collar districts receive substantive representation that is similar to that of their wealthier equivalents. As the proportion of their district's residents from low-income households grows, House members move away from constituent opinion at the same rate as they do for high-income groups. If anything, lower-income groups have more of an effect than do wealthier Americans on the behavior of senators. I also find that inequality results in polarization that is more symmetrical—and less rightward tilting—than much of the literature asserts.

The focus of chapter 9 and chapter 10 is descriptive representation. In chapter 9, I explore the question of whether lower-income, less educated, and blue-collar Americans care to receive representation from legislators more like themselves than are the current collection of wealthy members of Congress. I examine federal legislators and leverage new data on House candidates to both infer and observe directly district and individual-voter choice in elections where one candidate is wealthier than the other. Lower-income Americans—and indeed their wealthier compatriots—display ambivalence on the matter. In chapter 10, I examine legislators' behavior. I am interested in the relationship between member class—defined by net worth, education, and prior occupation—and roll-call voting. I find little evidence that the less affluent among them do more to advance the perceived interests of working-class citizens. I also show that less affluent legislators are a little less effective than are their colleagues. This finding suggests that working-class Americans are perhaps better off with wealthy representatives.

Chapter 11 looks specifically at educated and professional Democrats. We might expect these individuals to compensate for any lack of pressure for progressive economic policies placed on policymakers by lower-income citizens. I show that, for the most part, they do not. Highly educated Democrats are, compared to their Republican equivalents, supportive of spending on social-welfare policies and hostile to tax cuts. They are also to the left of their less educated blue-collar co-partisans, however. What is more, the progressive economic-policy preferences of professionals are limited largely to regulatory and distributive issues. Their views regarding redistribution and issues such as labor rights, the minimum wage, and social welfare tend to be more conservative. This tendency may have shaped the policies sought by Democrats who have been in government since the early 1990s.

In doing all this, I talk a great deal about Americans' financial situation—including that of political candidates and government officeholders. When I do, I use a variety of measures. Income, particularly at the household level, is the most prevalent. But I sometimes use broader indicators of wealth like net worth, which includes measures of assets and liabilities unrelated to income. The two indicators are distinct but often highly correlated, at least in the United States (Pfeffer and Waitkus 2021). In places, I use other indicators of class. These are mainly occupation and education, but I also occasionally look at things such as union membership. I do so as a supplement to the measures of a person's financial situation. In these cases, I make the uncontroversial assumption that people with little formal education who work in blue-collar jobs and join unions generally have lower incomes and little wealth.

I also deploy a wide variety of social science methods and tap a vast reservoir of data. These sources include congressional roll-call votes, indicators of district opinion, gauges of ideology, effectiveness scores, hearings, and member personal financial reports (to name just a few measures of legislative behavior and attitudes). I utilize population patterns from the Census; surveys like the American National Election Studies (ANES), Cooperative Election Studies (CES), and General Social Survey (GSS); polls done by Gallup and many others; and information collected and graciously provided by political-science colleagues across the country. I often use the latest data available. All of the analyses, however, cover much of the period since 1980—a time Bartels (2008) labels "The New Gilded Age."

I think some parts of the argument constitute contributions in themselves, but together they make an important claim that has been lost on what has become the dominant view. Our democracy is not perfect, but it is largely fair—or at least considerably more equitable than critics argue. If you do not like economic inequality and seek policy remedies, altering public opinion will likely be more fruitful—and less commingled with unintended consequences—than overhauling our political institutions.

Public Opinion and Economic Policy

System Responsiveness and Attentiveness

Much of the political-science literature asserts that national economic policy is contrary to the interests of working-class Americans. Comparatively speaking, for example, their government collects little in revenue and is uninterested in redistribution. It regulates to further the interests of business, not workers. The "neoliberal" policies established in the Reagan years and extended in the decades following worsened the financial health of Americans at the bottom of the socioeconomic ladder, at least relative to compatriots (Hacker and Pierson 2016; Harvey 2005). Even when the federal government has acted to initiate social policy—on issues like pensions, health care, and home ownership—outcomes have favored the better-off (Faricy 2015; Howard 2007; Mettler 2011; Morgan and Campbell 2011; Page and Gilens 2017, 36–49).

This critique makes a number of assumptions about the American economy, government action, and the interests and policy preferences of less affluent citizens that I tackle throughout the book. At its core, however, is the belief that, in some fundamental way, American democracy is broken (Achen and Bartels 2016; Grumbach 2022; Page and Gilens 2017). Because lawmakers overlook or consciously oppose the interests of a large socioeconomic group—one that constitutes perhaps even a majority of Americans—important economic policy decisions do not reflect national sentiment. When policy is contrary to the views of the general public, it tends to be conservative and provides the country with lower spending, lower tax rates, and less regulation than it seems to desire. Such policies help the wealthy and contribute to inequality.

The political-science literature analyzes three basic concepts related to the representation of public views in policy (Canes-Wrone 2015; Wlezien 2017).

Responsiveness describes a general sensitivity of policy to mass opinion. Because intermediary institutions like elections, parties, and the media filter inputs, and because legislatures and administrative practices subject responses to veto hurdles and counter-majoritarian procedures, outputs in a representative democracy necessarily approximate rather than replicate the position and movement of mass attitudes. In any given period, moreover, policy and opinion likely start from different points. If the public's views lurch perceptibly to the left or right, however, responsive policy should move away from its current position in that direction, and to a similar extent.

Policy–opinion congruence describes a more precise "matching" of policy outputs to public views at just about the same point in space at just about the same point in time (Canes-Wrone 2015; Erikson et al. 1993; Wlezien 2017). The public should have what it wants, and it should have it now. Congruence therefore holds democratic governance to a higher, arguably unreasonable standard.

The third concept is *attentiveness*. In a representative democracy, policymakers should work on issues that the public feels require scrutiny. Here, the precise direction of policy produced is secondary; an attentive government is one that spends much of its time and effort considering and possibly enacting laws in a policy area about which the public signals it cares.

There are numerous models of responsiveness, congruence, and attentiveness. Some claim the public can form what we might consider "rational" and coherent opinions and, in some logical way, bring information to bear on their core interests and an assessment of the real world (Page and Shapiro 1992). Others are skeptical of Americans' capacity to do this (Achen and Bartels 2016; Althaus 2003; Luskin and Bullock 2011). Much of the work debates whether public opinion drives policy or, alternatively, politics proceed in the reverse (Zaller 1992), but most scholars suggest a bidirectional and mediated relationship. Mass attitudes and government interact continually. Factors such as elections, parties, the media, interest groups, and feelings toward the president further complicate the relationship between public opinion and a particular policy (Atkinson et al. 2021; Bovitz and Carson 2006; Burstein 2014; Canes-Wrone 2006; Erikson et al. 2002; Gilens 2012, 124–92; Lenz 2012; Soroka and Wlezien 2010, 2022; Stimson 2004; Wlezien 1995).

A study of the political roots of economic inequality should examine the extent to which economic policy is responsive and congruent and policymakers attentive, regardless of how public opinion is derived. If government decisions on economic matters are broadly reflective of mass attitudes across time and issues, we have evidence consistent with a procedurally equitable democracy. Such a finding does not engage directly with the argument that the affluent disproportionally shape economic policy outcomes but suggests we should not worry especially about it.[1]

I examine economic policy responsiveness and attentiveness—and to a lesser extent congruence—in this chapter and the next. My approach is to compare public opinion directly with outputs. I am uninterested in economic conditions. The policy of the federal government does not exert full control over them, and besides, there is very little temporal variance in aggregate American public opinion about the goals of economic policy. We always seem to want growth, low unemployment, and manageable inflation.

I am also less interested at this point in intermediaries like the political parties, although I suggest the data show they play important roles. To the extent that the political-science literature on inequality has addressed these institutions, it has cast the Republicans as "the bad guys." Bartels (2016, 33–73) shows that the US economy generally enjoys more growth and higher employment under the left-of-center policies of Democratic administrations. Redistribution increases under them, and tax rates for Americans at the lower end of the socioeconomic ladder decline. The literature argues that the wealthy do well under Republicans and that inequality increases with that party enacting conservative policy out of the White House (Bartels 2016, 69–73; Kelly 2009, 79–117; 2019).

At least in these two chapters, I am agnostic on the derivation of mass attitudes. As noted, the literature makes a strong case that the public does not behave rationally and that elites can manipulate its views (Achen and Bartels 2016; Lenz 2012; Zaller 1992). This stance might be antidemocratic to those with a robust view of democracy. Still, we have no reason to believe it is anything but a fixture of American politics across time, across both Democratic and Republican governments, and across liberal and conservative economic policymaking.

I do assume there exists a perceptible public position on economic issues, however. This position is expressed by a majority or plurality of the population and is understood by policymakers through their interpretation of mass political behavior and attitudes. In this chapter—and others too—I generally deploy polls as the medium. If a majority or plurality support a position and especially if this support is large relative to other positions, the government should be aware—to be attentive—and should move existing policy toward it—to be responsive. A government's policy is congruent when it moves to meet public opinion.

I do not discern precise causal mechanisms, but I sometimes speculate as to whether public views drive policy outputs or the reverse. My goal is to see whether we can make a reasonable case that economic policy outputs reflect American public opinion in the post–World War II period.

Economic Policy Responsiveness in the Aggregate

I start by exploring whether basic indicators of federal economic policy mirror changes in ideological measures of public opinion over a lengthy time series. The approach is general but provides useful insight into the extent of government's responsiveness to Americans' opinions on the economy.

To investigate this question, I employ a widely used measure of "public mood" to approximate Americans' broad ideological views about economic policy. This measure, devised by James Stimson (Ellis and Stimson 2012, 38–46; Erikson et al. 2002; Stimson 1998, 2015), essentially aggregates responses to thousands of national survey questions about policy matters over a long time series since the early 1950s.[2] Higher values indicate greater preference for liberal policy. The scores correlate strongly with other potential measures of basic public opinion (Enns and Kellstedt 2008). Scholars of mass attitudes have repeatedly used Stimson's mood measure as an indicator of the general public's ideological position, including its views about economic issues (Enns and Kellstedt 2008; Enns and Wlezien 2011, 9–15; McKee 2019, 276–80; Owen and Quinn 2014; Ura and Ellis 2012).

The first measure of policy output is David Mayhew's (2005) indicator of "important laws enacted" by Congress since the end of World War II. Mayhew identifies these laws using two "sweeps" through records of legislative production, a "contemporaneous" approach scouring journalistic summaries of a Congress and a "retrospective" approach deploying historical analyses of policy areas. I include "first-sweep" laws because the entire postwar period is subject only to that method.[3] I then identify whether we should consider a law primarily economic. The "economic" category captures three basic types of laws: taxes (including tariffs), redistributive or social welfare (many of these laws are about health care and Social Security), and regulatory policy (including labor relations). I omit bills that have economic implications but are ostensibly about other matters—civil rights, crime, immigration, and reform to the workings of government constitute a large proportion of such bills. I code each piece of economic legislation as conservative, liberal, or neither/both, and I calculate a score for each Congress by subtracting the number of conservative laws from the number of liberal laws (excluding those considered neither or both). Ellis and Stimson's (2012, 42) discussion of federal economic policy and conservative and liberal positions on them guides this part of the analysis. My approach is similar to that of Erikson, MacKuen, and Stimson (2002, 325–80) in their work on the "macro polity."[4]

Figure 2.1 reports the results of the relationship between mood and policy observed by Congress. It is clear that the body of economic legislation produced by the postwar Congresses is progressive—in the majority of Congresses, the net number of liberal laws is positive. This result might be a function of coding, but it also corroborates Mayhew's (2005) story that a huge expansion of government spending and reach into economic affairs characterizes the post–World War II period, at least up until the 1980s.[5] Erikson, MacKuen, and Stimson (2002, 328–36) do not identify a single conservative law in the Mayhew dataset in the 1960s and 1970s.

As for government responsiveness, the public appears to be more conservative than economic policy output in the 1960s and 1970s and to the left of it in the 1950s, 1980s, and 1990s.[6] Generally, however, the two types of indicators—mood and the three measures of Mayhew's legislation (all laws, all laws but with the historical ones double-weighted, and first sweep–only laws)—move in tandem, making appreciable leftward and rightward turns at approximately the same time. The current era, particularly since the financial crisis of 2008, is the most obvious outlier. Here, as the public moved in a conservative direction, policy became more liberal—with the conspicuous exceptions of the Obama 112th Congress, which produced a surprisingly conservative body of work, and the Trump 115th Congress, where mood and policy outputs moved in the reverse. The discrepancies are possibly attributable to mass opinion's thermostatic quality and the public's tendency to push against government action when it feels it is moving too far on a particular course (Atkinson et al. 2021; Grossmann and Wlezien 2024; Soroka and Wlezien 2010, 2022; Wlezien 1995). Erikson, MacKuen, and Stimson (2002, 325–80) and Grossmann and Wlezien (2024) notice this tendency in their analyses of public mood and Mayhew's laws as well.

In sum, this showing is not bad. Correlations between mood and each of the three legislative-output measures reveal the strongest relationship to occur when policy outcomes are lagged by one Congress. This finding is suggestive of a responsiveness model. The correlation coefficients produced when I deploy the data this way are .535 ($p < .05$) for the basic measure of legislative output, .552 ($p < .05$) when the number of historic laws is doubled, and .564 ($p < .01$) when sweep-two laws are excluded.[7] These figures are .216, .232, and .279 respectively when observations are made in the same Congress and –.016, .005, and .023 when we observe mood in the Congress following policy outputs.

Still, given the general historical congruity, the divergent trajectories of public mood and legislative output in recent years—a time of heightened

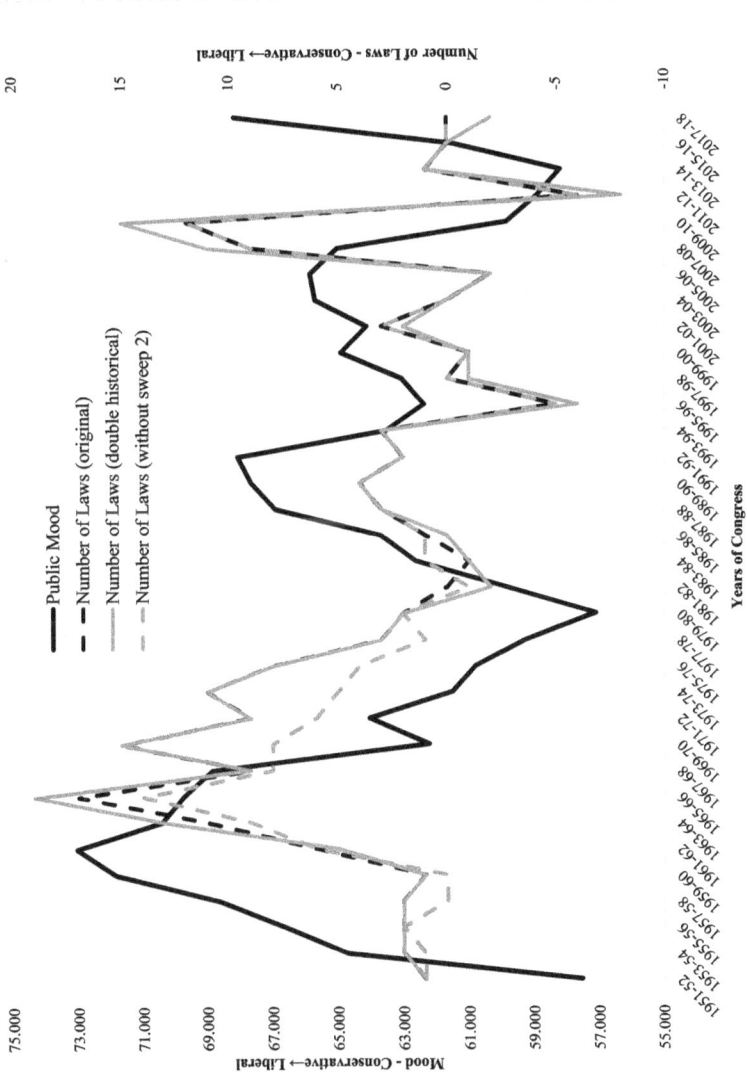

FIGURE 2.1. Public mood and the ideological content of important laws dealing with the economy, 1951–2018

awareness of inequality—are interesting and possibly concerning. Scholars argue that political institutions attenuate the responsiveness of policy to mass opinion, and it is plausible their intermediary effects are unusually significant now. The intensifying polarization of the major American parties in Washington has been well documented (McCarty et al. 2006; Theriault 2008). When the parties switch control of Congress or the presidency under such conditions, the result is a kind of "leapfrogging," with policy outcomes moving dramatically from an extreme conservative position to an extreme liberal position or vice versa (Bafumi and Herron 2010). Others have noted that the Senate filibuster, an obstructionist device increasingly deployed by the body's ideological and partisan minorities, impedes the federal government's capacity to respond to public desire for action and, in turn, facilitates the general drift of economic policy in a conservative direction (Enns et al. 2014; Kelly 2019, 129–42). Perhaps we have entered an era of reduced responsiveness, although as the record since the financial crisis suggests, policy outputs under these conditions can have liberal as well as conservative biases.

Figure 2.2 plots the Stimson public-mood measure against the average first-dimension DW-NOMINATE score of the sponsors of all important bills on economic policy passed into law during each Congress to see whether this generally optimistic assessment of the federal government's responsiveness holds.[8] The output data come from E. Scott Adler and John Wilkerson's "Congressional Bills Project," which identifies the policy area of each bill and whether or not it is considered "important."[9] The figure resembles figure 2.1 but is suggestive of less responsiveness—and indeed the correlation, with or without a lag, does not reach levels of statistical significance. As measured by the average DW-NOMINATE score of bill sponsors, the economic legislation produced from the lengthy period of the late 1960s to the late 1980s remained relatively constant and left-of-center as public mood was quite conservative— although there is a perceptible move downward to meet public mood in the early 1980s. By the mid-1990s, policy had moved sharply rightward, with a magnitude that seems to have exceeded the public's conservatism.

This measure of policy outputs also illustrates the leapfrogging effect discussed above. With House—and increasingly Senate—majorities effectively monopolizing the floor agenda and their members sponsoring most of the bills destined to become law (Cox and McCubbins 2005; Den Hartog and Monroe 2011; Gailmard and Jenkins 2007), changes in party control of the congressional chambers under polarized conditions led to huge tacks in the ideological direction of policy. This finding, in turn, demonstrates that Democratic control of government best serves progressive public moods and Republican control conservative moods, or at least such has been the case since

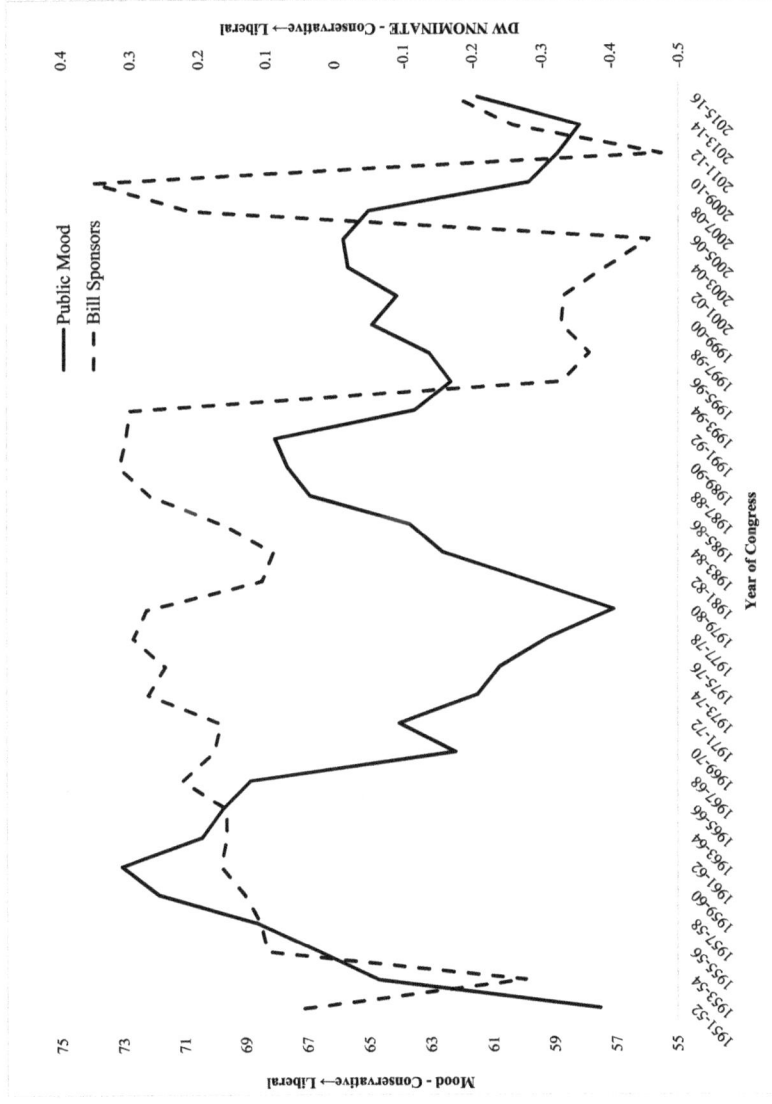

FIGURE 2.2. Public mood and economic policy as measured by average DW-NOMINATE score of bill sponsors, 1951–2016

the 1980s. According to Stimson's measure, from about 1990 to the financial crisis, mass opinion was relatively moderate and stable. It did not therefore always receive the policy response it should have.

There are additional important broad gauges of federal economic policy we can use to assess Washington's responsiveness to public opinion. Figures 2.3, 2.4, and 2.5 reveal examinations of three such measures: the average annual change in non-defense federal discretionary spending, the average annual change in the proportion of pages in the Code of Federal Regulations, and the average annual effective federal tax rate. I observe all indicators by Congress and compare them to the mood data. The first measure captures government expenditures undertaken through the congressional-appropriations process on domestic policy operations. Although it excludes the mandatory and considerable expenditures on programs like Social Security and Medicare, the measure conveys a central feature of federal fiscal policy. The Code of Federal Regulations reveals rules promulgated by the departments and agencies of the federal government and, as such, represents a good measure of the change in regulatory environment for economic actors.[10] The effective rate at which Americans pay taxes, both income and payroll, to the federal government provides a succinct indicator of the tax burden.

The relationships these indicators have with mood are less robust than the one enjoyed by Mayhew's measure. This weakening is particularly the case for the effective tax rate, which correlates negatively with mood—largely because rates and public opinion moved in opposite directions from the early 1960s to mid-1980s. In fact, Atkinson et al. (2021, 28–31) show public opinion on taxes to be especially thermostatic. Spending and regulation map fairly well, however. Of all the decades in the time series, the 1970s is probably where policy is most unresponsive; the mood was increasingly conservative, but spending, tax, and regulatory policy were progressive and becoming more so. The opposite is true of the early 1980s, when President Ronald Reagan and his congressional allies cut taxes, regulations, and domestic expenditures in the wake of growing public liberalism. Perhaps the conservative or "neoliberal" policies of the period play an important role in the inequality bemoaned by much of the political-science literature. But, with the possible exception of regulations, I think the figures show that government in the 1980s was less out of touch with public opinion than it had been in the decade before. The lines tend to be closer together in the 1980s. Indeed, the same could be said when comparing the 1970s and 1980s in figure 2.1 and figure 2.2.

From roughly the mid-1980s to the middle of the first decade of the 2000s, both policy and mood are relatively stable and, with the exception of regulations, at historically moderate levels for the time series. They were stable

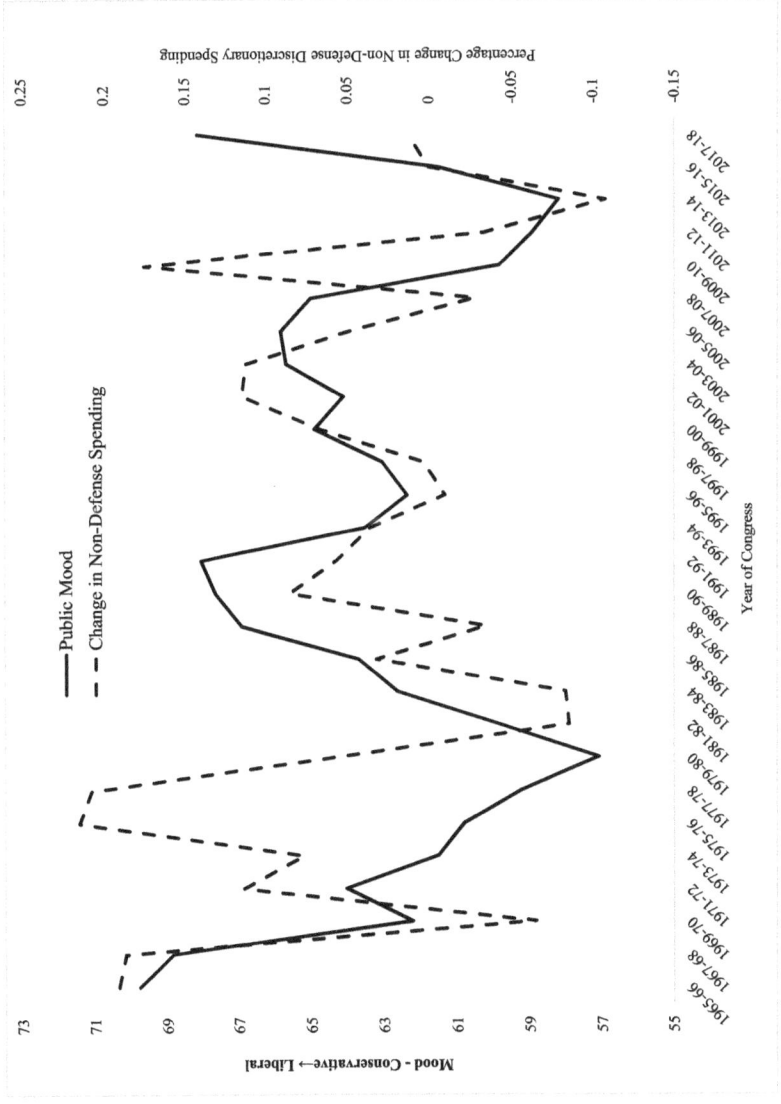

FIGURE 2.3. Public mood and changes in non-defense discretionary spending (constant 2012 dollars), 1953–2018

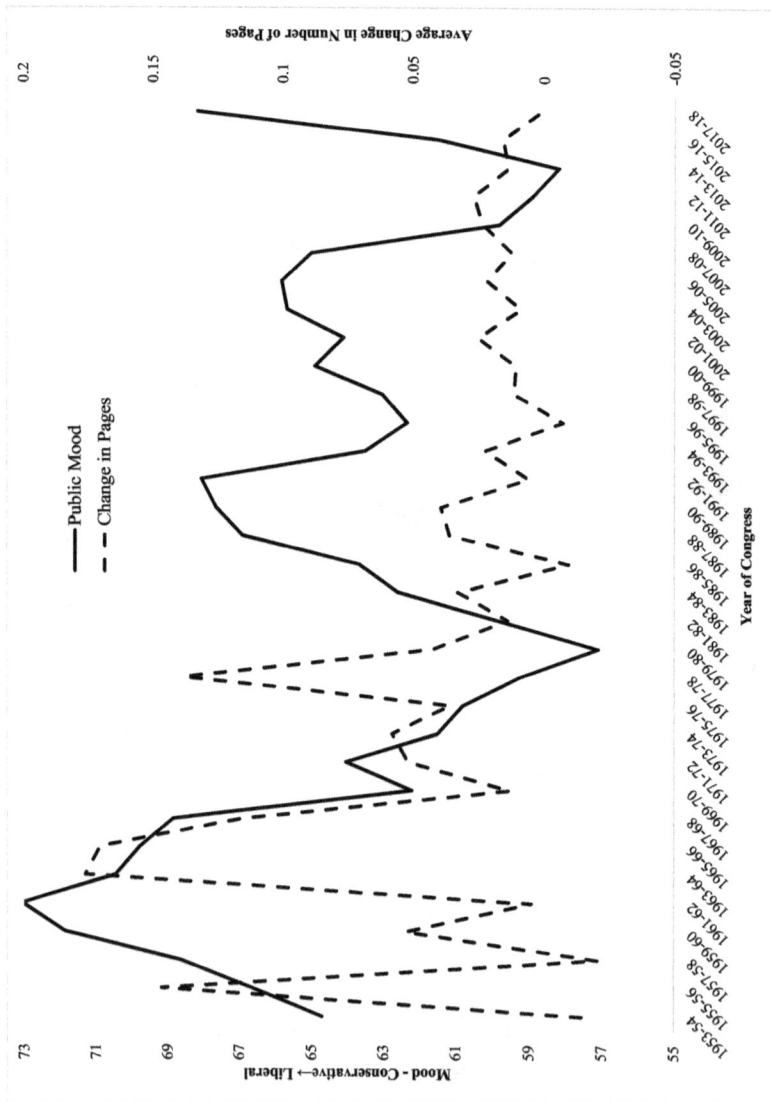

FIGURE 2.4. Public mood and changes in the proportion of pages in the Code of Federal Regulations, 1953–2018

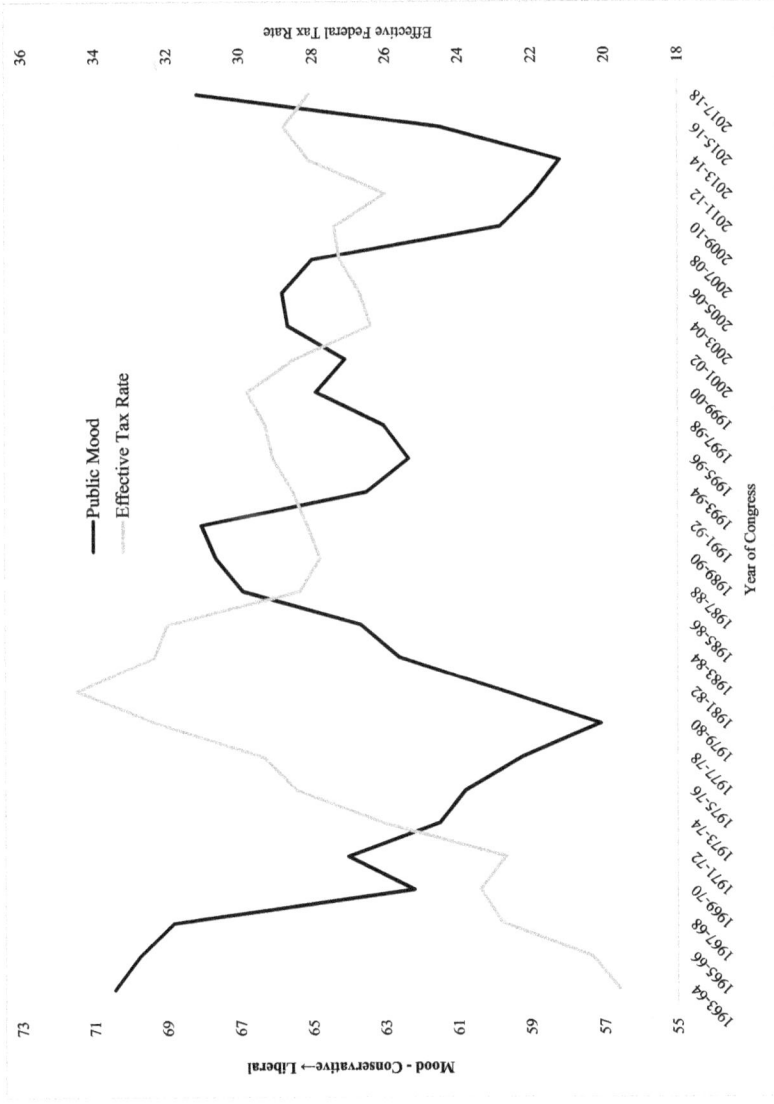

FIGURE 2.5. Public mood and changes in average effective tax rate (income and payroll), 1953–2018

despite the Republican Revolution in Congress and all the partisanship of the Clinton and George W. Bush years. The Great Recession in 2008 naturally generated a spike in spending, but any separation of economic policy from public opinion since that time, at least as measured by these important indicators, is the result of a volatile mood and largely unchanging course of government action.

At the most aggregate of levels and in the broadest of terms, the ideological character of postwar federal economic policy appears to have been reasonably responsive to public opinion. Its most important enactments have generally tacked leftward and rightward with the views of Americans, or remained relatively stable and moderate at times the public has evidently wanted it to—most notably for the twenty or so years following the mid-1980s. There have been periods when Washington has passed legislation dissonant with mass attitudes. Of these periods, the 1970s, the first half of the 1980s and the decade since the 2008 financial crisis stand out. Only in the shortest of these episodes—basically the first Reagan term—did the federal government give Americans conservative economic policy they did not seem to want— although there had been a clarion call for such policy as the president was elected. During the other two episodes, economic policy enactments were evidently to the left of the public's views.[11]

Responsiveness and Attentiveness to Individual Issues

Stimson has calculated mood scores for over a dozen issues during the postwar period.[12] In this section, I take individual issue areas I consider economic and try to gauge policy responsiveness to public opinion. As an initial exercise, I plot the mood scores for each issue over time (by annual average for a Congress). I use the ten issues I consider economic above—that is, those from the Congressional Bills Project, which are analyzed in figure 2.2.[13] The issues are macroeconomics, health care, labor, education, environment, energy, transportation, social welfare, housing, and domestic commerce. Again, higher scores denote liberal moods. Figure 2.6 reports the results.

It is interesting to compare the issues and see the changes over time. There is significant temporal and cross-sectional variance in Americans' attitudes, a richness often missed by studies of public and elite ideology (Broockman 2016). Labor was viewed as prominent enough to be one of the few issues worthy of measurement in the early postwar Congresses. An initial leftward spike—possibly in reaction to the Taft-Hartley Act of 1947, which restricted labor—precedes a slow but steady movement to the right. Recently, public opinion of the issue has become relatively conservative, and—possibly as a

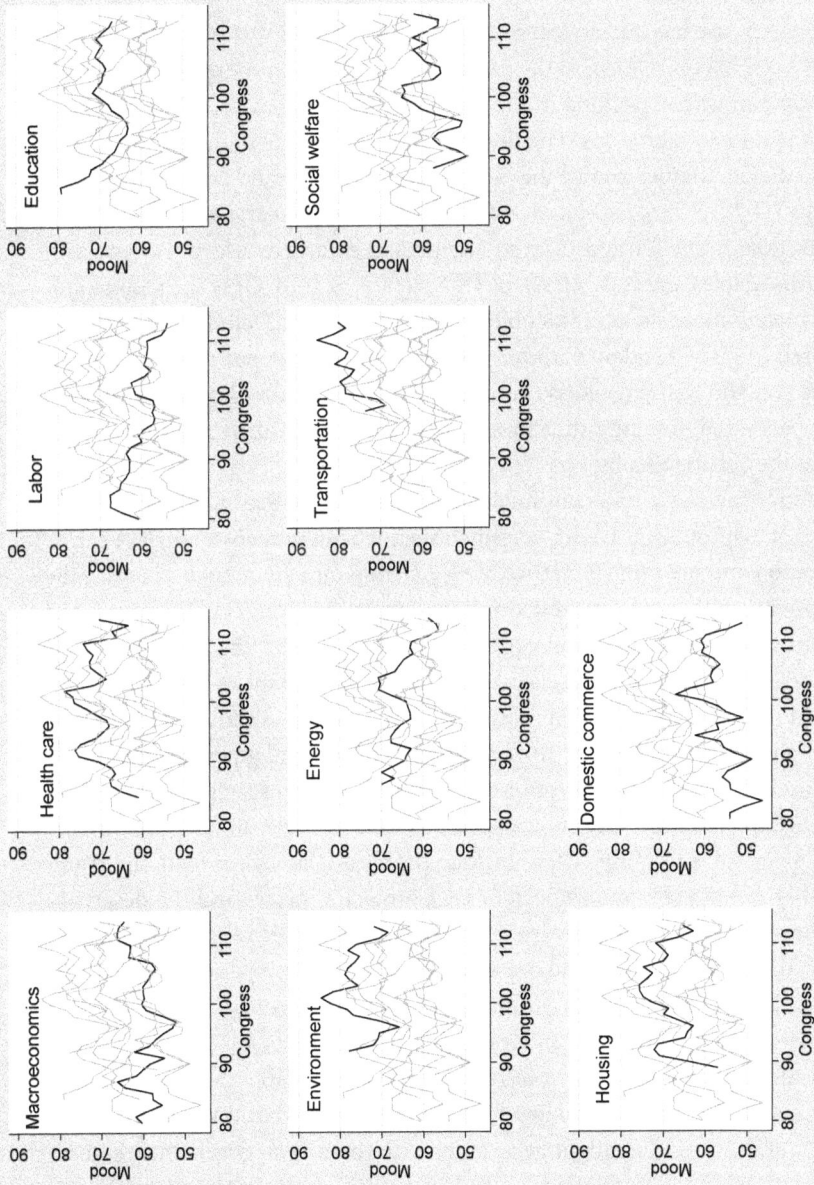

FIGURE 2.6. Public mood on ten economic issues, 1947–2016

Mood score (with higher values indicating liberalism) is on the vertical axis; Congress number is on the horizontal axis.

result—labor seems to have dropped from the radar screens of policymakers in Washington. Americans' attitudes toward labor policy since the mid-1970s are presumably related to unions' declining membership and political influence (Francia 2006).

Health care has had an interesting ride. The mood surrounding it has always been liberal relative to the other issues, although progressive sentiment has gone in waves, peaking in the late 1960s and early 1970s, the early 1990s, and the mid-to-late 2000s. The three periods coincide with the establishment of Medicaid, Medicare, and the Nixon administration and Senator Ted Kennedy's (D-MA) 1975 legislation establishing HMOs (health maintenance organizations); the aborted Clinton attempts at extensive reform in 1993; and the Affordable Care Act (ACA), or Obamacare, of 2010. Only the second episode met without meaningful policy response after the Democratic Congress refused to give President Clinton what he wanted (Skocpol 1996)—although there was the Kennedy-Kassebaum insurance portability legislation in 1996 that permitted, among other things, workers to keep their health coverage when they changed jobs.

Americans have had continually, perhaps even increasingly, liberal views about transportation. We have seen comprehensive and costly surface transportation and broader infrastructure legislation on a frequent basis since the early 1980s, although these outcomes are largely the product of the routinized congressional appropriations and authorizations cycles that govern policymaking on the issue. Still, several transportation bills make Mayhew's dataset.[14] Public mood on the environment looks similar. Although today many on the left express repeated frustration with the federal government's efforts to combat climate change, the height of public progressivism on the issue in the late 1980s and early 1990s seems to have brought about many important pieces of legislation. These include the Clean Air Act of 1990, the Water Quality Act of 1987, and important laws protecting water and the deserts in California in the first three years of the 1990s. A series of laws designed to clean the water and air in the decade from 1965 to 1975, a period that also saw the establishment of the Environmental Protection Agency, addressed—and possibly satiated—growing environmental liberalism.[15]

Federal policy appears to have responded reasonably to mood on education as well. Note that progressivism erodes somewhat through the 1950s, 1960s, and 1970s. This might be a response to the federal government's insertion of itself into K–12 public education by providing resources to schools with the National Defense Education Act of 1958 and Elementary and Secondary Education Act of 1965. Since then, the federal government has remained an important funding source for schools in poor and minority jurisdictions, but it has not increased its share of national education spending and has instead focused more on academic accountability, as the No Child Left Behind Act of 2001 best illustrates (Abernathy 2007). This state of affairs is consistent with Americans' recent relatively conservative views on the issue.

Housing and energy are more difficult to explain. Motivated by significant media coverage of the limited supply and squalor of urban development, several important housing laws were passed in the 1950s, before these data begin (Hays 1995). The Housing and Community Development Act of 1974, an effort to move federal policy to block grants and provide vouchers for private housing, coincides with a sharp elevation of mass liberalism. The energy mood starts off as moderate but—like that of labor and education—grows more conservative. It is not inconsistent with recent important legislation on the matter, such as the 2005 Energy Policy Act—which increased market regulation in the wake of Enron's collapse but also provided tax incentives for providers and unleashed fracking—and the lifting of the ban on oil exports in 2015.

In a relative sense at least, mood on three of the issues is consistently conservative during the postwar period. The issues are not trivial. Social-welfare policy, which includes programs like Social Security, Aid to Families with Dependent Children, and nutrition assistance, invokes right-leaning attitudes throughout the time series. Supporters of these programs have been playing defense for most of the period since the 1980s, after expansion in the 1960s and 1970s (Zelizer 2015)—when, for example, food-stamp coverage grew, eligibility and benefits for Social Security increased, and the Supplemental Security Income program commenced.[16] Reflecting the data presented here, Wlezien and Soroka (2021) reveal slightly elevated public preferences for greater welfare spending in the first decade of the 2000s, but there is no doubt that, compared to other issues, American public opinion on social welfare leans right. Interestingly, by deploying the public's mean preference over an extended period as a "neutral point," the authors argue that current progressive views remain largely congruent with actual spending on welfare programs (Wlezien and Soroka 2021).

If anything, opinion about domestic commerce, which embraces the financial system and much regulatory policy as defined by the Congressional Bills Project, is even more conservative. The liberal wave of the 1960s and 1970s identified by Mayhew (2005) does not spare this issue, despite public attitudes to the contrary. Significant consumer safety laws on matters like food, consumer products, and pesticides were passed during the period. Since then, policy has more often matched the mood. The Financial Modernization Act of 1999 was widely seen as a repudiation of New Deal–era banking regulations (Omarova 2013). However, despite opinion on the issue moving rightward, the financial crisis was met with liberal government action. The Troubled Asset Relief Program (TARP) and Wall Street reform legislation, the former passed in the dying embers of the Bush administration and the latter seen as a triumph for President Obama and the chairs of the two congressional banking committees, Senator Chris Dodd (D-CT) and Representative Barney Frank (D-MA), involved a considerable commitment of federal resources and greater regulation.

The third "conservative" issue is the macro-economy. It includes many important economic matters, fiscal policy and measures explicitly designed to combat unemployment and inflation chief among them. Although the public mood on the issue is generally to the right, there are times when it is toward the middle of the pack and attitudes become relatively more progressive. These times seem to be when the government is interested in combating unemployment or spending public funds to realize social policy. The mid-1950s to about 1970 and the period following the 2008 financial crisis are when the macroeconomic mood is relatively liberal. It is at its most conservative during the rampant inflation of the 1970s and early 1980s and the "roaring" 1990s. Some of the policies to combat the rising cost of living, including President Nixon's wage and price controls, are progressive in nature, but Americans have traditionally trusted Republicans to deal with the problem of inflation—possibly because of their administrations' record on the matter (Hibbs 1977). The robust growth of the early internet age under President Clinton led the public to believe that Washington should leave the economy alone.

Let us turn now to attentiveness. Elected officials cannot intentionally respond to mass opinion if they are unconcerned with a matter. Figure 2.7 plots, for each issue, its rank on two lists. The first is Gallup's "most important problem" survey data, made available by the Policy Agendas Project (Jones et al. 2023).[17] Each data point represents a biennial Congress for which I have averaged these public-opinion survey annual scores. I rank only among my economic issues. If an issue is unmentioned, I rank it last. The second ranking is of the issue's share of all economic bills passed into law in that congressional session. These data come from the Congressional Bills Project I used earlier. I consider "jobs," "taxes," and "the economy" macroeconomic issues, and since together they are always deemed the most important economic problem by the public—with the exception of the 80th Congress (1947–1948), when labor was number one—I omit that issue from the analysis. I also omit transportation. Survey respondents rarely mention the issue, but because Congress packages it into small and frequent authorization and appropriations bills, transportation is often the issue targeted by the largest proportion of all the bills that become law.

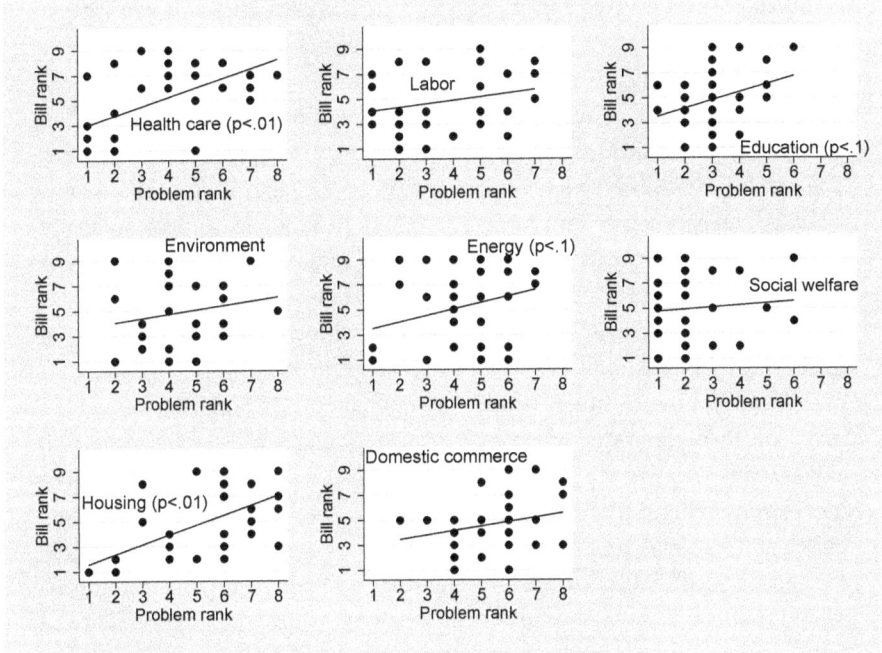

FIGURE 2.7. Government attentiveness to eight economic issues, 1947–2016
Rank of the issue's share of all economic bills passed in a given Congress is plotted along the vertical axis; rank of the issue as the public's "most important problem," as reported to Gallup, is plotted along the horizontal axis.

The results suggest that Congress is reasonably attentive to the economic issues the public cares about most. Four issues generate positive correlation coefficients that are statistically significant at the $p < .1$ level, and the relationship between the rank of the most important problem and proportion of economic bills passed is particularly robust for health care and housing. The relationships on health care and energy are noteworthy because of their volatility in the most-important-problem rankings. Americans have generally overlooked energy, except for the period from the mid-1970s to the mid-1980s, when it spent a decade as (or nearly) the most important issue besides the macro-economy. At least in a relative sense, health care was seldom important to Americans even in the mid-1960s, when Medicare and Medicaid were established. It shot to prominence in the late 1980s, however, and has since tussled with social welfare—and to a much lesser extent education—for the number two slot, behind the macro-economy. Congress paid most attention to housing in the 1950s and early 1960s, a time when Americans regularly viewed it as among the country's top three or four problems.

Of course, we need to explain why Congress is not constantly sensitive to the public's desire to see government deal with matters like jobs and taxes. Before 1980, the macro-economy's average rank in the proportion of economic bills passed by Congress was third; since that time its rank has fallen to nearly eighth. This drop in rank seems a function of three developments. The first is the use of reconciliation to bundle fiscal policy measures into omnibus bills. The Reagan administration initially recognized the advantage of using the procedure this way, and presidents and congressional majorities have deployed the technique regularly since, not least because the vehicle is immune from the Senate filibuster.[18] Second, with the obvious exception of the Great Recession and COVID-19 pandemic, the country has enjoyed relatively healthy rates of inflation and unemployment. Even during periods of very low unemployment, when policymakers are apt to leave the issue well alone, many citizens are still talking about taxes and jobs. Finally, government seems focused more on monetary policy as an instrument for economic health and less on countercyclical fiscal policy. Whatever the cause—possibly the increased difficulty of passing bills that address polarizing macroeconomic matters, possibly because of high levels of debt—Congress and the administration look more to the Federal Reserve for economic leadership (Binder and Spindel 2017, 201–31).

However, if we plot the public mood around an issue against, for that same issue, the mean first-dimension DW-NOMINATE score of the sponsors of each bill that became law and that the Congressional Bills Project considers "important," the results—which I do not report—are unimpressive. For eight of the issues, the relationship does not reach statistical significance, and for six of them the line of fit is almost perfectly horizontal or slopes upward, denoting that as the mood generates higher values and gets more liberal, so sponsors have higher DW-NOMINATE scores or get more conservative. Only the correlation coefficients of energy and labor are significant and of the correct sign.

Setting aside obvious measurement differences, we might ask: Why, at the individual-issue level, are economic-policy outputs attentive but less responsive to public mood? One plausible explanation revealed itself in the analysis of the Mayhew data and ideology of bill sponsors above. The parties, extreme and unified over the past thirty years or so, are increasingly mediating the effect of public opinion. Under these conditions, Democratic and Republican elected officials respond differently to the public's ideological mood or position on an issue (Broockman and Skovron 2018; Butler and Dynes 2016; Jones et al. 2019, 213–26). When they set the legislative agenda, Democrats accommodate liberal movement in mass opinion but stand firm in the face of greater conservatism. Republicans do the opposite. Bills may pass to demonstrate the governing party's sensitivity to an issue of public concern, but their content will be largely consistent with that party's ideology. This observation is similar to one Bartels (2008, 2016) makes in his influential work. He argues that policy is especially unresponsive—but not necessarily divergent—in the current era of inequality because the Republicans have generally been in control of government since the mid-1990s.

Second, and again somewhat speculatively, although the aggregated policy records of the parties reveal postwar Democrats to be consistent liberals and Republicans conservatives (Poole and Rosenthal 1997), studies of congressional roll-call voting show that member preferences on many economic issues load along several dimensions that shift over time and frequently reveal intraparty heterogeneity or interparty commonality (Jochim and Jones 2013). At the finer-grained individual-issue level, there is, in other words, greater volatility. Issues like education, energy, and transportation, for example, have some ideological character but are also distributive and often subject to bipartisan coalition building (Jochim and Jones 2013). On these issues, public mood is likely to increase policy output but not particularly shape its content.

A final observation is worthy of mention. Figure 2.7 shows mood to be, in relative terms at least, consistently progressive on five issues: health care, education, environment, transportation, and housing. As noted above, there are three routinely conservative issues: macroeconomics, social welfare, and domestic commerce. The policy areas where we see the public's liberal views are largely distributive. Political scientists often consider them valence issues, those that typically evoke nonideological responses and around which broad consensus often forms (Jacoby 1994). To be sure, expanding the government's scope and directing its resources on housing and education is likely to help low-income Americans disproportionately, but better-off citizens can benefit from such policies as well. Spending on transportation infrastructure is visible to the general population—and can often help business—and environmental regulations, although seen as consistent with a progressive agenda, have few discernible immediate material benefits exclusively for the less affluent. Whereas only health care seems genuinely redistributive in nature among the liberal issues, the conservative issues of macroeconomics and social welfare have potentially large redistributive effects. Domestic commerce also deals with regulation over broad swaths of the economy. Outside the environmental arena, the public seems largely skeptical of government intervention. Americans, therefore, tend to be more conservative on the "big" issues—I have noted that the macro-economy is always number one and that social welfare has held the number two or three slot as Gallup's "most important problem" when it comes to economic concerns solidly since the early 1960s. I suspect Americans' right-of-center views do not exert less practical influence on policy outputs than do their liberal attitudes. We tend to lean right on the issues that do most to shape the nation's economy.[19]

Conclusion

This chapter presents an analysis of the responsiveness and attentiveness of federal economic policy to American public opinion in the postwar era. Is the record a strong one? It is certainly not spotless, particularly if we use certain measures of policy content, like the ideology of members of Congress who sponsored legislation. There are also times when policy seems unresponsive and conservative. During the Reagan years, for example, data suggest Washington was producing what was, to that point at least, the most conservative economic policy of the postwar period. At this time, the public's mood was rapidly liberalizing. The first Trump presidency was also a moment when mass attitudes and government policy on the economy seemed out of step.

But it is surely unreasonable to focus on short periods. It is also unfair to assess this aggregate record in an absolute sense. To what are we comparing it? If compared to the assertion that federal economic policy since World War II, and especially in the recent era of inequality, has been made with little regard to the public's interests as understood by its expressed preferences, then the performance revealed here is creditable. On balance, outputs do reasonably reflect public wishes, and they certainly do so more than the political science of economic inequality would have us believe.

Mine is not an especially novel interpretation. Others have concluded that federal economic policy has been responsive to American public opinion since World War II, particularly prior to the 1990s (Bartels et al. 2016; Erikson et al. 2002; Page and Shapiro 1992; Stimson et al. 1995). Some have suggested a thermostatic relationship between mass attitudes and government action (Atkinson et al. 2021; Wlezien 1995), but even then Americans are often in the driving seat and force policy to tack back in their direction. The public is, recent scholarship shows, assisted with surprising aptitude by a media that elucidates economic policy choices for voters (Soroka and Wlezien 2022).

If ideological bias exists in American postwar economic policy, evidence suggests it is liberal and redistributive rather than conservative. Critics of modern American democracy overlook the period of the 1960s and 1970s, when policy was often discernibly to the left of public opinion. There is a clear disconnect between Washington and the public as mass attitudes moved rapidly to the right in the second half of the 1960s, while Lyndon Johnson completed his Great Society and Richard Nixon executed policies that continued to expand the government's budget and scope. This disconnect is revealed by analyses of public opinion and economic policy at the aggregate level as well as by the effective federal tax rate, discretionary domestic spending, and regulations. These policies also seemed to have few compensatory features. To be sure, this was a time before inequality accelerated, but macroeconomic conditions deteriorated, culminating with the debilitating stagflation of the early-to-mid-1970s. Many policies of the 1960s and 1970s, including health care programs, environmental regulation, and an expanded Social Security system remain fixtures of the American economy.

Those who suggest that the recent period of inequality is a function of Republicans crafting economic policy to fit their own and patrons' interests may have a case. The early Reagan years and the decade between the party taking command of Congress in 1994 and the conclusion of George W. Bush's first term are times of conservative economic policy. But these right-of-center policies were not dramatically at odds with Americans' stable and far-from-liberal views at the time. Compared to their positions on other issues, moreover, Americans have been consistently conservative on welfare, macroeconomic, regulatory, tax, and labor policy—all matters formative of a nation's economic character. The post-1980 era also witnessed its fair share of liberal bias. The government's response to the financial crisis during the Obama years, for example, was to move economic policy to the left as the public shifted in the opposite direction.

Particularly since the mid-1990s, the lack of responsiveness to the public's economic policy wishes appears largely a function of elite partisanship. While mass attitudes have been moderate in a historical sense, the party of government pushes for policy outcomes that are close to its increasingly extreme preferences. In this way, recent Democratic presidents and congressional majorities and Republican presidents and congressional majorities are not as responsive as their predecessors, at least not to the general public, consisting as it does of many independents, ideological moderates, and supporters of the opposition (Grossmann et al. 2021). At the macro level, the past couple of decades are not ones of considerable economic policy responsiveness. But they are also not suggestive of an innate rightward bias or a tendency to impose on Americans unwanted policies that exacerbate economic inequality.

Public Opinion and Economic Policy

Episodes and Issues

The claim that federal economic policy is reasonably responsive to public opinion must survive a deeper dive into postwar history, and particularly into our "New Gilded Age" of inequality. That is the endeavor of this chapter. I turn first to episodes in recent American political history that take the form of comprehensive and coherent economic packages enacted by the federal government and generally pushed by individual presidents. I look at four of these episodes, focusing on the current period of inequality and presumed unresponsiveness that many suggest began in the 1980s. The choice of episodes is not exhaustive, but these examples represent important bursts in which Washington presented and passed a program of policies designed to alter the economy in some fundamental way. The goal is to understand whether the packages adopted were responsive to the desires of the public at the time. Again, I am generally uninterested in the source of mass attitudes and the motivations of policymakers. The treatment is inevitably limited, but I think it is extensive enough to make a case for my argument.

The Reagan Revolution

The election of Ronald Reagan as president in 1980 and the subsequent enactment of much of his economic agenda have been ascribed a pivotal role in any understanding of America's economy, including its level of inequality (Bartlett 2009). Commencing immediately after his inauguration, the administration and its congressional allies moved a package of legislation into law that reduced income taxes and domestic discretionary spending dramatically (Morgan 2009, 76–121; Peterson and Rom 1988; Shuman 1992, 249–76; White and Wildavsky 1989). The famous Economic Recovery Tax Act (ERTA) of

1981 constituted, at the equivalent of over 2 percent of GDP, the largest tax cut in American history. Individual income tax brackets were indexed for inflation and reduced considerably—the top rate came down to 50 percent from 70 percent. The 1981 Omnibus Budget Reconciliation Act (OBRA) cut federal expenditures on domestic programs by an unprecedented $38 billion. Defense spending grew by more than 40 percent from 1980 to 1984. To be sure, there were significant reversals later in Reagan's first term. These were brought on by pressure from a ballooning budget deficit—it increased to more than $200 billion in 1983. The president signed tax hikes nullifying provisions of ERTA in both 1982 (the Tax Equity and Fiscal Responsibility Act) and 1984 (the Deficit Reduction Act). But the enactment of Reaganomics is universally viewed as having moved the country's economy in a decidedly conservative—critics often call it neoliberal—direction. As noted in the last chapter, it is also emblematic of a period when policy appeared out of step with mass attitudes.

Public views of fiscal policy were evolving in the late 1970s. At that time, Gallup's regular polling on the amount of taxes respondents felt they paid reported unusually elevated proportions of "too high" answers—between 65 and 70 percent across the decade.[1] The figure peaked in the 1980–1982 period for the National Opinion Research Center's (NORC) version of the question. Researchers have argued that Republican leaders in Congress and conservatives in the policy community adopted aggressive tax-cutting positions prior to the public's shift on the issue (Burns and Taylor 2000). That may be so. But it was not until Reagan's election and the attainment of these levels of mass discontent with the federal government's fiscal stance that actual policy outcomes were brought into line with public opinion. Confirming Associated Press/NBC News polls taken in the winter and spring of 1981, which showed that around 60 percent of respondents supported Reagan's tax cuts, Enten (2017) found ERTA to be popular when passed. Indeed, Americans approved of it more so than any other comparable tax cut legislation since, with the possible exception of the first extension of the George W. Bush cuts under Barack Obama in 2010. A Gallup poll in August 1981 revealed that only 26 percent of respondents opposed ERTA.

With regard to spending, the American National Election Studies (ANES) survey has asked Americans if they would prefer to "cut government services and spending" or have "more" of them for many years. The mean on a seven-point scale fell closest to the "cutting" pole in 1982—with the exception of 1994 and 1996, during the time of the "Republican Revolution" in Congress.[2] Higgs and Kilduff (1994) show in a systematic analysis of contemporaneous polls that Americans' call for greater resources for national security spiked to a quarter-century high in 1980 before retreating fairly quickly to 1970s levels. It is significant that the largest annual hike in the defense budget in both percentage and dollar amounts (17 percent and $27 billion) came following Reagan's first budget.

Moreover, as the new administration embarked on a program of deregulation, the public saw government interference in business as debilitating—a message that Reagan's predecessor, Jimmy Carter, also seemed to have received, given policies lifting restrictions on the airline and trucking industries passed in 1978 and 1980. A September 1981 Gallup poll reported that 58 percent of respondents opposed increased government interference with business. A CBS/New York Times poll of the same year showed that 65 percent believed "government has gone too far in regulating business."[3]

Very few people believed the budget deficit was of concern as Reagan entered office. Surveys taken at the end of the 1980 campaign continually reported inflation, unemployment, and the Cold War to be the top issues of interest to voters. Thirty-one percent of respondents to a CBS News/New York Times poll in October 1980 offered "inflation" as the "most important problem facing this country today." Of twenty issues mentioned as replies to an open-ended Gallup poll posing the same question that summer, not one had anything to do with budget deficits.

Americans, however, quickly changed their minds about the president's approach. An ABC News/Washington Post poll in February 1982 revealed that only 35 percent of respondents thought he should "stick" with his economic program (Sussman 1982). Other regularly administered surveys like ANES do not reveal quite such a dramatic reversal, but it is clear support for reducing taxes and spending on domestic programs decreased appreciably around that time. Simultaneously, the federal deficit became an issue of concern. A September 1983 Gallup poll revealed that 76 percent of respondents felt its accelerated growth constituted a "threat" (whether "great" or "somewhat"), although by large numbers Americans opposed solutions such as increasing taxes and cutting Social Security, Medicare, or Medicaid. By the 1986 midterms, the federal deficit had become the most important issue to voters, according to the ABC News/Washington Post exit poll.[4] Reagan's about-face and deficit-reduction focus reflected transformed public sentiment.

Clinton's Focus on Deficit Reduction

Many Democrats hoped that Bill Clinton, the first Democratic president for twelve years, would use traditional Keynesian principles to bolster domestic spending after the relatively lean Reagan-Bush period. But the new administration made deficit reduction the focus of fiscal policy, and the OBRA, passed over monolithic Republican opposition because of its tax hike, was the highlight of 1993 (Drew 1994; Quirk and Hinchcliffe 1996).[5] Clinton ground out victory on the bill, believed to risk the reelection chances of vulnerable congressional Democrats, and needed the tie-breaking vote of Vice President Al Gore in the Senate to get it to his desk.

Many accounts of the administration's decision to move quickly and decisively on deficit reduction attribute it to the strong showing of H. Ross Perot in the 1992 campaign (Drew 1994). Perot referred to the country's fiscal health continually while on the stump. Surveys revealed that many more Americans thought he was the candidate "best at handling the economy" than would end up voting for him (Frankovic 1993, 125). Knowing that Perot opposed Clinton's effort to secure congressional approval of the North American Free Trade Agreement (NAFTA), the president felt he could not upset the Texas businessman's supporters with his budget (Harris 2005). Given six choices in a Cambridge Reports/Research International poll of January 1993, 29 percent of respondents wanted the incoming administration to tackle the deficit, placing the course of action in second place just behind reducing unemployment. An ABC News/*Washington Post* poll reported that 45 percent of participants believed "a major reduction in the federal deficit" should be, when "thinking about the economy," the "most important goal for Clinton during his first term in office." This compared to 27 percent who desired a "middle-class tax cut" and 22 percent who wanted "short term spending to boost the economy," policies traditionally more appealing to voters.

Public opinion therefore helps explain Clinton's "New Democrat" or "Third Way" approach to fiscal policy.[6] It certainly encouraged him to push through OBRA. A CBS News/*New York Times* poll, administered soon after the administration's proposal was released in February 1993, suggested that the public's usual desire for tax cuts and other spending increases had diminished. Only 41 percent of respondents supported the president's opponents and thought the first draft of OBRA was just "another way to raise taxes"; 51 percent perceived it positively as a "new way of attacking the deficit."

It is not surprising, however, that OBRA took a tortuous journey to passage. The president ultimately got his roughly $500 million in deficit reduction when he signed the bill in August, but over the summer Congress forced him to jettison the infamous energy tax—an ABC News poll in July showed that 54 percent of respondents opposed a gas levy—and swallow greater cuts on programs like food stamps and the earned-income tax credit (CQ Almanac 1993, 107–24). A June 1993 NBC News/*Wall Street Journal* poll revealed that only 10 percent of respondents wished the legislation to pass in the form it then took, 54 percent desired fewer tax increases and more spending cuts to maintain deficit reduction levels, and 27 percent wanted to keep the tax proposals and decrease spending further so as to squeeze even more deficit reduction from the plan. A poll by the same organizations the following month reported that 61 percent of respondents felt that "cutting spending more" was the best way to bring congressional doubters and the administration to agreement. Public distrust of his opponents and support for the painful but necessary act of lessening the deficit strengthened Clinton's resolve to get the bill passed, however. A survey taken by CBS News just prior to the vote on the final version of the legislation showed that 62 percent of respondents felt that continued Republican opposition was motivated by selfish "political gain."

Clinton's dogged pursuit of deficit reduction during the first eight months of his presidency marked a departure from the usual economic agenda of post–New Deal Democratic administrations. Public concern for the country's broad fiscal health, intensified by the Perot campaign, seem to have convinced him and his congressional Democratic allies to force OBRA into law.

The Response to the Financial Crisis

In the early fall of 2008, during the run-up to the presidential election, a number of financial institutions wobbled, and a couple—American Insurance Group and Lehman Brothers—collapsed. The effects on financial markets were devastating. Stock indices declined by roughly one-third, and the value of some money-market shares dipped below the hallowed one-dollar mark. Banks and large corporations from other sectors of the economy clamored for government rescue.

The response by two administrations and two Congresses was rapid. Outgoing Bush Treasury Secretary Henry Paulson and Fed Chair Ben Bernanke, working with the Democratic congressional leadership and in consultation with the presidential campaigns of Barack Obama and John McCain, pushed a broad legislative package designed to shore up the economy. The centerpiece was the Troubled Assets Relief Program (TARP), which had at its disposal about $700 billion to buy up mortgage-backed securities and preferred stock of many different corporations, including the banks Citigroup and Bank of America and the auto giants General Motors and Chrysler. The money was to be invested according to certain guidelines. The agreements were to be transparent and limit executive compensation, the government was to recoup funds, and home ownership was to be preserved so as to minimize foreclosures. A new oversight board would administer the program.

TARP was large, complex, and speedily enacted—it became law on October 3, 2008, just eighteen days after Lehman's disintegration.[7] As such, it is difficult to see how public opinion could have shaped it dramatically. But as McCarty, Poole, and Rosenthal (2013, 234–37) demonstrate, the initial reaction to the legislation's passage was supportive—55 percent of respondents in a September 2008 CNN poll approved of "the millions that have been given in aid," for example. This public endorsement was also bipartisan and only eroded appreciably following enactment and with Obama in the Oval Office for a couple of months. By then, TARP was losing significant support among Republicans (McCarty et al. 2013, 235–37).

Once inaugurated, Obama set immediately to work completing the federal government's response. Although drafted by the congressional Democratic leadership prior to the president's assumption of office, the American Recovery and Reinvestment Act (ARRA), frequently known at the time as the Recovery Act or stimulus bill, benefited from the weight thrown behind it by his administration. ARRA was, until 2020, the largest piece of fiscal legislation ever enacted outside the budget process.[8] It passed over unified Republican opposition; not a single member of the House GOP voted for it, and the administration leaned heavily on three moderate GOP senators from the northeast to secure the approval necessary to defeat a filibuster in the upper body. The legislation later became a target of the emerging Tea Party movement. But ARRA enjoyed greater support among the public. The media's coverage and just about all of the survey questions about the stimulus linked it to Obama. Monthly Democracy Corps polls from December 2008 to February 2009 showed at least 62 percent of respondents "strongly" or "somewhat" favoring "Obama's economic recovery plan," yet Americans supported ARRA without the president's name attached. Fifty-one percent of subjects believed it was "critically important" that the "government pass an economic stimulus plan" in a Gallup poll of early February 2009. A further 29 percent stated that passing such a plan was "important, but not critical." The details did not seem to matter particularly. The public just wanted help and was prepared to support the legislative effort.

Republicans gambled in their obstruction. Whereas 25 percent of Americans disapproved of Obama's efforts on the issue, the same Gallup poll reported that 58 percent disapproved of the actions of the congressional GOP. Republicans' near-universal opposition speaks to how polarization in Washington has structured both parties' responses to movements in economic policy away from their ideological bases. Moves to the left in mass opinion about the economy seem less likely to be followed by Republicans in Washington than they were forty years ago. I noted this development in the previous chapter.

There was a third major legislative response to the financial crisis. Dodd–Frank—as it was named after its chief sponsors—consolidated a broad effort to reform the unpopular financial-services sector and ensure that it could survive the kind of threat it faced at the height of the 2008 meltdown.[9] It was enacted in July 2010. By then, the administration and congressional Democrats were focused on their health care initiative, and the Tea Party had sprung to life, helping Republican opposition to the Obama agenda gain traction. Still, there appears to have been enough residual anger or fear from the crisis to generate public support for regulating the banking system, even if Americans were not aware of Dodd–Frank's details. The legislation benefited greatly from being associated with Obama, who was consistently supported more than congressional Republicans on the issue—an April 2010 ABC News/*Washington Post* poll revealed he was "trusted" by 52 percent of respondents "to do a better job handling regulation of the financial industry"; his opponents on the Hill were only trusted by 35 percent of respondents.

As McCarty, Poole, and Rosenthal (2013, 237–39) note, mass opinion was favorable through 2009, but by the time the Senate considered Dodd–Frank in the spring of 2010, people had begun to worry about the government's capacity to act in the nation's interests and not the banks'. Republican support for the reform dissipated entirely. At first opposition was manifest in increasing numbers of respondents claiming to be unsure of the legislation—56 percent had "not heard enough" about the bill in a February CBS News/*New York Times* poll, 51 percent in an April Resurgent Republic survey. It soon took the form of outright hostility. As early as March, a CNN/Opinion Research Council poll showed that 62 percent of Republican voters objected to the measure. It was at this point that public opinion took its palpable move to the right—a move I discussed in chapter 2. Americans were then to deliver a victory to the Republicans in the 2010 midterm elections.

Trumponomics

There are numerous interpretations of Donald Trump's narrow victory in the 2016 presidential election. Beyond just the (lack of) major-party candidates' personal appeal, political scientists have pointed to cultural, economic, and racial causes (Sides et al. 2018). But Trump had a message that contained within it an economic agenda. It was not especially coherent, but it constituted something resembling a program he pursued in office. The principal elements were his trade policy, a broad program of deregulation, and a large tax cut.

Trump's term in office saw the country involved in a number of confrontations over trade. The most publicized were with Canada, Mexico, the European Union, and, particularly, China. The administration's trade team—notably US trade representative Robert Lighthizer and the "hawk" Peter Navarro—pursued a consistent policy of imposing tariffs on imports in order to pressure governments to provide more favorable conditions for American exporters. In the China case, the government used complaints about that country's theft of intellectual property, manipulation of its currency, forced technology transfer, and dumping and subsidy policies to justify several rounds of tariffs, beginning in January 2018, on an array of Chinese goods, including appliances, steel, televisions, and parts for aircraft. China's retaliation mainly targeted American agriculture (Zumbrun et al. 2020).

Trump's stance was in many ways inconsistent with public views about the issue. As recently as 2008, a Gallup poll revealed that 52 percent of Americans saw foreign trade as a "threat" to the country's economy. The Trump years saw them embrace free trade (Edwards 2021, 101–6). In February 2016, 58 percent of subjects in the same survey saw foreign trade as an "opportunity for growth" and that number climbed to 79 percent in February 2020—with only 18 percent believing that the stance constituted a threat. With regard to the "war" with China, the public seemed to have little doubt who would suffer. In a May 2019 Monmouth University poll, 62 percent of respondents suggested that "American consumers" would "bear more of the costs" of the tariffs on China; only 23 percent that Chinese companies would bear those costs. A July 2018 NBC News/*Wall Street Journal* poll revealed that only 26 percent supported the use of tariffs because "they will help" rather than "hurt" the "average American."

But when the issue was put differently, the public supported the administration. As Trump was elected in late 2016, polls suggested broad dissatisfaction with existing trade policies. A November 2016 Quinnipiac poll showed that 64 percent of respondents supported "renegotiating" trade agreements with other major countries, and a CBS News poll of the following month indicated that Americans believed trade policy "loses more jobs" than "creates more jobs" by a 48 percent to 29 percent margin. Americans also seemed to agree with the president's general approach to put US economic interests before others'. A February 2017 Gallup poll showed that 71 percent of respondents agreed that "promoting favorable trade policies for the U.S. in foreign markets" was a "very important" foreign-policy goal. This goal ranked above defending the security of allies, working with the United Nations, and other policies that imply placing American interests at the same level or below those of other countries.

Americans' views of trade at the time were therefore complex and heavily dependent upon how researchers worded surveys. In the abstract, free trade was good, but polls revealed a nagging sense that the international regime benefited others at the expense of American businesses, workers, and consumers. The public disliked the trade policies Trump criticized in the campaign, but it hardly welcomed his alternatives. On balance, it is hard to avoid the conclusion that Trump's aggressive revision to a general trade policy that had spanned several decades and both Republican and Democratic administrations was at least somewhat unresponsive to public opinion.

Not surprisingly, Republicans supported the administration's policies more than Democrats did. Researchers have suggested that a "Trump effect" helped generate protectionist views among the president's strongest supporters, even those who might otherwise have supported free trade (Essig et al. 2021). Pew Research polls reveal that whereas at the beginning of the Obama years slightly more Republicans (57 percent) than Democrats (53 percent) believed that free trade agreements with other countries were generally "a good thing," in May 2018 the difference was twenty-four percentage points, with Democrats (67 percent to 43 percent) more likely to approve of such arrangements. The transformation corroborates a recurring theme of public opinion and economic policy responsiveness in the past decade or so. Greater polarization has encouraged presidents and congressional majorities to push for policies central to their party's platform. This trend makes government less responsive to the views of the median American.

Largely through executive order and administrative rulemaking, but also sometimes using the legislative process, Trump reversed an array of government regulations on environmental, labor, health care, telecoms, financial, energy, and transportation issues. Deregulation played a role in the 2016 campaign, and in his widely publicized Executive Order 13771—issued just ten days into his presidency—Trump established a policy by which executive agencies were required to rescind two regulations for every new one proposed. The goal, regardless of how realistic it was, was to reduce the cumulative cost of these policies.[10]

Gallup annually surveys Americans about their views on the extent of government regulation of "business and industry," and partisan responses are predictable, with a greater proportion of Republicans routinely replying they feel there is "too much" of it. In October 2017, the gap between Republican and Democratic subjects was forty-eight percentage points. The same poll reported that 45 percent of all respondents felt there was "too much" regulation and only 23 percent "too little," a result barely unchanged over the previous five years. But if the broad program had public support, certain elements did not seem to. According to a CBS News poll in April 2017, 51 percent of subjects characterized the rolling back of environmental regulations by the Trump administration "a bad thing."

Trump's signature domestic legislative achievement was the passage in December 2017 of the Tax Cuts and Jobs Act (TCJA). Its principal effects were to alter individual income tax brackets and lower rates, incentivize greater use of the standard deduction, and reduce the corporate tax rate from 35 percent to 21 percent. Much of the media narrative and clearly the view of most Democrats in Congress was that Trump and GOP allies on the Hill moved ahead with the legislation despite considerable public opposition (Balz 2017; Edwards 2021, 73–79; Hacker and Pierson 2020, 149–52). A battery of surveys fielded from roughly November 2017 to February 2018 found that the proportion of subjects who disliked the tax bill was anywhere from about ten to twenty percentage points larger than the proportion who supported it. A Quinnipiac poll released a few days into the New Year, for example, put the percentage of respondents as disapproving at 52 percent, those who approved at 32 percent.

Partisanship drove much of this opposition. In a January 2018 CBS News poll, 80 percent of Republicans felt TCJA was "fair"; only 13 percent of Democrats did. But opposition was also driven by a general suspicion that politicians promote the interests of other people. In the same poll, 50 percent of respondents felt that the tax bill was "unfair" to people like themselves, 42 percent "fair." In direct contradiction to the facts, many even believed their own taxes would "go up." A CBS poll the previous month reported that 41 percent of respondents thought their taxes would increase. At the same time, and as the bill was debated in Congress, an NBC News/*Wall Street Journal* poll reported that only 7 percent of subjects felt the legislation would mostly help "the middle class," 63 percent "the wealthy and corporations." Given his background, Trump might not have been the best person to lead a tax bill of this type. A CNN poll in December reported that 63 percent of respondents felt that the president and his family would be better off under the new law.

Another prominent feature of American culture, a pervasive dislike of taxation, provided TCJA a tailwind, however. As the legislation passed, Americans were evenly split between believing the amount of tax they paid was "about right" and "too much" in Gallup's poll.[11] According to a Monmouth University survey fielded at the same time, although only 29 percent of respondents wanted the legislation enacted, just 24 percent wished to "leave the tax system where it is." Thirty-nine percent called on Washington to work on a "new plan."

In fact, once established, people were more accepting of the new tax policy. The proportion who approved of the legislation increased by ten percentage points (from 26 percent to 36 percent) in the Quinnipiac poll between December 2017 and March 2018 and was up to 44 percent in the January 2018 Monmouth poll. By April 2019, Gallup found that 40 percent of poll participants approved of the law. Some of this effect was likely attributable to reduced withholding in paychecks and the realization that the economy was not hurt, at least in the short term. The law also surely benefited from its new status as existing policy and the public's innate skepticism of plausible alternatives.

The biggest challenge to Trump's presidency came with the COVID-19 pandemic in the spring of 2020. The virus effectively closed the economy, shuttering hundreds of thousands of businesses and forcing unemployment above 20 percent. The Federal Reserve led much of the government's response by injecting hundreds of billions of dollars of liquidity into the economy. But Congress also passed a series of bills to alleviate the economic harm. It enacted four "phases" under Trump, including the third-phase, $2.2 trillion Coronavirus Aid, Relief, and Economic Security (CARES) Act, which provided direct relief to many large businesses like hospitals and airlines, supplied cash payments to individuals and small businesses, increased unemployment assistance, bolstered collective bargaining and sick leave, and forgave some loans.

Congressional leaders of both parties authored the critical COVID legislation under Trump. They then built coalitions to ensure floor passage (Lee 2023). During 2020, the policy response to the pandemic was therefore neither a component of any presidential agenda nor the product of concerted executive action. Moreover, the shock was so jarring and sudden that there was no time for public opinion to form around specific recommendations for government action. Policymakers acted without precedent or cues from mass attitudes. Americans did chime in after the fact, however. A Gallup poll fielded just after Trump signed the CARES Act reported that 77 percent of respondents approved of the legislation.

President Joe Biden had more time to formulate an approach. Before he. had spent two months in office, he signed the American Rescue Plan Act, which provided $1.9 trillion in economic stimulus despite the solid opposition of congressional Republicans. The bill extended unemployment benefits, provided direct payments to individuals, expanded the child tax credit, funded school reopening, and paid for an ambitious program of COVID-19 vaccinations, testing, and treatment. A Pew Research poll released as the bill passed revealed that 70 percent of respondents supported it.

Public Opinion and Economic Policy:
Individual Issue Responsiveness and Congruence

I have argued that policy hews quite closely to public opinion and that there exists a reasonable case for responsiveness. In this section, I also attempt to investigate whether economic policy outputs are congruent with public attitudes. To do so I look separately at seven economic issues during the post-1980 period of heightened inequality. They are important and generally easy for citizens to understand. They frequently have quantitative features that permit the kinds of direct comparisons between mass attitudes and policy that facilitate an evaluation of the extent to which the two are congruent as well as responsive.

MINIMUM WAGE

Both editions of Bartels's influential work on the subject of the political sources of American economic inequality have chapters devoted to what he calls the "eroding minimum wage" (Bartels 2008, 223–51; 2016, 198–232). His argument is that the real (or inflation-adjusted) value of the minimum wage has declined greatly over time and that policymakers have only rarely elevated its nominal amount. The last time Congress altered the federal minimum wage by statute was 2007. The last time the nominal amount rose—as a consequence of the 2007 legislation—was in 2009, to $7.25 an hour. Republicans have often used the presidential veto and congressional procedures like the filibuster to block efforts to link the minimum wage to inflation.

They have done so despite substantial public support for increasing the minimum wage—support that extends through most of the postwar period. As Bartels points out, there are a number of recent polls where large majorities of respondents support particularly sizable increases, well above $7.25. A December 2013 ABC News/*Washington Post* poll allowed respondents to set the minimum wage; the median response was $9. Several surveys administered by CBS News/*New York Times* through 2014 and 2015 saw around 70 percent of respondents favoring a minimum wage at $10.10. By the time Trump first became president, surveys suggested Americans were amenable to a $15-an-hour minimum wage, the amount advocated by the 2016 Democratic Party platform and the central feature of a bill passed by the Democratic House in 2019. A January 2019 *The Hill*/Harris X poll reported that 55 percent of respondents supported raising the minimum wage to that level; an April 2021 Pew Research poll had the figure at 62 percent. In November 2020, when Floridians approved a referendum, their state became the eighth to formalize plans to elevate the minimum wage to $15. In January 2022, President Biden issued an executive order raising the minimum to that amount for federal workers and contractors. Later that year, voters in several states, including Republican Nebraska, approved ballot questions raising the minimum wage.

Bartels (2008, 2016) and others like Witko et al. (2021, 230–58) are correct. The evidence on this issue is strong. Federal policy has been neither responsive nor congruent. I will add two important caveats. They hardly exonerate the government, but they do mitigate the offense somewhat. The first has to do with the conditions under which Americans consider the minimum-wage issue. Most questions ask respondents to think of the matter unadorned and without a request to weigh plausible effects. Of course, although economists debate the effects of the minimum wage, changes to the rate have potentially significant impacts on the broader economy. When interviewers inform respondents of potential costs, they profess very different views. A March 2014 Bloomberg poll revealed that 57 percent of subjects deemed "unacceptable" a "tradeoff" of increasing the "incomes of 16.5 million Americans" while costing "500,000 jobs"—a figure that, a Congressional Budget Office report stated, would be the result of raising the minimum wage to $10.10 over three years. Only 39 percent of respondents supported a minimum-wage hike in a 2014 Reason-Rupe poll stipulating that the policy would "cause[] some employers to lay-off workers or hire fewer workers."

Second, raising the minimum wage is just not important to many Americans, including, as we shall see in chapter 11, professionals who make up an increasingly critical bloc of Democratic voters. The public does not have intense feelings about the issue, and as a result there is little pressure on policymakers to give it great attention. According to Heffington, Park, and Williams's (2017) "Most Important Problem" (MIP) dataset, the percentage of Americans who saw "wages" as the most important problem between 1960 and 2015 exceeded 1 percent in only three years—1969, 2009, and 2015—and in all of these cases, the number was still below 1.5 percent.[12] "Inflation," which is the issue revelatory of Americans' concerns for a high cost of living and therefore—if indirectly—an indication that they place a greater emphasis on prices than on wages, was the choice of at least 5 percent of respondents in every year from 1966 to 1984.[13] More people picked inflation than wages as the most important problem in every year after 1959 except 1965, 2009, 2010, and 2015.

A Third Way poll in December 2015 is consistent with this finding. It showed that in response to an open-ended question about "the most important issue that you want the President and Congress to make a priority," "raising" or "increasing" the minimum wage was thirteenth, garnering many fewer responses than issues like immigration, terrorism, and gun control. In fact, only 3 percent of Democrats had it as their first choice. The poll also revealed that the mean response for "raising the minimum wage" on a ten-point scale gauging whether a policy would help the subject and her family a "great deal" was less than the mean for all of the following: "improve worker and job training," "roll back government regulation to free up business," "require business to publish salaries so men and women are paid equally for equal work," "break up Wall Street banks," "offer free pre-K education for three and four year olds from low- and middle-income families," "lower interest rates on college loans," "reduce the federal budget deficit," "invest more in infrastructure like repairing roads, bridges and building out our energy grid," "make community college tuition free," "require that employers contribute a small amount to a private retirement account so every employee has savings beyond Social Security," "improve the quality of college and technical training for those preparing to enter the workforce," and "change campaign finance rules to get money out of politics." It was, in fact, dead last and the issue that respondents seemed to believe affected their lives the least.[14]

The results of a Pew Research poll of September 2019 revealed ambivalence specifically among lower-income respondents—categorized by Pew from their income, family size, and place of residence. Forty-nine percent felt that "increasing the minimum wage" would do a great deal to reduce income inequality. This was less than the proportion that felt "making college tuition free," "increasing taxes on the wealthiest Americans," "expanding Medicare so that it covers Americans of all ages," "ensuring workers have the skills they need for today's jobs," and "eliminating college debt" would have the same effect. Only "reducing illegal immigration," "expanding government benefits for the poor," and "breaking up large corporations" were thought to have less of an impact.

In many ways, the general lack of interest is unsurprising. It is difficult to know what proportion of workers feel they would benefit personally from an increase in the federal minimum wage, but according to 2024 numbers from the Economic Policy Institute, a rise in compensation to $15 per hour would increase the pay of slightly fewer than one in eight workers. The figure continues to decline as wages rise and states and municipalities take the lead on the policy. Only about 2 percent of all American workers in 2024 earned less than $10 an hour—a reduction of seventeen percentage points since 2010.[15]

TAXING THE RICH: THE ESTATE TAX
AND THE TOP RATE OF INCOME TAX

I look at two related issues here. The first is the estate tax. Congress considered proposals to eliminate or greatly reduce the levy during the late 1990s. In

2001, as part of a broader tax cut package, President Bush and congressional Republicans were able to eliminate the estate tax for the remainder of the decade. On two different occasions after 2010, when it was about to snap back to rates as high as 55 percent on estates valued at more than $1 million, Congress passed legislation under President Obama to cushion the blow significantly. After the 2017 tax overhaul, the federal rate applied only to estates with values above about $11.25 million.

Scholars have studied the recent politics surrounding this issue quite carefully. Graetz and Shapiro (2005) argue that the successful efforts in the first decade of the 2000s to eliminate the estate tax and then prevent its reversion to 1990s levels were largely the product of a manipulation of public opinion as well as energetic and astute lobbying by conservative political interests of a responsive Republican administration and Congresses. The asymmetric intensity of feeling on the issue was crucial as well, with repeal proponents, particularly small-business owners and farmers, working assiduously to elevate the issue to the forefront of the political agenda at a time when most Americans cared little about it. Piston (2018, 82–88, 132–35) focuses on the public's lack of knowledge about who pays the tax and attributes its opposition to an erroneous belief that millions of Americans are liable. Bartels (2016, 170–97) devotes an entire chapter to the topic. Critiquing the Graetz and Shapiro account, he says that working- and middle-class Americans never really liked the estate tax (as demonstrated from data going back to the 1930s) because it violates their understanding of the relationship between work and reward. Instead, Bartels (2016, 181–93) says the views of most Americans on the issue were immaterial to what the federal government would do about it. What mattered was that Republican elites wanted repeal and when they got control of federal policymaking—the first prolonged period of Republican unified government since the 1920s came to power in 2001—they did precisely that.

What scholars like Bartels, Graetz and Shapiro, and Piston recognize is that surveys show that the American public consistently oppose the estate tax. Public policy on the issue has largely been responsive over the past couple of decades. It has not, however, been particularly congruent. During the congressional debate over the 2017 tax cut, CNN asked subjects what they thought of repealing the inheritance tax, reminding them at the time it applied only to people with estates valued at more than $5.5 million. Fifty-six percent in the November poll said they opposed that effort.

Policymakers have altered the top rate for the federal individual income tax several times in the current period of enhanced inequality (Scheve and Stasavage 2016, 54–71). ERTA reduced it from 70 percent to 50 percent in 1981 and five years later, the Tax Reform Act decreased it to 28 percent, in this case by eliminating a large number of breaks and "loopholes" of which top earners were taking advantage. Under Clinton, the rate went up to 39.6 percent, only to be cut again to 35 percent with the Bush tax cut package of 2001—legislation, like Bush's 2003 tax bill, that had significant support among the general public (Bartels 2016, 144–50). Under Obama it reverted to the Clinton-era level, but an added 3.8 percent ACA tax made the effective rate 43.4 percent. This level was reduced by the 2017 Trump tax cuts down to 40.8 percent—37 percent plus the 3.8 percent ACA supplement.

A few surveys help us gauge whether this policy has been responsive to and congruent with public opinion. It appears that, for the most part, it has. In an ABC News poll of August 1993, 70 percent supported OBRA's provision increasing the top rate of income tax. By 1998, with the rate still at 39.6 percent, 38 percent wanted to maintain it, 39 percent increase it, and 6 percent reduce it, according to a February Zogby poll. A 2012 poll conducted by *The Hill* just as the Obama administration was contemplating increasing the top rate from 35 percent asked respondents what income tax rates families earning over $250,000 should pay. Eighty-eight percent said 35 percent or lower— with 21 percent saying less than 20 percent and 23 percent recommending a 25 percent rate. As Trump and Republicans pushed their tax bill in the second half of 2017, by which time many Democrats had started to push energetically for increasing taxes on the wealthy, a Pew Research survey revealed that Americans had moved back to the left a little on the issue. Forty-three percent of respondents felt that income taxes on households making more than $250,000 annually should be raised. But 29 percent felt that they should stay the same, and 24 percent felt that they should be lowered. In addition, more Republicans with incomes under $75,000 said income taxes on high earners should be decreased than increased.

A desire to increase taxes on the rich appears to have intensified in the 2020s (Zacher 2024a).[16] A surtax on the wealthy such as that proposed by Biden in late 2021 to pay for his Build Back Better plan was quite popular— although the package ultimately enacted in 2022, known then as the Inflation Reduction Act (IRA), contained only minimal tax hikes on stock buybacks and selected large corporations. An October 2021 Vox–Data for Progress poll reported that about 70 percent of respondents supported measures such as raising income and capital gains taxes on the very wealthy. An April 2023 Pew survey reported that 61 percent of respondents approved of raising tax rates on households that made more than $400,000 annually. Forty-three percent of Republicans said it "bothers" them "a lot" that "some wealthy people don't pay their fair share" but only 19 percent felt the same way about "some poor people."

But Americans historically oppose tax rates that seem punitive. There has been, for example, little appetite to go back to the rates of the 1960s and 1970s. After the tax increase in 1993, the GSS survey reported a significant drop in those who favored increasing taxes on Americans with high incomes. There was a decline of roughly twenty percentage points between 1987 and 1996, suggestive of a thermostatic response to tax policy by the public (Atkinson et al. 2021; McCall 2013, 197–99). An April 2019 Quinnipiac poll reported general support for increasing taxes on the very wealthy but a majority in opposition to raising the rate of income tax on incomes above $10 million to 70 percent, an amount proposed with much publicity by the progressive House Democratic freshman, Rep. Alexandria Ocasio-Cortez (D-NY).[17]

These findings are similar to those of Ballard-Rosa, Martin, and Scheve (2017). Their 2014 YouGov survey found that whereas public support for taxes on lower-income Americans declines monotonically as rates go up, Americans' attitudes toward the levies paid by the wealthy are clustered. Respondents in the study found a rate around 35 percent, roughly the top rate of income tax today and therefore congruent with actual policy, most appealing. The mean response to a question asked by YouGov for Ellis and Faricy (2021, 40–44) in 2019 about the tax rate participants thought the top 1 percent of earners should pay was 40 percent.

Finally, the public supports reducing the tax breaks that wealthier citizens receive. The 2023 Pew poll revealed that 59 percent of Republicans and 49 percent of Democrats say that the "complexity of the federal tax system" "bothers them a lot." A December 2012 Bloomberg poll asked whether the wealthy's tax rate should be raised or the amount they "can claim in tax breaks, such as mortgage interest and charitable contributions" limited. Fifty-two percent chose restricting the tax breaks. The 2017 TCJA reflected—although may not have fully addressed—these sentiments.

TAX EXPENDITURES

The wealthy do enjoy many tax breaks or special deductions, credits, or exemptions that we often characterize as "loopholes." These are "tax expenditures," to use the formal term, and they constitute incentives for certain kinds of—presumably socially desirable—activities. They "cost" around $1.3 trillion, or just shy of 30 percent of federal expenditures, in 2019, according to the Center on Budget and Policy Priorities (CBPP). The biggest tax expenditures include exclusions for employee-provided health care, imputed rental income, and capital gains; deductions for mortgage interest, defined-contribution and defined-benefit pensions, and state and local taxes; and credits for earned income and children. CBPP estimates that the top quintile receive nearly 60 percent of these expenditures and the top 1 percent almost one-quarter.

Political scientists have written a great deal about tax expenditures (Ellis and Faricy 2021; Faricy 2015; Hacker 2002; Howard 1997; Mettler 2011). They characterize them as reversing redistributive policies and elevating inequality— Faricy (2015) calls it "welfare for the wealthy." The earned-income tax credit is redistributive in nature, but wealthier Americans tend to take advantage of most other tax expenditures.

TCJA aside, tax expenditures have flourished. Whereas Democrats prefer direct payments to citizens and use of the spending side of the federal ledger to redistribute wealth down the income ladder, Faricy (2015) shows that Republicans have generally enacted these tax expenditures to reward the more affluent Americans who often vote for their candidates. Not surprisingly, the rise in tax expenditures coincides with the frequency of Republican presidencies and congressional majorities starting in the 1980s (Faricy 2015, 105–17, 134–49).

The success of these policies is consistent with my argument, however. They are more popular than equivalent policies that provide direct payments to individuals. Ellis and Faricy (2021) present data from a series of YouGov polls about tax expenditures and reveal that large majorities consistently support "tax breaks" for things such as "health care contributions," "mortgage interest," "saving for retirement," "student loans," and "dependent care." They also present findings of an experiment where they presented subjects with policies framed as either tax expenditures or direct government spending. In five of the six cases—tax credits or deductions for "mortgage interest," "retirement savings," "student loans," "paying for health care," and using "green energy"—more survey respondents supported the tax expenditure and opposed the direct spending. The distinction on the green-energy question was not statistically significant, but only on "paying for necessities" was there no discernible difference: The participants split evenly, with 55 percent supporting both types of policy response.

This result also fits a narrative that, ceteris paribus, Americans prefer tax cuts to spending increases. As Ellis and Faricy (2021, 103–6) show in their discussion of the 2014 CES, more respondents—by twenty-one percentage points (47–26)—wanted to increase the earned-income tax credit than wanted to increase spending for welfare. The 2014 CES also asked over forty thousand respondents to address the budget deficit by offering a combination of "tax increases" and "spending cuts." The mean answer was by getting 59 percent of it from spending cuts and 41 percent from tax increases. CES asked the same question in 2016, and the means were 57 percent and 43 percent.

DOMESTIC SPENDING PRIORITIES

Americans tend to believe that the federal government spends too much money. Krimmel and Rader (2021) found that even a plurality of Blacks and Latinos feel the federal government spends "too much"—as opposed to "too little" or "about the right amount." But by large margins—generally in excess of twenty percentage points—respondents to the 2018 GSS said "too little" rather than "too much" was directed to programs addressing specific issues like education, health care, Social Security, childcare, protecting the environment, and "highways and bridges."[18]

It is unclear whether these views on particular policies are informed by an understanding of how much is actually expended on these matters and the need to raise revenue to pay for them. Regardless, surveys can tell us something about the public's spending priorities and the extent to which federal fiscal policy is congruent with them. Since the early 1970s, the GSS has been asking the same questions about the amount the federal government spends on policies and programs.[19] Unsurprisingly, the GSS results mirror the Gallup "most important problem" data I used in the previous chapter in the analysis of attentiveness. At the beginning of the time series, issues related to crime and drugs top the list. After about 1990, education and health care emerge as the top spending priorities according to the GSS, with Social Security elevated from about mid-ranking to the top four or five and the environment rising a little as well. Issues like welfare, solving the problems of big cities, and assistance to Blacks consistently fall toward the bottom. Defense, which is not of direct interest here but is a matter that consumes a great share of the government's expenditures, is invariably in the bottom half. Foreign aid, which is also not our focus but sees relatively little in the way of federal spending, is nearly always last.

Of course, the federal government's spending has increased tremendously over the last forty-five years. But the priorities revealed by fiscal policy have not materially changed. Spending on entitlements like Social Security and the health programs Medicare and Medicaid are by some distance the largest single items on the list of government outlays and only grow in the proportion of the budget they consume. The GSS surveys suggest this kind of spending is popular—in 2018 the proportion who said government spending on health care was "too little" was forty-nine percentage points larger than that claiming it was "too much"; the figure for Social Security was twenty-four percentage points larger. Federal education spending is less than 2 percent of the budget, but Washington provides only about one-twelfth of the money for K–12. Law enforcement is a similar story, with most of the approximately

$210 billion spent annually in the United States on policing and incarceration coming from states and municipalities.[20] Both policy areas also seem under-funded by the federal government, according to GSS surveys.

On the other hand, although Wlezien and Soroka (2021) have noted an increase since 2000 in the proportion of survey respondents who want the government to spend more on welfare, Americans consistently oppose increased spending on "safety-net" programs—such as Supplemental Security Income, food stamps, and unemployment benefits (McCall 2013, 193–209; Shaw 2009–2010). This opposition does not mean they want to stop funding entirely. Page and Jacobs's (2009, 70–72) comprehensive "inequality survey," undertaken in 2007, showed that nearly 70 percent of respondents felt that "government must see that no one is without food, clothing, or shelter." Even 71 percent of Republican respondents favored their "own tax dollars" going to "help pay for . . . Food stamps and other assistance to the poor." But as recently as 2014, the difference in the percentage of respondents to the GSS survey who said that "too much" was spent on these kinds of policies and those who said "too little" was as large as thirty percentage points.[21]

A credible argument can be made that fiscal-policy priorities adequately reflect the public's views. It should be noted, however, that public knowledge of federal budget matters is notoriously poor—a January 2011 CBS News poll revealed that 30 percent of subjects thought foreign aid constituted more than one-fifth of the budget, and 48 percent thought the government directed less than 20 percent of its expenditures to Social Security. Whether policymakers should even consult American attitudes on precise levels of domestic spending is an open question.

EXTENDING COVERAGE FOR HEALTH CARE

Since the creation of Medicare and Medicaid in the mid-1960s, the federal government has made numerous efforts to extend health care coverage to more Americans. These efforts include the establishment and subsequent encouragement of HMOs in the 1970s and 1980s, the Clinton administration's failed attempt to furnish universal coverage in 1993, the 2010 ACA, and ongoing efforts by Republicans to erode "Obamacare." Throughout, a central issue addressed by policymakers has been whether the government should mandate that more Americans have some kind of insurance, regardless of provider.

Polls suggest why presidents and Congresses have often hesitated to have the government compel and finance greater coverage, despite public support for health care spending. Gallup regularly surveys Americans about their views of the issue and, since 2000, sizable majorities have rated their coverage as "excellent" or "good." In September 2009, as President Obama formally kicked off his project to overhaul the system, 59 percent of respondents said that "controlling costs" was the most important feature of any reform effort, 39 percent "extending coverage." Sixty percent in that poll thought that Obama's efforts to get more people insured would lead to tax increases on the middle class or an overall decline in the quality of health care.

Gallup's surveys also reveal the public's conflicting views on whether or not it is the federal government's "responsibility to make sure all Americans have health care coverage." At the beginning of the century, a perceptible majority felt this way—in fact, 67 percent of participants in an October 1999 NBC News/*Wall Street Journal* poll said the government "should guarantee health insurance coverage." But as the ACA was written, debated, and passed, a slim plurality and sometimes a majority began to oppose the statement, possibly unnerved or satiated by the new policy. In Gallup's November 2013 poll, for example, 56 percent of respondents believed it was not the government's job to provide coverage—although by the 2020s the same proportion were stating that providing coverage was indeed the government's responsibility.

The complexity and multitude of potential approaches to health care policy likely complicate matters for the public, making consensus difficult and plausibly slowing and attenuating the government's response. A Harvard School of Public Health/Robert Wood Johnson poll of January 1994 is illustrative here. Researchers asked participants who should be responsible for providing health insurance. Thirty-five percent responded "employers," 30 percent "individuals," and 27 percent "government." And, not surprisingly, opinions are increasingly motivated by partisanship. Some of this partisanship is ideological and principled; for example, a January 2017 Pew Poll revealed that 66 percent of Republicans believed it was not the responsibility of the government to ensure all Americans had health care coverage, while 81 percent of Democrats believed that it was. But much was surely driven by public views of a president pushing for expanded coverage, as significant Democratic support for and deep Republican opposition to the Clinton and Obama proposals starkly demonstrate (Kriner and Reeves 2014; Tesler 2012).

Hopkins (2023) argues in a recent book about the ACA and its aftermath that the salience and complexity of health care have meant that Americans' views on the issue are largely stable and immune from elite manipulation. Atkinson et al. (2021, 28–32) and Soroka and Wlezien (2010, 111–19) claim that attitudes on health care are thermostatic, potentially checking efforts to move the policy decisively in a particular direction. Both models are consistent with a story in which the ACA is anomalous—and arguably enacted against

the public's will—and in which entrenched public opinion stymies government efforts to extend health care coverage significantly.[22]

The Personal Responsibility and Work Opportunity Reconciliation Act
(PRWORA) of 1996 transformed the principal federal social-welfare program Aid to Families with Dependent Children (AFDC) into Temporary Assistance for Needy Families (TANF). The most important change required
participants to work for benefits—the regulations stipulated that recipients
engage in "work activities" and subjected them to a five-year eligibility limit.[23]
At the time, many critics framed the development as an unwarranted shift in
established policy and betrayal of American values. Three influential administration officials resigned in protest when President Clinton signed the bill.[24]

As I report above, however, public attitudes about social welfare have
been consistently conservative relative to other economic policies. Numerous surveys spanning several decades reveal that Americans generally agree
that recipients of benefits should work for them. A *Los Angeles Times* poll in
April 1985 reported that 51 percent of respondents viewed "workfare" (a government program requiring "poor people" to work before "they can receive
poverty benefits") favorably, only 5 percent unfavorably. The attitude was
apparent as Washington began debating welfare reform during the Clinton
years. An ABC News/*Washington Post* survey of January 1994 showed that
89 percent of respondents supported a "law limiting welfare recipients to a
maximum of two years of benefits, after which those who are able to work
would have to get a job or do community service." PRWORA did little to alter
views. Fifty-seven percent of respondents to a *Washington Post*/Kaiser/Har-
vard 2000 Election Values Survey in September 2000 supported the five-year
eligibility limit, even for beneficiaries who are "willing to work but cannot
find a job." The legislation made policy more congruent with mass opinion.

Support for a policy of working for benefits is presumably grounded in
Americans' views of welfare recipients (Cook and Barrett 1992). An ABC
News/*Washington Post* December 1985 poll reported that 52 percent of respondents agreed that "most able-bodied people on welfare prefer to sit at
home and collect benefits even if they can work." As Republicans took control
of both bodies of Congress for the first time in forty years in January 1995,
the same question asked by the same polling outfit showed the figure to have
increased to 57 percent. The sentiment remains widespread. An August 2017
Politico/Harvard Public Health poll revealed that 72 percent of respondents

supported work requirements for Medicaid.[25] When Congress tightened work requirements for TANF and the Supplemental Nutrition Assistance Program (SNAP) or food stamps—but not Medicaid—in the debt-ceiling extension legislation of June 2023, an Axios-Ipsos poll showed that 63 percent of respondents "strongly" or "somewhat" supported a policy that Medicaid and SNAP beneficiaries should show proof of work to receive benefits.[26]

MAJOR TRADE AGREEMENTS

I have not talked a great deal about trade to this point. It is not fully domestic in nature, but it does have significant effects on the economy. Americans have often been wary of trade, but their opinions on the issue fluctuate over time. A frequently fielded Gallup question asking respondents if they believe trade provides an "opportunity for growth" or poses a "threat to the economy" reveals that citizens have been most supportive of liberalization recently—in fact, especially during the first Trump presidency, a period when policy turned in a protectionist direction. An NBC News/*Wall Street Journal* survey furnishes similar results, with the proportion of subjects claiming that "free trade" has "helped" (and not "hurt") more than doubling—from 23 percent to 50 percent—between November 2010 and August 2018. The only period when those replying to the Gallup poll seeing trade as a threat outnumbered their more upbeat fellow respondents was, roughly, from 2005 to 2008. This followed the Bush administration's approval of a series of regional agreements (Irwin 2017, 672–81).

Indeed, reactions to individual accords generally drive mass views on trade. In September 1992, during the run-up to the ratification of NAFTA, the Gallup poll cited above revealed that a greater proportion of respondents felt trade posed a threat to the economy than believed it offered an opportunity for growth. This result presumably reflected concern about the agreement, as expressed by candidates Pat Buchanan and Ross Perot on the presidential campaign trail that year. Once Clinton was elected, he set to work revising the broader plan by making it more palatable to labor and environmentalists. In concert with the administration, congressional supporters of NAFTA—most of whom were Republicans—mobilized public opinion for their cause. In September 1993, an NBC News/*Wall Street Journal* poll revealed that only 42 percent of Americans backed the agreement; by November, this figure was 53 percent. Uslaner (1998) suggests that the change was attributable to citizens focusing on the issue and being persuaded by arguments about the value of trade. But the most successful single effort on behalf of NAFTA was probably Vice President Al Gore's "defeat" of Perot in a debate about the issue broadcast by CNN in early November. A Gallup poll before the show revealed that 38 percent of respondents opposed NAFTA and only 34 percent supported it. Following Gore's performance and just eight days prior to the House vote, 57 percent of the same sample said they would support the agreement. Legislators broke very late in favor of the trade deal as well (Box-Steffensmeier et al. 1997). Recent work suggests that members of Congress were more responsive to the views of organized interests than to constituents over the course of 1993 (Lee et al. 2023). Overall, however, I think it is fair to say that the literature sees the adoption of NAFTA by Congress as broadly consistent with Americans' wishes (Holian et al. 1997; Uslaner 1998; Wink et al. 1996).

Clinton also pushed to grant China Permanent Normal Trade Relations (PNTR) so that it could join the World Trade Organization (WTO) in 1999 and 2000. A Gallup poll in January 2000 showed 50 percent of subjects approving of this effort, 40 percent opposed. Other surveys posing similar questions revealed a narrow margin in favor of PNTR. By the time the measure was voted on by Congress, the gap had widened, with 56 percent in favor according to Gallup. Nearly twice as many House Democrats voted against the agreement as did for it, perhaps reflecting the Clinton administration's decision early in the process to quit lobbying co-partisans from blue-collar industrial districts in the Midwest and northeast (Irwin 2017, 667–68). The public's general approval of the measure possibly buoyed its congressional supporters.

PNTR seems to have encouraged a surge in imports from China and a reduction in American manufacturing jobs, especially in low-skill and labor-intensive industries located in the South and Midwest. When President George W. Bush pushed Congress to adopt the Central American Free Trade Agreement (CAFTA) in 2005, public support of trade was low. In Gallup's generic survey of attitudes about trade, 49 percent saw it as a "threat" to the American economy, only 44 percent an opportunity for growth. The agreement with countries like Costa Rica, El Salvador, and Honduras was perceived as especially troublesome for the textile industry. By the time Congress voted, however, a clear plurality of Americans seemed to approve of CAFTA. A June 2005 Program on International Policy Attitudes/Knowledge Networks survey reported that 50 percent of respondents supported the agreement, while 39 percent opposed it.

Although there is no clear temporal pattern to Americans' general views of trade—and they are certainly not vocal supporters of its most liberalized forms—NAFTA, PNTR, and CAFTA, possibly the three most important regional or bilateral trade agreements of the last forty years, all passed with public approval. When mass views appeared opposed to the agreements, elite supporters worked earnestly for revisions and to galvanize mass support. It is not coincidental that a potential fourth regional trade agreement of the era, the Trans-Pacific Partnership (TPP) died under the Obama and Trump administrations. Although there was support among the public during 2014 and 2015, surveys showed it to be at best lukewarm. Most Americans were unaware of TPP, and it was not prominently covered by the news media like NAFTA, PNTR, and CAFTA had been—a May 2015 CBS News/*New York Times poll* showed that 48 percent of respondents had "heard nothing at all" about the agreement. As the 2016 presidential campaign moved into high gear, Trump continued to erode public confidence in the country's liberal trade regime. A July 2016 TIPP/*Business Investor's Daily* survey reported that 60 percent of subjects wished Congress would reject TPP, while only 27 percent wished that it would approve the agreement. When thought of as a series of separate agreements presented for public approval or rejection, recent American trade policy has been reasonably responsive to and congruent with mass attitudes.

WHAT THESE ISSUES TELL US

American opinion on these economic issues, as on many others, can be uninformed and, therefore, open to persuasion. On occasion, it acts as a thermostat, reactive to and tempering rather than driving policy. Comparing a measure of presidential party with Stimson's mood scores for various issues, Atkinson et al.'s (2021) recent book reveals that American public opinion behaves thermostatically on economic issues—or certainly more than it does on other kinds of issues. Overall, however, these vignettes show Americans to be quite conservative, displaying a pervasive view that government programs and tax policy should interfere only moderately to redistribute wealth and affect economic outcomes. For its part, Washington has generally crafted policy accordingly. This is certainly the case on particular domestic spending priorities, social-welfare policy, and tax expenditures, but it is also true of the estate tax and the rate at which the wealthiest pay income tax. Progressives might argue that the federal government is too unaccommodating of public attitudes about health care coverage, entitlement spending, and the minimum wage, although the last of these is not of importance to most citizens.

The case for congruence is naturally harder to make than that for responsiveness. Not only is the bar higher, we just do not have as much serviceable data. Again, the minimum wage, a popular staple of the literature on how policymakers have failed the American people and economy, emerges as a black mark. But there are numerous examples of appreciable congruence between public opinion and policy output here. I suggest that they include the top rate of income tax, tax expenditures, "workfare," and major trade agreements.

Conclusion

I think the discussion of important episodes and issues I present above provides further evidence that federal economic policy has been reasonably responsive—and on occasion quite congruent—with American public opinion. I examine four episodes, the Reagan economic revolution, Clinton's focus on deficit reduction, the Bush–Obama response to the Great Recession, and the policies of the first Trump administration. None of the four, it is fair to say, was universally popular. But each was broadly consistent with public opinion. Reagan's tax cuts were well received, but Washington quickly detected Americans' discomfort with the budget deficit and reversed course on fiscal policy as the 1980s wore on. Clinton was vindicated in his approach to the deficit, despite his repudiation of Democratic New Deal Keynesian orthodoxy. Although public sentiment turned against the Obama agenda through 2010, efforts to address the deep financial crisis the president faced on his first day in office found popular support. Trump's economic nationalism was polarizing, but he took advantage of Americans' contemporaneous and deep concerns on trade and tax policy.

If anything, however, Obama and Trump's programs were less responsive to mass sentiment than those of Reagan and Clinton. This difference seems a function of greater partisanship and ideological division within the public. In the 1980s and 1990s, many—presumably moderate—Democrats and Republicans could support the kinds of economic policies they might expect from a president of the opposition party. They appeared more likely to approach economic problems in practical ways. Since then, Americans' views of economic conditions and potential policy adjustments have become an extension of their personal ideology and entrenched opinion of the president and his party.

I look also at seven issues. Of these, policymakers seem most out of step on the minimum wage, a subject at the center of influential analyses of how American politics disregards public opinion and contributes to inequality. I suggest, however, that political science research overstates the issue's importance to Americans. On the other six issues, policy seems quite responsive and occasionally congruent. Americans have generally opposed punitive taxes on their wealthy compatriots, although they prefer that taxes be increased on the rich rather than on themselves. They have welcomed spending on health care, education, and housing, much of it benefiting the middle class. They dislike welfare spending. They tend to support incentives for socially desirable behavior that come in the form of tax advantages rather than direct payments. Americans sometimes want health care coverage extended to others, but they are wary of losing their own if the government makes too radical a move. They believe that welfare recipients should work for benefits. Indeed, the value of industry is consistent with support for the minimum wage, preference for tax benefits over direct assistance, and reluctance to tax the estates and incomes of the well-off.[27] Americans' views of international trade fluctuate, but they have been supportive of all the major bills approved by Congress over the past quarter of a century. Sometimes these views appear latent and require activation. In most instances, however, policy has moved to reflect public opinion.

I continue to examine Americans' views of economic matters in the next chapter, but break the population down into socioeconomic strata, largely using measures of income. Do low-income Americans have materially different views about economics and important economic-policy issues? The evidence serves again to challenge the consensus about the contribution of American politics to economic inequality.

4

Less Affluent Americans' Views of the Economy

Substance

Postwar federal economic policy appears reasonably responsive to American public opinion. This observation does not mean, however, that elected officials are as receptive to the views of the less affluent as they are those of the wealthy. Because the well-off participate actively in politics and are capable of amplifying their attitudes, their preferences and interests might appear to be those of the median American or a majority of all citizens. If this is the case, reelection-minded politicians act on the desires of the rich rather than the wishes of others.

Such a model is problematic if Americans' opinions of economic policy vary materially by class or income. But if working-class, middle-class, and wealthy citizens have similar attitudes, it does not matter particularly to whose cues policymakers respond. So long as government is sensitive to general public opinion, less affluent Americans will have their views reflected in economic policy. It is of secondary importance that their representation may be "coincidental" (Enns 2015) or that we may enjoy what Page and Gilens (2017) have called "democracy by coincidence."

The conventional wisdom is, however, that Americans' opinions on economic policy are heterogeneous and driven significantly by their class status or financial circumstances (Beramendi and Rehm 2016; Rehm et al. 2012; Meltzer and Richard 1981). Income, education, and occupation are robust determinants of economic-policy preferences and ideological type and therefore party voting.[1] Lower-income, blue-collar, or working-class Americans prefer redistribution and government management of the economy as a function of largely progressive economic-policy preferences that lead them to vote frequently for Democrats. Wealthier citizens' policy preferences drive their economic conservatism and support for Republicans. These differences are considerable and should be clear to policymakers. The observation also shapes much of the literature on the political causes of economic inequality (Bartels 2016; Gilens 2012).

There are different arguments. Observers have identified confounding effects that cause individuals to display preferences for economic policies that do not seem consistent with their situation. Frank's (2004) *What's the Matter with Kansas?* is probably the most widely known. He advances the claim that lower-income Americans' views of religion and cultural matters drive their conservatism on economic issues. Ellis and Ura (2011) show that the party voting of lower-income and less educated Americans is more influenced by concerns about cultural preferences than the voting of their wealthier compatriots is. Others see an attenuated link between real personal financial situation and political attitudes, blurring the distinctions in the economic-policy preferences of the rich and poor. This weakening is a function of factors such as group identity (Shayo 2009), altruism and patriotism (Dimick et al. 2018; Gilens and Thal 2018; Williamson 2017), fluctuations in the overall level of inequality (MacDonald 2020a, 2020b; Trump 2018) or the tendency to compare oneself with compatriots who are not as affluent (Cansunar 2021; Condon and Wichowsky 2020; Lupu and Pontusson 2011). Education is increasingly countering, rather than enhancing, the effect of income in the formation of economic-policy preferences (Grossmann and Hopkins 2024; Zingher 2023). Enns and Kellstedt (2008) disaggregate public opinion over a long time series to show there is little difference in the economic-policy views of Americans with few formal educational credentials and those who hold college and postgraduate degrees.

I address the variance of economic policy attitudes by income—and sometimes other indicators of class—in this chapter. I show that, to the extent that government's responsiveness to lower-income and working-class Americans is deficient, the situation does not incriminate American democracy as much as the literature asserts. There are differences in attitudes regarding economics and economic policy across Americans of various income groups and classes, but they are few and often negligible.

Income and Americans' Aggregated Economic Policy Views

Political scientists often assume that public attitudes about matters of economic policy, particularly redistribution or the transfer of wealth to the less affluent, are heterogeneous. Americans with lower incomes are more likely to have progressive views at both the ideological and individual-issue levels (Bartels 2016; Gilens 2012). Material self-interest suggests they should support redistribution. In its simplest terms, an influential model developed by

Romer (1975) and Meltzer and Richard (1981) proposes that individuals with incomes below the median will prefer a tax rate at 100 percent, while those with incomes above the median will prefer no taxes at all. The wealthy experience a net loss in income when the state pools and redistributes revenues, those below the median a net gain. The work provides theoretical underpinnings to the argument that redistribution is consistent with the interests of lower-income citizens.

I look in this first section at whether macro-level data reveal differences in the economic-policy attitudes of rich, middle-income, and poor Americans. To do so, I redeploy Stimson's "mood" measure (Ellis and Stimson 2012; Stimson 2004). We cannot derive mood scores by income group directly, but scholars have utilized other methods as a close approximation. Enns and Wlezien (2011, 9–12) take survey questions that Stimson (Ellis and Stimson 2012; Stimson 2004) uses to construct the mood measure where individual participant responses are available. These questions constitute about 15 percent of all Stimson's survey questions but roughly 30 percent of all question-sequences (these are items asked multiple times during the time series). Deploying respondents' income and Stimson's method of converting question responses into mood, Enns and Wlezien (2011) construct scores for three income groups—the top and bottom quintiles and the middle 60 percent—over the 1956-to-2006 period. Ura and Ellis (2008) aggregate GSS questions about spending on ten domestic policies as a proxy for mood and then form scores for different income groups—here, by quartile. Their indicator is highly correlated with Stimson's mood score.

Figure 4.1 reveals these authors' findings, with the Enns–Wlezien scores on the left and the Ura–Ellis scores on the right. Over the half century spanned by the Enns–Wlezien data, temporal variance greatly exceeds cross-sectional variance. There are minimal differences in the three groups' ideological moods from about 1960 to the mid-1970s and from the late 1980s through the mid-1990s. There are also occasions when the middle-income group is to the left of the lowest-income group and the right of the highest-income group. Through the 1980s until the mid-1990s, the middle-income group was discernibly closer to the higher-income group than to the lower-income group, suggesting public pressure to push economic policy in a conservative direction. The low-income group's liberalism scores range from the low 50s to the low 80s, while the high-income group's scores range from the high 40s to the low 70s. The widest gap between these two groups' scores is about ten points and was present only during the period of progressive economic policy in the 1960s and 1970s.

The Ura–Ellis data tell a similar story. The spread is considerably broader in its temporal than cross-sectional form. Again, from roughly the mid-1980s

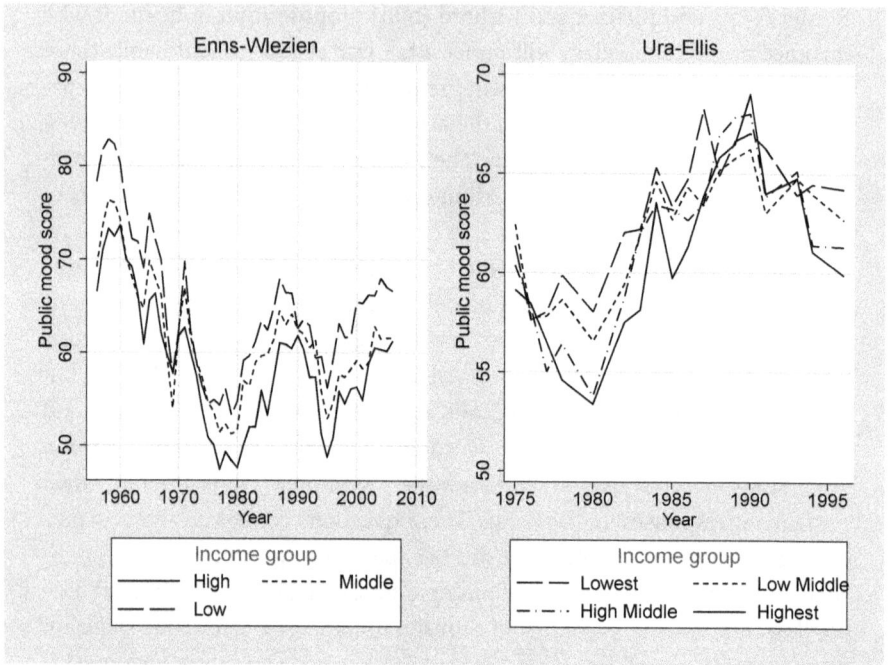

FIGURE 4.1. Economic policy mood of different income groups, 1960–2010
Enns and Wlezien (2011) data are in the left-hand figure; Ura and Ellis (2008) data are in the right-hand figure.

to mid-1990s, the gap between the groups is particularly narrow. Not least because Ura and Ellis divide the population into four groups that are equal in size, there are more occasions when lines cross. Those in the second-highest and second-lowest quartiles switch positions frequently, and there are instances when those middle groups are either to the right of the wealthiest quartile or to the left of the poorest cohort.

These findings all suggest that Americans in different income strata hold different views of economic policy but that these differences are not particularly large most of the time. Note also that the groups move together. The income groups trace each other's leftward or rightward moves. This observation tells us nothing about the congruity of policy and public opinion but suggests that economic policy is roughly responsive to the various cohorts in equal amounts. The conservative economic policy of the early 1980s and mid-1990s might be a reply to rightward moves by the wealthiest Americans, other income groups, or the general population.

We come to analogous findings using Gilens's (2012; Gilens and Page 2014) comprehensive dataset of just over 1,800 survey questions collected from the

1980s to early in the first decade of the 2000s. Gilens imputes the proportion of respondents of groups located at the 10th, 50th, and 90th percentiles by income who were in favor of change on a particular policy.[2] Very often the wealthy, middle-class, and poor agree. When we define clear positions as those where more than 55 percent or less than 45 percent of respondents in a group favor policy change (and therefore exclude groups' neutral stances, when between 45 and 55 percent favor change), any two of the three groups take oppositional stances on only 8.3 percent of the questions. On roughly one-third of those questions (therefore just under 3 percent of the total), two of the groups take a clear position against the other and none is neutral. Of those, the lowest-income group was most likely to be in conflict with the other two, but such conflict only arose on 1.6 percent of all questions. This result is consistent with Enns's (2022, 116–18) observation that the Gilens data reveal a significant amount of consensus between income groups on public policy.

Gilens (2012, 97–122; Gilens and Page 2014) identifies his survey questions by policy type. If we take the imputed response of the groups at the 10th, 50th, and 90th percentiles of income for the survey questions on economic policy and use Gilens's scores, the estimated proportion in favor of change is correlated in excess of $r = .9$ for the poor-middle and middle-rich pairings. This finding applies for issues including taxes, the minimum wage, and unemployment benefits. In the case of social-welfare policy, the correlations for these pairs are greater than $r = .93$.[3] The scores are just about as high as they are on issues that are not economic in nature, like foreign policy and gun control, where, theoretically at least, income or class should have less effect on preferences. Interestingly, the rich and poor agree more on economic and social-welfare policy ($r = .812$ and $r = .858$) than they do on religious and moral policies ($r = .776$). I will return to the Gilens data at the end of this chapter.

Affluence and Americans' Views of Important Economic Concepts

In this section, I look at Americans' views on three concepts that constitute important features of a national economy. They are broader than individual policies and distinct from ideology. I examine aggregate public opinion, but I am most interested in differences across income or class groups.

INEQUALITY

Economic inequality is a social condition, not a policy.[4] The exercise of understanding public attitudes surrounding it is tricky. Still, material self-interest assumes that affluent citizens should be less concerned by its presence than their lower-income compatriots should be. Some well-off Americans, especially those who enjoy their wealth by virtue of investments or inheritance, are more likely to be uncomfortable with inequality than others (Cohn et al. 2023). There may also be situations when the rich grow perturbed by high levels of economic polarization—perhaps if the poor tend to be white (Newman et al. 2022; Wager 2024), or there exist negative externalities such as worrying crime rates (Rueda and Stegmueller 2019), or government coffers are flush and the country can afford to direct resources to the poor (Cavaillé 2023). But in general, wealthy citizens' tolerance is presumably higher for significant differences in affluence unaddressed by government action (Cohn et al. 2023).

Many academic analyses of survey data suggest this is not the case. Not only do the poor dislike inequality, so generally do the middle class and rich. Page and Jacobs (2009) wrote a book exploring Americans' attitudes about inequality using data collected just prior to the financial crisis. Seventy-two percent of their respondents agreed that "differences in income in America are too large," including 60 percent of wealthier subjects—those with annual family incomes over $80,000 (Page and Jacobs 2009, 40–46). The Harris poll shows no material change since the early 1970s in the proportion of respondents who believe "the rich are getting richer and the poor are getting poorer" (Strain 2019). The figure is consistently about 70 percent, implying broad consensus across income groups. The ANES survey routinely asks whether respondents perceive "the difference in incomes between rich people and poor people in the United States today [to be] larger" than it was twenty years ago.[5] Between 2002 and 2012, the percentage of affirmative responses was in the 74–80 percent range, with a slight shift toward those saying the difference was "much"—rather than "somewhat"—larger toward the end of the time series (Bartels 2016, 118–20). Condon and Wichowsky (2020, 13–15) show the mean score on a seven-point scale of responses to GSS's question regarding whether the "government in Washington should reduce the income differences between rich and poor" as holding practically static, at about 3.5, since the late 1970s. Whereas they see indifference, Witko et al.'s (2021, 105–7) interpretation of this question notes a bias in favor of remedial action since 2000. McCall's (2013) comprehensive study of public opinion and economic equality draws similar conclusions. Majorities, albeit slim, generally believe assertions such as "inequality continues to exist to benefit the rich and powerful" and "large income differences are unnecessary for prosperity" (McCall 2013, 99–102; McCall and Kenworthy 2009). McCall also sees few differences in views about inequality across class indicators like income and education—with the exception of the 1990s, when the proportion of higher-income Americans who believed there was a lot of inequality decreased (McCall 2013, 106–12).

If Americans' opinions of inequality are so disparaging and consistent across groups and time, we should expect government to respond. Why have public attitudes wielded such minimal effect? I think there are several largely overlooked explanations. First, inequality might not appear to be as large and important in this country as political scientists think. A number of economists argue that observers exaggerate American inequality because their calculations omit factors such as Medicaid, Medicare, transfer payments, and taxes. Early (2018) suggests that accounting for government redistribution of income would have reduced the United States' Gini coefficient in 2016 by about 40 percent. More recent analyses posit that the Gini indicator has been flat over the past half century and may have been lower in 2017 than it was in 1967 (Ganz and Brill 2020; Gramm et al. 2022).[6] Although apples-to-apples comparisons are difficult, these calculations greatly diminish the difference between the United States and its advanced industrial peers. According to Ganz and Brill (2020), the United States is still quite unequal but not perceptibly more so than countries like Ireland, New Zealand, South Korea, Italy, and Spain.

Even if America's inequality is objectively large, Bartels (2016, 121–23) shows that a significant proportion of Americans—nearly a third in the 2002 and 2004 ANES—have neither "thought about" nor acquired any real understanding of inequality in the United States. Since 2001, Gallup has asked periodically what people consider to be the "most important problem" facing the country. Economic inequality has garnered an average of 1.5 percent of responses.[7] According to Heffington, Park, and Williams's (2017) "Most Important Problem" (MIP) dataset, the annual average percentage of Americans who saw "poverty/inequality" as the most important problem between 1957 and 2015 is 2.72 percent—a figure that peaked at 9.5 percent in 1991.[8] By comparison, the "budget deficit" annual mean is 3.95 percent and the crime mean is 6.82 percent.[9] In the summer of 2020, in the midst of a presidential campaign, the issue tied for ninth place in importance among Democrats, according to a Pew Research poll.[10] The September 2019 Pew Research American Trends survey revealed that 42 percent of respondents characterized "reducing economic inequality" as a top priority, well below the proportion describing "dealing with terrorism" and "reducing gun violence" the same way.[11] Another 2019 Pew Survey, here on "Trust and Distrust in America," reported that 52 percent of subjects saw "the gap between rich and poor" as a "very big problem," but 67 percent viewed "ethics in government" and 62 percent "the ability of Democrats and Republicans to work together in Washington" the same way.[12] As the country emerged from a pandemic widely thought to have widened the economic divide, a June 2021 Harvard University–Harris poll reported that only 7 percent of respondents put "income inequality" in their three "most important issues facing the country today." This figure was seventeen percentage points behind immigration, seven percentage points less than the national debt and federal deficits, and two percentage points lower than "political correctness and cancel culture."[13] A 2017 Organization for Economic Cooperation and Development (OECD) survey of citizens in its thirty-two member countries placed Americans thirtieth in the proportion who believed income differences in their country were too large. At 63 percent, the US topped only the Netherlands and Denmark, two countries with Gini coefficients about 65–75 percent of ours (OECD 2021).

To be sure, some research suggests that Americans do have a grasp of growing income differentials in the country (Stimson and Wager 2020, 58–59). But they have little understanding of the true distribution of wealth across the population. Norton and Ariely (2011) asked respondents to estimate the proportion of the country's wealth held by various groups of citizens. The average participant guessed that the top fifth held about 58 percent, a good twenty-five percentage points lower than the actual amount.

Geography, moreover, obscures inequality. Many Americans live in economically homogeneous communities (Ellis 2017). They do not often interact with people who are much better or worse off. When rich and poor do encounter one another, our informal and increasingly egalitarian culture blurs traditional social distinctions that in the past conveyed large economic differences (Cansunar 2021; Page and Jacobs 2009, 30–31).

Inequality would also be more apparent if an association with a particular class was important to Americans. It is not, however. A *New York Times* national survey taken in 2018 revealed respondents placed "social class" last of ten groups they most identified with (Badger and Bui 2018). Their family role, religion, occupation, gender, nationality, and age were all considerably more important to their sense of self. In fact, only 2 percent of respondents stated that social class was the most important factor in describing who they were. This result seems attributable to Americans' aspirations. Romantic images and misconceptions about wealth accumulation inspire rather than anger (Page and Jacobs 2009, 26–28). Kim's (2023) work on reality television reveals that exposure to "rags-to-riches" stories inoculates frequent viewers from concerns about inequality. Condon and Wichowsky (2020, 125–68) demonstrate that Americans "look down" rather than "look up," in a psychological need to appreciate their own standard of living.

Second, many Americans view inequality as a condition that policy cannot or should not alter. Bartels (2016, 106) rejects the notion that people find the phenomenon "natural and unobjectionable," but I think the sentiment constitutes a reasonable interpretation of his findings. Both he (Bartels 2016, 118–23) and McCall (2013, 102–5) argue that public recognition of inequality is temporally stable, even in the face of the rapidly and dramatically changing economic circumstances of the past half century. McCall (2013, 140–84) uses a great deal of data, and her argument is nuanced, but it would also be fair to say that she believes many Americans accept inequality as a form of "system justification," as if criticism of its existence were unpatriotic. She reveals that citizens think executives are paid too much and unskilled workers too little, but that they believe much of this income gap is attributable to natural ability and that the responsibility to reduce the gap does not belong to the government. Lendway and Huber's (2023) experimental study shows that Americans are significantly more accepting of income differences when informed of job responsibilities and qualifications.

Other survey data are consistent with this interpretation. The same September 2019 Pew Research American Trends survey cited above reported that 70 percent of respondents—including 59 percent of low-income subjects—"believed some amount of inequality is acceptable."[14] Gallup polls over the past twenty years reveal that roughly half of respondents think "the fact that some people in the United States are rich and others are poor" is "an acceptable part of the economic system," while the other half consider it "a problem that needs to be fixed"—although by whom it is not clear.[15] Even the expression of a desire for government to reduce differences between rich and poor is unlikely to result in policy if a majority cannot agree on a solution.

Many political scientists assume that public recognition of inequality as an important problem is a sufficient condition for government action (Bartels 2016; McCall 2013; Witko et al. 2021). Stasis frustrates them, and they argue it is evidence of a malfunctioning democracy. But perhaps the public knows that government has been trying for decades to alleviate inequality without much success. Americans recognize its existence but plausibly believe that government action is futile and potentially counterproductive.

Third, as McCall (2013) notes, inequality's abstractness means that Americans' attitudes about it translate poorly into actual policy preferences, and therefore public views of the condition produce ambiguous cues for policymakers. Inequality often manifests as a kind of injustice or a worrying sign of diminishing opportunities, but the sign provides little practical direction to those who would like to address it. When the public makes concrete connections between inequality as a problem and policy prescriptions, moreover, they frequently plump for conservative responses. Piston (2018, 57–76) argues that political scientists exaggerate the extent to which Americans oppose downward distribution because the public generally holds positive views of the poor and resent the rich. Unlike McCall (2013), he (2018, 147) suggests that "divisions in attitudes toward class groups map onto divisions in policy preferences" and that pro-poor people are liberal and pro-rich people are conservative. He concludes, therefore, that policymakers misread or ignore public opinion. But *poor* and *rich* are themselves abstractions, and I suspect people imagine these as conditions. Being poor is worse than being rich, and individuals will therefore direct their sympathy to the disadvantaged. As we shall see, however, Americans, more so than people in other countries, believe that these circumstances are a function of personal behavior and that government assistance to alleviate them should be contingent on a demonstrated effort by the subject to address their personal situation—by working for benefits, joining a job training program, or getting an education, for example. The analysis in the previous chapter revealed that Americans may have compassion for the poor, but they seem to prefer people who work, regardless of their financial situation, over those they believe do not.

Fourth and finally, as Hochschild (1981) noted forty years ago, there is a significant amount of evidence showing that even those who would benefit from redistribution are uninterested in equality. Hoy and Mager (2021) report that informing poorer Americans they are in the bottom two quintiles by income has no material effect on either their attitudes toward inequality generally or what, if anything, government should do about it. In the September 2019 Pew poll used extensively in this section, 52 percent of lower-income respondents believed that "reducing economic inequality" was a "top priority," the same proportion of the group that viewed "addressing climate change" similarly. A larger proportion of lower-income respondents believed that "reducing gun violence," "dealing with terrorism," and "making healthcare more affordable" were top priorities. In fact, a much larger proportion of upper-income respondents (twelve percentage points) believed that making health care affordable should be a top priority than lower-income respondents thought reducing income inequality should.[16]

Historical analyses furnish similar findings. Heffington, Park, and Williams (2017) break their MIP data down to the individual-respondent level. They have responses from 710,429 subjects for whom they also have information about income. Of course, these individuals spread unevenly across surveys and time, but they provide some insight into whether lower-income Americans care, in both relative and absolute senses, about inequality. The proportion of respondents from the bottom income quartile who stated that "poverty/inequality" was the most important issue was 3.4 percent for the 1957–2007 period. This figure compares to 3.1 percent for the second-lowest quartile, 2.7 percent for the second-highest quartile, and 2.2 percent for the highest quartile. For comparison—and, again, this result is of aggregated individuals, regardless of the time they were surveyed—twenty-eight more subjects in the lowest quartile said the "budget deficit" was the most important problem than named poverty/inequality (4,628 to 4,600).[17] Witko et al. (2021, 89–91) deploy some of the same data to make the case that citizens in the lowest income quartile care significantly more about poverty or inequality than they do about the budget deficit. But their analysis is from the period after 1995, one that excludes eight of the top ten years for the budget deficit in the list of America's most important problems—the issue is particularly concerning to survey participants from 1984 to 1994. Even without these years, the authors are only able to show that the proportion of individuals in the lowest quartile who thought that poverty/inequality was the most important problem exceeded those selecting the budget deficit by about 1.5 percentage points.

In fact, when analyses reveal that Americans' concerns about inequality differ by income, the relationship can be in the positive rather than negative direction. Interestingly, although he does not discuss it, Bartels (2016, 124–35) uses a measure of family income in examinations of questions in the 2002 and 2004 ANES asking respondents whether they felt inequality had grown and whether they believed this growth was detrimental. After controlling for ideology and levels of political information, of those who recognized increasing inequality, respondents with higher incomes were more likely to express concern.

ECONOMIC AGENCY

Americans tend to believe they can affect their personal economic circumstances, an extension of an individualistic culture believed to be a hallmark of our country's politics (Hartz 1955). This tendency leads them to think that the causes of inequality and poverty are dispositional rather than situational and that policy responses are unnecessary and possibly counterproductive. We believe that characteristics like hard work, intelligence, and ambition should and do shape people's financial position and that factors such as race and family background should not and do not (Bower-Bir 2022). In short, we believe that we have economic agency and that that is a good thing. The 2019 Pew Global Attitudes survey found that 67 percent of American respondents "mostly" or "completely" disagreed that "success in life is pretty much determined by forces outside our control." This proportion was more than that found in all but one—Australia—of the thirty-three other countries where Pew asked the question. In the 2014 survey, 73 percent of respondents said it was "very important . . . to work hard in life to get ahead." This percentage was larger than the ones found in forty-one of forty-three other countries, the exceptions being Argentina and Colombia.

These attitudes are stable across time. Since 1994, Pew's Trends survey has asked respondents whether they think "most people who want to get ahead can make it if they're willing to work hard" or "hard work and determination are no guarantee of success for most people." The proportion who agreed with the latter statement is generally in the 30–40 percent range, hitting that highest number only once, in 2011. Around the turn of the century, it was in the low to mid-20s. Pew's question asking respondents whether they believe success in life is outside their control has behaved similarly. Since 1987 when it was first posed, a minimum of 56 percent of respondents have disagreed. The figure was particularly high from the late 1990s until about 2010 and increased a little again in the late 2010s. To some extent, such minimal fluctuations are surprising given researchers' beliefs that the elevated inequality we currently experience leads people to become more fatalistic about their circumstances and less confident they can attain the "American Dream" (Chetty et al. 2017; Wolak and Peterson 2020).

Most of those who believe that individuals shape their own economic situations tend to be affluent. Suhay, Klašnja, and Rivero (2021) show that high-income individuals, particularly the very wealthy, attribute economic success to matters like "intelligence" and "hard work" rather than to being "lucky" or coming from a "wealthy family." Bower-Bir (2022) reveals that low-income, non-white, and older citizens tend to give greater credence to situational determinants of economic outcomes. Still, socioeconomic differences on the causes of disparities are not as large as we might imagine. Page and Jacobs's (2009, 51–53) study reveals at most very small differences in Americans' attitudes across income groups regarding statements like "It is still possible to start out poor in this country and become rich" and "Our freedom depends on the free enterprise system." In both cases, a healthy majority (70 percent and 65 percent) of low-income respondents agreed. Pew's September 2019 Trends survey question about the value of work is also illustrative. Sixty-four percent of upper-income participants sided with the belief that diligent people can prosper, but so did 55 percent of lower-income respondents, with the middle class roughly halfway between.

Less affluent Americans are also considerably more likely to believe in the importance of work to success than are wealthy foreigners. This finding suggests a broad belief in the capacity of Americans to shape their personal economic situations. In its 2012 Global Attitudes Survey, Pew asked its usual question about work and success. Seventy percent of low-income Americans agreed that "most people can succeed if they are willing to work hard," a proportion larger than that of high-income Britons and Germans who felt the same.[18]

In fact, today Americans seem more divided by partisanship than by wealth or class on the importance of agency to economic outcomes (Suhay et al. 2022). Democrats tend to accept that personal circumstances are the result of an unfair system or bad luck. Pew's American Trends panel reveals that these attitudes are polarizing along party lines. Up until roughly 2010, a comfortable majority of Democrats disagreed that "hard work and determination are no guarantee of success for most people." By 2019, a slight majority agreed.[19] Moreover, whereas for Republicans the relationship between income and the argument that affluence is the result of industry and ability is positive, the higher the Democratic respondent's income, the less likely they are to attribute economic outcomes to dispositional matters. Again, the 2019 Pew Trends survey is useful. Fifty-eight percent of Democrats with family incomes above $100,000 believed that hard work and determination did not ensure success, but only 51 percent of Democrats with incomes less than $30,000 did.

GOVERNMENT AND MARKETS

Perceptions of the institutions likely to generate desirable economic outcomes should vary across socioeconomic groups (Kenworthy and McCall 2008; Meltzer and Richard 1981). The wealthy presumably prefer markets. Their less well-off compatriots favor purposive state action. Government might not always make less affluent citizens better off, but elected officials generally propose economic policy intervention to restrict freedom of action and redistribute resources in some way. All things being equal, markets are more likely to maintain the advantages enjoyed by the well-to-do.

Survey researchers have produced a great deal of polling data on Americans' attitudes about whether the market or government is the institution most capable of securing desirable economic conditions. In every election from 1992 to 2016, ANES asked participants to choose whether they thought a "strong government" was required "to handle today's complex economic problems" or whether "the free market can handle these problems without government being involved." The responses suggest that the public prefers intervention. Those siding with the government outnumber those wanting market-generated solutions by about 3 to 2, and sometimes nearly 2 to 1. Respondents' views differ little by income, though. Higher incomes are associated more with support for markets, but not by much. In fact, in 1992 and

2016 a majority of respondents in every family income group—and ANES uses more than twenty of them, ranging in 2016 from under $10,000 to more than $250,000—chose "strong government." In every year that ANES posed the question, correlations between the income categories and the "strong government" response varied from only about $r = .05$ to $r = .1$.

ANES has also asked the question, "Is less government better or are there more things government should be doing?" Majorities still tend to side with government action, but these majorities are considerably slimmer than the ones in the survey's question about markets—with generally around 55 percent of respondents favoring more government, except in the early 1990s when the number was about 60 percent. In fact, the 2012 and 2016 respondents split evenly. Income is more highly correlated on this item. The strength of the relationship has diminished greatly over time, but it was as high as $r = .24$ in 1992.

Question wording appears crucial in shaping public views about the comparative value of government and markets, however. This point may have to do with the abstract and depersonalized nature of the market—which individuals probably find more difficult to comprehend than they do government. Results often seem contradictory. A George Mason University Mercatus Center poll of American adults in 2019 revealed that 57 percent of respondents agreed that "the freer a market is, the more likely it is to serve the general public." The same poll registered an average of 4.4 on a seven-point scale ranging from "no involvement" to "significant involvement," with a "moderate involvement" middle, in describing the level of activity government should have in "economic matters."[20] An August 2014 *Reason*–Ruppe poll demonstrated that respondents were considerably more favorable toward the "free market" than toward a "government-managed economy"—"very favorable" and "mostly favorable" assessments of the free market were thirty-nine percentage points greater than for the "government-managed economy."[21] A RealClear Opinion Research survey taken in 2019 reported that a majority—58 percent—of participants rejected greater government involvement and agreed that "capitalism and free markets are too heavily regulated in the U.S. today" or "capitalism and free markets are generally working well in the U.S. today."[22] This survey was administered before the COVID-19 pandemic struck but three years into a Trump administration that had cut taxes and reduced regulations and was quite unpopular to boot. A Gallup poll the same year reported that 43 percent of participants thought socialism was a "good thing." But at a point in Gallup's time series when socialism's popularity was as high as ever, a majority continued to choose the "free market" for eight of the ten issue areas where interviewers asked respondents whether they preferred the "free market" or "government" to be "primarily responsible for what happens." These areas included "the distribution of wealth," "the economy overall," "wages," "higher education," and "healthcare."[23]

Government action is also less popular when respondents are called on to assess it in isolation. Since 1992, Gallup has asked whether people "think government is trying to do too many things that should be left to individuals or businesses" or whether "it should do more to solve the country's problems." Most of the time, and often by margins as large as fifteen to twenty percentage points, the public agrees that government does too much. The occasions when it narrowly sided with greater government action were in 1993; immediately following 9/11; and in the midst of a pandemic, just prior to Joe Biden's election as president in the fall of 2020.

It appears that Americans are skeptical of the proposition that abstract markets deliver more desirable personal economic effects than their own talents and hard work do, and there is clearly some desire on their part for government to play a role in the economic arena. Still, it is also accurate to state that at a conceptual level, public support for government intervention in the economy, particularly to equalize outcomes and including among the working and middle classes, is equivocal and, in a comparative sense, tepid.[24]

Income and Americans' Views of Redistributive Policy

WELFARE SPENDING

Here I look at attitudes across income and other groups toward more-concrete economic policies. I am interested in two important policies designed largely to redistribute wealth. I start with spending on welfare programs. The existing literature suggests that there is perceptible variation in the views of Americans on this issue across income and class groups. Enns and Wlezien (2011, 5–9) and Soroka and Wlezien (2008; Wlezien and Soroka 2011, 288–92) use GSS survey data from 1973 to 2008 to show little difference in the attitudes that low-, middle-, and upper-income citizens have about federal spending levels on a whole array of issues, including health care, education, and the environment. The differences in the net support for increased spending are relatively large for welfare, however. Low-income Americans are appreciably more likely to be supportive. Yet even for this group, approval is only positive for a few years in the time series—particularly in the late 1980s and the middle of the first decade of the 2000s. It averages close to −10; that is, the proportion of low-income participants calling for decreased spending on welfare is about ten percentage points greater than the proportion wanting more.

Gilens (2012, 113–23) generates similar findings from the data I discussed earlier in this chapter. I noted previously that he finds little difference between the views of people in various income groups on matters of social-welfare policy. What is more, positions of people in all groups tend to be what we might call "conservative." Participants at the 10th, 50th, and 90th percentiles by income all reveal significant support for work requirements and job training for welfare recipients. Although to a lesser extent than those at the median and high-income thresholds, low-income respondents also approved of setting time limits on welfare benefits. Like Wlezien and his colleagues, Gilens reveals a material difference between respondents in the different income cohorts in the extent to which they support cuts to welfare. Still, on average a majority of poorer survey participants endorsed reduced expenditures.

To explore this matter further, I examine responses to a question ANES asked about federal spending on welfare from 1992 to 2016—"Should federal spending on welfare programs be increased, decreased, or kept about the same?" The time series represents a healthy chunk of our current era of inequality. For every year the question was asked, I deploy an ordered logit model with supporters of increased spending designated the lowest values and supporters of decreased spending the highest values.[25] I use a variety of theoretically important independent variables, including income and two other class-related measures—education and whether or not the respondent or someone in their household belonged to a labor union.[26] Consistent with other surveys, participants generally opposed greater welfare spending—with the exception of 1996 and 2008, the proportion who replied "increase" was around one-fifth and even a little less, but "keep about the same" was often the plurality response.[27]

Figure 4.2 reveals the coefficient plots for the gauges of socioeconomic status for all seven elections. Income has a steady positive and material effect, meaning that the higher the respondent's income, the more likely they are to believe that government should decrease welfare spending. In 2008, for example, the model predicts that a respondent in a household with an annual income of $20,000 has a 22.6 percent chance of supporting a cut to welfare spending, a respondent in a household making $100,000 a 35.2 percent chance. Household union membership has no such effect, however— although there are occasions in recent elections when union affiliation is close to a statistically significant association with support for cuts in welfare spending. The finding is different from that of Franko and Witko (2023a), who argue in an analysis of GSS data that less affluent Americans are appreciably supportive of redistribution when they are conscious of their class through union membership. The relationship between education and welfare

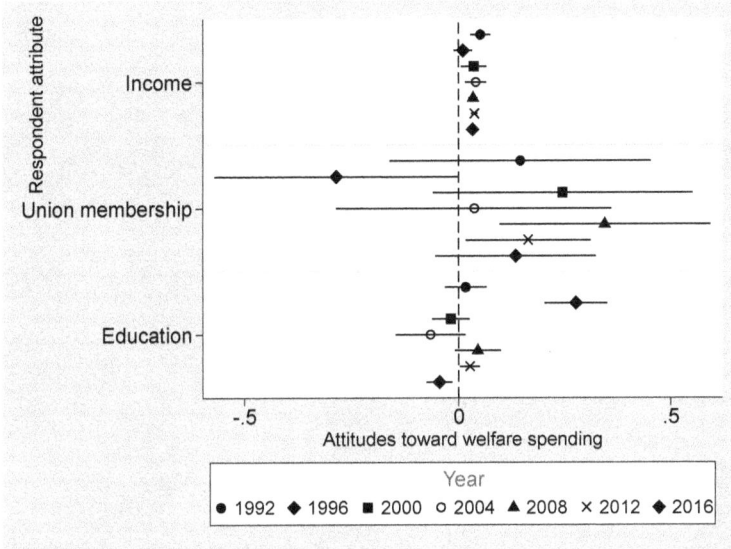

FIGURE 4.2. Effect of income, union membership, and education on attitudes regarding welfare spending, ANES 1992–2016
Higher values represent support for decreasing welfare spending. Bars represent 95 percent confidence intervals. ANES data can be found at https://electionstudies.org/.

spending is counterintuitively negative in 2004 and 2016. This finding appears to muddle the link between socioeconomic status and attitudes toward welfare spending.

Partisanship is increasingly modifying and reducing the influence of socioeconomic status (Auslen and Phillips 2024; Suhay et al. 2022). Figure 4.3 shows how party identification conditions the effect of income on the preference to decrease welfare spending in each of the presidential elections—that is, specifications of the model where I interact income and party identification. The steep lines in 1992 and 2008 reveal that income was most important to respondents' attitudes in those years. Young Democratic presidential candidates won both elections—Bill Clinton the former, Barack Obama the latter—with energetic campaigns focused on economic problems. Notice how little income contributes to attitudes in 1996, after Clinton had delivered on welfare reform and, even for many Democrats, the issue appeared to have been addressed. Partisan differences were at their widest in 2012 and 2016, when the proportion of highest-income Democrats wishing to decrease welfare spending was considerably less even than the proportion of lowest-income Republicans who preferred the same policy. According to Cavaillé (2023, 190–98), high-income Democrats—or what are often called

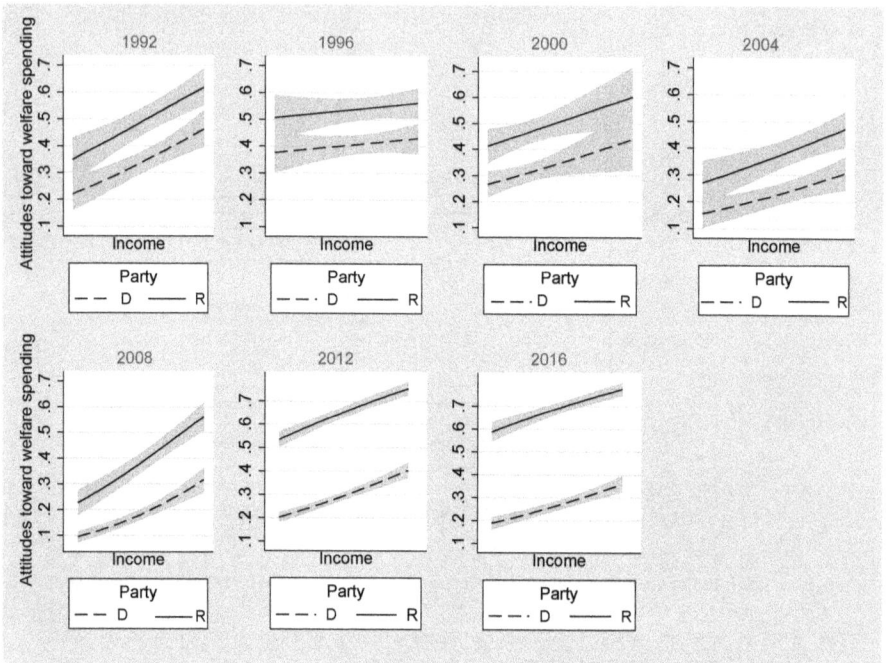

FIGURE 4.3. Effect of income when conditioned by party on attitudes regarding welfare spending, ANES 1992–2016

Republicans are shown in the solid line, Democrats the dashed line. Higher values represent support for decreasing welfare spending. Gray areas are 95 percent confidence intervals. ANES data can be found at https://electionstudies.org/.

"bleeding-heart liberals"—constitute an important counterbalance to lower-income conservatives who care little for redistribution.

TAXES

Many of the questions researchers ask about taxes produce intuitive responses. In Gallup's extensive time series on the subject, less than 5 percent believe they pay "too little" and a majority nearly always believe they pay "too much."[28] The GSS survey repeatedly shows this trend is the same for all income groups, with even a majority of low-income respondents consistently believing their own taxes are "too high"—the figure for middle-income and upper-income respondents is generally above 60 percent (Enns and Wlezien 2011, 5–9; Soroka and Wlezien 2008).

If there is a group that pays too little, Americans agree it is the wealthy. From the early 1990s on, a plurality of respondents to Gallup's poll tended to believe that lower-income people paid "too much." The proportion saying that middle-income Americans paid "too much" or their "fair share" battled for top spot, but the amount claiming that upper-income people paid "too little" was always a sizable majority, even if that majority declined after 2000.[29] Gilens (2012, 113–5) reports that survey respondents at the 90th income percentile support, by amounts in excess of 65 percent, both cutting income tax rates for low- and middle-income Americans and raising levies upon themselves. Bartels (2016, 116–8) shows that according to the 2002 and 2004 ANES surveys, even a majority of rich people believe they "pay less than they should" in taxes. This belief could arise out of a sense of civic responsibility or patriotism (Williamson 2017). Regardless, nearly everyone seems to realize that when the policy concerns revenues, it makes sense to go after people with money.

The evidence therefore suggests less variance of opinion across income groups on taxes than on welfare spending. It is only on cutting capital gains taxes and instituting a flat tax, for example, that attitudes fluctuate markedly, according to Gilens (2012, 113–15), with the poor generally in opposition and wealthy wanting both—and, as history has shown, experiencing limited success on the former and clear failure on the latter. To further explore the extent to which affluence drives individuals' views about tax policy, I use questions that presumably get respondents to think of revenue broadly and tax hikes or cuts as trade-offs against other policy objectives.

Figure 4.4 reveals coefficients from logit or ordered logit analyses of questions asked by ANES in presidential elections from 1992 to 2004. The questions vary across the years, and I use two in 2004. They essentially ask respondents what government should do with tax policy when dealing with budget deficits or surpluses.[30] Higher values denote approval for decreasing taxes or opposition to increasing taxes. I use the same independent variables I did in the model of social-welfare policy above. Party identification is the most robust performer, with Republicans taking the strongest position in favor of tax cuts. Of the reported measures, income and union membership have no material effect on attitudes. The results confirm a recent analysis of state tax policy using a similar approach. Donovan and Bowler (2022) show that income has little to no direct effect on respondents' preferences for tax increases over spending cuts as a way to resolve a budget deficit. Education performs more dependably. In every case except the question in 2004 asking respondents if they would prefer cuts in domestic programs to cuts in taxes, subjects with less education are supportive of policies reducing or holding the line on taxes.[31]

Figure 4.5 reveals the results of the same model applied to questions about taxes asked by the CES from 2012 to 2018—I do not use 2008 and 2010 because

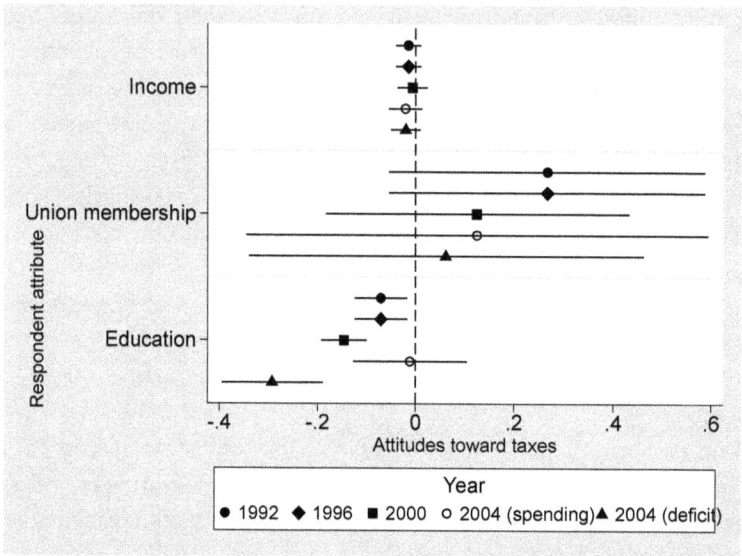

FIGURE 4.4. Effect of income, union membership, and education on attitudes regarding taxes, ANES 1992–2004

Higher values represent support for decreasing taxes/opposition to increasing taxes. Bars represent 95 percent confidence intervals. ANES data can be found at https://electionstudies.org/.

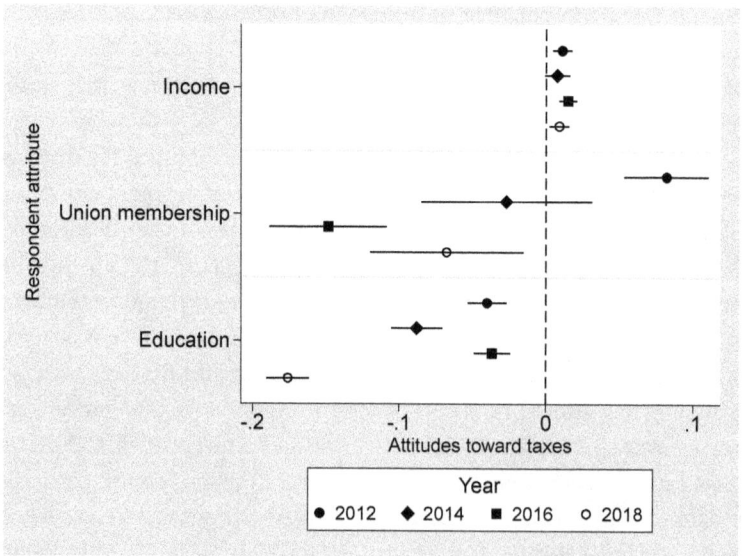

FIGURE 4.5. Effect of income, union membership, and education on attitudes regarding taxes, CES 2012–2018

Higher values represent support for decreasing taxes/opposition to increasing taxes. Bars represent 95 percent confidence intervals. CES data can be found at https://cces.gov.harvard.edu/.

the survey's only tax items were those analyzed by Donovan and Bowler (2022).[32] The questions are unavoidably heterogeneous and different from those posed by ANES, but they do get at subjects' opinions about taxes. Again, I code the position most in favor of tax cuts or against tax increases highest, whether the dependent variable be dichotomous or have three values.[33] With the exception of 2014, income and a desire to cut or oppose increases to taxes enjoy a statistically significant positive relationship, even though the substantive effect seems small. In 2016, for example, when the variable's coefficient is largest, a member of a family with an income of $20,000 had a 38.9 percent chance of ranking a tax increase as the least desirable option when addressing the budget deficit, one from a family with an income of $100,000 a 41 percent chance. In 2016 and 2018—and 2014 if we use a 90 percent confidence interval or 5 percent on each tail—union membership is associated with a greater tolerance of hiking or holding the line on taxes.

Once again, however, education has a negative effect. Respondents with lower levels of education are more likely to support reductions and oppose increases in taxes. The finding provides an interesting complication to the traditional story of class and tax policy preferences, but it comports with observations of a "diploma divide" in which education increasingly explains Americans' vote choice and in which college graduates are becoming more Democratic and those without degrees more Republican—a divide seen particularly in the first decade of the 2000s (Grossmann and Hopkins 2024; Zingher 2022a).

Figure 4.6 shows race and ethnicity to play interesting roles. In every year for the CES data, both Blacks and Latinos were statistically more likely to support tax cuts or oppose tax hikes when compared to whites. To be sure, the substantive effects are not always strong, particularly for Latinos. But they do generally grow over the 2012–2018 period and are larger than the effects of indicators we would intuitively believe to be important. In 2014, for example, the predicted probability of a Black respondent supporting the Tax Hike Prevention Act was 29.2 percent; for a non-Black it was 24.8 percent. In the case of Latinos, these figures were 34.6 percent and 25 percent, respectively. In 2016, Blacks were more likely than non-Blacks—by eight percentage points—to place raising taxes as their last choice of options to address the budget deficit, but they were less likely than non-Blacks—by 5.6 percentage points—to recommend the policy as their first choice. The differences between men and women and Southerners and non-Southerners were between one and two percentage points for both the first- and third-choice alternatives. The multivariate analyses reveal, therefore, Blacks and Latinos to have views on taxes that are more in line with those of men, Southerners, the

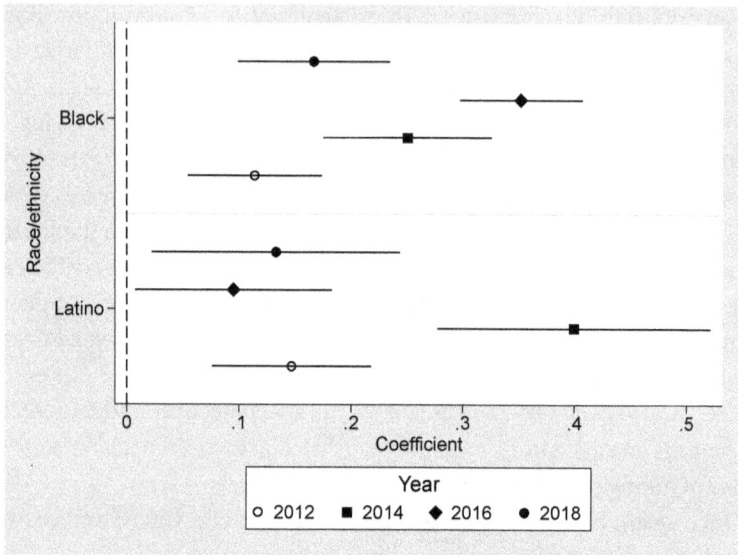

FIGURE 4.6. Effect of race and ethnicity on attitudes regarding taxes, CES 2012–2018
Higher values represent support for decreasing taxes/opposition to increasing taxes. Bars represent
95 percent confidence intervals. CES data can be found at https://cces.gov.harvard.edu/.

religious, the wealthy, and Republicans than women, non-Southerners, the
agnostic, the poor, and Democrats. Tax policy attitudes appear to mitigate
against the argument that marginalized racial and ethnic groups take consistently progressive positions on redistribution.

Income and the General Responsiveness of Economic Policy

I have argued that the economic-policy views of low-, middle-, and high-
income Americans are quite similar. However, elected officials may still be
responsive more to the wealthy than the poor. If so, the outcomes we witness
are a function of Page and Gilens's (2017) "democracy by coincidence." If, and
when, the attitudes of income cohorts diverge, government will be most responsive to the group or groups with the most influence.

I look at the matter of which income groups or classes receive greater
representation at the dyadic level—by individual members of Congress—in
chapter 8. For the time being, I am interested in aggregate policy responsiveness. I wish to discover which income groups' preferences are most faithfully
represented by economic-policy outcomes.

One approach is to see whose views correlate most with policy change. Researchers have been waging a robust debate on this subject for around fifteen

years. Many argue that the rich tend to "win" (Bowman 2020; Gilens 2012; Gilens and Page 2014; Hajnal 2020, 120–41). A small group of scholars dispute the claim, suggesting that the picture is unclear and that there are occasions and issues when less affluent Americans have their preferences reflected in policy outcomes (Branham et al. 2017; Enns 2015; Wlezien and Soroka 2011; Ura and Ellis 2008). I do not have much to add, but by examining some of the established data in a new way, I come down on the side of the contrarians.

To be more specific, I use the Gilens (2012; Gilens and Page 2014) data examined earlier in the chapter and, similar to Branham, Soroka, and Wlezien (2017), compare the capacity of Americans at the 10th, 50th, and 90th percentiles by income to alter policy areas that Gilens identifies as important. I am, of course, largely uninterested in social, foreign, and cultural policy, so I evaluate only two of his policy types, economic and social-welfare. Figure 4.6 reveals the mean annual scores of the three income groups where the government responded with change on an issue in the policy area and where it did not. I calculate these scores based upon the proportion of the group's members who supported policy change on the issue.[34] Positive values indicate that a majority of the group supported change on an item, negative values that a majority opposed policy change. Of course, I do not model causation, but the data should be revelatory nonetheless.

At face value, the results are consistent with the argument that policy reflects the views of wealthier Americans better than it does those of their middle- and lower-income compatriots. The higher the proportion of Americans in the richest group to want change on the issues, the more likely a policy will change. The differences in the means are not statistically significant at the 95 percent confidence level, however, and substantively a score between one and two—received by all income groups—reveals on average that between 55 percent and 60 percent of the group's members supported change. We can hardly describe the differences as material. Note also the results when it comes to economic and social-welfare policies where change did not occur. With lower values demonstrating greater opposition to change and therefore support for the status quo, the highest-income group did seem to get its way more on economic policy—although again inter-cohort distinctions are not statistically significant—but not on social-welfare policy. In fact, on that issue the lowest-income group gave the least support for change on matters government left untouched, and the differences between the means for the highest- and lowest-income group approaches statistical significance. Wlezien and Soroka (2011) confirm this finding. Using data from GSS and the federal budget, they suggest that government expenditures on social-welfare programs are more sensitive to views on the issue—conceptualized as whether there was "too

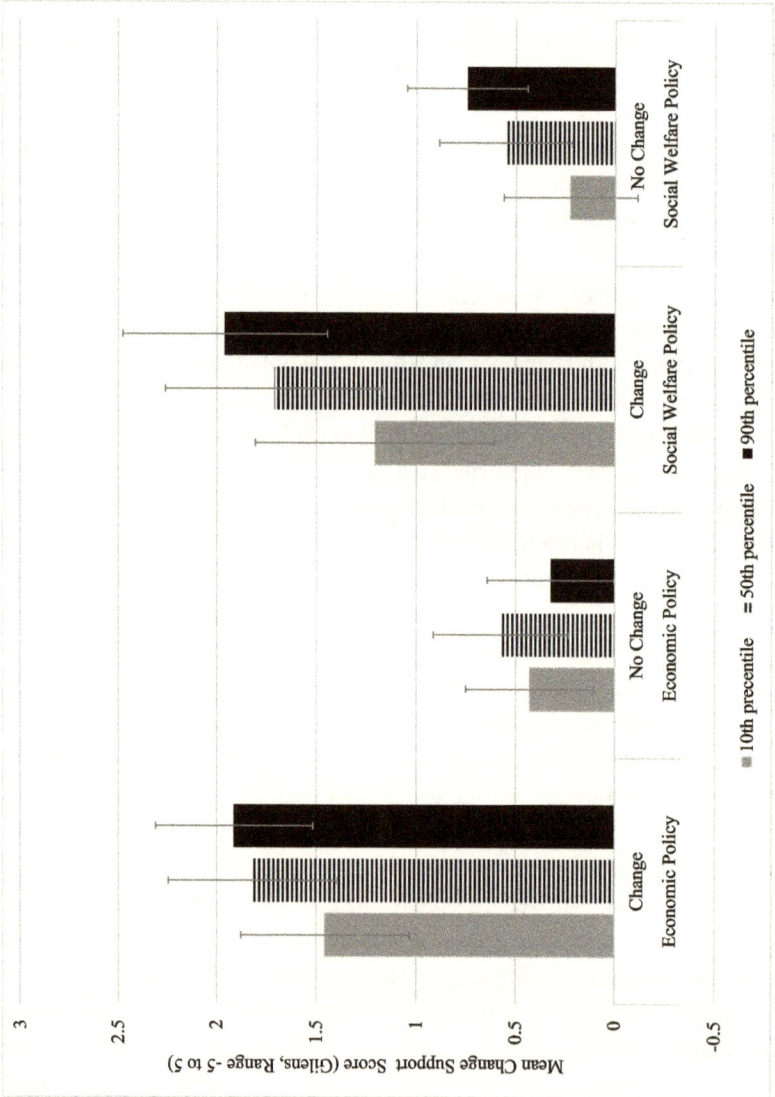

FIGURE 4.7. Attitudes of different income groups toward economic and social-welfare policy change, 1981–2002. Capped lines denote 95 percent confidence intervals. Data is from Gilens (2012) and Gilens and Page (2014).

Legend: 10th precentile   50th percentile   90th percentile

Y-axis: Mean Change Support Score (Gilens, Range - 5 to 5)

Y-axis values: -0.5, 0, 0.5, 1, 1.5, 2, 2.5, 3

X-axis categories: Change Economic Policy, No Change Economic Policy, Change Social Welfare Policy, No Change Social Welfare Policy much," "too little," or "the right amount" of spending—of low-income citizens than of high-income citizens.

We should pay attention to other findings. Although there is no statistically significant intergroup difference in mean support for change or stasis, for both economic and social-welfare issues the support of each group for change is materially greater when new policy is enacted than when it is not. Second, in all cases the values are above zero. This result suggests a bias in all groups for policy change over continuity. Third, with the exception of the richest cohort, citizens are more supportive of the status quo on social-welfare policy.[35] Bowman (2020) argues that this observation exaggerates the influence of Americans with the lowest incomes because the absence of policy change, as opposed to its occurrence, is more a function of the system's inertia than of genuine political sway. Presidential vetoes, a bicameral legislature, and the Senate filibuster, among other features, stymie public desire for new policy as much as do the competing views of fellow citizens. As I show in chapter 2, however, economic policy—including social welfare—moved markedly to the left in the postwar period up until the late 1970s, just as Gilens's time-series data begin. We might claim, therefore, that any success achieved by lower-income Americans' support for existing social-welfare policy in response to efforts since the early 1980s from conservative sentiment and Republican policymakers to push it to the right is, even if assisted by counter-majoritarian political institutions, intentional and material.

Gilens (2012; Gilens and Page 2014) also measures the length of time in years (from two to four) it takes government to approve the policy change expressed in the survey item.[36] With that information, I take the questions in the economic and social-welfare "policy change" categories used above and calculate, for all three income groups and both issues, the correlation between the score and the time until policy change. In all six instances, the correlation coefficients are negative, meaning that as the proportion of the group that wants change increases, so the time it takes to achieve the change goes down. There are no statistically significant differences across groups, but although the strongest negative correlation on social-welfare policy was for the highest income group ($r = -.073$, compared to $r = -.008$ for lowest and $r = -.029$ for middle), on economic policy the strongest was for the lowest-income group ($r = -.122$, compared to $r = -.017$ for highest and $r = -.042$ for middle).[37]

Conclusion

Less affluent Americans' expressed economic-policy preferences are not as progressive as observers often believe. Cross-sectional and temporal analyses of survey data on the attitudes of Americans from various classes and income cohorts show marginal differences in the views of the rich, the poor, and the middle class. As such, economic policy outcomes, at least at the aggregate level, cannot inordinately reflect the views of any one particular socioeconomic group.

Americans of all types are frequently conservative in their outlook on the economy and its operations. They tend to support economic freedom, be tolerant of inequality, and place their faith in their own abilities to make a living. This claim holds true in both comparative and historical senses. Less affluent citizens may be more supportive of spending for social welfare than wealthier compatriots are, but they are still skeptical of such programs. Partisanship increasingly shapes opinions on the issue, and lower-income Republicans are often more supportive of cuts than wealthy Democrats are. There is a strengthening inverse relationship between education and social-welfare policy preferences as well. Although wealthier Americans are supportive of cuts and hostile to hikes in taxes, so are those with fewer education credentials. I also show that racial and ethnic minority groups can take conservative positions on matters of redistribution, especially taxes.

Finally, I reveal little apparent difference in the capacity of various income groups to affect policy change. Less affluent Americans' desire for and opposition to policy change on economic and social-welfare issues are as strongly correlated with the outcome as are the views of their wealthy compatriots.

Less Affluent Americans' Views of the Economy

Clarity

I continue an examination of affluence and economic policy attitudes in this chapter, but I now look at the extent to which individuals in different socio-economic groups hold clear views and the extent to which group members collectively hold coherent views. Lower-income Americans might exert less influence because they send policymakers weak signals. Elected officials cannot act confidently on behalf of individuals whose personal opinions are unformed or unintelligible. Groups whose members express conflicted attitudes might also receive less vigorous representation. This response by government is not self-evidently an act of bias. It seems unreasonable to ask policymakers to divine constituents' wishes. In a democracy, they will serve individuals and groups who give them discernible cues.

Note that I am uninterested in the conduits through which Americans transmit their attitudes. I do not look at voting, campaign contributions, or other behavior. We tend to think of these as a kind of "megaphone" and that affluent citizens' greater resources provide them with a louder voice in politics through their votes, dollars, and organizational capacities. I am interested in the enunciation of opinions, not their amplification. Are those of lower-income Americans mumbled or incoherent? If so, such garble might help explain the underrepresentation of their supposed progressive interests in economic-policy outcomes. The inability of less affluent Americans to speak clearly, moreover, is not particularly the fault of our democratic process and institutions.

I examine the strength of Americans' political and policy attitudes in two ways. First, I classify individuals by income and examine the clarity of their views. A person who does not hold a distinguishable opinion cannot convey an intelligible request to policymakers. A person whose views contradict their actions or seem inconsistent across issues is similarly disadvantaged. Second, I compare the views of individuals within income cohorts. If these attitudes are heterogeneous, the group's communication of its collective preferences is ambiguous.

Party Identification, Ideology, and Affluence

My analysis relies primarily on two kinds of political attitudes, party identification and ideology. When outwardly displayed, both viewpoints succinctly and effectively impart an individual's stances to others, including elected officials, on an array of issues, including the economy. Party identification and ideology are the most rudimentary of citizens' views about politics and policy. Democrats have recognized positions on many policies, so do conservatives. The former, along with liberals, typically desire a larger role for government in the economy. They believe it should regulate business and use fiscal policy to redistribute. Republicans and conservatives tend to want limited government intervention in addition to tax and spending cuts. Many Americans recognize in themselves and express an identification with a major party and an established ideology.

There are theoretical reasons to think that low-income Americans' expressed political views will be unformed or muffled and as a group will be inconsistent and consequently incoherent. A person's party and ideological identification are products of motivation and cognition, the latter an exercise reliant upon political information and the capacity to process it. As the canonical literature reports, less affluent Americans have traditionally revealed little interest in politics (Campbell et al. 1960; Delli Carpini and Keeter 1996). This work has shown that levels of ability to understand ideology, party identification, individual policy issues, and the relationships between them are closely related to formal education and socioeconomic status (Converse 1964; Kinder and Kalmoe 2017).

To be sure, political scientists believe party identification to be a type of social identity, formed through associations and affinities, both positive and negative, and based on emotional as much as intellectual ties (Achen and Bartels 2016; Elder and O'Brian 2022; Green et al. 2002; Huddy et al. 2015; Greene 1999; Mason 2018). But it can also be thought of as a heuristic for policy stances, used as a shortcut by citizens who, at least when it comes to politics, are "cognitive misers" (Cohen 2003; Downs 1957; Fiorina 1981; Kam 2005; Rahn 1993). Party identification has an intellectual quality, and people frequently use it to convey complex collections of policy positions they and others hold parsimoniously.

Today, American politics are so polarized that scholars even talk of ideological identities (Cayton and Dawkins 2020; Halliez and Thornton 2021; Levitin and Miller 1979; Mason 2018). In other words, the terms "liberal" and "conservative" convey a sense of tribalism or status as much as they project policy preferences. The label "conservative" is often viewed as more socially desirable than "liberal," for example (Cayton and Dawkins 2020; Claassen et al. 2015; Ellis and Stimson 2012, 72–77; Schiffer 2000). But ideology is inherently more abstract than party identification. Parties with their organizations, leaders, and politicians are "material realities in a way ideologies are not," and "the language of partisanship pervades political discourse" (Kinder and Kalmoe 2017, 133). Ideology does less than partisanship to drive Americans' broader views of politics as well as their voting behavior (Kinder and Kalmoe 2017, 92–114), but it is still a personal political belief system, the integration of an individual's positions on separate policy issues into a coherent whole as defined by a broadly understood intellectual framework.

For many people, identifying one's own or another's ideology is to detect a pattern in a variety of issue stances and then evaluate it against types. In America, ideology is typically arrayed on a continuum with liberal and conservative poles, the distinctions blurred by a moderate classification that lies somewhere between. It is spatial more than categorical. To express one's own ideology confidently and accurately suggests motivation to understand, access to information, and cognitive skills. The ideological, Philip Converse (1964, 216) wrote in the 1960s, "rely in some active way on a relatively abstract and far-reaching conceptual dimension as a yardstick" against which they can evaluate politics.

The "average," perhaps working-class, American's inability to understand ideology has been a consistent theme of political science for a hundred years. The Almond-Lippmann consensus placed little faith in the capacity of ordinary people to organize their thoughts about politics generally.[1] Converse (1964) expanded upon this position to suggest that most Americans are "innocent of ideology," given their disinclination to follow politics and the complexity of analyzing even simple conventional ideological categories of conservative and liberal and relating them to positions on individual issues. Much recent social science suggests that Converse's view is an accurate description of twenty-first-century American politics (Broockman 2016; Elder and O'Brian 2022; Kalmoe 2020; Kinder and Kalmoe 2017). We have reason to believe that those who are broadly knowledgeable about politics—generally the well-to-do and highly educated—are more likely to understand and logically organize its abstractions, particularly ideology (Abramowitz 2010; Barber and Pope 2018; Jewitt and Goren 2016; Lupton et al. 2015). Low-income

Americans without college educations are increasingly aligning ideology with party and positions on particular issues as well (Hare 2022), but even in the partisan and polarized twenty-first century, they do not do so as adroitly as their more affluent and often more politically knowledgeable compatriots do (Halliez and Thornton 2021; Kozlowski and Murphy 2021).

Do Less Affluent Americans Have Clear Political Views?

I deploy several tests to examine whether affluence contributes to individuals' capacity to identify and express their partisanship and ideology. The first is to ask Americans simply what their own ideology is. It is standard practice for surveys to provide participants with the opportunity to reply with "don't know" or "unsure" to requests for them to self-report their ideology. There is some dispute as to what such responses mean. Several researchers are concerned that those who select "don't know" may actually know more than those who choose to guess (Mondak 2000), although a significant amount of research has pushed back against this possibility (Jessee 2017; Sturgis et al. 2008). Berinsky (2004) argues that participants who answer "don't know" often do so because the responses presented by surveys leave them confused or without an alternative for which they feel they can express support. Regardless, I am not particularly interested in these survey questions as measures of political knowledge. I use "don't know" responses as an indicator of those who do not lucidly and forcefully impart their political views to policymakers. An omitted response to such a simple question asked by a pollster, I suggest, constitutes a reasonable proxy.

Figure 5.1 and figure 5.2 report the results of the proportion of the subjects in particular family-income categories who stated they did not know their own or the sitting president's ideology when asked in the CES surveys from 2008 to 2020.[2] The five available responses range from "very liberal" to "very conservative," with a moderate midpoint. Consistent with Berinsky (2004), a much larger proportion of lower-income participants state that they do not know their personal or the president's ideology than do survey participants at the highest ends of the income scale. Those with the lowest incomes offer this reply particularly frequently. The similar pattern of responses to both items suggest we should reject the possibility that lower-income subjects' answers to the personal-ideology question are a function of a peculiar difficulty in or unwillingness to self-categorize given the choices presented. Less affluent respondents appear more likely not to understand what ideology is or how to apply it. The results are consistent with the theory that, as individuals,

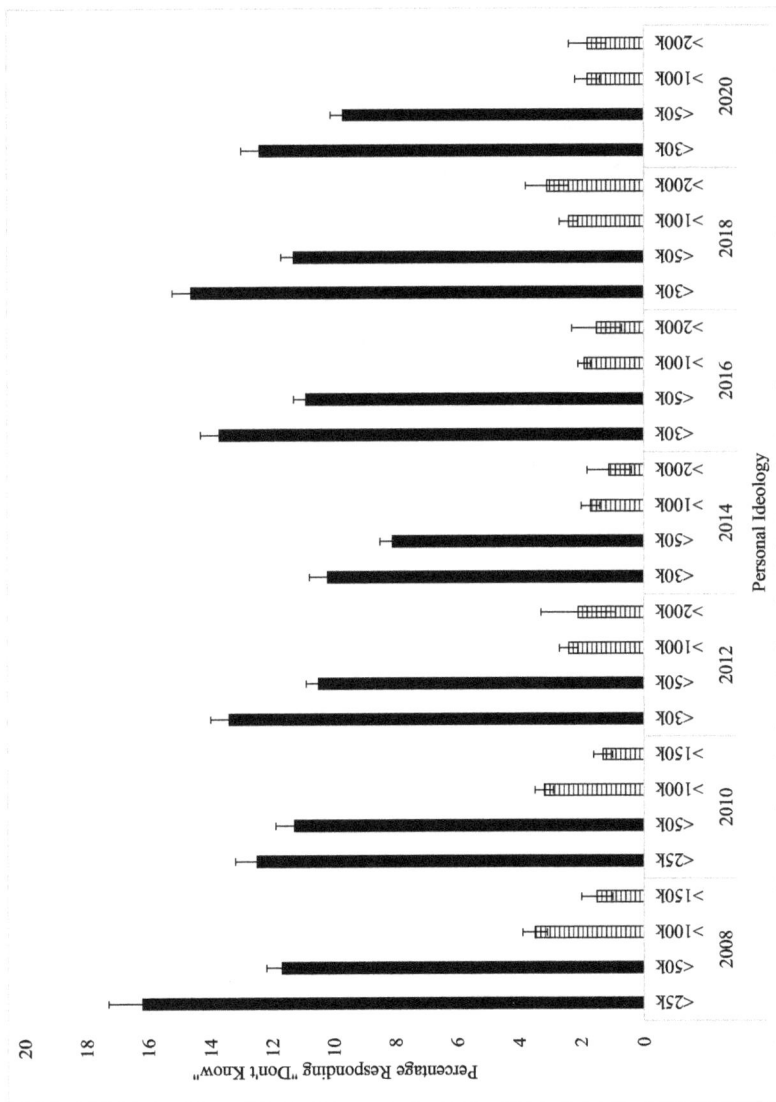

FIGURE 5.1. Percentage of respondents in various income groups reporting "don't know" to questions about personal ideology, CES 2008–2020

Lower-income groups are denoted by solid bars. Capped lines represent 95 percent confidence intervals. CES data can be found at https://cces.gov.harvard.edu/.

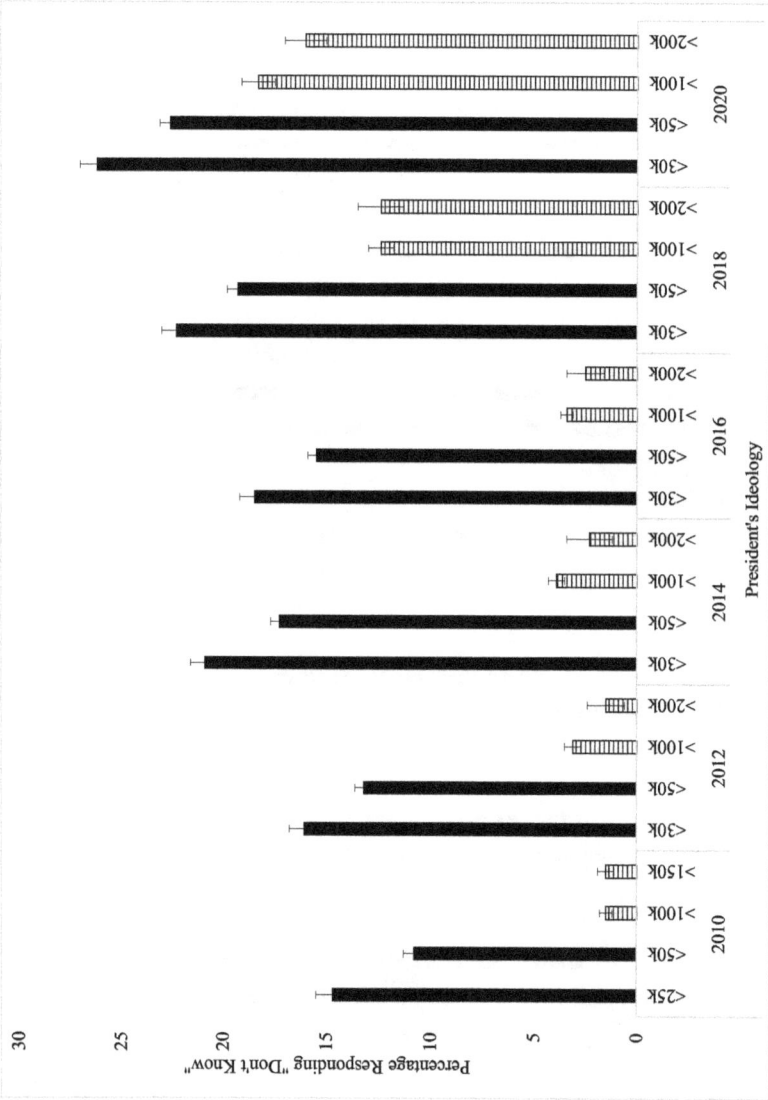

FIGURE 5.2. Percentage of respondents in various income groups reporting "don't know" to questions about presidential ideology, CES 2010–2020

Lower-income groups are denoted by solid bars. Capped lines represent 95 percent confidence intervals. CES data can be found at https://cces.gov.harvard.edu/.

lower-income Americans communicate their ideological stances less clearly than do their wealthier fellow citizens.

The data in figure 5.1 and figure 5.2 furnish one additional interesting finding. For 2018 and 2020, they show that respondents of all income levels, especially the highest, are less sure of the president's ideology than they were in earlier years. This finding suggests a kind of "Trump effect." Trump's novelty and general disruption of national politics made him difficult to place within the country's established ideological framework, especially in the minds of the wealthy and generally most attentive and knowledgeable (Barber and Pope 2019).

Figure 5.3 highlights this Trump effect further. It shows the proportion of respondents in two income cohorts—below $50,000 and above $100,000—who claimed not to know the president's ideological placement and that of each of the two major parties. The findings are consistent with the basic argument; lower-income Americans are materially less likely to know the ideology of important political figures and institutions. Moreover, for all the years Obama was in office, a great deal more of the subjects in both groups claimed to know the president's ideology than claimed to know the ideology of both the Democratic Party and Republican Party—interestingly, a larger percentage of respondents always claimed to know the Democrats' ideology than claimed to know the Republicans' ideology. In 2018 and 2020, however, significantly more survey participants stated that they did not know the president's ideology than stated that they did not know either of the parties' ideologies. Americans, including the most affluent, seemed incapable of identifying Trump's ideology when compared to that of other presidents and political institutions.

Lower-income Americans' greater ignorance of ideology is not merely a twenty-first-century phenomenon. Using ANES data, which has many fewer cases than CES, figure 5.4 illustrates that the importance of income to an understanding of one's own ideology goes back to the earlier years of the post-1980s era of inequality. It shows, controlling for the usual battery of demographic controls, the predicted probability of a respondent being "not sure" of her own ideology at different levels of family income in 1988, 1992, and 1996.[3] The differences are arguably considerable: Around a third of respondents in the bottom cohorts but only one in five in the top cohorts claimed to be ignorant of their personal ideology. These differences are especially large in the 1990s.

As noted, we think of ideology as a broad system in which positions on issues integrate into a logical whole, fitting together in a commonly recognized pattern within a framework broadly deployed to make sense of American

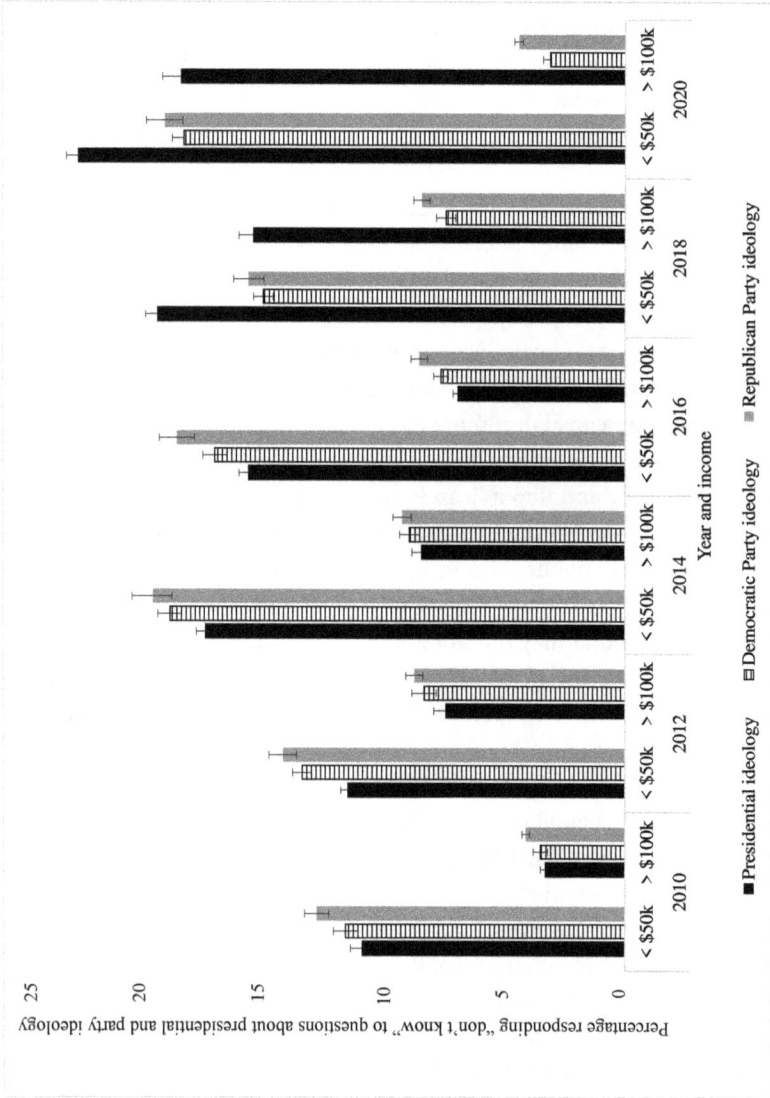

FIGURE 5.3. Percentage of low-income and high-income groups who did not know the ideology of the president and the two parties, CES 2010–2020

Lower-income groups are denoted by solid bars. Capped lines represent 95 percent confidence intervals. CES data can be found at https://cces.gov.harvard.edu/.

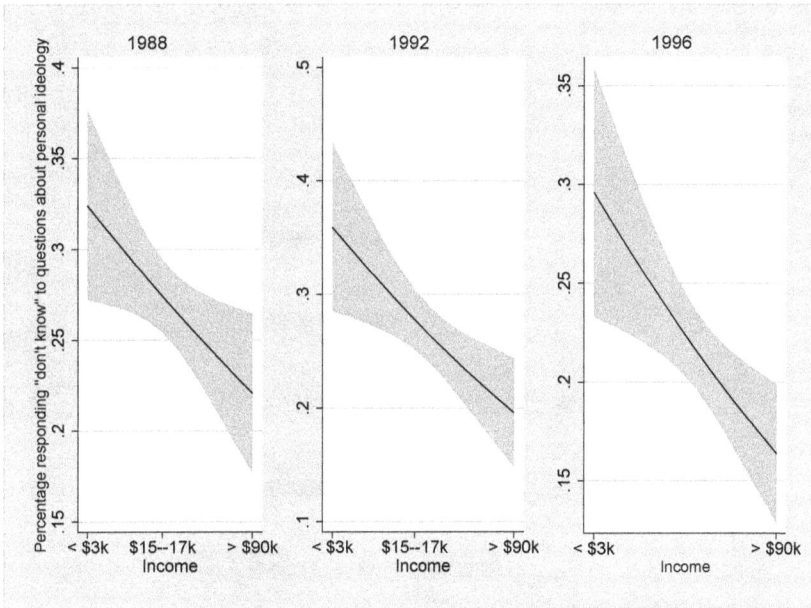

FIGURE 5.4. Effect of income on a respondent's knowledge of their own ideology, ANES 1988–1996 Shaded area represents 95 percent confidence intervals. The vertical axis denotes the predicted probability of a respondent replying "don't know." ANES data can be found at https://electionstudies.org/.

politics. Individuals who hold and proclaim views considered ideologically consistent across prevalent political issues practice what researchers call "ideological constraint" or "issue alignment" (Baldassari and Gelman 2008; Jacoby 1995; Kozlowski and Murphy 2021 Sullivan et al. 1978; Zingher 2023). They have policy preferences that appear consistent and that can be anticipated. With this point in mind, I examine responses to a series of questions about four issues asked by CES from 2010 to 2020 in a further test of the clarity of the political opinions of individuals from various income groups. The issues, all at the center of public debate about economic policy, are the environment, immigration, taxes, and health care. CES poses a number of questions on each issue—ranging from three to six—and asks respondents whether they "oppose" or "support" a stated position. I code each position taken by a subject as consistent with broader liberal or conservative ideology and determine the number of answers given by survey participants in each ideological category on each issue for the year. I then report the number of "wrong" answers given by a survey participant; that is, the number of responses in the non-modal ideological category.[4]

Figure 5.5 reveals the results of the scores for respondents who live in households with incomes less than $50,000 and those with incomes above

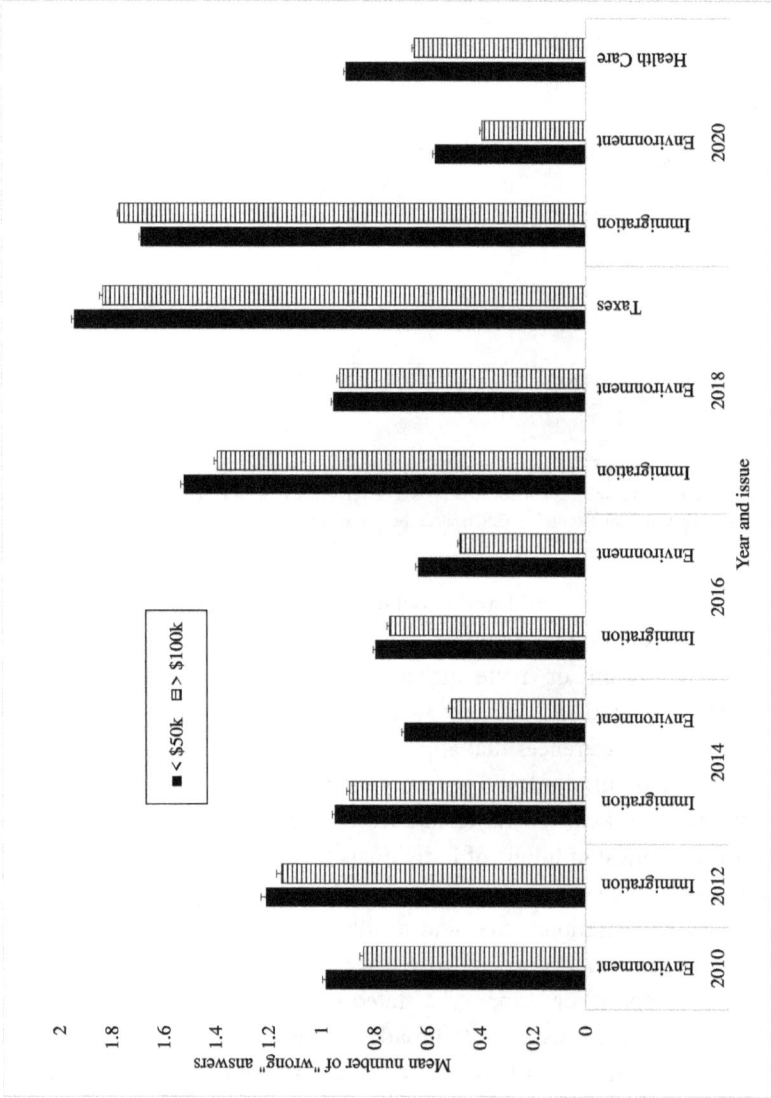

FIGURE 5.5. Number of ideologically inconsistent answers to questions about certain issues by income group, CES 2010–2020 Lower-income groups are denoted by solid bars. Capped lines represent 95 percent confidence intervals. CES data can be found at https:// cces.gov.harvard.edu/.

$100,000. Although the differences between the two often do not look substantively large, the error bars show them nearly always to be beyond 95 percent confidence intervals—a finding consistent with the work of Zingher (2023). With the exception of 2018, the differences on the environment issue are particularly great, with lower-income Americans being more ideologically conflicted or inconsistent.

Again, it is interesting how the first Trump presidency appeared to reduce the differences between how the affluent and those less well-off think in ideological terms, especially on immigration. Indeed, in 2020 respondents in the higher-income group produced materially more inconsistent responses on the issue than did those in the lower-income group. As a polarizing figure, Trump plausibly clarified American politics in the minds of citizens (Baldassarri and Gelman 2008; Layman and Carsey 2002). Placed within the conventional liberal-to-conservative ideological framework, however, his unique candidacy and tenure confused many Americans.

Political scientists also associate ideological moderation with inconsistent positions across issues and, consequently, incoherent directions to policymakers (Ahler and Broockman 2018; Kinder and Kalmoe 2017). Moderates, some of the literature asserts, lack or are unwilling to activate the cognitive skills required to process abstract concepts like ideology—which differs from concrete concepts like the party, an institution that features more frequently in public debates about politics. As Kinder and Kalmoe put it (2017, 71), "the moderate category seems less an ideological destination than a refuge for the innocent and the confused." Its occupants are unlikely to influence economic policymaking much, especially when Washington is polarized and candidates motivated to attend to the engaged and informed and their parties' reliable base voters (Campbell 2016, 207–18).[5]

Unlike moderates, however, political observers consider citizens unaffiliated with party or independents to be strategic and effective—in short, potentially critical to election outcomes and consequently influential to policymaking (Klar and Krupnikov 2016, 29–33).[6] If there is a party equivalent of the nonstrategic and ineffectual moderate, it is the reflexive partisan, who habitually votes Democrat or Republican regardless of personal views about policy or any assessment of changes in the broader political landscape. Observers of politics see independents as growing in size and influence—as demonstrated by registration statistics across the country—while polarization inevitably squeezes self-described moderates. Klar and Krupnikov (2016) demonstrate that in an era of deep polarization and mistrust, citizens have rational reasons to hide any true partisan affiliation. Independents frequently hold partisan and ideological views that drive their voting behavior, but they are turned off by polarization and do not want to advertise their allegiance to a political party (Klar and Krupnikov 2016; Smidt 2017). They are also rational and persuadable. Parties and candidates covet their support and take their opinions seriously, strategically shifting positions on policies to accommodate them, particularly in frequently competitive contests for the presidency and party control of Congress (Hillygus and Shields 2008; Mayer 2008). Political scientists seldom accuse unaffiliated voters of innocence and confusion regarding their partisanship. In contrast to moderates, they seem capable of clearly communicating policy preferences, capturing the attention of elected officials, and shaping policy outcomes.

Figure 5.6 explores the proposition that less affluent Americans are disproportionately represented among moderate partisans, a group thought of as lacking political influence. This does seem to be the case. Using CES data from 2008 to 2020, it reveals the proportion of respondents in the under-$50,000 and over-$100,000 groups who self-identify as "moderates" and "independents" and place themselves at the midpoints of the five-point ideology and three-point party identification scales. With the exceptions of 2012 and 2016, a materially larger proportion of lower-income respondents consider themselves "moderates." Roughly 30–45 percent of those in the cohort characterize themselves this way, demonstrating the recognized link between working-class Americans and ideological indifference and ambiguity. Affluent respondents, on the other hand, are more likely than are lower-income compatriots to claim that they are unaffiliated with a party.

An analysis of party identification further illustrates the relationship of income to the clarity of an individual's political views. Figure 5.7 reports the predicted probability of a respondent in three income cohorts stating they were a "strong" Democrat or Republican or a "lean" Democrat or Republican—subjects also reported themselves as "not very strong" (which is between "strong" and "lean") or "independent" (which is suggestive of no party affiliation). The model contains the usual battery of demographic variables as well as a control that folds a five-point liberal-to-conservative ideology measure, so that I code respondents as "moderate," "ideological," or "very ideological."[7] It is quite clear that as household income rises through the cohorts, the likelihood of a person claiming to be a "strong" identifier with either party rises monotonically and appreciably even after accounting for ideology. The opposite is true of self-identified "leaners." Although the differences appear smaller, the error bars show that in every year, as household income grows the predicted probability of the subject considering themself a "leaner" goes down. The statistical models for each year show income to have a material relationship with the propensity of respondents to convey a solid attachment

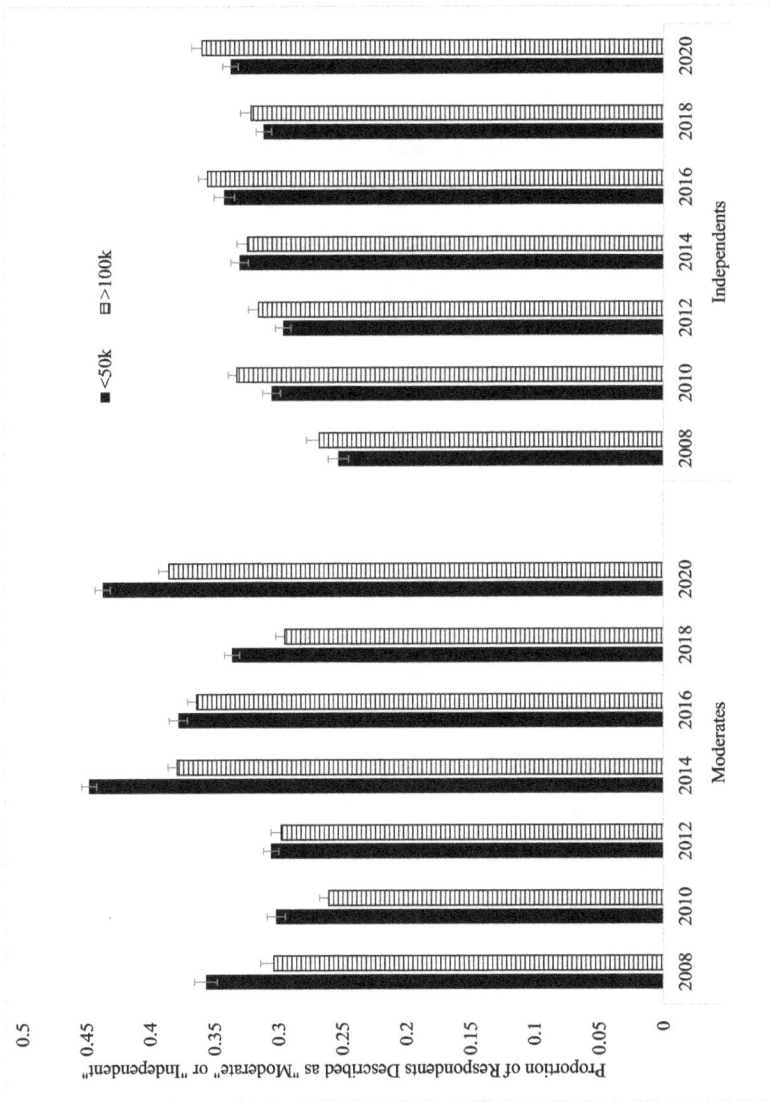

FIGURE 5.6. Proportion of self-identified moderates and independents by income group, CES 2008–2020 Lower-income groups are denoted by solid bars. Capped lines represent 95 percent confidence intervals. CES data can be found at https:// cces.gov.harvard.edu/.

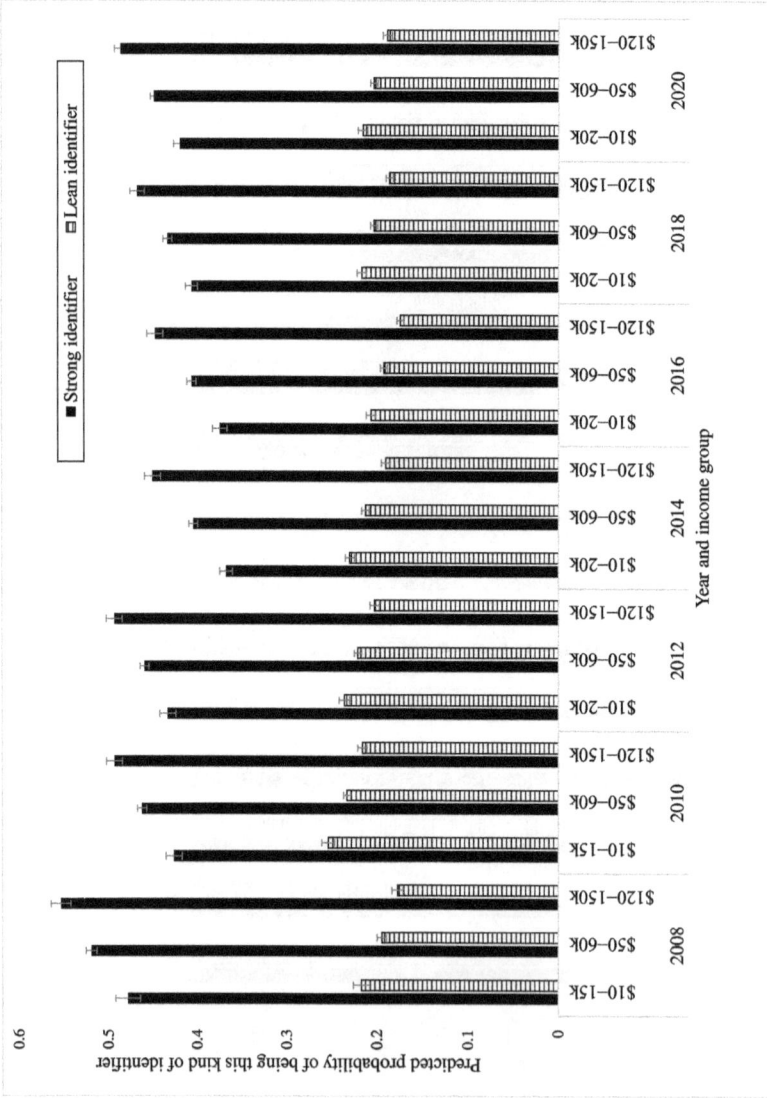

FIGURE 5.7 Predicted probability of respondents exhibiting "strong" and "lean" identifiers by income group, CES 2008–2020 Solid bars denote respondents who consider themselves strong identifiers. Capped lines represent 95 percent confidence intervals. CES data can be found at https://cces.gov.harvard.edu/.

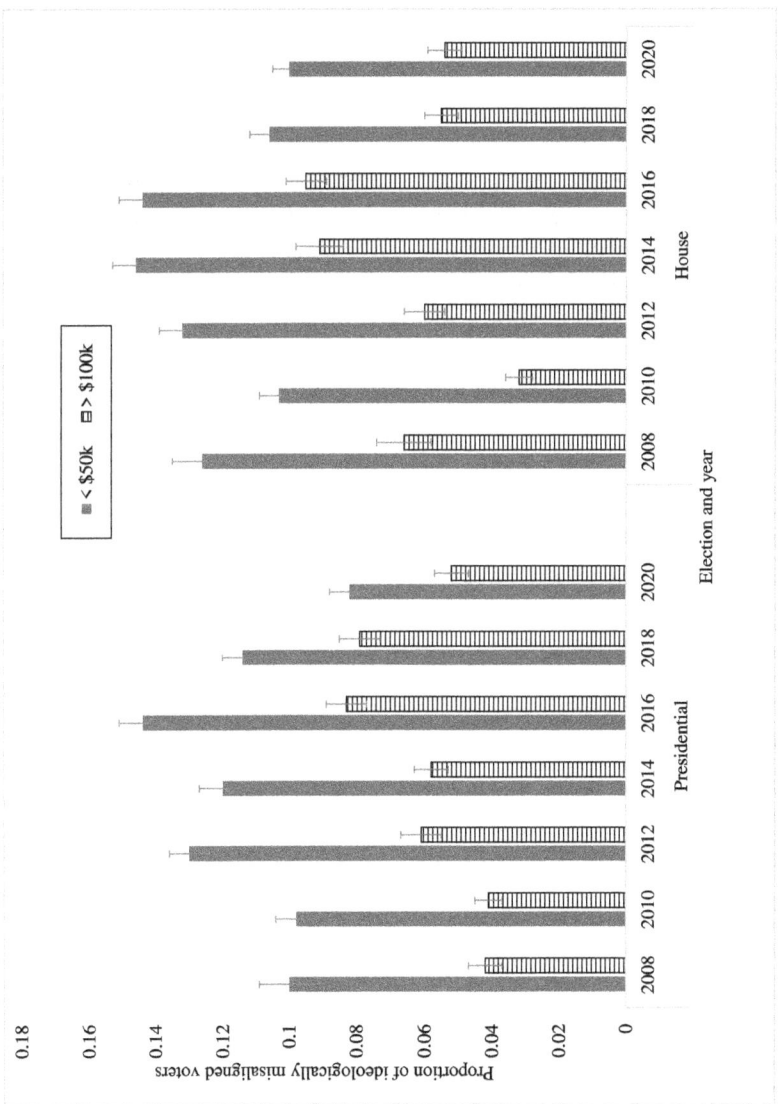

FIGURE 5.8. Proportion of ideologically misaligned voters in presidential and House elections by income group, CES 2008–2020. Lower-income groups are denoted by solid bars. Capped lines represent 95 percent confidence intervals. CES data can be found at https:// cces.gov.harvard.edu/.

to one or the other of the two major parties. Lower-income Americans tend to be ideologically moderate loose partisans, a designation that political science—and presumably the parties, candidates, and policymakers—views as confused, nonstrategic, indecipherable, and inconsistent.

One final way I wish to understand the clarity of the signals that individuals of various income levels convey about their policy preferences to elected officials is to examine whether self-reported views are consistent with personal political behavior, a form of what is called "correct voting" (Lau and Redlawsk 1997; Robison 2021). When voting contradicts ideology, individuals seem confused and conflicted, especially in polarized politics where ideology and party are closely aligned and the positions of candidates, in general elections at least, are distinct. When vote choice constitutes an apparent extension of policy positions, citizens communicate their wishes more clearly. They demonstrate an ability to make connections between their own views and those of candidates and are likely to be considered sophisticated, motivated, and reliable supporters worth rewarding with policy (Lau et al. 2008; Robison 2021).

Figure 5.8 utilizes the CES data and reports the proportion of ideologues misaligned with party from the less-than-$50,000 income group and greater-than-$100,000 income group. These individuals are self-identified liberals who voted for Republican candidates or self-identified conservatives who voted for Democratic candidates in presidential and House races.[8] To be sure, even lower-income respondents seem to be increasingly selecting the "correct" party (Zingher and Flynn 2019), but throughout the time series they are always more likely to be misaligned than wealthier compatriots. They frequently vote incorrectly by over twice as much as higher-income subjects in the survey. Again, we have evidence that elected officials should have less confidence in knowing how to respond to the wishes of their less affluent constituents.

Do Less Affluent Americans Have Homogeneous Political Views?

Political scientists traditionally conceptualize constituency as unitary and understand its preferences to be expressed by a majority of its members or, when using a spatial approach, its median (Erikson et al. 2002; Kalt and Zupan 1984; Kingdon 1989; Shotts 2002). Many congressional scholars, however, have proposed an alternative understanding of representation, stating that legislators are, at different times and on particular issues, disproportionately influenced by various sub-constituencies (Bishin 2000, 2009; Clinton 2006; Fenno 1978; Miler 2007, 2010, 2018; Miller and Stokes 1963). Lawmakers do not see a singular geographic constituency and attempt to ascertain its collective preference; rather, they divine different groups of constituents based upon their demographic attributes, socioeconomic characteristics, distinct interests and opinions, or unusual attentiveness to certain policies. Lawmakers then weigh the positions of the various, often competing, sub-constituencies. Income-, wealth-, or class-based sub-constituencies are presumably as perceptible as any other large and important group; as Miler (2010, 62) notes, "sub-constituencies are not necessarily organized interest groups; rather they are defined by their common policy interests." In standard versions of sub-constituency theory, high-income, wealthier, or upper socioeconomic sub-constituencies are likely to have greater influence over their representatives' policy decisions because they are more active and therefore especially visible in political settings (Bishin 2009; Miler 2010, 32–45; Miler 2018).

Legislators' responsiveness to the wishes of a sub-constituency is conditioned by their party, ideology, policy interests, and indubitably other factors. Representatives' actions often amplify the policy demands of groups with congruent attitudes and discount those of groups who tend to oppose them (Broockman and Skovron 2018; Butler and Dynes 2016). In this way, the economic-policy views of working-class residents are likely to be more salient to Democratic lawmakers than to their Republican colleagues. Moreover, we would expect sub-constituency organizational capacity to have a significant effect on a legislator's behavior and responsiveness to the group's policy preferences. It is for this reason that many believe the demise of labor unions diminishes the influence of the working class (Becher and Stegmueller 2021; Flavin 2018).

The uniformity of a sub-constituency's views is important, too. Policymakers are more likely to be responsive to groups whose members collectively form a coherent position on an issue (Olson 1965). Divided sub-constituencies do not provide an intelligible cue to lawmakers. A lack of coherence on an issue manifests in two ways. First, many members of the group may not have a position at all. This state of affairs conveys the impression of abstention even if those remaining group members who do express a view are united. I have shown earlier in the chapter that as individuals lower-income Americans are less likely than others to express a position on an issue. Second, most members of the group might take individual positions, but collectively these positions are heterogeneous. Such diversity conveys the impression of inconsistency and conflict. It is this second point I analyze in this section.

I look first at the distribution of self-identified ideology across economic groups using the CES data. Here, I omit "don't knows" and use the five-point measure of ideology coded 1–5, from "very liberal" through to "very

conservative." Figure 5.9 reveals the coefficient of variation (standard deviation divided by the mean) of this measure for various income groups. Higher
values of the indicator represent greater heterogeneity of views within the
group.

There is generally greater variance within less affluent groups and a visibly linear relationship between income and ideological coherence between
2008 and 2016. Lower-income Americans are therefore not only less likely to
express a personal ideology and, when they do, to call themselves moderates
and weak partisans; they are also, as a group, generally more heterogeneous
in their attitudes. They are indeed a little more likely to be liberal than those
with higher incomes, but they are also more likely to choose a different ideology than their supposed "natural" or "usual" one—the ideology seen by
others as most consistent with their economic interests. Lawmakers receive
conflicting signals from their less affluent sub-constituencies.

There are two outliers, however. In 2018 and 2020, the relationship between income and intragroup ideological homogeneity greatly attenuates. In
2018, every group reveals its greatest level of incoherence in the time series.
In 2020, there is no visible relationship between income and ideological cohe-
sion. Whereas historically the large proportion of moderates diversified the
ideological position of low-income Americans, recently this quality has made
the group more homogeneous than the wealthy, who seemed to have been
both polarized and confused by Trump's ascendancy.

Next, I turn to group or sub-constituency coherence on individual issues.
Here I borrow from the 2019 Democracy Fund Voter Study Group (DFVSG)
data. This data came from a large-N internet survey (of about eight thousand
subjects) administered by YouGov, where most of the subjects were "panel-
ists" included in each of the annual studies.[9] I select three issues on which
lower-income Americans ought to take particular interest. They would potentially receive direct and possibly large benefits from these policies. High-
income citizens are likely to oppose them, although any implied costs to the
wealthy are presumably diffuse. Consistent with Olson's (1965) canonical
argument about interests, the intensity of feeling on these policies should
therefore be asymmetrical. In other words, the policies described in the question seem biased in favor of greater homogeneity of responses among lower-
income voters.

The prompts asked participants if they "strongly favored," "somewhat favored," "somewhat opposed," or "strongly opposed" the following policies:
"tax credits for lower-income workers," "making it easier for unions to organize," and "raising the minimum wage." I intentionally avoided questions
about the 2017 TCJA and Republicans' legislation designed to overhaul the

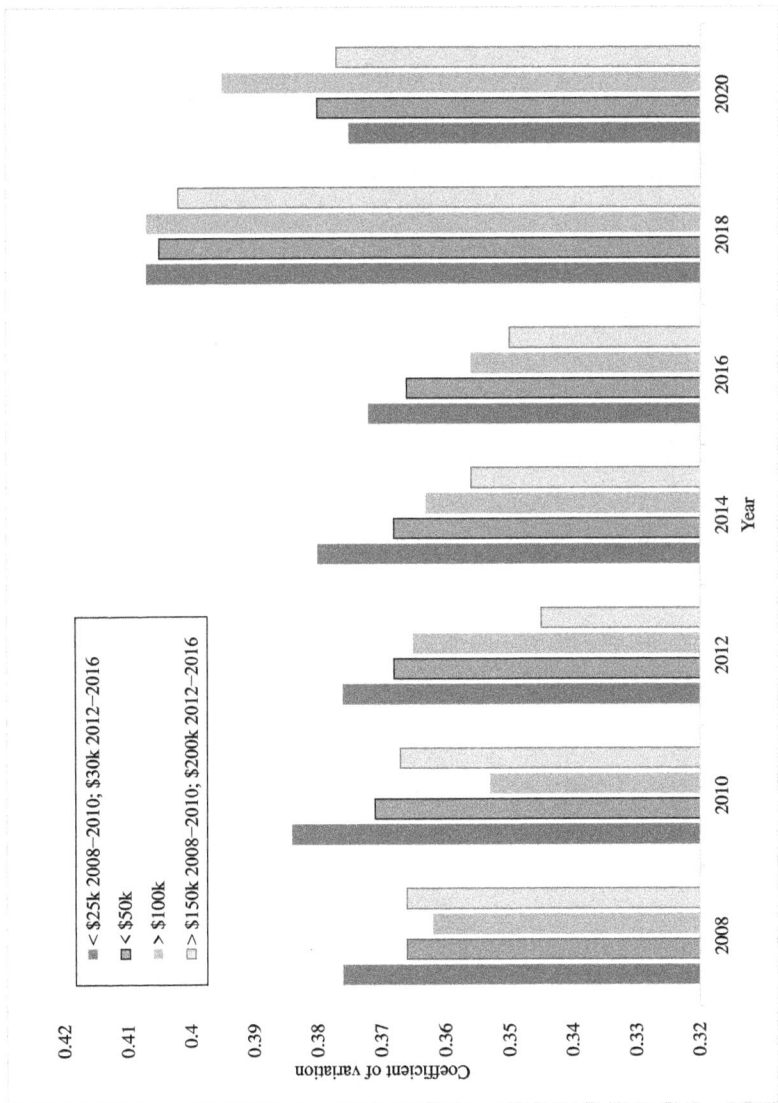

FIGURE 5-9. Ideological heterogeneity of various income groups, CES 2008–2020
The bars represent the coefficient of variation (standard deviation/mean) of individual group members' scores on the five-point ideology scale. High scores represent greater heterogeneity. CES data can be found at https://cces.gov.harvard.edu/.

ACA—because of their links to Trump and Obama and because of the baggage these connections carried in the minds of respondents (Lerman et al. 2017; Tesler 2012). Figure 5.10 reveals the coefficient of variation of the responses of four income groups—those with median household incomes below $30,000, below $50,000, above $100,000, and above $200,000. The results show that even on these important individual economic-policy issues where the intensity of opinion ought to be asymmetrical, higher-income respondents, with less at stake, tend to have more homogeneous views. We can make a case that lower-income survey participants are more coherent only on the union-organization item, and there any difference is negligible.

As a group, lower-income or blue-collar Americans have views that are more heterogeneous, and therefore less intelligible, than those of other, more affluent socioeconomic groups. Their representatives should therefore receive fewer intelligible cues from them. We would expect, in turn, legislators with a greater proportion of lower-income constituents to have voting records that are more difficult to categorize. Pulled in various directions by conflicting messages from an important sub-constituency, members with sizable proportions of working-class households will respond by constructing an aggregate voting record that conforms less to the increasingly rigid confines of American politics' conventional ideological framework (Hare 2022). When compared to colleagues who represent affluent districts, these members should take diverse ideological positions over the course of a Congress.

I address this question by examining the determinants of members' first-dimension DW-NOMINATE error scores from 1973 to 2014 (Poole and Rosenthal 1997, 27–34). This score is the proportion of all a member's roll-call votes in a Congress not correctly classified by the DW-NOMINATE model. First-dimension DW-NOMINATE scores explain a great deal of the variance in members' voting—between 80 and 90 percent over the past half century. The scores closely approximate an economic liberal-to-conservative ideological dimension. We can therefore think of legislators with more errors as constructing voting records that do not fit well into that dominant framework of American political life.[10]

In the analysis reported in table 5.1, I deploy a conventional battery of control variables that measure legislator characteristics, all of which generate statistically significant coefficients in analyses with large numbers of cases. The performances of these variables reassuringly make sense. The majority leadership's control and resultant political manipulation of the agenda and capacity to reward and punish have the potential to pull members of the minority away from solid and reflexive ideological opposition. Senior and electorally vulnerable legislators are more likely to break from any ideological

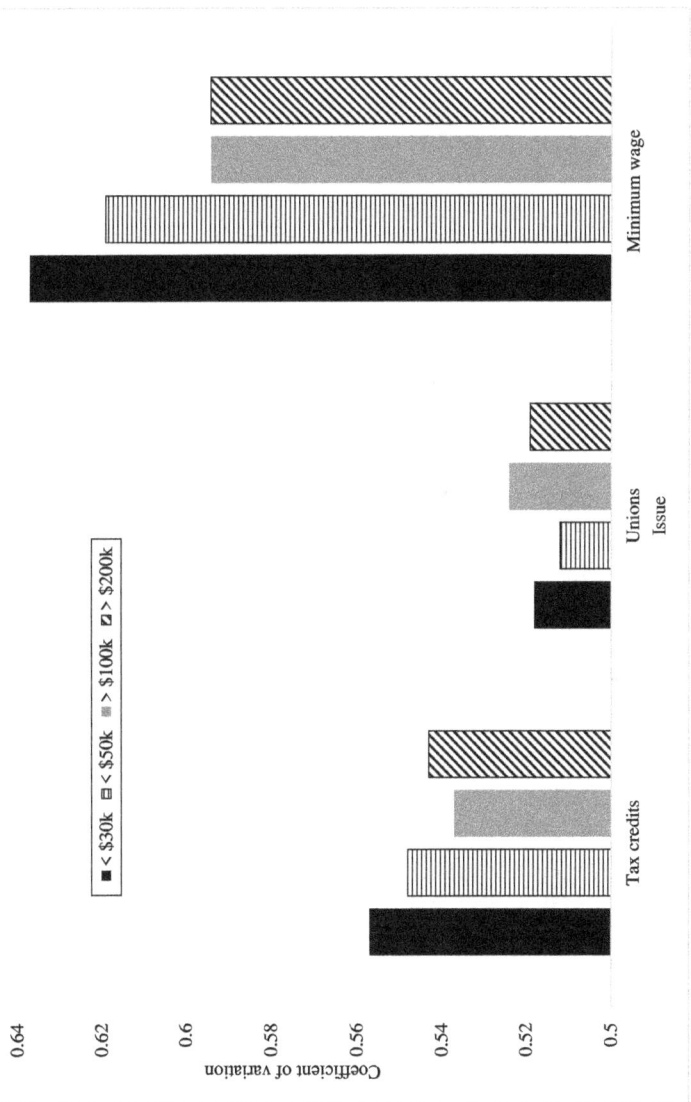

FIGURE 5.10. Heterogeneity of views of members of various income groups on three issues, DFVSG 2019

The bars represent the coefficient of variation (standard deviation/mean) of individual group members' scores on a four-point scale. High scores represent greater heterogeneity. DFVSG data can be found at https://www.voterstudygroup.org/data.

TABLE 5.1. Constituent income and the ideological consistency of
House members, 1973–2014

Median household income	−.0005 (.0001)*
Seniority	.0006 (.0002)*
Majority party	−.030 (.002)*
Ideology	.013 (.003)*
Leader of either party	−.020 (.003)*
Committee chair	−.018 (.003)*
Female	−.007 (.003)*
Black	−.027 (.003)*
Latino	−.014 (.004)*
Vote share	−.0002 (.0000)*
Constant	.189 (.005)*
Adjusted R^2	.413
N	8,544

Notes: OLS estimation with robust standard errors clustered by
member in parentheses. Dependent variable is the geometric mean
probability of a member's DW-NOMINATE estimate. Congress fixed
effects are not reported. *$p < .05$. Tests are one-tailed.

orthodoxy imposed by their party, and leaders and committee chairs build records that are more consistent than those of the rank-and-file. Moreover, even after controlling for these many factors, female, Black, and Latino members tend to be more ideologically consistent.[11]

I also use a measure of district income, the median household income. As hypothesized, legislators from jurisdictions with a lower median income acquire voting records that are inconsistent and harder to predict by the DW-NOMINATE model of ideological voting. The substantive effect is not especially great. It takes an increase of about $105,000 in median household income to reduce the proportion of votes in error by about five percentage points or roughly one standard deviation (the mean is 11.1 percent). Still, the coefficient does reach levels of statistical significance. The members with the most incoherent voting records represent the least affluent districts.

I examine an additional way a sub-constituency might communicate its views. Regardless of the sub-constituency's position on a policy, it presumably conveys its concern that government pay close attention to its preferences when it believes an issue to be particularly important. The higher a group collectively ranks an issue, the greater the chance that representatives will focus on it as they draw up and consider legislation. Policy outputs on an issue should also be closer to the preference of a sub-constituency that believes the issue is important than that of a group that does not (Hayes and Bishin 2012; Jones and Baumgartner 2004: Miler 2018). Income groups that do not prioritize an issue will not convey as strong a cue to policymakers that it should be the government's focus.

Organized interests convey their policy priorities through lobbying, campaign contributions, endorsements, and the adoption of public positions (Esterling 2007; Grossmann and Pyle 2013). Income groups are inevitably less unified and structured. It is reasonable, however, to assume that legislators who are attentive to the concerns of an informal group because they generally share its preferences or believe its support is important to their personal political advancement will expend resources writing and approving legislation on issues in which the group has demonstrated a significant interest.

In this analysis, I examine the economic-policy priorities of various cohorts of Americans identified by income using the 2016 CES and 2019 DFVGS. The data constitute recent snapshots and record the attitudes of a large number of individuals in many income groups.[12] Interviewers asked CES respondents whether they believed each of fifteen political issues was of "very high importance," "somewhat high importance," "somewhat low importance," "very low importance," or of "no importance at all." DFVGS participants were asked about twenty-three political issues and whether they thought each was "very important," "important," "not very important," or "unimportant" to them. Figures 5.11 and 5.12 are bump charts revealing the ranking of these issues to each of four income groups—those below $30,000, below $50,000, above $100,000, and above $200,000—determined by the proportion who believed it was "very important" or of "very high importance." The issues ranked at the top (a ranking of 1 denotes that it comes first) are the most important to the group.

The priorities of the four income groups do not differ tremendously. The top five issues are common to all groups in both surveys. Particularly in the DFVSG data (figure 5.12), the higher-income cohorts place a greater premium on the broad and rather nebulous issue of the economy. It is their most important issue. They also rank jobs slightly higher than do the other cohorts. The lower-income groups view Social Security and health care as the most important issues, and Medicare as the third–most important issue in the DFVSG survey. The higher-income groups place greater emphasis on national security in the CES survey. Although, again, there are slightly different priorities, the bottom five issues are common to all income groups in both surveys—issues like abortion, gay rights, and racial and gender equality.[13]

The middle stratum of issues displays some volatility, particularly in the DFVSG survey. "Poverty" is, like "the economy," a broad term that might have various policy prescriptions attached to it. Not surprisingly, the two low-income groups rank it higher than do the two affluent groups.[14] It is also

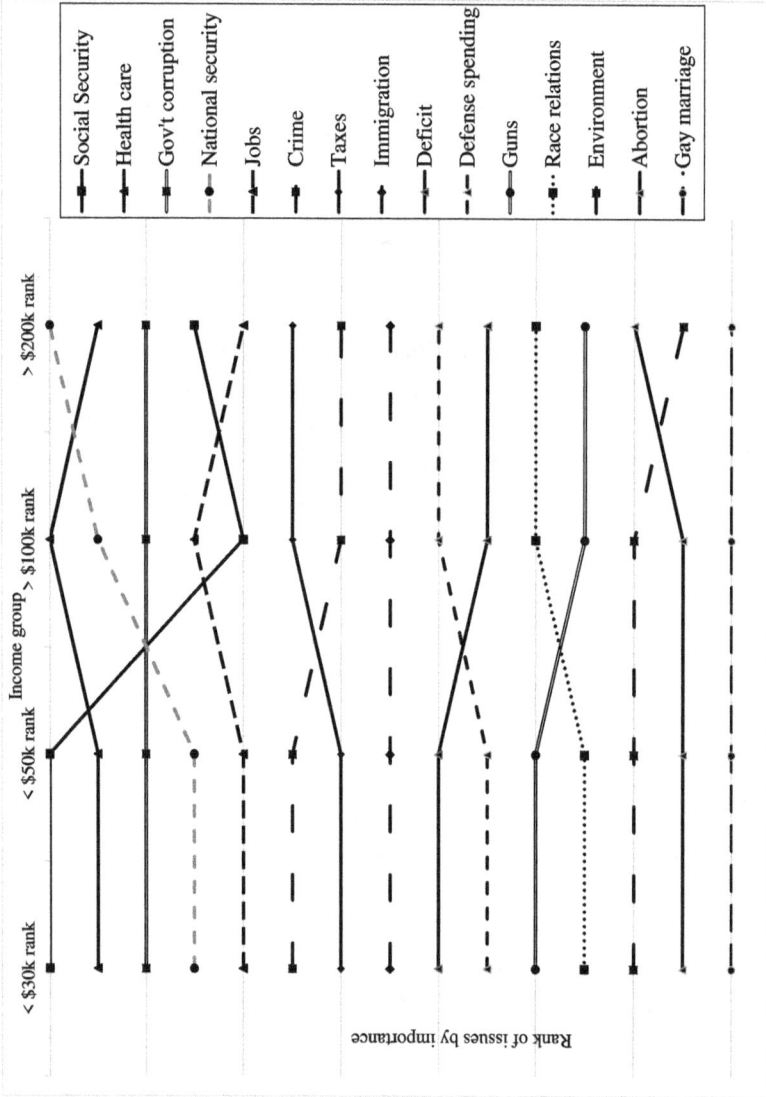

FIGURE 5.11. Importance of various issues to different income cohorts, CES 2016
Lines denote issues ranking, with most important issues at the top. CES data can be found at https://cces.gov.harvard.edu/.

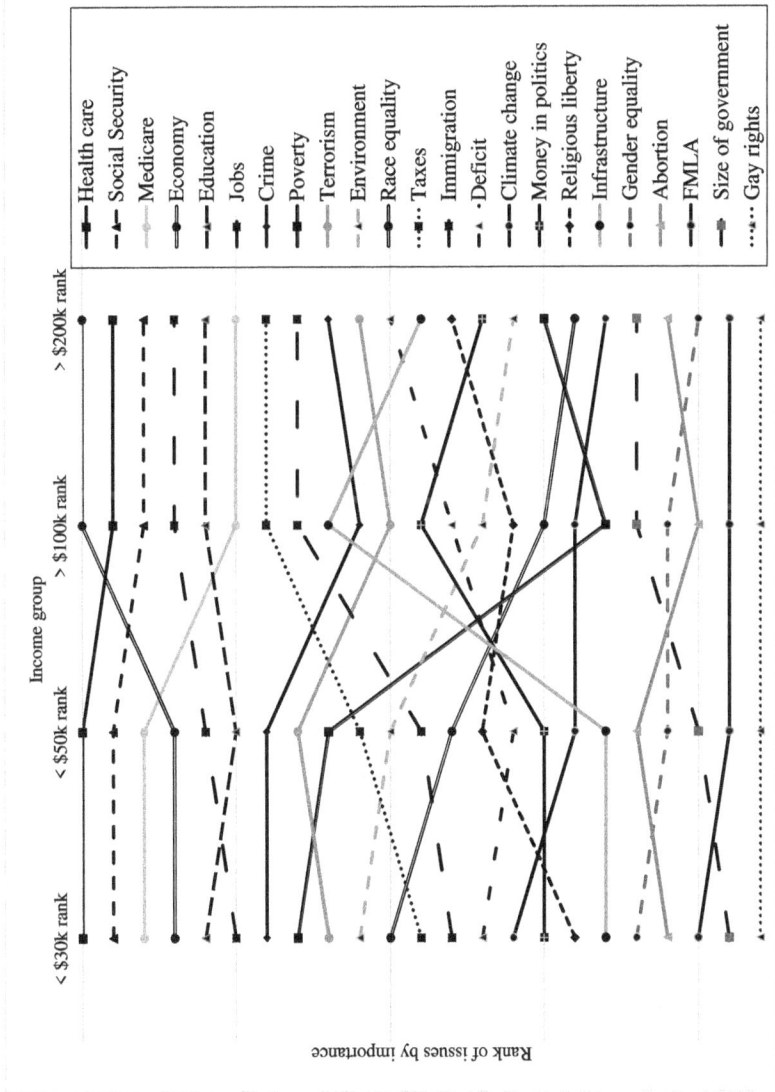

FIGURE 5.12. Importance of various issues to different income cohorts, DFVGS 2019

Lines denote issues ranking, with most important issues at the top. DFVSG data can be found at https://www.voterstudygroup.org/data.

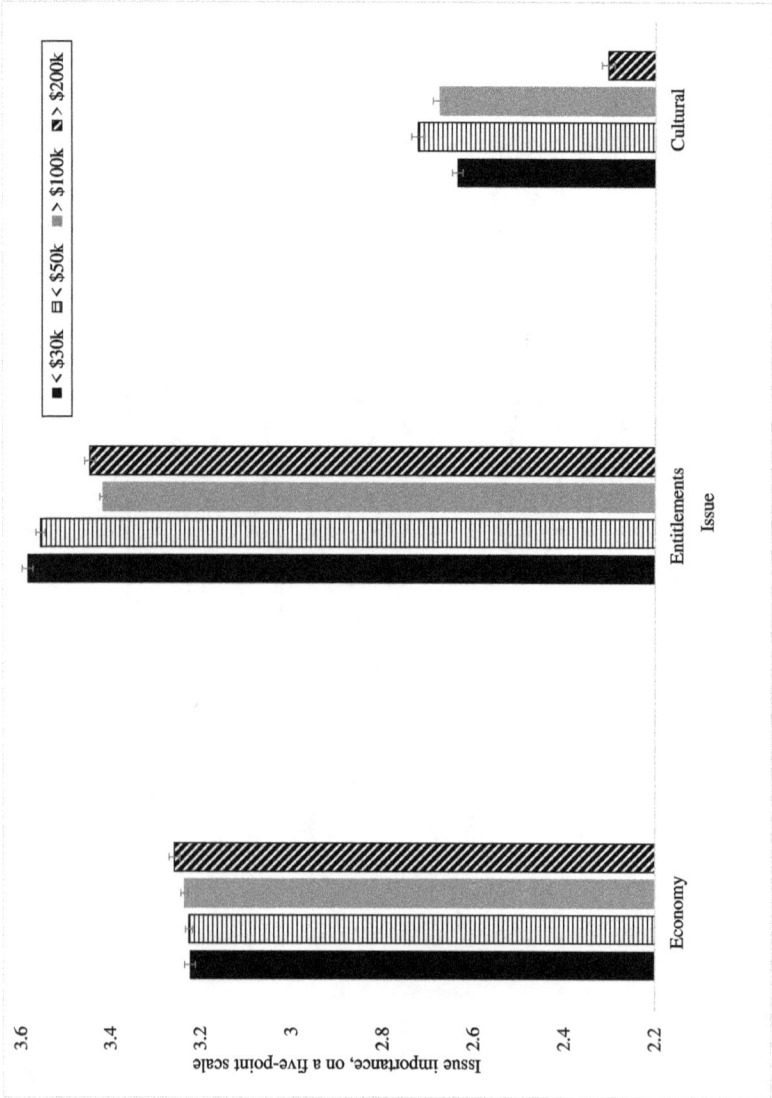

FIGURE 5.13. Importance of certain issues to different income groups, CES 2016
Capped lines represent 95 percent confidence intervals. CES data can be found at https://cces.gov.harvard.edu/.

striking that lower-income Americans are relatively more concerned about crime and terrorism but—perhaps contradicting a feeling pervasive among political commentators after the 2016 election—possibly less worried about immigration. Taxes are visibly more important to the wealthy, and the environment to those making less than $50,000 a year.

Figure 5.13 examines the 2016 CES study and the various income cohorts' views of the issues. The data report the mean scores for individuals of each group for ten of the issues, which I then put into one of three categories. I rank responses from "very high importance" to "no importance at all," and the average is taken for all participants in a group and then for all the issues in a category. "Economic" issues are taxes, jobs, and the budget deficit. I consider "Entitlements" to be Social Security and health care. "Cultural" issues are guns, abortion, crime, race relations, and gay marriage. Groups with higher scores care about the issue type more. Note that there is no material difference between the groups on the economy, echoing the argument I made in chapter 4. It would also be fair to say that the less affluent are more concerned with cultural issues and entitlements. As I noted in previous chapters, the concern less affluent Americans have for Social Security and health care may help explain why, unlike for issues like taxes and regulation, federal policy on them has not moved perceptibly to the right since 1980.

Conclusion

Critics who argue that the views of less affluent Americans have little influence on policymakers point frequently to class differences in voter participation rates, levels of political activism, and financial contributions to campaigns. It is, however, plausible that any variance in the capacity to shape decisions made in Washington is the result not so much of the relative inability of lower-income citizens to amplify their views on economic policy but of the largely silent or incoherent nature of them. Under such circumstances, any enhancement or elaboration of policy attitudes will do little to give them effect.

To explore income-based differences in the consistency of Americans' political views and policy preferences, I focus on both individuals and groups. Less affluent citizens are less likely to be sure of their own and others' political views. They reveal themselves as less capable of structuring their policy preferences within the conventional framework used to communicate attitudes in American politics. Lower-income Americans are also less likely to hold strong ideological and partisan attachments; in other words, they tend to consider themselves moderates and weak partisans, two characteristics scholars believe are typical of politically confused and ineffective citizens. Notably, the less affluent are less likely to vote in a manner consistent with their ideology, presumably leaving politicians they support unclear as to their instructions on how to govern.

At the group level, lower-income cohorts are more heterogeneous in their political attitudes. This heterogeneity makes them appear more incoherent. Such apparent incoherence is evident in the case of self-identified ideology. It is also true for issues, even those like raising the minimum wage that should be more salient to them. As a result, it is perhaps not surprising that the House members who represent districts with lower median incomes tend to have, in an ideological sense, more incoherent or inconsistent voting records. Finally, although as with their substantive views high and low-income Americans tend to rank issues in a similar order of importance, wealthier citizens place a little more emphasis on economic issues than do their compatriots.

There are other potential tests of my argument and surveys of American public opinion I could analyze. But I am interested only in establishing correlation and I think it is clear that the preponderance of evidence in my basic survey of the partisan, ideological, and economic policy attitudes of Americans of different income groups shows that the less affluent are more conflicted and unsure as individuals and heterogeneous and therefore incoherent as a group. All these findings jibe with an argument that our democratic system functions better than the political-science literature on economic inequality assumes. Even if lower-income Americans have distinctly progressive views on economic policy—and chapter 4 casts doubt on the proposition—they are less effective than their wealthier counterparts at communicating those views to officials in Washington. Lawmakers are naturally inclined to take cues from sub-constituencies that speak more confidently and sonorously.

Distribution and Less Affluent Americans' Views of Politics

In the 1970s, Ted Lowi (1972) proposed a categorization of public policy that profoundly influenced the way social scientists study the subject. *Redistributive policies* refer to issues where government is taking and giving substantial resources from and to distinct and large groups. Progressive taxation and Medicaid are examples. So are programs that entail direct payments to individuals. *Regulatory policy* refers to government implementation of rules that stipulate behavior, as labor, environmental, and civil rights policies usually do. Here government is using its legal authority to direct societal practices.

The focus here is on a third type, what Lowi called *distributive policy*. It describes circumstances where a distinct and finite group receives resources from government, often in the form of a contract, grant, subsidy, or tax break. Although the good distributed by the federal government may appear public, the policy is not redistributive because, in geographic terms generally, the benefits are concentrated and the costs dispersed widely across the broader population. Funding for the construction of a bridge, government procurement of equipment from a local manufacturer, and a grant to an area nonprofit are all examples. Whereas redistributive policymaking activates large social blocks generating political conflict, distributive policymaking involves narrower parochial interests and gives rise to logrolling among elected officials.

Americans seem to approve of distributive policy. They subscribe to a delegate model of representation and frequently appear to want those they elect to focus on their proximate interests rather than national concerns (Cain et al. 1987, 36–40). The single-member district simple-plurality electoral system where candidate nomination is by primary further incentivizes such policymaking.

Working within this cultural and institutional framework, members of Congress seek to maximize the "personal vote"—the proportion of their vote

attributable not to their party affiliation but their own individual accomplishments and attributes (Cain et al. 1987; Fiorina 1977; Herrera and Yawn 1999).
Bipartisan and near-universalistic coalitions historically form in support of
congressional appropriations, an especially popular form of distributive policymaking (Groseclose and Snyder 1996; Niou and Ordeshook 1985; Shepsle and
Weingast 1981; Weingast 1979). Indeed, Gordon and Simpson (2018) reveal
that congressional appropriations have financed local projects since the late
eighteenth century, despite the federal nature of the system. Members worked
hard to secure funding for the construction of lighthouses, post offices, and
military forts and the dredging of rivers and harbors during the Republic's
formative years.

Scholars assume a significant and constant demand for federal government
funding on typically distributive matters like transportation, schools, scientific research, defense goods, and grants to nonprofits. Everybody should want
more money—including through customized breaks on the revenue side—for
themselves and their family, company, neighborhood, city, congressional district, or state. It is not surprising, therefore, that the focus of research on distributive politics has been on variance in the capacity of policymakers to supply
particularistic benefits to their constituents.

A number of such studies suggest that presidents do much to direct favors and federal resources to certain states, cities, and counties, despite their
national constituency and a theoretical preference for universalism over
particularism (Berry et al. 2010; Dynes and Huber 2015; Kriner and Reeves
2015; Taylor 2008). Rules governing presidential nominations and the Electoral College with its winner-take-all principle for distributing electoral votes
produce incentives for presidents to push federal money to competitive and
supportive states. Congressional scholars reveal a variety of determinants for
the geographic distribution of grants, procurement, and other discretionary
spending. Members of the majority party are especially capable of securing
funds for their constituents (Albouy 2013; Cann and Sidman 2011; Carroll and
Kim 2010; Curry and Donnelly 2021). Incumbents in marginal seats also do
well (Bickers and Stein 1996; Engstrom and Vanberg 2010; Lazarus 2009, 2010;
Stein and Bickers 1995), as do members of the appropriations committees
and the authorizing panels whose jurisdictions contain the substantive issue
related to the expenditure (Berry and Fowler 2016; Carsey and Rundquist
1999; Lazarus 2010; Weingast and Marshall 1988). The malapportionment of
the Senate advantages smaller states in allocations (Ansolabehere et al. 2003;
Clemens et al. 2015; Larcinese et al. 2013; Lee 2004), and the institution's stag-
gered elections mean members whose terms are expiring at the end of the
current Congress are successful (Shepsle et al. 2009). In an era of partisan

polarization in which ideology is salient to voters, Republicans dip into the pork barrel less frequently (Sidman 2019).

There is, however, some interesting theoretical and empirical work on what we might call the "demand side" of distributive politics. It makes the case that the appetite for federal largesse varies across the public. One argument is that in comparison to more affluent individuals—and possibly redistributive policy—less affluent Americans prefer favorable distributive policy outcomes and the kind of legislator and legislative behavior more likely to steer these benefits to them.

Affluence and Distributive Policy: Theory and Existing Research

I lean on this body of work here. It begins with the assumption that lower-income Americans prefer distributive policies more than do their compatriots because any government assistance constitutes a larger share of their income (Elkjaer and Iversen 2023; Harden 2016, 36–37; Stokes et al. 2013). In Dixit and Londregan's (1996, 1143) words, "the incremental dollar means more" to those less well-off. Improved transportation, new schools, better public health facilities, job training, federal buildings, and government contracts to local employers should have a greater material effect on the life of a lower-income citizen. Americans from poorer districts, regardless of their personal financial situation, are also likely to express support for distributive policy. Tromborg and Schwindt-Bayer's (2019) theory of "relative deprivation" posits that residents of low-income jurisdictions issue greater demands for distributive benefits—like job training, health care, transportation resources, and recreation facilities—because they find it difficult to attract for-profit businesses willing to supply them privately, at least not without government support.

To be sure, redistribution also favors less affluent Americans. Augmented Social Security, Medicare, and social-welfare spending, particularly when it comes in the form of transfer payments, compose a greater proportion of their income. Beneficiaries of programs like food stamps and TANF are frequently described as "lazy" and "unmotivated," however (Katz 1989; Soss and Schram 2007). These sentiments influence the views of poorer white Americans, particularly since welfare policy has deep racial connotations (Gilens 1999). Money spent on education, transportation, and health care clearly furthers a genuinely public good and is not perceived as a stigmatizing special favor to the undeserving. Such financing also constitutes a response to immediate and practical economic and social problems, not expensive efforts to address abstractions like inequality and systemic poverty.[1]

Because they frequently do not qualify for benefits but pay disproportionately through the progressive tax system, moreover, wealthier citizens are aware of the costs of redistribution relative to its benefits. Research shows that economic self-interest shapes preferences for redistribution (Campbell 2002; Kuziemko et al. 2015; Luttig 2013; Meltzer and Richard 1981). Such countervailing pressures do not exist in distributive policymaking. Citizens consume the products of public goods like roads, schools, and hospitals regardless of their economic situation, and while the benefits of these policies are geographically concentrated, the costs scatter widely across the entire country's population when they are paid for by the government. Individual distributive policy items can have materially positive effects on the daily lives of thousands of residents of a state or congressional district, especially the less well-off, but they are obscure lines in the federal budget.

A relationship between socioeconomic status and views of distributive policymaking has found empirical confirmation in the American context. Harden's (2016) comprehensive study of state legislators reports that lower-income citizens prefer their representatives to focus on constituency service like casework and the allocation of public goods and services to the district. Wealthier Americans, on the other hand, place greater emphasis on policies like those we generally consider redistributive and regulatory. Griffin and Flavin (2011) confirm these findings in their work on Congress. Beyond this work, however there is little research on whether variance in the attention of American federal legislators to particular spheres of representation is a function of the socioeconomic composition of the population they serve and greater demands to focus on the proximate needs of constituents placed upon them by less affluent citizens. David Mayhew (1974, 73–74) speculated this was so when he noted in the mid-1970s, "Congressmen from the traditional parts of old machine cities . . . devote a great deal of time and energy to the distribution of benefits." Grimmer, Westwood, and Messing (2014, 40–54) demonstrate that members from less affluent districts tend to claim credit for federal government expenditures. This does not mean they actually deliver, however.

I explore four propositions in the remainder of this chapter. First, I examine whether less affluent Americans have a stronger sense of "place" and allegiance to the physical community in which they reside than do the better-off. Evidence consistent with the proposition is suggestive of lower-income Americans' greater appreciation for particularistic and localized benefits. Second, I examine the postulate that lower-income Americans have a strong preference for their representatives to focus on matters of direct interest to their own constituents, such as government allocations to the district or state.

There is some established work in this area, and I add to it only by exploring recent data. The third proposition is that individual members of Congress respond to these concerns. I therefore analyze legislators' behavior, examining whether the affluence of their constituents explains any propensity to spend a disproportionate amount of time, effort, and resources on local matters and the allocation of federal funds to constituents. Finally, I examine actual distributive policy outputs and patterns in particular kinds of federal spending. It is with the last two propositions that I break some new ground empirically, by looking at, among other things, the nature of members' careers, assignment of staff to their district, membership of the House Appropriations Committee, and capacity to direct federal money to their constituents.

If these assertions are confirmed, we might agree with Griffin and Flavin's (2011, 529–30) statement that "disparities in representation across demographic groups may occur in part because citizens prioritize policy representation and other facets of representation differently and elected officials are sensitive to these differences." In other words, the conservative economic-policy outcomes that purportedly increase inequality could be a function of affluent voters' representatives advancing their redistributive policy preferences, as low-income voters call upon their receptive legislators to attend to distributive politics and the direct allocation of government finances and projects to themselves, their friends, and their neighbors. This point is an important one, and it has been largely neglected by the current literature on American democracy and economic inequality.

Constituent Affluence and Sense of Place

Recent research suggests that lower-income citizens place greater value on their personal relationships and people, such as family and neighbors, who live proximately in their physical communities (Hopkins 2018, 187–90; Piff et al. 2010). These relationships are often necessarily reciprocal and transactional (Walker 1995). Wealthier citizens, by contrast, are more cognizant of their geographic mobility and abstract matters of identity (Stephens et al. 2014). A recent study of millions of Facebook users reveals that less affluent Americans tend to make friendships in their neighborhood, whereas wealthier citizens are more likely to have friends, now dispersed across the country, they made while in college (Chetty et al. 2022).[2] Affluent lifestyles are more likely to produce allegiances to people who live further away—often overseas—and presumably outside tangible and proximate political communities.[3]

Observations like these have contributed to our emerging understanding of the antagonisms between globalization and populism illuminated by the events of the past decade, particularly the election of Donald Trump in the United States, the passage of Brexit in the United Kingdom, and the *gilets jaunes* movement in France.[4] Trump—famously for a Republican—did better in 2016 among white non-college-educated voters than he did among those with a college degree, by the tune of eighteen percentage points. He also won proportionally more votes from those who made $50,000–$100,000 a year than those who made over $250,000. He stitched together similar coalitions in 2020 and 2024.[5] Best estimates—given that there was no exit polling—suggest that the proportion of Britons without education credentials voting to leave the European Union was thirty-nine percentage points greater than the proportion of those with a college degree. The 2016 contests pitted arguments in favor of parochial interests and economic nationalism—central features of a populist platform—against policies of free trade and liberal immigration (Clarke et al. 2017; Sides et al. 2018). Those who voted for Trump and "Leave" tended to be what Goodhart (2017) calls "Somewheres," as opposed to the "Anywheres" who supported Hillary Clinton and "Remain." Working-class Somewheres—with whom the *gilets jaunes* also certainly sympathized—are much less geographically mobile and as a result are rooted, feeling stronger attachment to their local communities.[6]

This thinking, in turn, relates to a concept called *place identity* that political scientists are just beginning to investigate, especially in work done on Southerners (Cooper and Knotts 2017; Jacobs and Munis 2019). Place identity is a form of social identity that "refers to a sense of belonging to a group whose membership is defined by living in a particular place and having a psychological attachment of group-based perception with other group members" (Munis 2020, 40). Wong (2010, 75–93) reveals that attachment to place is a function of longevity and an individual's rootedness in a community, itself a result of work and family ties. Other research reports place of residence to contribute more to personal identity as educational attainment goes down (Hopkins 2018, 187–90). To be sure, the working class pick up their homes more often than do the wealthy, but people with fewer educational credentials and lower incomes are considerably less likely to move across state lines. For less well-off young adults—at a time in life when geographical mobility is most common—the physical proximity of parents and the financial resources and child support they can provide are powerful deterrents to relocation (Spring et al. 2017). Working-class Americans are therefore more likely to invest in the personal relationships and social institutions—softball leagues, church communities, the neighborhood bar—that intensify an allegiance to the place they live.

Place identity has a corollary, *place resentment*, which describes people disliking others because they live elsewhere (Agnew 1987; Jacobs and Munis

2019; Wong 2010). The political science here is more developed. Research has shown the feeling to be stronger in people who live in rural areas (Cramer 2016; Dawkins et al. 2023; Jacobs and Munis 2019, 2023; Jacobs and Shea 2024)—or at least that rural identity generates an anti-intellectualism that appears related to animus (Trujillo 2022; Trujillo and Crowley 2022). Since a sense of place identity seems necessary for an individual to possess place resentment, scholars suggest that we find more of it among rural and Southern residents, particularly the working class (Cooper and Knotts 2019; Munis 2020).

To explore whether socioeconomic status affects the extent to which Americans allow an allegiance to place to shape their political attitudes and behavior, I analyze data compiled by Charles Hunt (2022) on what he calls the "local roots" of representation in Congress. Hunt shows that formal connections to the district, such as being born, educated, or employed there, have materially positive effects on a candidate's capacity to raise money and generate votes. These effects exist even in the twenty-first century, a period of partisanship, ideological polarization, and the dominance of national issues. I am interested in what explains a district's selection of an individual who was born there to represent it.

The data are therefore at the district level and are of limited utility in understanding the preferences and decisions of individuals. The approach also involves matters of candidate emergence as well as voter choice. As I note in a deeper analysis of descriptive representation in a later chapter, however, within the universe of all members or challengers, a clustering of candidates with certain qualities in less affluent districts is suggestive of a relationship between district socioeconomic character on one hand and a preference for those kind of politicians—here people with local roots—on the other. If geographic affinity and connection are unusually important to less affluent Americans, districts with lower median household incomes are more likely to have members and major-party general-election challengers with credible claims to be neighbors or "one of them."

Table 6.1 reports the results of logit models using Hunt's data of US House members and congressional districts. I include election-year fixed effects and, in the incumbent specification, a time-trend variable (as per Hunt) and cluster standard errors by member. The data for members are from 1964–2020, for challengers from 2002–2018.[7] It is clear that native-born major-party candidates are appreciably more likely to represent and secure nominations in jurisdictions with lower median household incomes and proportions of college-educated residents, even after accounting for attributes like candidate race, gender, and party and electoral competitiveness. Males, Democrats, and members representing safe and white districts are also more likely to have

TABLE 6.1. District income and education and candidates' places of birth, 1964–2020

	Incumbent	Challenger
District median household income	−.209 (.071)*	−.188 (.056)*
District proportion of residents with bachelor's degree	−3.26 (1.06)*	−2.55 (1.04)*
District proportion Black	−1.13 (.492)*	−.570 (.448)
District proportion Latino	−1.86 (.496)*	−1.27 (.400)*
District proportion urban	.512 (.289)	.745 (.393)
Incumbent female	−.905 (.197)*	
Incumbent age	−.007 (.005)	
Incumbent non-white	−.011 (.249)	
Incumbent bachelor's degree	.473 (.310)	
Incumbent Democrat	.425 (.119)*	
Incumbent two-party margin of victory	.008 (.003)*	.008 (.003)*
Challenger quality		.531 (.113)*
Time	.050 (.013)*	
Constant	−.286 (.450)	−.295 (.302)
Pseudo R^2	.057	.032
N (years)	9,612 (1964–2020)	2,894 (2004–2018)
Method	Logit	

Notes: Data are from Hunt (2022). Logit estimations with coefficients reported and robust standard errors clustered by member in parentheses. Dependent variable is coded "1" if a subject was born in the district, "0" if not. Congress fixed effects are not reported. *$p < .05$.

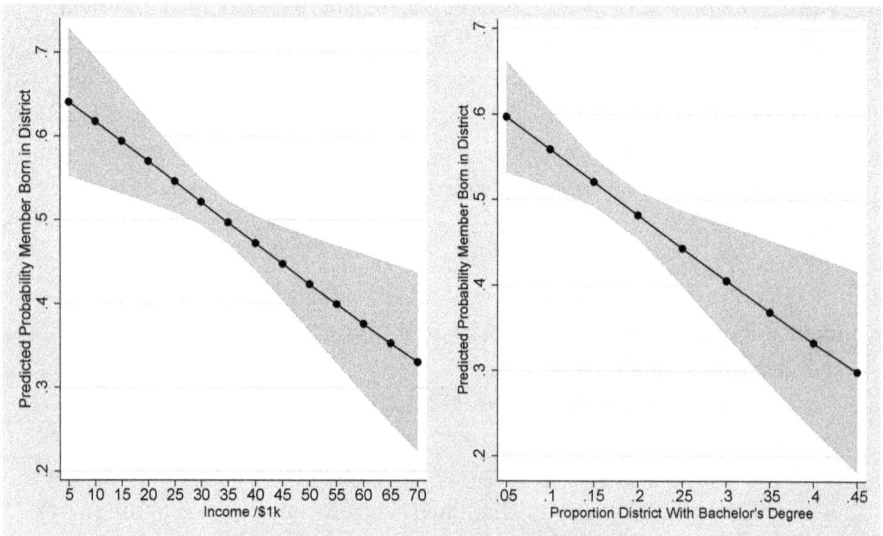

FIGURE 6.1. Substantive effect of district income and education on probability of a House member being born in their district, Hunt data 1964–2020
Shaded areas denote 95 percent confidence intervals. Data are from Hunt (2022).

been born there. Native-born challengers are disproportionately experienced in politics and run in districts where the incumbent is electorally secure.[8]

Figure 6.1 reveals the predicted probability of a district having a native son or daughter represent it at various levels of constituency income and education. For reference, in the entire data I analyze, just over one-half of members (51.1 percent) were born in their districts. For the districts with low incomes and relatively few residents with bachelor's degrees, the probability of having an incumbent representative born there is appreciably greater than 50 percent.

Affluence and Americans' Views of Distribution

Several scholars have explored citizens' preferences for the kinds of matters on which they believe their representatives should focus. Researchers generally divide legislators' activities into different types, including those that are especially attentive to constituents, such as casework and allocations of federal funds for local projects, and those that are explicitly more national in scope, such as overseeing the executive branch and researching, debating, and voting on important issues. Griffin and Flavin (2011) analyze the 2006 CES data and reveal that a greater proportion of lower-income Americans desire that their representatives engage in constituency service and distributive politics than do their wealthier compatriots, who instead prefer what the authors call "policy representation." Lapinski et al.'s (2016) analyses of Annenberg Institutions of Democracy data produce similar findings. Harden (2016, 50–59) asks respondents to read vignettes of legislators engaging in a particular activity and then explain how "warm" they feel about them on a thermometer that ranges from 0 to 100. He finds no statistically significant difference in the responses of poorest and wealthiest participants when they read about a legislator's constituency service, but low-income respondents have a materially more favorable reaction to allocation activity and a markedly cooler reaction to the policy condition. These results are replicated when respondents are coded by their employment status, with unemployed subjects much more enthusiastic about lawmakers who work on allocations for their districts than about those who work on broader policy matters. Interestingly, all three studies revealed marked racial and ethnic differences. Blacks and Latinos were considerably more receptive to particularism or distributive politics than were whites.[9] In both relative and absolute senses, whites strongly prefer representatives work on advancing their policy interests (Flavin and Griffin 2011; Harden 2016, 55–59).[10]

I have little to add to what I suggest are clear findings. Instead, I examine more recent data to see if they can be confirmed. The 2018 CES includes a

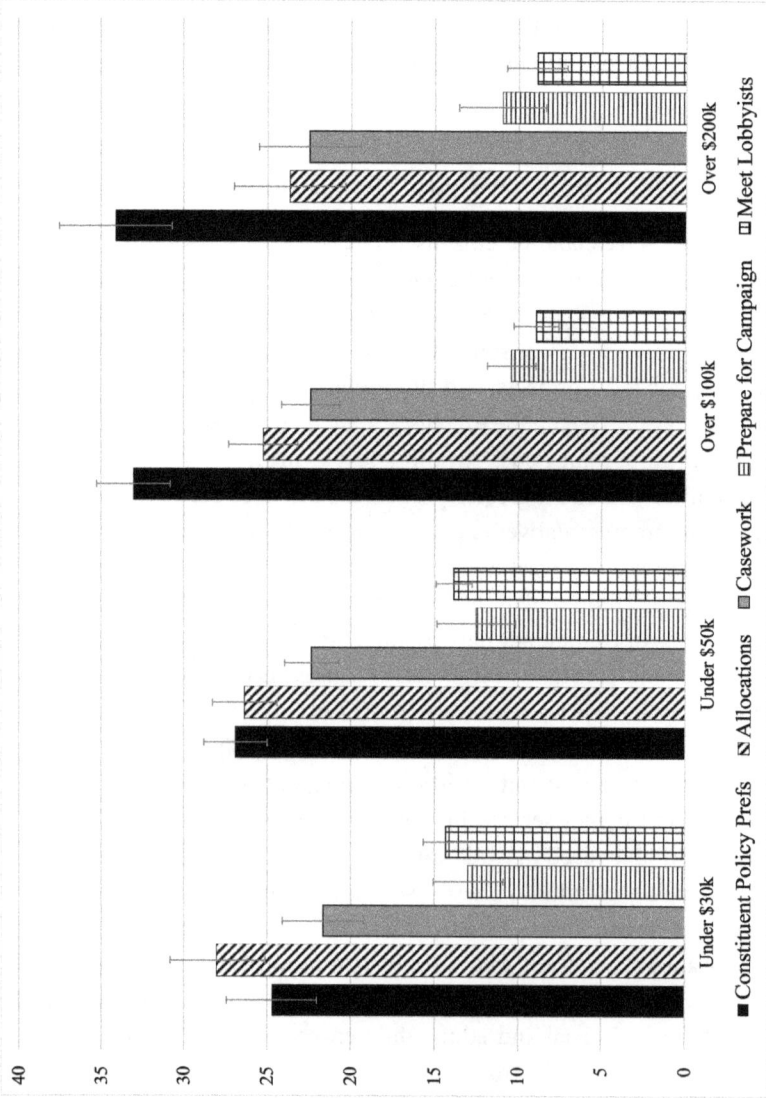

FIGURE 6.2. Income and individuals' preferences for how members of Congress spend their time, CES 2018 Capped lines represent 95 percent confidence intervals. CES data can be found at https://cces.gov.harvard.edu/.

question about how members should distribute their time among five spheres of activity. These are "learning and advocating for constituents' policy interests," "making sure his or her constituents get their fair share of government money and projects" (what I call "allocations"), "helping constituents who have problems with government agencies" (what I call "casework"), "preparing for the next election campaign," and "meeting with interest groups and lobbyists." Interviewers asked respondents how much time a member of Congress should spend on each activity.

Figure 6.2 demonstrates the importance of the different realms of activity to a series of income groups by displaying cohort means. No group prefers, above any other, that members spend time on allocating resources to the district, at least not to an extent that the difference is statistically significant. But higher-income respondents prefer their representatives to devote time to understanding and pushing for their policy interests. It is clearly these groups' most desired activity. Respondents with household incomes below $30,000 are the only cohort that wants legislators to spend a plurality of their time on securing government projects and money for constituents. The finding confirms two important points. Lower-income Americans prefer, if at times narrowly, their representatives to work on allocation and constituency service at the expense of matters with national implications. Wealthier citizens, on the other hand, place materially more emphasis on lawmakers advocating for their broader policy interests within the legislative process.

Constituent Affluence and Legislator Behavior

If less affluent Americans wish their elected officials to dedicate much of their time to matters like resource allocation, we should expect the legislators who represent them to oblige. Internalizing cues from their constituents, members of Congress interested in reelection will alter their professional activities to reflect what their voters want of them. We ought, therefore, to see patterns in lawmakers' behavior that are consistent with the findings above. Members from districts with lower median household incomes or greater proportions of poorer families will organize their legislative behavior to attend to local matters.

I look at several types of activities in an effort to understand whether legislators' work is consistent with this expectation. I first examine what Bernhard and Sulkin (2018) call a "gestalt" level of legislator behavior and the concept of a general "legislative style." Bernhard and Sulkin (2018, 42–60) identify five different styles from their analysis of a range of activities in which members engage during their time in office. "Policy specialists" are drawn mainly to

TABLE 6.2. Characteristics of district advocates, 1989–2008

	Median income	Lowest-income group proportion	Highest-income group proportion
District household income measure	.012 (.011)	.421 (1.85)	4.78 (2.34)*
Democrat	−.002 (.002)	−.002 (.002)	−.002 (.002)
Woman	−.193 (.248)	−.184 (.250)	−.249 (.247)
Black	−.820 (.382)*	−.936 (.392)*	−.788 (.378)
Latino	.269 (.418)	.139 (.416)	.333 (.410)
Margin	−.007 (.002)*	−.007 (.002)*	−.007 (.002)*
Seniority	.026 (.017)	.026 (.017)	.025 (.017)
Chair or ranking member	−.663 (.229)*	−.652 (.228)*	−.667 (.227)*
District in South	.246 (.160)	.208 (.164)	.231 (.158)
District percentage urban	−.022 (.004)*	−.019 (.004)*	−.024 (.004)*
Pseudo R^2	.058	.057	.061

Notes: Data are from Bernhard and Sulkin (2018). $N = 4,215$. Logit estimation with coefficients reported and robust standard errors clustered by member in parentheses. Dependent variable is coded "1" if a member is a district advocate in the Congress, "0" if not. Congress fixed effects are not reported. *$p < .05$.

substantive matters of national importance and spend a great deal of their time on a handful of issues. They regularly sponsor and co-sponsor legislation related to their interests. Both "party soldiers" and "party builders" are loyal to their party; the latter are also ambitious and wish to move up the leadership ladder. "Ambitious entrepreneurs" raise a great deal of money and work hard at cultivating a national image by appearing frequently on television and exploiting social media. The fifth style is that of "district advocates," members who operate "below the radar" and do not engage in what Bernhard and Sulkin (2018) call "showboating" or the seeking of media attention. District advocates are particularly high on what the authors call "homefront" indicators; that is, they tend to have several district offices and assign a large proportion of their staff to work there. Measures of roll-call voting and bill sponsorships reveal many of them to be ideologically moderate and the most likely of all types to vote against their party.

If our expectations about constituency preferences for legislative behavior are correct, the district advocate should be the style most likely to represent less affluent Americans. Table 6.2 reveals the results of a model of legislative style using a dichotomous measure indicating whether a member was a district advocate in a Congress.[11] The data cover the 101st–110th Congresses (1989–2008). They include a series of control variables—the member's party, race, gender, ethnicity, seniority (in years served), and margin of victory in the immediately previous election; the location of their district and the percentage of it that was urban; and whether or not they were a chair or ranking member of a standing committee. The independent variables of interest are those that measure district household income (divided by one thousand) and measures of the proportion of district households from the highest- and lowest-income cohorts. Here and throughout the rest of the book, I take advantage of detailed information from the US Census about incomes in congressional districts and use two sets of low- and high-income pairs, one narrow and the other reflecting a broader understanding of rich and poor. They are the proportion of a district's households that are in the very lowest- and highest-income brackets and the proportion in a larger number of brackets that also adjoin the bottom or the top. The former I call lowest- and highest-income groups, the latter low- and high-income groups.[12]

At first glance, there is little to recommend the hypothesis. In fact, members who represent districts with the largest proportion of highest-income households are more likely to be district advocates. A member from a district where only 1 percent of households is in the richest cohort has a 21 percent chance of being an advocate; one from a district where 9 percent of households are in the category has a 28 percent chance. Other variables explain legislators' choices to adopt the style better, however. Non-Black members are more likely to be district advocates, as are those who narrowly won election last time and legislators who do not have committee leadership positions. Note that lawmakers from urban districts are less likely to acquire the style. A member from a wholly urban district has a 16 percent chance of being a district advocate, one from a district that is one-fifth urban 52 percent.

This last observation is interesting. Mayhew (1974, 73–4) argued that urban politicians tended to focus on the kinds of activities that would make them district advocates. He saw them as cogs in the old party machines, attentive to their constituents and keen to distribute federal resources to their blue-collar and often ethnic voters. Some of the discrepancy is undoubtedly attributable to Bernhard and Sulkin's (2018) use of the number of district offices as a component of the district advocate measure—rural representatives require several offices to cover their geographically large districts. But it is also important to note that today, America's biggest cities are more socioeconomically diverse. Some urban districts are very wealthy (for example, New York's White Plains district, represented for years by Nita Lowey, and California's Silicon Valley district, represented by Anna Eshoo), others very poor (for example, New York's Bronx district, represented by Jose Serrano, and Michigan's Detroit district, represented by Carolyn Cheeks Kilpatrick and, more recently, Rashida Tlaib). The Democratic machines have also disintegrated (Trounstine 2008). During the ten Congresses for which Bernhard and Sulkin (2018) provide data, districts more than 75 percent urban are the

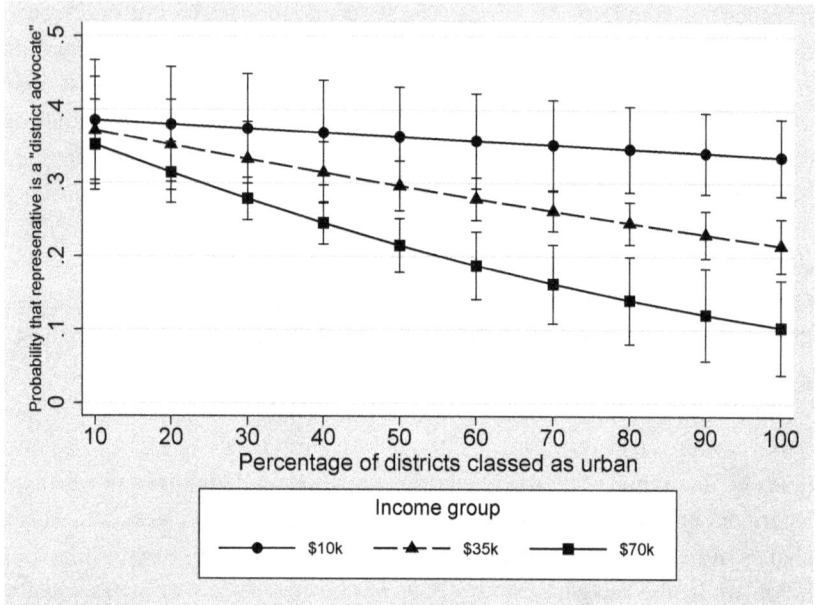

FIGURE 6.3. Effect of constituent income conditioned by the urban nature of a district on its likelihood of representation by a "district advocate," Bernhard and Sulkin data 1989–2008
Capped lines denote 95 percent confidence intervals. Data are from Bernhard and Sulkin (2018).

wealthiest and most unequal.[13] Rural districts are now generally poorer than urban equivalents, and, as these results imply, their residents seem more likely to want their legislators to focus on matters of particular interest to them.

With this finding in mind, figure 6.3 reports the marginal effects when the median household income is interacted with the proportion of the district that is urban. We can see that district advocates tend to represent rural areas. As the district becomes increasingly urban, however, household income becomes important. The lower the median household income of an urban district, the more likely its representative is to be a district advocate.

As noted, the percentage of a legislator's staff assigned to the district is a component of Bernhard and Sulkin's (2018) district advocate measure. Compared to their Washington-based colleagues, personal staff who work in the district tend to spend the bulk of their time on casework, assisting constituents in their dealings with federal agencies by, among other things, advising nonprofits on grant applications, locating lost Social Security checks, and facilitating veterans' efforts to receive benefits. Casework is not explicitly distributive policy but is a form of service to a member's constituents. It certainly has a parochial quality. An analysis of the extent to which legislators deploy staff in district offices ought, therefore, to provide some insight into the kinds

TABLE 6.3. Percentage of House members' staff based in the district, 1989–2008

	Median	Lowest-income group proportion
District household income measure	−.118 (.034)*	23.08 (7.34)*
Number of district offices	1.95 (.212)*	1.94 (.211)*
Democrat	2.16 (.541)*	1.90 (.536)*
Woman	−1.35 (.676)*	−1.23 (.689)
Black	3.12 (1.05)*	2.11 (1.05)*
Latino	.945 (1.29)	−.051 (1.32)
Margin	.006 (.008)	.004 (.008)
Seniority	−.180 (.065)*	−.193 (.066)*
Chair or ranking member	−1.38 (.804)	−1.29 (.794)
Party leader	3.13 (1.65)	3.24 (1.65)*
District in South	−1.38 (.524)*	−1.53 (.519)*
District percentage urban	.035 (.014)*	.047 (.015)*
Adjusted R^2	.106	.107

Notes: Data from Bernhard and Sulkin (2018). $N = 4{,}245$. OLS estimation with coefficients reported and robust standard errors clustered by member in parentheses. Dependent variable is the proportion of a member's staff in the district. *$p < .05$.

of lawmakers who feel a need to focus on their constituents and local issues, possibly at the expense of policy with national implications, on which staff in Washington spend much of their time working. Such an analysis has the additional virtue of constituting an unfiltered measure of what we might call "district attentiveness," a plausible category of legislator behavior that does not fit neatly into Bernhard and Sulkin's (2018) typology.

Table 6.3 reveals the results of a model of the percentage of members' staff based in the district from the 101st–110th Congresses calculated by Bernhard and Sulkin (2018). The data have a mean of 46.7 percent and standard deviation of 9.7 percent—half of legislators deploy between 41 and 53 percent of their staff in the district. I control for the number of district offices, itself a function of the geographic size of a member's constituency. There are several interesting findings. Democratic, Black, and junior members are more likely to situate staff at home. The same is true for Southerners and representatives from urban areas.

I am most interested in district socioeconomic characteristics, however. It is clear that members who represent less affluent places assign more of their staff locally. A decrease in the median household income of $30,000 increases the percentage of staff in the district by about 3.5 points. The indicator of the number of the poorest households is particularly robust. A six-percentage-point increase in the number of these households in a district (roughly the standard deviation) results in an approximately 1.5 percentage-point increase in the share of the member's staff not working in Washington. These results

contrast somewhat with those of Byers and Shay (2023), who argue that socioeconomic status (which for them is a combination of education and income)
has at best an indirect effect, influencing only members from low socioeconomic districts who assign a larger proportion of staff to the district as their
margin of victory in the previous election grows. The results are instead more
consistent with Kaslovsky's (2022) work. She shows that senators place more
staff and more frequently visit the counties in their states with lower median
household incomes.

House members can do other things that reflect the desire of their constituents for federal allocations. One is to advertise their legislative work on
the matter. With this point in mind, researchers have looked at the statements that lawmakers make in their newsletters and press releases. Using a
large and impressive dataset of every press release from every House member
between 2005 and 2010, Grimmer and colleagues (2012; 2014, 30–63) identify
press releases in which a member engages in "credit claiming" or "announces
an expenditure targeted to the district" (Grimmer et al. 2014, 36). The authors
reveal that just over 20 percent of press releases consist of credit claiming and
that there is a strong negative relationship between district median income
and the practice. This finding also holds true for education—House members representing fewer college graduates tend to have a higher proportion of
credit-claiming press releases (Grimmer et al. 2014, 42–45).

To examine whether this finding holds for a new and popular form of
communication, I examine data on nearly half a million social-media posts
placed by House members on their Facebook accounts from 2015 to 2018 and
collected by the Pew Research Center (van Kessell et al. 2018). The researchers
coded legislator posts in each of the two Congresses covered for the proportion they believed contained information regarding a "local topic."[14] Again,
this analysis is not a test of whether the socioeconomic status of a district
affects allocations of federal spending but of whether lower-income districts
with less educated constituents have representatives who wish to draw attention to matters of local concern.

Table 6.4 reports the results. The control variables include the distance
a member is from the chamber median first-dimension DW-NOMINATE
score. It is interesting to note that ideologically extreme members and those
from marginal districts devote more of their posts to local topics. So do junior legislators, those not in leadership positions, and Republicans. Moreover, although district household median income does not produce a statistically significant coefficient, the proportion of residents in the lowest-income
group and the proportion who have a college degree do, and in the hypothesized directions. In fact, an increase of five percentage points in the share of

TABLE 6.4. Constituent income and education and the proportion of members' Facebook posts on local topics, 2015–2018

	Proportion with bachelor's degree	Median income	Proportion poorest group
District socioeconomic measure	−.272 (.062)*	−.003 (.003)	.446 (.146)*
District proportion Black	−.034 (.046)	.015 (.046)	−.041 (.048)
District proportion Latino	−.008 (.039)	.063 (.036)	.040 (.036)
District proportion urban	−.051 (.031)	−.117 (.030)*	−.089 (.030)*
Democrat	−.029 (.013)*	−.039 (.013)*	−.041 (.013)*
Member committee chair	−.016 (.029)	−.021 (.029)	−.018 (.029)
Member party leader	−.126 (.053)*	−.125 (.054)*	−.133 (.051)*
Ideological extremism	.316 (.041)*	.334 (.040)*	.330 (.040)*
Two-party margin of victory	−.001 (.000)*	−.001 (.000)*	−.001 (.000)*
Member's terms served	−.003 (.001)*	−.003 (.001)*	−.003 (.001)*
Not on general-election ballot	−.053 (.016)*	−.028 (.014)	−.022 (.015)
115th Congress	−.046 (.006)*	−.044 (.006)*	−.047 (.006)*
Constant	.802 (.025)*	.784 (.028)*	.702 (.032)*
Adjusted R^2	.284	.264	.272

Notes: Data are from van Kessel et al. (2018). OLS estimations with coefficients reported and robust standard errors clustered by member in parentheses. "Ideological extremism" is the distance of a member's first-dimension DW-NOMINATE score from the chamber median. Dependent variable is proportion of posts concerning "local topics." $N = 858$. *$p < .05$.

households in the poorest group by income and a decrease of ten percentage points in the share of college graduates (roughly one standard deviation in both cases) elevate the proportion of posts on local matters by over two percentage points and nearly three percentage points, respectively.

House members can also recognize constituents' desire for federal expenditures by joining the Committee on Appropriations. This standing committee, formed out of Ways and Means in 1865, receives and reports all bills regarding, to use the words of the House's Rule X, the "appropriation of the revenue for the support of the Government." Given the panel's important role exercising Congress's "power of the purse," it is unsurprising that seats are coveted. Research has found that legislators who sit on Appropriations, particularly the powerful "cardinals" or chairs of its subcommittees, are capable of directing more federal funds to their districts (Berry and Fowler 2016; Clemens et al. 2010; Ferejohn 1974; Lazarus 2010; Lee 2003). The same seems to be the case in the Senate (Balla et al. 2002; Evans 2004; Payne 2003). According to congressional scholars' "Grosewart" scores of the value of committee seats, demand for slots on House Appropriations is second only to a seat on Ways and Means (Groseclose and Stewart 1998). Appropriations has also traditionally been the most active of the House's standing committees—at least as indicated by the number of hearing days per year (Adler 2002, 187–89).

TABLE 6.5. Determinants of House members' assignment to the Committee on Appropriations, 1973–2004

	Household median income	Lowest-income group size
District income measure	−.038 (.018)*	8.01 (2.33)*
Democrat	−.724 (.342)*	−1.05 (.375)*
Ideology	−1.12 (.397)*	−1.22 (.418)*
Woman	.059 (.323)	.046 (.322)
Black	−.509 (.478)	−.875 (.482)*
Latino	−.006 (.524)	−.068 (.545)
Seniority	.085 (.019)*	.088 (.020)*
Margin	.005 (.002)*	.004 (.002)*
District percentage with college degree	.046 (.013)*	.045 (.014)*
District percentage urban	−.010 (.004)*	−.008 (.005)*
Pseudo R^2	.045	.058
N	7,705 (93rd–113th Congress or 1973–2014)	5,974 (98th–113th Congress or 1983–2014)

Notes: Logit estimation with coefficients reported and robust standard errors clustered by member in parentheses. Dependent variable is coded "1" if a member is on Appropriations in the Congress, "0" if not. Ideology is member's first-dimension DW-NOMINATE score. Congress fixed effects are not reported. *$p < .05$.

Appropriations displays "uniform externalities" in that all House members should have roughly equal interest in its business (Adler and Lapinski 1997). But the discussion of affluence and attitudes toward distributive policy presented above gives us reason to believe that legislators from lower-income districts are more likely to request and receive an assignment on the committee. I test this hypothesis and report results in table 6.5. The explanatory variables of interest are the median district household income and the proportion of households in the lowest-income group. I deploy a variety of controls, most of which I used in the model of legislative style—indicators of member characteristics like race, gender, ethnicity, party, ideology, and seniority, as well as constituency characteristics such as the proportion of residents with a college degree, the proportion of the district classified as urban, and the margin of victory in the most recent election. The dependent variable is binary and denotes whether or not a House member sat on the chamber's Committee on Appropriations in a Congress. Data are from the 93rd to 113th Congress (1973–2014).[15]

Given the committee's prestige in the House, it is unsurprising that senior members are considerably more likely to sit on Appropriations. When controlling for party, there are a disproportionate number of liberals on the committee; a finding that again makes some sense when we consider that they are generally supportive of government spending. Most of the robust variables are indicators of district characteristics, however. Legislators from safe and rural districts are more likely to sit on the panel. More importantly from our perspective, so are those from relatively educated districts, a finding that seems inconsistent with the hypothesis. A relatively large share of the lawmakers on the committee are from lower-income districts, however. A district where 6 percent of households are from the lowest-income group has an approximately 10 percent likelihood of having its representative on Appropriations, a district with 16 percent of such households roughly double that.

House members only get to sit on Appropriations if the "steering" committees used by the parties to make assignments grant their requests. Placement on Appropriations is not, therefore, simply an expression of a member's interests. It requires the assent of their party's leadership. In fact, befitting its status as an important committee with universal appeal, the rate at which requests to be assigned to Appropriations are rejected is over 80 percent and only lower than that for Ways and Means among first-term members (Frisch and Kelly 2006, 126–30). With this in mind, I examine Frisch and Kelly's (2006) committee request data for the 93rd–103rd Congress (1973–1994).[16] The model is the same as that for actual assignments, but the dependent variables are whether or not a member made Appropriations their first choice and whether they requested it at all.[17] I include only members who Frisch and Kelly (2006) determine made committee assignment requests at the beginning of the Congress in the analysis; that is, principally freshmen. To make full use of the time series, I look only at the median household measure of district income. Table 6.6 reports results.

At least when it comes to assignments to Appropriations, the steering committees that make the selections seem biased by race, ethnicity, and gender—women and Latinos disproportionately request assignments but are no more likely to receive one, while Black legislators are no more likely to request but a little less likely to get appointed to the panel. But the committees also advantage members from lower-income districts. The results shown in table 6.5 and table 6.6 weaken the claim that freshman legislators with many less affluent constituents respond to their desire for government spending by requesting Appropriations, but they do suggest that the House is set up to facilitate the distributive-policy interests of members from poorer districts. Perhaps lawmakers from higher-income districts ask for Appropriations because their knowledgeable constituents pay attention to their assignment requests. Perhaps they often make Appropriations their first choice because they understand that their chances of obtaining a seat are not good. Regardless, the parties' steering committees seem to recognize the benefits—presumably electoral—of placing members from less affluent districts close to the machinery that directs the allocation of federal resources. It is presumably these legislators' constituents who truly appreciate the assignment.

TABLE 6.6. Determinants of House members' requests to be assigned to the Committee on Appropriations, 1973–1994

	First choice only	Chose at all
Median household income	.054 (.029)*	.033 (.027)
Democrat	−.519 (.369)	−1.03 (.338)*
Ideology	−.576 (.545)	−.518 (.498)*
Woman	.502 (.297)*	.866 (.279)*
Black	.337 (.394)	.275 (.369)
Latino	1.04 (.505)*	.902 (.549)
Seniority	−.061 (.036)*	−.167 (.040)*
Margin	.005 (.003)	.007 (.003)*
District percentage with college degree	−.012 (.014)	−.008 (.013)
District percentage urban	−.003 (.004)	−.003 (.004)
Pseudo R^2	.039	.057
N	1,302 (93rd–103rd Congress or 1973–1994)	1,302 (93rd–103rd Congress or 1973–1994)

Notes: Data are from Frisch and Kelly (2006). Logit estimation with coefficients reported and robust standard errors clustered by member in parentheses. Includes only members who made requests as identified by Frisch and Kelly (2006). Dependent variable is coded "1" if a member requested Appropriations in the Congress, "0" if not. Ideology is member's first-dimension DW-NOMINATE score. Congress fixed effects are not reported. *$p < .05$.

Constituent Affluence and Federal Spending

A heightened desire for allocations does not guarantee lower-income districts more federal money. Having representatives who focus much of their work on securing largesse does not necessarily secure dollars for jurisdictions with greater numbers of lower-income households, either. In the chapter's last section, I examine whether allocations reflect the distribution of lower-income districts across the country. I am not particularly interested in a causal mechanism, although I do limit the analysis to classes of federal spending that are particularly susceptible to congressional manipulation. I want to see whether patterns of allocations reflect the distribution of lower-income districts across the country.

Some research produces findings inconsistent with my hypothesis. Lazarus (2010) saw no relationship between unemployment in a district and either the number or value of earmarks its representative was able to secure prior to a moratorium on such activity in the early 2010s. Griffin and Flavin (2011) show that per capita income has no material effect on the percentage of federal contract allocations received by the district.

To examine my hypothesis, I use data on federal government spending from Dynes and Huber (2015), specifically the log of the amount spent annually for all federal outlays and what the authors call "high-variance programs." These latter programs are those where amounts fluctuate significantly across districts. As grants and loans, the programs in this category are less formulaic and more likely shaped by frequent congressional action than underlying and durable law.[18] Dynes and Huber (2015) do not claim that such programs are strictly distributive in the way the term is generally used. Indeed, the high-variance grant and loan programs include those for low-income housing assistance, Head Start, and Medicare prescription drugs—what we might call redistributive budget items. Others, however, are dedicated to the kind of spending that citizens, members, and political scientists think of as distributive. Among these are federal transit grants, airport improvements, environmental protection, and scientific research grants. I use the average for the Congress.

The data are from the 98th to the 111th Congresses (1983–2010), and in both specifications of the model I deploy a variety of controls that account for additional member attributes and important features of their districts. These variables are the size of the state's delegation (to account for spending on statewide projects), whether the district houses the state capital (since many federal programs distribute money through state governments), and whether the member shares party with, and therefore disproportionately benefits from the influence of, the president. I use Congress fixed effects and standard errors clustered by district (Dynes and Huber 2015). I also lag the dependent variable one Congress. I report results in table 6.7.

The results show that, regardless of the dependent variable used, districts with lower median household incomes and a greater proportion of lowest-income households obtain more funding. The effects are not trivial, and the indicator of households in the lowest-income group is particularly robust. Using raw dollars, an increase of ten percentage points in the proportion of households in the district that are from the lowest-income group is worth about $87 million in high-variance programs—the district mean for a Congress is $565 million. The median household income variable performs particularly well when we look just at the Congresses at the beginning of the time series—from the mid-1980s through to the early 1990s. In those biennia, a $1,000 decline in median household income is often worth as much as $4 million in high-variance program spending.

This effect of constituent income is beyond the clearly significant effect of ideology. The more liberal a member, the more their district gets in federal funds. It is also worth noting that a member's race and ethnicity seem important. Even controlling for district income and their ideology, white legislators capture more high-variance and overall spending for their districts. This is

TABLE 6.7. Constituent income and federal spending, 1983–2010

	All outlays (log)		High-variance programs (log)	
	Median district income	Proportion lowest income	Median district income	Proportion lowest income
Lagged dependent variable	.725 (.024)*	.719 (.025)*	.657 (.017)*	.651 (.017)*
District income measure	−.003 (.000)*	.660 (.089)*	−.002 (.001)*	1.16 (.233)*
Black	−.024 (.017)	−.043 (.017)*	−.005 (.049)	−.054 (.050)
Female	−.008 (.010)	−.008 (.010)	.033 (.028)	.040 (.028)
Latino	−.051 (.019)*	−.061 (.019)*	−.055 (.047)	−.095 (.048)*
Majority party	.004 (.005)	.003 (.005)	.006 (.014)	.003 (.014)
President's party	−.001 (.005)	.002 (.005)	.012 (.013)	.018 (.013)
Committee chair	−.000 (.008)	.000 (.008)	.042 (.026)	.043 (.026)
Appropriations	.004 (.007)	.001 (.001)	.032 (.024)	.025 (.024)
Seniority	.001 (.001)	.001 (.001)	−.002 (.003)	−.003 (.003)
Ideology	−.047 (.009)*	−.042 (.009)*	−.182 (.027)*	−.173 (.027)*
Electoral margin	.0002 (.0000)*	.000 (.000)	−.000 (.000)	−.000 (.000)
District in state capital	.126 (.014)*	.133 (.014)*	.619 (.046)*	.638 (.047)*
State delegation size	.000 (.000)	.001 (.000)*	.0013 (.0008)*	.002 (.001)*
Constant	16.43 (.165)*	16.34 (.156)*	15.80 (.091)*	15.64 (.088)*
Adjusted R^2	.849	.850	.786	.787

Notes: Method is OLS. $N = 5,521$. Standard errors clustered by district in parentheses. Fixed Congress effects included but not reported. *$p < .05$.

especially the case when they are compared to Latino members, but it also holds, if slightly, when they are compared to Blacks. Together with the appropriations committee data, this finding conceivably constitutes evidence that if congressional members and procedures exhibit biases against certain legislators and the people they represent, these biases appear to disadvantage racial and ethnic minorities but not the poor.

It is interesting that, although legislators with less affluent constituents are more likely to be on Appropriations, sitting on the panel does not seem to result in meaningfully greater government spending for its members' districts. The effect of district income on allocations is beyond any formal institutional advantages that legislators who represent poorer districts might enjoy.

Conclusion

This chapter explores the effect that individual and constituent income has on distributive politics—the process by which government allocates public funds for matters like education, transportation, construction projects, defense programs, and scientific research. Existing work assumes that demand for these resources is constant across the citizenry and political jurisdictions. Researchers posit that any geographic variance in patterns of allocations is therefore principally a function of supply. Senior legislators in formal positions of influence who share party affiliation with the president or chamber majority are especially proficient.

I have demonstrated a connection between citizen and district income and distributive politics, however. Deriving this link from theoretical work on the value of public goods to personal well-being and from cultural trends derived from geographic mobility and place identity, I show that lower-income Americans and districts are more inclined to want their representatives to focus on local matters, including distributive policy. These legislators respond favorably and capture a disproportionate amount of federal allocations.

More specifically, members from lower-income districts often spend much of their time and resources on the allocation of federal expenditures and constituency service. The decision to publicize their work on local matters and keep more of their staff at home demonstrates the concern that representatives from less affluent districts have for the practical needs of the people they serve. These members are also more likely to sit on the important Committee on Appropriations because they receive favorable treatment when legislators are being assigned to the panel. They secure more in the way of federal resources from "high-variance" budget items, or the type associated with grants and contracts, and not just the spending that takes the form of direct payments to individuals via means-test.

Most of the work on distributive policymaking in Congress—and constituency service in the form of activities like casework—overlooks the relationship between constituent affluence and member behavior. Political scientists often assume that poorer citizens are naturally interested in national issues and redistributive policy. Like Griffin and Flavin (2011), I think a preference for distributive politics and constituency service is a potentially important reason why members of Congress representing affluent districts and states appear to have disproportionate influence over matters of national scope with redistributive effects—that is, why major economic policy often seems conservative. Their colleagues with working-class constituents are perhaps more likely to have progressive preferences regarding redistribution, but they work fruitfully on other matters, including distributive policy. They wish to ensure that people in their jurisdiction have access to public goods such as jobs, infrastructure, and education. They seem to want to advance the interests of the families and neighbors they represent as much as they do people across the country with whom their constituents might share merely an abstract class identity.

The Substantive Representation of Affluence

Apportionment and Effectiveness

The findings so far do not preclude the possibility that less affluent Americans receive inferior representation in Washington. Policymakers might make decisions regardless of the views of working-class citizens. If so, the policy preferences of lower-income Americans are immaterial and the extent to which outcomes reflect them just plain luck or the result of their similarity to the preferences of wealthier compatriots. Elected officials are disconnected from this large section of the population and will remain insulated from pressures exerted by those at the lower reaches of the socioeconomic spectrum. Economic policy outcomes will not reflect any movement to the left among the less affluent, should it come. Any democracy we have is, to quote Gilens and Page (2014), purely "coincidental."

This point essentially brings us back to the literature's central argument about the political roots of economic inequality. Wealthier citizens turn out to vote in higher proportions, give more to federal campaigns, display elevated levels of political knowledge, participate more frequently in interest group politics, and contact their representatives more often. Either as individuals or as a discernible group, Americans with higher incomes are therefore able to bring policy outputs more closely in line with their views than their fellow citizens who make less.

By way of response, I develop my argument in this and the following chapter by exploring the relationship between affluence and substantive representation in Congress—or, put differently, the tendency of our federal legislature to make formal decisions that reflect the economic policy preferences of their constituents. In this chapter, I attempt answers to two questions that seem central to any investigation of the link between constituent affluence and congressional decision-making.

The first question concerns the design of Congress. I examine whether congressional design distorts national public opinion in a way that would likely produce economic policy outcomes unfairly biased against poorer citizens. More specifically, I ask: Is the House districted and the Senate apportioned to disadvantage less affluent Americans? As the Founders intended, federalism and separation of powers prevent the government in Washington from reflexively transforming the views of a majority of the population into outputs. The counter-majoritarian institutions of Congress, the focus of this chapter, have a particularly distorting effect. Economic policy could well be very different, and plausibly more aligned with the preferences of less affluent Americans, if made by a differently apportioned legislature.

The other question is the subject of the chapter's second half: Are members of Congress who represent less affluent Americans inferior to or treated unfairly by colleagues? For whatever reasons, poorer districts might elect less capable or influential legislators. I explore the possibility that legislators from states and districts with higher proportions of less affluent constituents are ineffective by analyzing the capacity of members to push measures they introduce personally through the legislative process. I also evaluate the ability of members with significant numbers of lower-income constituents to attain formal positions of authority within Congress. Because the Senate and, especially, the House are large organizations, they have felt compelled to centralize power and provide some members with greater authority than others (Taylor 2012, 35–118). The constituents of legislators who occupy positions in party and committee leadership have reason to expect favorable policy outcomes.

Do Congressional Districting and Senate Malapportionment Disadvantage Less Affluent Americans?

There are 435 full-voting members of the House of Representatives. Each represents a single congressional district, an area carved out within the boundaries of a state containing about 760,000 Americans. There are one hundred senators, each representing a state, and every state, regardless of population, has two senators. Individual federal legislators have constituencies that are considerably smaller than the country as a whole.

American electoral institutions therefore make the precise geographic distribution of groups of voters important to an understanding of their influence over election outcomes and presumably national policy. We tend to think of this dispersal in partisan terms, as the presidential victory of Donald Trump in 2016 attests. Although Hillary Clinton won about 2.9 million more popular votes across the country than Trump did, Republican voters were distributed in such a way as to give Trump thirty states and a majority of electoral votes. This kind of thing happens in congressional elections as well. In the 2012 House contests, for example, Democrats won about 1.4 million votes more than Republicans nationally but only 201 seats overall, thirty-three less than the opposition.

But we can conceptualize citizens as members of important demographic groups as well. For example, since the 1960s Blacks have received considerably greater representation in the House than the Senate. This trend is a function of the Black population's distribution (Lee and Oppenheimer 1999; Malhotra and Raso 2007; Griffin and Newman 2008). In states with many Blacks there have traditionally been several congressional districts where they constitute a meaningfully large proportion of the voters—perhaps a majority or close to it, perhaps a plurality when considering other minority groups. Statewide, however, Blacks have always been a clear minority, even in the Deep South. After the 1990 census, moreover, many states with sizable percentages of minority residents were compelled to set aside a proportionate number of House districts in which minorities—that is Blacks or Latinos—constituted a majority.[1] This redistribution and concentration of the Black population brought about a 40 percent increase in Black House members following the 1992 elections.

Members of a particular group can be apportioned in a certain way for the purposes of maximizing (or minimizing) their influence over national policy outcomes. When we think of such groups in binary terms (generally Democrat and Republican or perhaps white and non-white), the manipulation of political boundaries to advance the interests of one of the groups is clear. Those charged with drawing district maps should ensure that their preferred group's voters constitute a majority in as many jurisdictions as possible. This aim is executed through a strategy of efficient use of votes or "packing" opponents in a small number of districts so that favored candidates either win narrowly or are defeated heavily.

Even if American policymakers configured state lines to advance certain interests—as was arguably the case with the Missouri Compromise of 1820— they did not do so with an eye to the politics of our time. Still, we can examine whether, like congressional districts, the Senate is "gerrymandered" and placement of state boundaries benefit particular groups. The Senate is also grossly malapportioned. The populations of its jurisdictions vary considerably in size. Thus, individual residents of little Nevada ought to have more influence over their senators and therefore national policy outcomes than do people in neighboring and huge California. For the purposes of influencing Senate decision-making, it is beneficial for particular groups of voters to be concentrated in states with small populations (Dahl 1956).[2] Research on distributive policymaking has shown that residents of small states receive more benefits per capita than those who live in large states do (Ansolabehere et al. 2003; Clemens et al. 2015; Hauk and Wacziarg 2007; Larcinese et al. 2013; Lee 2004). Other work reveals that the movement of minorities out of smaller states has resulted in the underrepresentation of Black and Latino interests in the Senate (Griffin 2006a; Malhotra and Raso 2007).

A number of scholars argue that congressional redistricting and malapportionment advantage Republicans and therefore hobble the economic policy interests of less affluent Americans (Hacker et al. 2022a, 36–37; Kelly 2019, 70–72). Republicans, particularly in the 2010 cycle, gerrymander more (Hacker and Pierson 2020; McGann et al. 2016) and benefit from Democratic voters' concentration in cities (Rodden 2019). With regard to the Senate, Republican candidates appear to do better in small states that are home to more than their fair share of rural and small-town Americans (Lee and Oppenheimer 1999). It appears that, at least since the 1980s, Republicans get more of their legislative agenda passed through the upper body than do Democrats on votes when the winning coalition of senators represents less of the American population than does the losing coalition (Evans 2024).

I am uninterested in partisanship and voting but simply explore the distribution of different income groups across House districts and the states. To evaluate the proposition that this distribution hurts poorer Americans, I administer three tests that examine the composition by income of congressional districts and states from the current period of inequality—that is, the 1980s onward. In a first test, I assume that for their interests to be best represented in Congress, the House and Senate should be "gerrymandered" and that—when thought of dichotomously as high-income and low-income—the less affluent group should constitute a majority of the residents in a majority of districts or states. The best way to achieve this end is to divide the population into two groups of equal size, rich and poor or those whose households have incomes above the national median and those whose incomes are below.

Figure 7.1 shows the percentage of House districts and states in which the median household income at the beginning of the decade was below the national number according to the Census. The House data refer to the maps drawn immediately following the 1980, 1990, 2000, 2010, and 2020 censuses. Bars pointing upward denote decades when at least one-half the states or districts had a median household income below the national median; those pointing downward denote decades when this was the case for less than 50 percent of states or districts. The only decade when the majority of jurisdictions do not have median incomes below the national measure is the 1980s, when this is the case for both bodies. The 1980s stand out as a time when

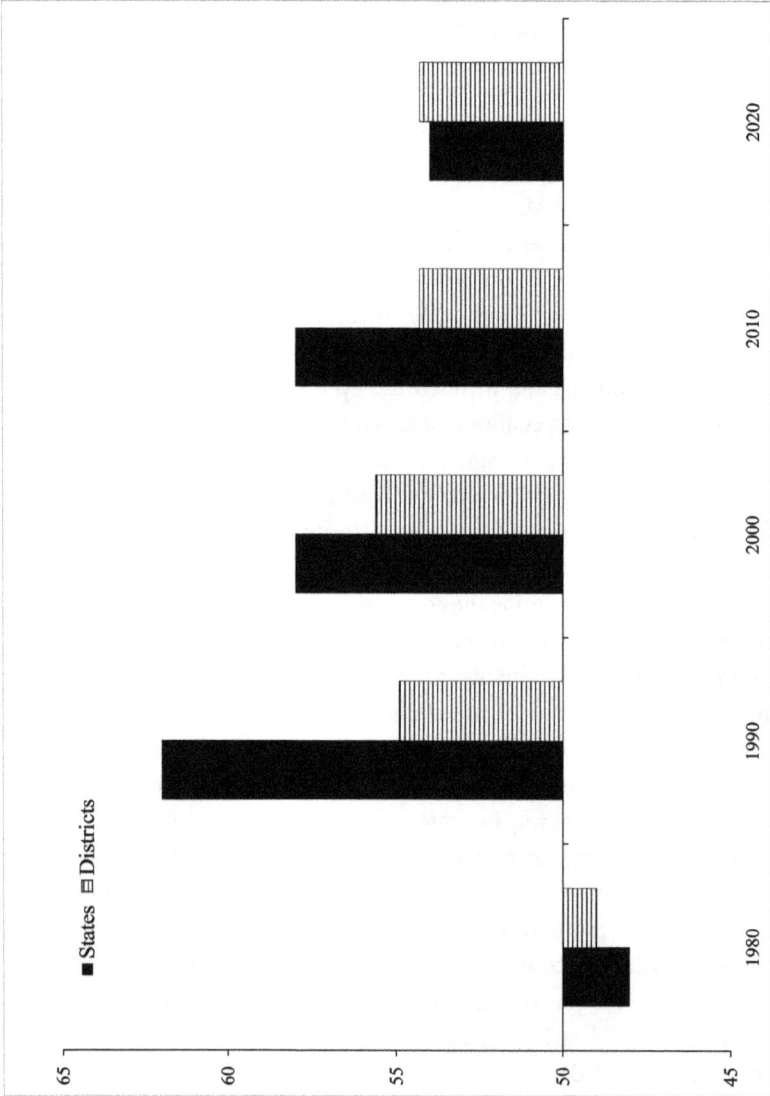

FIGURE 7.1. Percentage of states and districts in which median household income is below the national median, 1980–2010. Income data are from the census.

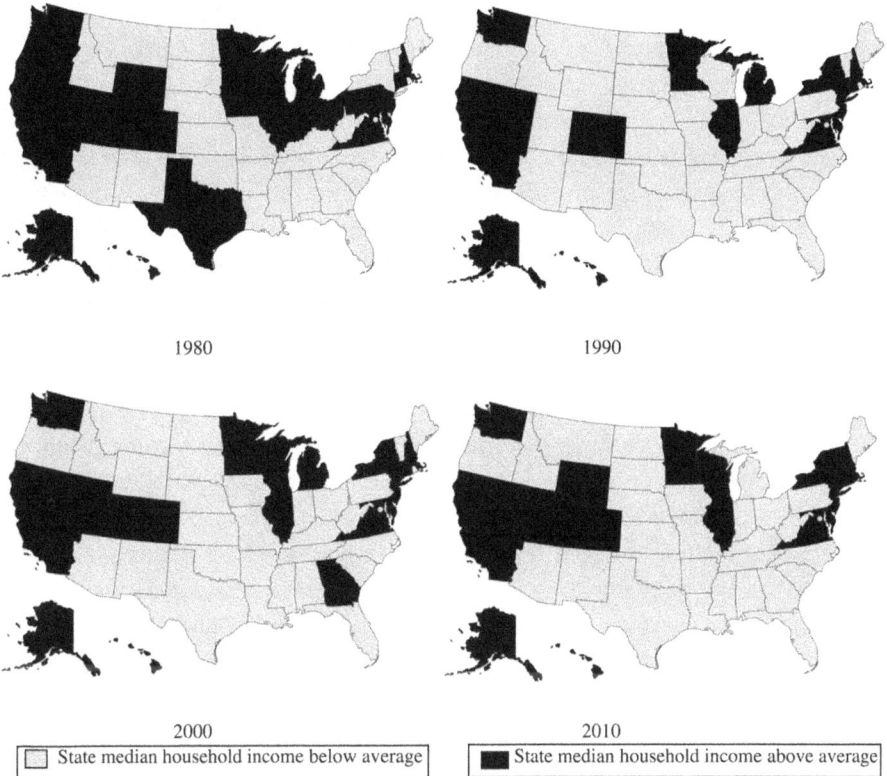

1980   1990

2000   2010

| State median household income below average | ■ State median household income above average |

FIGURE 7.2. State median household incomes relative to the national median household income, 1980–2010
Income data are from the census; states above the median are in black.

the House and Senate do not particularly favor either of these two large and equal-sized income groups. By the 1990s, if a "gerrymander" existed, it clearly favored low-income Americans.

Figure 7.2 reveals the states that were above and those that were below the national household median income at the commencement of the four decades of the 1980s, 1990s, 2000s, and 2010s. The states above the median generally remain in the group throughout the time series, although there is a clear drop below the threshold in the Midwest. The increased low-income "bias" caused by Senate malapportionment is somewhat attributable to smaller states becoming relatively poorer in the 1980s. They tended to be rural and their economies based on natural resources and manufacturing. Indiana, Iowa, Oregon, and Wyoming are examples of states that slipped from above the national median household income to below, although, with the oil bust and significant immigration, so did Texas, a big state.[3]

Significant regional variations in income complicate conclusions we can draw from these findings. In a modification of this first test, therefore, I take only states with three or more House seats and record the proportion of these districts in each decade that are below their state's median household income. Figure 7.3 reveals the results. Again, notice that the redistricting across the decades benefits lower-income Americans. After every census, most households in a clear majority of these districts have incomes below their state's median. As figure 7.4—a map of congressional districts following the 2000 redistricting, separated into national quintiles by median household income—shows, the concentration of the wealthy that seems to be making these patterns is particularly prevalent in well-off coastal states. Whereas less affluent Deep Southern and Midwestern states are quite monochromatic, denoting a tendency to divide congressional districts fairly evenly by income group, poorer Americans predominate within a number of districts in states like California, Maryland, New Jersey, New York, Pennsylvania, Texas, Virginia, and Washington—notice a few black and dark gray blotches there. These states tend to be the most unequal and where certain urban and suburban districts have become domains of the wealthy (Franko and Witko 2018, 51–59). The logic of population density that has undercut the power of cities in American politics for over a century hurts affluent urban and suburban dwellers today (Rodden 2019).

For groups that constitute a small minority of the population, it is less clear what represents an optimal distribution across electoral jurisdictions. These groups cannot form a majority in a majority of states or districts. Is it better for them to be concentrated and constitute a majority or near-majority in a few jurisdictions or to be more uniformly dispersed and have a small but discernible presence in many or most? The literature on group size and representation is conflicted. Some of the work on race and representation in the United States suggests that it is better for the policy interests of Blacks and Latinos that their populations concentrate within jurisdictions (Fine and Avery 2014; Lublin 1997). Research suggests the same of lesbian, gay, and bisexual citizens (Hansen and Treul 2015). Others have argued that a backlash—motivated by the threat posed by population size and the political gains that come from it—makes it more advantageous for minority demographic groups to disperse more evenly across jurisdictions (Avery and Fine 2012; Enos 2016; Griffin and Newman 2008; Haider-Markel 2010; Preuhs 2007). When they do, lawmakers notice them, and they gain capacity to influence or build broad coalitions in favor of their legislative interests (Bailey 2001; Chase 2015; Rogowski 1989). One reason the national security budget has been so healthy over the past half century is that weapons manufacturing

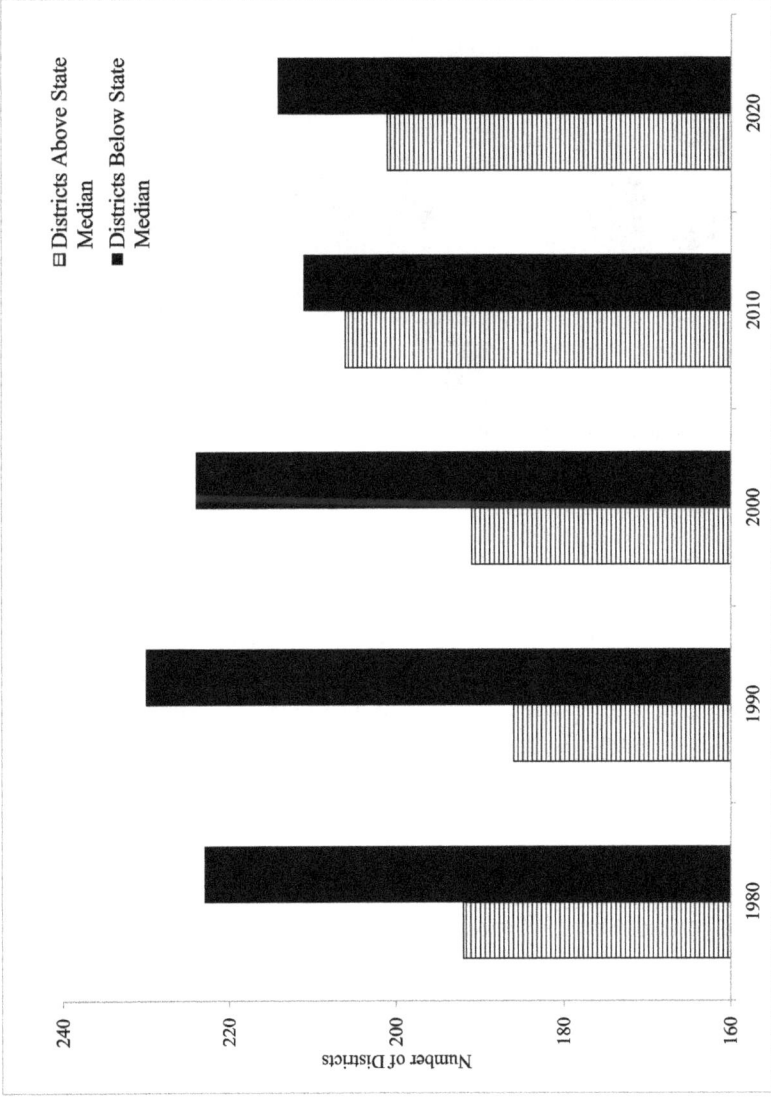

FIGURE 7.3. Number of districts above and below the state median household income from states that have three or more House seats, 1980–2020

Income data are from the census.

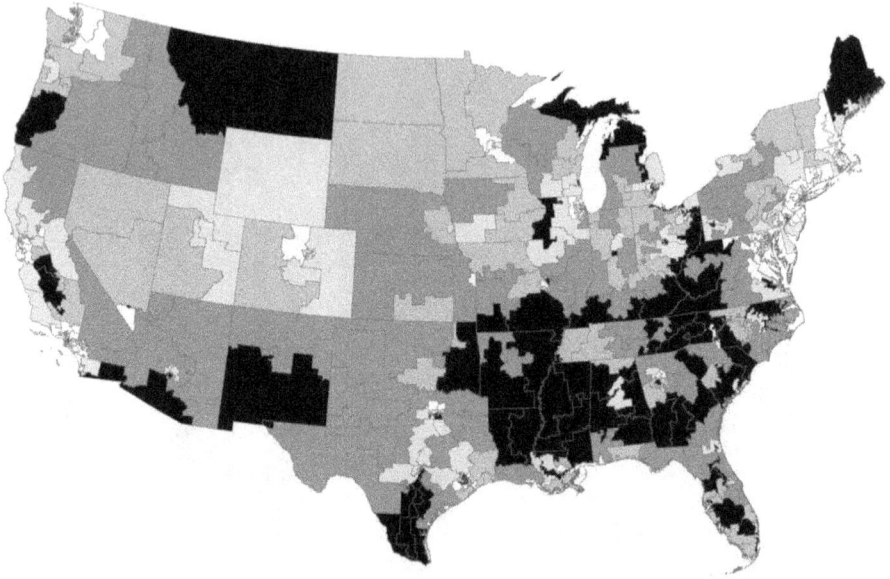

FIGURE 7.4. District median household incomes, 2002
Income data are from the census; districts are divided into quartiles. The darker the shade, the lower the district median household income.

and military bases are located in the districts of so many members of Congress. Although the sector rarely reaches a level of dominance within a district's economy, its broad presence provides it with the ability to build large legislative coalitions in favor of defense spending (Goren 2003; Thorpe 2014).

Because there is no definitive answer to this question of population dispersion, in the second test I take two pairs of groups by income and compare the distribution across states and districts of the low-income categories with their high-income equivalents. Are the patterns of the compared groups similar or different? Do the patterns suggest that low-income groups are disadvantaged—or possibly advantaged—by their distribution across districts?

The groups within a pair must be small enough that their patterns of distribution will not be interdependent. I therefore use the two low- and two high-income groups I introduced in chapter 6. I deploy the coefficient of variation (standard deviation as a proportion of the mean) to compare the distribution of the income groups in each decade from 1980 to 2010. The higher the coefficient, the greater the variance in the data. Figure 7.5 reveals the results with both the lowest- and highest-income groups and the larger low- and high-income groups. The two income cohorts disperse differently. The higher coefficient of variation for wealthier groups shows that they tend to be more unevenly distributed than their less affluent equivalents. This

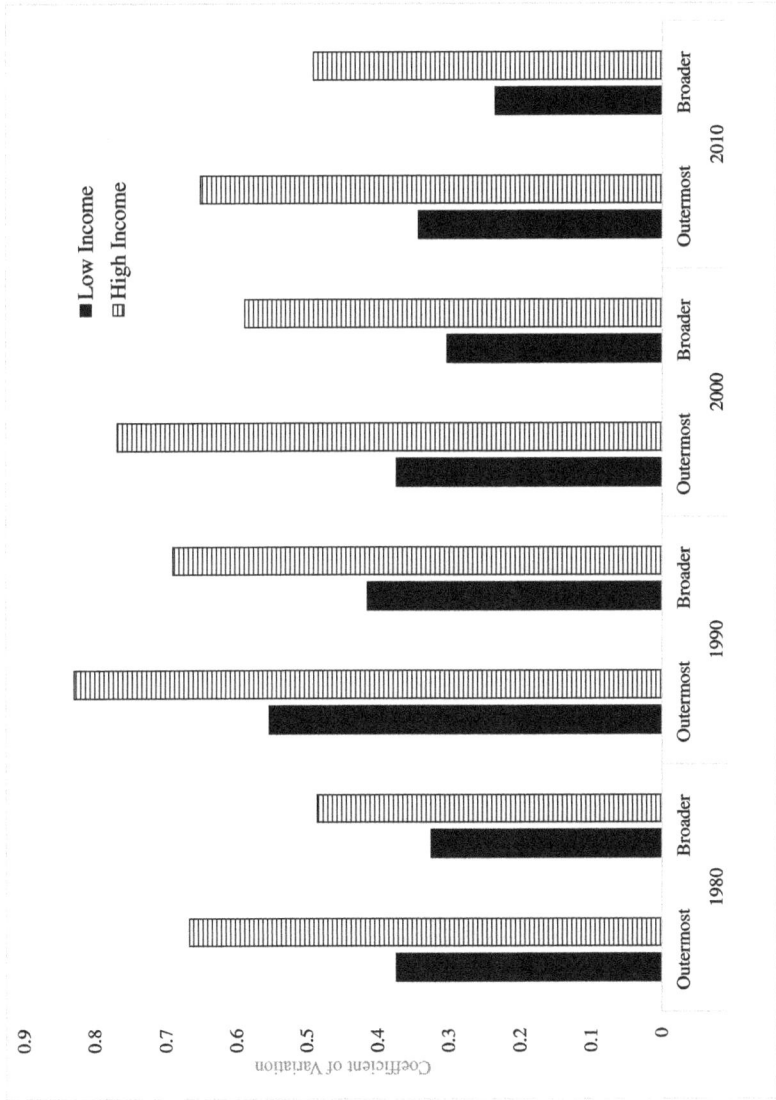

FIGURE 7.5. Distribution of low- and high-income households across congressional districts, 1980–2010 Income data are from the census. "Outermost" denotes smallest groups, "broader" the more expansive definition. Coefficient of variation is the standard deviation divided by the mean, with higher scores suggesting greater variance.

pattern is a feature of modern congressional districts, touched upon above in the discussion of median household income.

What are the takeaway points from this analysis? When we think of lower- and higher-income Americans as small groups at the extremes, the wealthier find themselves more concentrated in congressional districts. It is they who are "packed," to use redistricting vernacular. Less affluent voters spread more evenly or possibly "crack." Although the broad literature on group size and political influence appears agnostic on to whose benefit this distribution is exactly, some literature on affluence and policy outcomes suggests that lower-income Americans are better off evenly dispersed. In his treatment of inequality and its effects on members of Congress, for example, Ellis (2017) argues that the more visible poorer Americans are to more members of Congress, the greater the impact they will have on representatives' behavior.[4] This trend is to some extent a function of population density and is therefore largely an urban phenomenon, but as Ellis (2017, 78) notes, "regularly interacting with people of different economic groups . . . serves to humanize people of different income groups, and promote a shared sense of fate and circumstance." Personal observations or exposure to the expressed preferences of their constituents can sensitize members of Congress to the interests of low-income citizens. The more members who are exposed to these groups, the greater the impact such groups have on policy outputs.

Other political science is consistent with this interpretation. Dimick, Rueda, and Stegmueller (2018) show that "other-regarding" behavior intensifies among the wealthy under growing inequality, resulting in their greater support of redistributive policy in the most unequal American states. Xu and Garand (2010) demonstrate that people who live in states with higher income inequality are cognizant of it as a national problem. Franko and Witko (2018, 58–72, 75–95) argue that economic diversity within political jurisdictions is beneficial for the representation of the interests of those with low incomes.

I administer a final test in this section to examine whether the Senate's malapportionment hurts low-income Americans. I take the state-level version of the income data used in the House analysis above and calculate the mean percentages of both pairs of the lower- and higher-income groups for the smallest twenty-five states by population and the largest twenty-five states by population. I then subtract the amount for the largest states from that for the smallest states. Bars above the horizontal axis line denote results that are positive numbers; bars below the line denote negative numbers. Given that all states enjoy equal representation in the Senate, it is more efficient for higher- and lower-income American households to constitute a larger proportion of

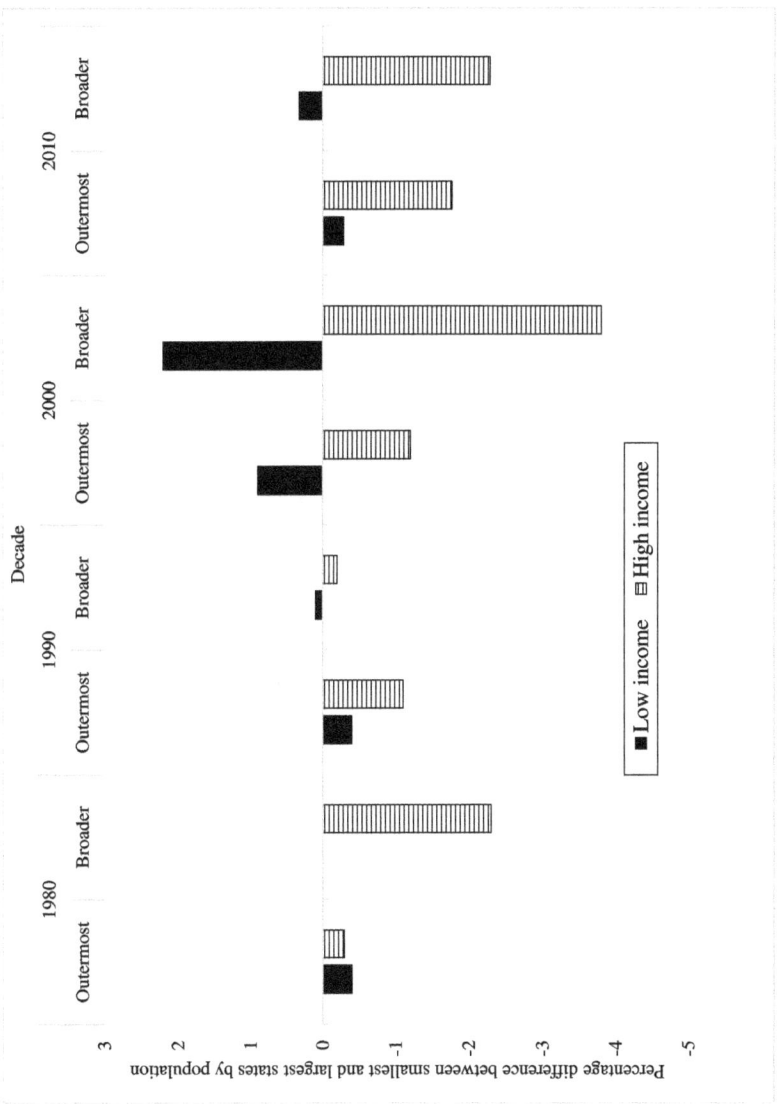

FIGURE 7.6. Difference between smallest and largest 25 states by population in mean percentage of households in high- and low-income groups, 1980–2010

Income data are from the census. "Outermost" denotes smallest groups, "broader" the more expansive definition.

all households in the least populous states than in the most populous states. The groups, therefore, should want bars above the line.

Figure 7.6 reveals the greater inequality of large states given the number of bars below the zero line. With regard to less affluent citizens specifically, it presents a mixed picture. In three of the decades, large states have a greater proportion of the outermost groups or very poorest households (2000 being the exception), but when we expand the definition to include the broader group of lower-income households, the least populous states have a larger proportion of the poor for all decades except 1980, when the figures for both types of states are identical (and the difference is zero). Matters are clearer at the other end of the income scale. The big states consistently display significantly greater proportions of wealthy households than the small states do. In other words, compared to their less affluent compatriots, the nation's higher-income households disperse more inefficiently across the states for the purposes of influencing Senate policymaking.

This result is interesting in light of the prevailing wisdom in political science. I noted earlier that research finds that the Senate's equal treatment of states benefits whites at the expense of Blacks and Latinos (Griffin 2006a; Malhotra and Raso 2007). When Johnson and Miller (2023) weight senators' votes on selected important legislation from 1961 to 2019 by their states' populations, they discover that Democrats would have enjoyed many more policy victories. This was especially the case on social issues—although notably not economic matters. I suggest that if Senate malapportionment—and therefore to some degree the Electoral College and presidential-election process—benefits certain socioeconomic groups, it is those at the lower end.

This situation is unlikely to change soon. Poorer Americans tend not to move as far, and although the better off have been leaving some large states like Illinois and New York, many of their popular destinations are growing rapidly—places like Arizona, Georgia, Florida, North Carolina, and Texas. Incidentally, the result is the same when we use states' median household income. In every decade, the mean was lower in the twenty-five least populous states than in the twenty-five most populous states. The difference in constant 2010 dollars was $1,741 in 1980, $2,201 in 1990, $3,610 in 2000, and $1,185 in 2010. By 2021, the gap in nominal amounts was $3,531.

Are Less Affluent Americans Represented by Ineffective Members of Congress?

Much of the literature on the advancement of less affluent Americans' interests in Congress focuses on dyadic representation—the relationships between single legislators and their own constituents. In that vein, I now look at whether members of Congress representing low-income districts and states are, for whatever reasons, less capable and occupy formal positions of lesser influence than their colleagues with better-off constituents. I evaluate the proposition that low-income Americans' dyadic substantive representation is inferior because the members of Congress who represent them are inferior.

I first examine legislative effectiveness—the name given by congressional scholars to the capacity of legislators to turn policy preferences into outcomes.[5] It is possible that the members of Congress who represent lower-income districts and states get fewer of their policy proposals through the legislative process and are therefore relatively ineffective. They might just not be very skilled or, alternatively, they might be subject to the biases of leaders and colleagues. Either way, their constituents receive substandard representation that can help explain why policy does not reflect the economic interests of less affluent Americans.

Volden and Wiseman (2014, 17–28) have constructed an extensive and useful dataset of individual members' legislative-effectiveness scores, calculated from the bills each has introduced in every Congress since 1973. The bills are placed into three categories based upon their importance—"commemorative," "substantive," and "substantive and significant"—and five categories depending on the length of their journey within the legislative process—each was subject to "introduction," but many progressed further and received "action in committee," "action beyond committee," "passed the House/Senate," or even "became law." Volden and Wiseman (2014) give greater weight to the more important bills and later stages of the process. It is these scores I utilize to help us understand the effectiveness of poorer Americans' congressional representation.[6]

Table 7.1 presents a model of the Volden and Wiseman House legislative-effectiveness scores for House members from 1973–2014. With the exception of variables that measure the income of districts' residents, I replicate the model they present in chapter 2 of their book (Volden and Wiseman 2014, 38–51, 59).[7] I use measures of district income I have deployed before: the median household income (divided by one thousand), the proportion of constituents who fall in my highest-income category, and the proportion who fall in my lowest-income category. As noted, the second and third variables are available only after the 1980 census. Per Volden and Wiseman, I place all the variables into two specifications, one including and the other omitting a measure of legislative effectiveness that is lagged one Congress. I cluster standard errors in the regression model by member and incorporate, but do not report, fixed effects by Congress.

TABLE 7.1. Constituent income and legislative effectiveness of House members, 1973–2014

Median household income	.006 (.003)*	.005 (.002)*				
Highest income			2.01 (.621)*	1.66 (.479)*		
Lowest income					-1.53 (.610)*	-1.40 (.467)*
Lagged effectiveness		.437 (.032)*		.391 (.036)*		.393 (.036)*
Seniority	.063 (.008)*	.011 (.006)*	.065 (.009)*	.020 (.007)*	.067 (.009)*	.021 (.007)*
State legislative experience	-.089 (.073)	-.050 (.053)	-.014 (.073)	-.018 (.056)	-.020 (.074)	-.023 (.056)
State legislative experience × legislative professionalism	.465 (.235)*	.316 (.164)*	.326 (.233)	.269 (.167)	.325 (.234)	.269 (.168)
Majority party	.453 (.050)*	.316 (.044)*	.545 (.063)*	.412 (.052)*	.541 (.063)*	.409 (.052)*
Majority-party leadership	.494 (.171)*	.326 (.114)*	.378 (.152)*	.360 (.123)*	.374 (.151)*	.355 (.122)*
Minority-party leadership	-.144 (.055)*	-.038 (.050)	-.128 (.058)*	-.061 (.049)	-.134 (.059)*	-.067 (.050)
Speaker	-.806 (.282)*	-.558 (.144)	-.782 (.248)*	-.667 (.147)*	-.756 (.256)*	-.646 (.160)*
Committee chair	3.12 (.241)*	2.20 (.182)*	2.99 (.245)*	2.30 (.199)*	2.99 (.246)*	2.30 (.199)*
Subcommittee chair	.764 (.074)*	.542 (.055)*	.667 (.081)*	.489 (.063)*	.664 (.081)*	.488 (.062)*
Power committee	-.206 (.053)*	-.106 (.035)*	-.264 (.057)*	-.161 (.038)*	-.257 (.057)*	-.153 (.037)*
Distance from median	-.023 (.122)	-.162 (.097)*	-.035 (.142)	-.145 (.110)	-.038 (.142)	-.146 (.109)
Female	.059 (.052)	.046 (.035)	.020 (.046)	.040 (.037)	.038 (.047)	.056 (.038)
Black	-.295 (.084)*	-.184 (.066)*	-.202 (.080)*	-.131 (.065)*	-.147 (.086)*	-.078 (.070)
Latino	.072 (.118)	.032 (.076)	.097 (.119)	.052 (.078)	.106 (.125)	.071 (.083)
Size of delegation	-.003 (.002)	-.002 (.002)	-.004 (.002)*	-.003 (.002)*	-.004 (.002)*	-.003 (.002)
Vote share	.016 (.010)	.030 (.011)*	.015 (.011)	.030 (.011)*	.014 (.011)	.030 (.011)*
Vote share²	-.000 (.000)	-.0002 (.000)*	-.000 (.000)	-.0002 (.000)*	-.000 (.000)	-.0002 (.000)*
Constant	-.462 (.364)	-.974 (.385)*	-.480 (.386)	-1.05 (.408)*	-.200 (.393)	-.826 (.408)*
Adjusted R²	.424	.536	.420	.521	.419	.521
N	8,965	7,220	6,850	5,840	6,850	5,840

Notes: OLS estimation with robust standard errors clustered by member in parentheses. Congress fixed effects are not reported. *$p < .05$.

The findings are robust and compatible with the conventional wisdom about income and representation. Districts with higher median household incomes and more high-income residents have the most effective legislators. Less effective lawmakers, on the other hand, represent districts with large numbers of residents in the lowest income category. The results hold if I use the more relaxed definitions of high- and low-income households. Moreover, the substantive effect of income is hardly trivial. The impact of increasing a district's population in the highest-income category by twenty-five percentage points or decreasing the lowest-income category by thirty-five percentage points—that is, adjusting them from roughly their lowest to highest values or vice versa—is about the same as the impact of replacing a member from the minority party with one from the majority party.

What explains this finding? One answer might be that colleagues in some way discriminate against representatives of the less affluent. They may, for example, deprive them of appointments to powerful positions that would provide greater opportunities to turn policy preferences into outputs. Indeed, Miler (2018, 163–80) shows that legislation promoting the interests of the poor is most likely to pass if advocates occupy formal positions of institutional authority. In the modern House, such positions include the Speaker, floor leader, committee chair, and seats on important committees. The Speaker and floor leaders enjoy critical procedural powers that permit them to set the floor agenda and manipulate floor proceedings (Cox and McCubbins 1993; 2005; Rohde 1991; Sinclair 2012). They effectively control the assignment of members to standing committees and can raise considerable sums for their colleagues' campaigns (Cann 2008; Heberlig and Larson 2012). Committee chairs and their minority-party counterparts, the ranking members of the minority, have great power, at least within their panels' jurisdictions (Deering and Smith 1997; Maltzman 1997). It is rare for panels to report bills without the chair's consent (Cox and McCubbins 2005, 149–70). Rank-and-file members who do not occupy these formal positions of authority desire membership on what are often called the "power" committees—generally viewed as those with jurisdictions covering the most important matters facing members and that Volden and Wiseman (2014) list as Appropriations, Rules, and Ways and Means. We discussed the importance of Appropriations in the previous chapter. Members of Rules have significant influence over the floor agenda (Cox and McCubbins 2005; Monroe and Robinson 2008).

I explore the proposition that members from low-income districts are systematically excluded from positions of influence in the House using Volden and Wiseman's (2014) data and report the results in table 7.2. There are three sections to the table. The left-hand section reveals the results for logit model

TABLE 7.2. Constituent income and institutional positions of House members, 1973–2014

	Leader of either party			Committee chair			Member of power committee		
Median household income	.008 (.012)			-.001 (.012)			-.006 (.008)		
Highest income		1.50 (2.61)			-.569 (2.84)			.477 (1.96)	
Lowest income			-4.14 (2.66)			-.186 (2.59)			2.38 (1.70)
Majority				6.57 (.947)*	6.34 (.938)*	6.32 (.939)*			
Seniority	.095 (.021)*	.071 (.022)*	.074 (.022)*	.343 (.021)*	.323 (.023)*	.323 (.023)*	.105 (.014)*	.108 (.017)*	.107 (.017)*
State legislative experience	-.694 (.436)	-5.42 (.458)	-.598 (.465)	-.248 (.388)	-.206 (.383)	-.209 (.385)	-.228 (.247)	-.187 (.263)	-.172 (.261)
State legislative experience × legislative professionalism	1.59 (1.11)	1.11 (1.19)	1.24 (1.21)	.668 (1.06)	.742 (1.01)	.757 (1.02)	1.23 (.708)*	1.18 (.741)	1.15 (.731)
Distance from median	1.14 (.294)*	.992 (.291)*	.960 (.286)*	.694 (.615)	.717 (.644)	.704 (.646)	-.552 (.217)*	-.680 (.211)*	-.649 (.211)*
Female	.741 (.316)*	.655 (.341)*	.666 (.330)*	-.502 (.376)	-.611 (.389)	-.621 (.382)	.006 (.209)	.033 (.222)	.053 (.219)
Black	-.009 (.519)	-.028 (.547)	.200 (.552)	.991 (.374)*	.820 (.402)*	.840 (.430)*	-.293 (.318)	-.271 (.309)	-.449 (.325)
Latino	.346 (.598)	.336 (.608)	.506 (.606)	.755 (.505)	.681 (.478)	.708 (.490)	-.293 (.376)	-.111 (.379)	-.274 (.384)
Size of delegation	-.012 (.009)	-.011 (.010)	-.013 (.010)	.004 (.008)	.010 (.009)	.010 (.008)	-.004 (.006)	-.005 (.006)	-.003 (.006)
Vote share	.141 (.069)*	.216 (.081)*	.216 (.081)*	.056 (.059)	.100 (.064)	.101 (.065)	.121 (.027)*	.126 (.031)*	.128 (.031)*
Vote share^2	-.001 (.000)*	-.001 (.001)*	-.001 (.001)*	-.000 (.000)	-.001 (.000)	-.001 (.000)	-.001 (.000)*	-.001 (.000)*	-.001 (.000)*
Constant	-9.93 (2.64)*	-12.56 (3.04)*	-12.01 (3.07)*	-14.33 (2.42)*	-15.34 (2.73)*	-15.36 (2.76)*	-6.44 (1.01)*	-6.59 (1.17)*	-6.94 (1.17)*
Pseudo R^2	.065	.059	.062	.412	.400	.400	.058	.061	.062
N	8,965	6,850	6,850	8,965	6,850	6,850	8,965	6,850	6,850

Notes: Logit estimation with robust standard errors clustered by member in parentheses. Congress fixed effects are not reported. *$p < .05$.

specifications where the dependent variable denotes whether a member was a leader of either party (conference/caucus chair and up), the middle section whether they were a chair of a full standing committee, and the section on the right whether they sat on one of the three power committees. I use control variables from Volden and Wiseman (2014) that I deem important to a model of attainment to these positions and again deploy measures of district income.

The results show that members with more low-income households are not, at least for the time period I study, underrepresented in any of these most important and influential formal positions in the House. It is the most senior and entrenched members who secure these prizes, with ideological extremists rising to positions in the leadership and moderates disproportionately selected for the power committees. Institutional advantages do not appear to explain the greater effectiveness of legislators from high-income districts. So what does? Do the poor just get poor representation?

Table 7.3, I believe, provides us with an answer in the negative. It examines two categories of bills used by Volden and Wiseman (2014)—all bills and those they call "substantive and significant"—and models their passage through each of the five stages of the legislative process the authors identify as important. In the top section, the dependent variable is the number of each member's bills in a Congress in the category. In the bottom section, the dependent variable is the proportion of a member's bills that passed each of the four stages beyond introduction. The count and regression models reveal an interesting story. It is clearly the case that members from districts with high-income constituents introduce many more bills than do colleagues who represent the less well-off. A five-percentage-point increase in the proportion of residents from the highest-income group, for example, brings an increase of about 1.5 substantive and significant bills introduced by a member when the mean is approximately 0.8. Indeed, the greater legislative effectiveness of members from districts with higher-income constituents is essentially attributable to their propensity to introduce more bills, particularly on the most important issues. Any advantage that members with wealthier constituents have in effectiveness has largely dissipated by the time bills go to the floor of the House and pass into law.

As revealed in the top section, it is true that when we perceive of bills in raw numerical terms, members with high-income districts advance appreciably more legislation of substantive and significant kind through the later stages of the legislative process and lawmakers with low-income constituents markedly less. However, if we use a measure that is the proportion of bills introduced—something we might consider a kind of "batting

TABLE 7.3. Constituent income and success of House members' bills, 1973–2014

| | Number of category bills introduced by a member | | | | |
	Introduced	Action in committee	Action beyond committee	Passed House	Became law
Median household income					
All bills	.015 (.002)*	.002 (.004)	.003 (.004)	.002 (.003)	−.000 (.004)
Sub & sig	.013 (.005)*	.011 (.005)*	.010 (.005)*	.008 (.005)	.009 (.007)
Highest income					
All bills	3.00 (.530)*	1.59 (.770)*	1.44 (.803)*	1.09 (.778)	.657 (.994)
Sub & sig	3.42 (.806)*	3.07 (.930)*	2.84 (.894)*	2.82 (.936)*	3.18 (1.31)*
Lowest income					
All bills	−2.41 (.484)*	−1.66 (.647)*	−.922 (.658)	−.675 (.649)	.274 (.719)
Sub & sig	−2.39 (1.14)*	−2.24 (1.27)*	−2.00 (1.19)*	−1.72 (1.27)	−1.46 (1.41)
	Percentage of category bills introduced by a member				
	Introduced	Action in committee	Action beyond committee	Passed House	Became law
Median household income					
All bills		−.082 (.023)*	−.083 (.020)*	−.054 (.015)*	−.012 (.000)*
Sub & sig		.035 (.042)	.010 (.038)	.001 (.027)	.008 (.042)
Highest income					
All bills		−17.44 (5.16)*	−17.50 (4.41)*	−12.86 (3.34)*	−21.85 (5.78)*
Sub & sig		14.25 (9.69)	12.55 (8.89)	5.95 (6.83)	7.25 (9.83)
Lowest income					
All bills		16.66 (6.18)*	17.77 (5.67)*	13.73 (4.01)*	18.14 (6.97)*
Sub & sig		−13.69 (10.95)	−6.61 (9.96)	1.59 (6.57)	−9.16 (11.38)

Notes: N = 8,695 when median household income is used; 6,850 in other cases. Cell entries in the first part of the table are coefficients from negative binomial regression analyses using the control variables in the model specifications reported in table 7.1, but here the dependent variables are the number of a member's congressional bills that traversed the various hurdles in the legislative process, and the lagged measure of legislative effectiveness has been omitted. Cell entries in the second part of the table are coefficients from OLS regression analyses using the same independent variables, but here the dependent variables are the percentage of all bills in the category introduced by the member that traversed the various hurdles in the legislative process. "Sub & Sig" denotes substantive and significant legislation. *$p < .05$.

average"—members from less affluent districts seem more effective. At least when it comes to the broader definition of bills—that includes, of course, largely symbolic commemorative legislation—members with low-income constituents get a larger proportion through all stages of the legislative process, including into law. This result is not, of course, an argument these members influence policy outputs disproportionately. It is a function of a smaller numerator and their reluctance to introduce bills. But it does suggest that members with wealthier constituents appear more effective than they really are.

In chapter 6, I revealed that less affluent Americans appear to direct their representatives to distributive policymaking and the allocation of federal resources to their constituents. These are activities best pursued through committee work, the appropriations process, and the lobbying of executive agencies (Evans 2004; Fiorina 1977; Mayhew 1974). The findings here flesh out a logical corollary: Members with wealthier constituents focus more on lawmaking and substantive policy matters. Yet these members exert disproportionate influence only at the beginning of the legislative process. At this stage, individual lawmakers can control outcomes. Unlike the floor agenda, what we might call the "bill agenda" is unrestricted, and any member can introduce any bill on any topic at any time the House is in session. It is true that members cannot have bills become law if they do not introduce them. But, perhaps to signal to their attentive constituents that they care about certain issues, legislators from affluent districts introduce, much more often than do their colleagues with low-income constituents, bills that do absolutely nothing to alter public policy.

Volden and Wiseman (2018) have recently collected and analyzed legislative-effectiveness scores for the Senate. Figure 7.7 shows simple scatterplots and lines of fit for the state median income and legislative-effectiveness scores of senators in each Congress from the 97th (1981–1983) to the 114th (2015–2017). On balance, there is a bias toward states with higher incomes, but it is slight. The correlations are only significant at the $p < .05$ level in four Congresses—the 99th (1985–1987), 107th (2001–2003), 110th (2007–2009), and 111th (2009–2011).[8] These are the only instances when more effective senators represented more affluent states.

It may be that legislative effectiveness is not a particularly good indicator of influence in the Senate. Individual senators exercise power by ways other than advancing bills through the legislative process. With the filibuster, hold, and prevalence of unanimous consent, obstruction is an effective strategy in the upper chamber (Koger 2010). With fewer formal rules, the Senate also seems shaped more by convention and norms like apprenticeship than the House. Its members enjoy more committee assignments, and floor leaders and panel chairs exercise far less authority than in the House (Den Hartog and Monroe 2011). In 2006, the magazine *Time* ranked the ten best senators of the contemporaneous Congress (Bacon and Calabresi 2006). Of "those who make a difference," four were not even in the top half of their parties' membership, according to Volden and Wiseman's scores.

Sen. Robert Byrd (D-WV) provides an example of how these effectiveness scores may not capture the true influence of senators as well as they do that of

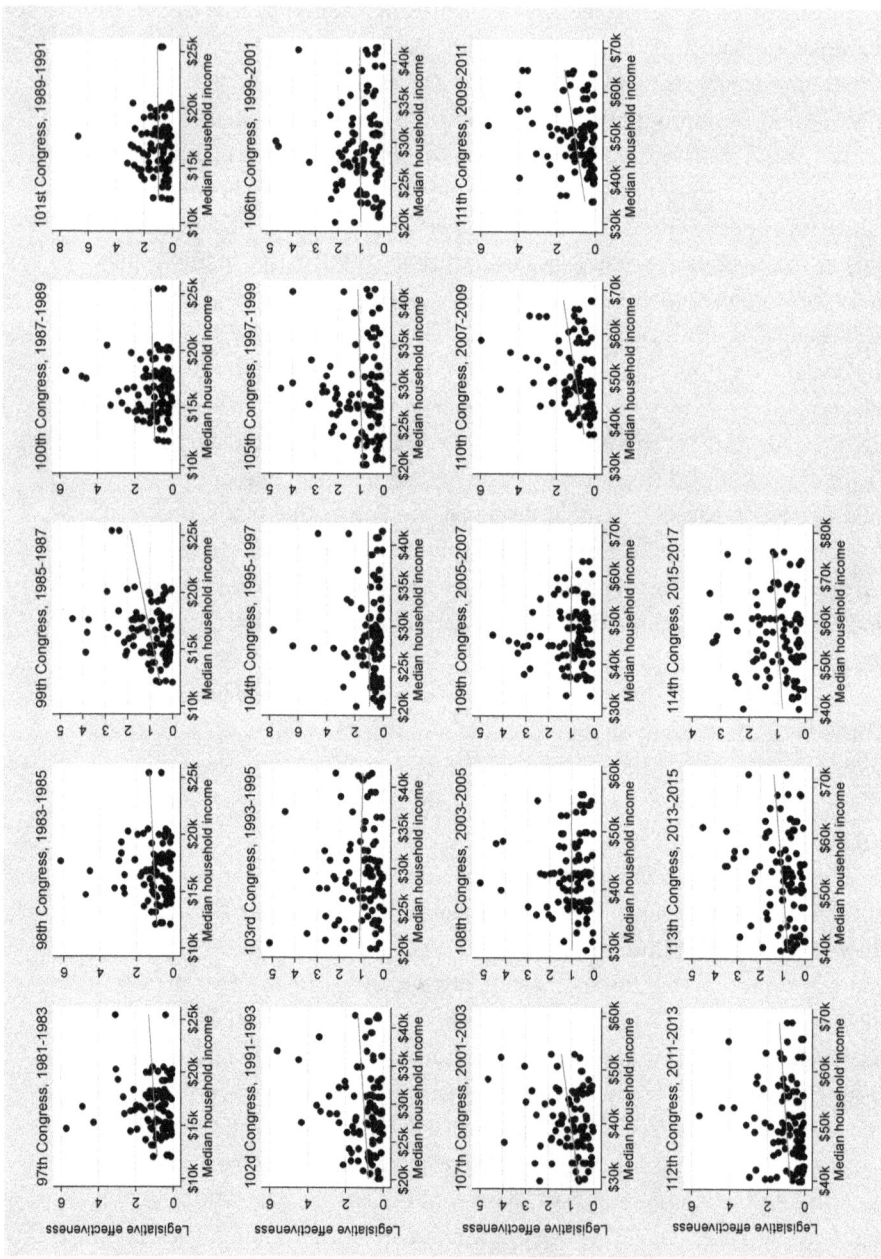

FIGURE 7.7. Legislative effectiveness and household median income in the Senate, 1981–2017. Data points represent individual senators. The lines denote the line of fit for state median income and legislative effectiveness scores. Data are from Volden and Wiseman (2014).

House members. Byrd was the longest-serving senator in American history and, despite representing one of the country's poorest states, widely regarded as powerful. He spent many years as Democratic leader and whip, often in the majority, and as chair of the Committee on Appropriations. His legislative-effectiveness scores, even at the height of his career in the 1970s and 1980s, were routinely among the very lowest in the body.

Volden and Wiseman (2018) show that, as was the case in the House, majority-party status is a critical determinant of legislative effectiveness in the Senate. The rich state–poor state pair of Sen. Ted Kennedy (D-MA) and Sen. Jesse Helms (R-NC) illustrate this nicely. In the last Congress before the "Republican Revolution" of 1994, Kennedy was the Senate's second most effective member; Helms ranked in the seventies. In the Congress immediately following the election that brought about a new Republican majority, the two just about switched places.

Presence in leadership positions surely constitutes evidence of influence in the Senate, and both parties have had, in recent decades, formal floor leaders from poorer states—in addition to Byrd, Tom Daschle (South Dakota), Trent Lott (Mississippi), and Mitch McConnell (Kentucky) come readily to mind. Less affluent states are also home to many important committee chairs who have presided over economic policymaking during the past half century—for example, Max Baucus's (Montana) long reign at Finance and the significant hold Deep Southern and Appalachian-state senators have had on the top position at Appropriations since 1968.

Conclusion

The case presented in this chapter adds to my general argument that formative work and conventional thinking exaggerate the magnitude of wealthier Americans' influence over Congress. Both parties complain frequently that the House is gerrymandered in favor of their opponents. Democrats—despite their control of the upper body but not the House in 2011–2014 and 2023–2024—insist that the Senate is malapportioned in favor of the Republicans, mainly because small states tend to be rural. But during the current period of inequality, the design of congressional jurisdictions has not facilitated any meaningful representational bias by affluence. If there are perceptible differences in the geographic distribution of Americans by income, it is that less affluent citizens are dispersed across House districts and more concentrated in smaller states than their wealthier compatriots. If anything, these patterns are suggestive of representational advantages for the interests of less well-off Americans.

There is also no evidence to suggest that less competent House members and senators represent poorer Americans. Median household income and the size of low- and high-income cohorts do contribute to lawmakers' legislative effectiveness in the House, but not because legislators from less affluent districts and states are incapable or shut out of important formal positions of influence; rather, these legislators introduce fewer bills. As discussed in chapter 6, members from lower-income districts are more likely to focus on distributive policy than their colleagues are—work often done outside traditional lawmaking. Members with higher-income constituents get more bills through the various stages of the legislative process, but when we account for the number of measures they sponsor, House members with more lower-income constituents often perform better.

The Substantive Representation of Affluence

A Dyadic Analysis

Less affluent Americans are not directly victims of malapportionment or gerrymandered House districts. The legislators who represent them are not disadvantaged or incapable. But these points do not mean that these citizens will influence policy as much as their wealthier compatriots will. We return to the issue that poorer citizens' representatives might simply ignore them. I have argued that the claim that federal postwar economic policy has been out of step with public opinion and made with purposeful disregard for the views of the working class is exaggerated. In this chapter, I take a dyadic approach to the evaluation of policymakers' responsiveness to the economic interests of Americans from different financial circumstances.

I am not the first to take such an approach. The existing work is thorough, sophisticated, and imaginative. In recent years, researchers have gathered data from hundreds of survey questions asked of the American public to determine estimates of the opinion of constituents and households at different income levels for individual congressional districts and states (Bartels 2016; Gilens 2012; Lax et al. 2019; Rhodes and Schaffner 2017; Tausanovitch 2016). Some of the work looks at how House members respond to their constituents' policy preferences (Bartels 2016; Ellis 2012, 2013, 2017; Miler 2018, 91–130; Rhodes and Schaffner 2017; Tausanovitch 2016). Some of it analyzes the Senate (Bartels 2016; Hayes 2013; Lax et al. 2019; Tausanovitch 2016). The work uses roll-call data to determine lawmakers' behavior relative to the preferences of different groups of constituents. Overwhelmingly, this literature on dyadic representation asserts that legislators in both the House and Senate are appreciably more responsive to their affluent constituents (Bartels 2016, 235–49; Ellis 2017, 99–104; Griffin and Newman 2013; Hayes 2013; Miler 2018, 91–130; Rhodes and Schaffner 2017; Tausanovitch 2016).[1]

Are Members of Congress Less Responsive
to their Less Affluent Constituents?

I take a different tack from this impressive body of work, although one informed by several important implications it makes. First, I do not directly observe constituents' application of influence on their representatives but measure constituent preferences and legislator behavior and make inferences about the relationship between the two. In doing so, the approach assumes constituents exert pressure directly. Legislators might be sensitive to public opinion conditioned or amplified by intermediaries like parties, interest groups, and the media, but they also respond to the demands citizens make themselves through various mediums at their disposal—campaign contributions, emails, phone calls, social media, personal conversations, responses to surveys, etc.

Second, because affluent constituents make demands more frequently, robustly, and competently I am open to the claim that lawmakers are more responsive to their wishes than to those of their low-income equivalents. Americans with higher incomes are more likely to vote, so any promise to hold members accountable for their response to policy requests is more credible than threats made by constituents of lesser means. Wealthier individuals are also more likely than lower-income citizens to form organized groups among themselves, and given what we know about the importance of collective action in American politics, such formal coordination enhances their opinions significantly (Baumgartner and Leech 1998; Miler 2018, 91–130; Olson 1965; Schlozman, Verba, and Brady 2012, 265–443).[2]

Third, the quantity of demands and therefore magnitude of the influence of a particular income cohort will be commensurate with its size relative to other groups. As Jaeger (2019) argues in a study of state legislators, a subconstituency's sway may fluctuate across issues, but it is generally a function of its size. Less affluent constituents exert influence that increases as the group does, even if on a per capita or household basis it may not be as great as that of a higher-income group. It is also likely that legislators have information about the size and potential influence of an income group. Here individual citizens have not expressed their opinions or lobbied, but lawmakers respond using information about group size—gleaned from their personal observations and general knowledge of their constituents—in anticipation of pressure and electoral adjudication of their performance in office. Ellis (2017, 78) has such an effect in mind when he describes methods by which poorer constituents influence members' behavior.

Fourth, and finally, legislators make presumptions about groups' opinions and interests that may or may not be consistent with any expression of policy preferences. In the case of socioeconomic status, these presumptions are that affluent constituents generally desire conservative economic policy, whereas less well-off constituents want liberal or progressive economic policy.

As I note, most of the literature that examines the responsiveness of members of Congress to the views of different income cohorts within their constituency utilizes expressed policy preferences. Here I infer the ideological positions of constituents from their income, with Americans in low-income households assumed to be liberal, those in high-income households conservative. I then build the analysis around the relative size of various income cohorts in congressional districts and states.

HOUSE MEMBERS' RESPONSIVENESS
AND THE SIZE OF DIFFERENT INCOME GROUPS

I introduced the concept of sub-constituency in chapter 5 and explained how legislators discern various groups and that characteristics like income or class are used to categorize constituents this way. There, I argued that legislators were likely responsive to groups that took clear positions on issues rather than to those that abstained or were divided. Here I argue that sub-constituency size is an important determinant of influence over a member of Congress. The approach is simple, novel—at least in this context—and does not suffer from potential measurement errors that naturally afflict an effort to discern from a national sample the collective views of a sub-group of a congressional district's residents.

My approach roughly replicates Bartels's (2016, 239–42) analysis of the capacity of various income groups to influence the behavior of House members, replacing measures of policy preferences with indicators of size. To measure the size of income groups, I deploy the different measures of high- and low-income households in a district used previously. Like Bartels, I measure member behavior, the dependent variable, using first-dimension DW-NOMINATE scores—a scaling procedure that deploys roll-call votes to place members in each Congress on a similar, single, ideological liberal-to-conservative dimension with poles of -1 and $+1$ (Lewis et al. 2024). The dimension captures a great deal of congressional voting and "almost always picks up the fundamental economic issues that separate the two major political parties of the time" (Poole and Rosenthal 1997, 27). I control for general-constituency views that presumably constrain elected representatives and vary across districts even with similar demographic profiles. I do so using scores created by Tausanovitch and Warshaw (2013; Tausanovitch 2016), who estimate the public's policy preferences by applying item response methods to a series of questions on a number of large-scale surveys of Americans done between 2000 and 2014. The measure is broad, but questions on economic matters make up a significant part. Multilevel regression and post-stratification of the responses by individual participants generate district-level ideology scores (Tausanovitch and Warshaw 2013, 333–35). In imitation of DW-NOMINATE scores, these also have effective poles of −1 (most liberal) and +1 (most conservative). They are available for six Congresses (108th–114th, or 2003–2016) and therefore permit me to extend this analysis beyond the period examined by Bartels.[3] Scores remain the same for a district throughout a decade—that is, between redistricting cycles—so that a constituency has identical scores for the 108th–112th Congresses but a different one for the 113th and 114th Congresses.[4]

Table 8.1 reports the results of the entire dataset for all four measures of higher- and lower-income households. In most specifications, I include additional controls for party and for geography (a measure indicating whether the district is in the South).[5] Unsurprisingly, the indicators of constituency opinion and party pull most of the weight. Critically for our analysis, the proportion of lower-income households has an appreciable effect on members' ideology in the liberal direction, whether or not I control for the proportion of higher-income households in the district. To be sure, the percentage of households that are from the highest-income cohort performs well, with members becoming more conservative as it grows. But over the course of all the specifications, it would be fair to say that increases in the different measures of low-income constituents explain about as much of the movement of members in a liberal direction as growth in high-income households does for their rightward shift. Given the similar profiles of the low- and high-income variables, the raw coefficients suggest that the substantive effects are similar. What is more, in the analysis of the pair of broader groups, the higher-income variable does not have a statistically significant coefficient in the specifications where we control for the size of the lower-income group.

Figure 8.1 reveals the effects when party is interacted with the lowest- and highest-income variables (the smaller outermost groups). The results are from specifications that include the measures of the other income cohort and the South as a control. Republicans become markedly more conservative as the proportion of highest-income households increases, Democrats more liberal as the proportion of lowest-income households goes up. But Republicans with more lowest-income households in their districts are also more conservative and Democrats with more highest-income households more liberal than co-partisans. Districts with relatively high proportions of rich or poor households appear to contribute to the House's partisan polarization. If we accept the conventional wisdom about the income groups' ideological views,

TABLE 8.1. Constituent income and House member ideology, 2003–2016

	Outermost	Broader	Outermost	Broader	Outermost	Broader	Outermost	Broader
Higher-income group	.958 (.280)*	.312 (.218)	.459 (.094)*	.230 (.047)*			.280 (.127)*	.051 (.095)
Lower-income group	−.764 (.315)*	−.536 (.252)*			−.466 (.095)*	−.282 (.050)*	−.259 (.126)*	−.231 (.103)*
Constituency opinion	1.40 (.038)*	1.13 (.037)*	.375 (.019)*	.369 (.019)*	.336 (.020)*	.347 (.019)*	.360 (.021)*	.353 (.021)*
Democrat			−.675 (.011)*	−.675 (.011)*	−.674 (.012)*	−.673 (.011)*	−.672 (.011)*	−.672 (.011)*
South			.036 (.010)*	.039 (.010)*	.048 (.010)*	.048 (.010)*	.043 (.010)*	.046 (.010)*
Constant	.143 (.061)*	.181 (.100)*	.335 (.011)*	.324 (.012)*	.427 (.016)*	.433 (.015)*	.380 (.025)*	.412 (.041)*
Adjusted R^2	.604	.602	.923	.923	.923	.924	.923	.923

Notes: $N = 3,085$. OLS estimation with robust standard errors clustered by member in parentheses. Dependent variable is first-dimension DW-NOMINATE score. "Outermost" refers to very highest- and lowest-income cohorts; "broader" to my more relaxed definition of the cohorts. Congress fixed effects calculated but not reported. *$p < .05$.

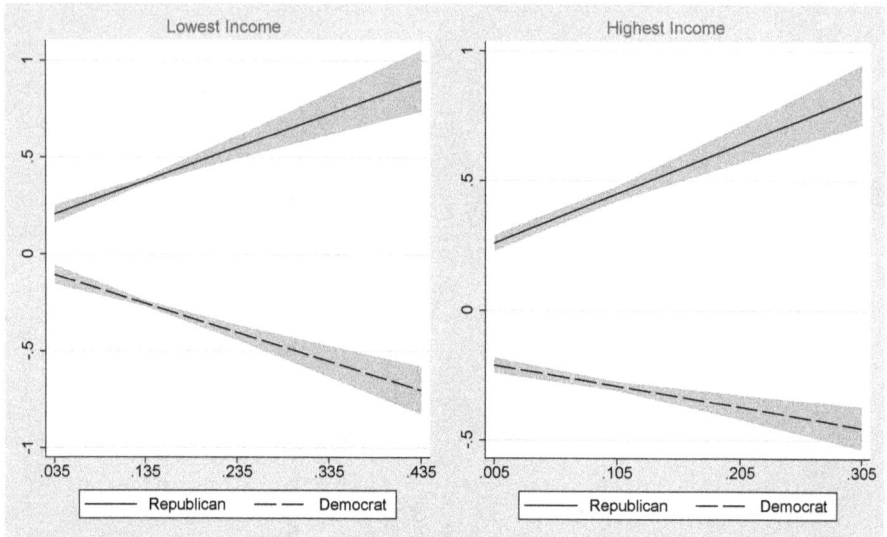

FIGURE 8.1. Effects of highest- and lowest-income groups on House member ideology when conditioned by party, 2003–2016
Shaded areas denote 95 percent confidence intervals. Income data are from the census.

a comparison of the slopes' angles indicates that Republicans do a greater disservice to lowest-income households as their presence in a district grows than Democrats do to highest-income households as they become more numerous.[6]

Figure 8.2 adds information about region to my analysis. Here I separate districts into thirds (tertiles) for each Congress by the size of the highest-income group (left-hand panel) and lowest-income group (right-hand panel). The darker the shade, the wealthier the district (the higher the proportion of highest-income households or the lower the proportion of lowest-income households). Members from Southern states are denoted by letters in lower case, those not from Southern states upper case. I plot constituent ideology on the vertical axis and member DW-NOMINATE scores on the horizontal axis. Both parties have members from all types of districts on both sides of the line of fit—that is, those who are more liberal (above the line) and more conservative (below the line) than we should expect given constituent ideology. But the Democrats, as a result of the greater ideological range of their districts, are particularly interesting. There are a number of jurisdictions where representatives are reasonably far to the left of their constituents—that is, well above the line. Many of these districts are Southern and poor and often where Black members serve sizable numbers of Black constituents. Rural examples from recent Congresses include districts represented by Sanford Bishop (D-GA), Jim Clyburn (D-SC), Artur Davis (D-AL), Terri Sewell (D-AL), and Bennie Thompson (D-MS). More urban—and often a little wealthier—districts include those of Alcee Hastings (D-FL), Al Green (D-TX), Sheila Jackson-Lee (D-TX), Eddie Bernice Johnson (D-TX), John Lewis (D-GA), Cedric Richmond (D-LA), Bobby Scott (D-VA), and Frederica Wilson (D-FL).[7]

There are also a number of districts where Democratic members are below the line and therefore to the right of their constituents. Many have large numbers of highest-income households but appear to have a reasonable percentage of lowest-income households as well. The districts are found mainly outside the South in urban and suburban areas in states like California, Connecticut, Illinois, Massachusetts, Maryland, New Jersey, and New York. In recent Congresses, their representatives have included reliable progressives such as Elijah Cummings (D-MD), Danny Davis (D-IL), Christopher Murphy (D-CT), Jerrold Nadler (D-NY), Bill Pascrell (D-NJ), Nancy Pelosi

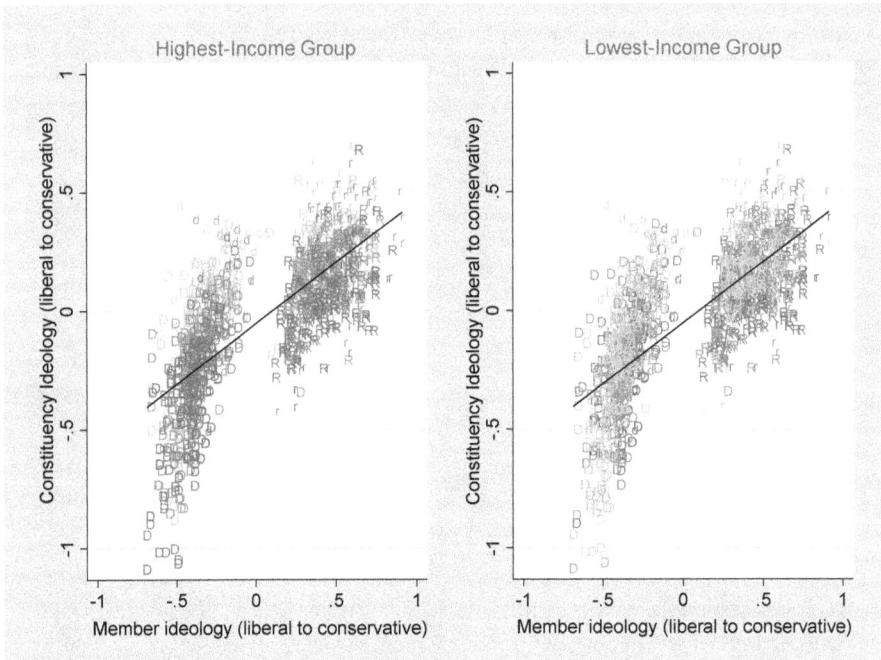

FIGURE 8.2. Affluence, party, and region of districts plotted by constituent and House member ideology, 2003–2016

Constituent ideology is plotted on the Y-axis, member ideology on the X-axis. Districts (observations) are split into tertiles. The darker the district, the wealthier it is (most highest-income households or fewest lowest-income households). Upper case denotes Democrats and Republicans from outside the South, lower case those from the South. Income data are from the census.

(D-CA), Ro Khanna (D-CA), and John Tierney (D-MA). From this list, it seems that at least some of any possible overall conservative bias in the House comes from the moderation of very liberal districts by liberal members.[8]

These findings do not contradict the literature on the dyadic congressional representation of the less affluent. The work I cite at the beginning of the chapter approximates the expressed economic-policy preferences of individual constituents and measures their effect on representatives' behavior. Instead, I make assumptions about citizens' economic-policy attitudes based on their household income. We should note, however, that in previous chapters, I revealed many low-income Americans to have what we might consider moderate or conservative preferences. If these citizens' preferences for economic policy are more conservative than generally thought, my findings suggest that lawmakers may be moving too far to the left in an effort to accommodate them. Regardless, members move in a liberal direction as the proportion of less affluent households in a district increases.

Of course, what the findings in this section most dramatically reveal is that any effect of the size of particular income groups in a district is, in a relative sense, small. This appears particularly the case for Democrats who, as figure 8.2 demonstrates, are clustered tightly along the horizontal planes measuring member ideology but have observations spread up and down the vertical dimensions that denote constituency ideology. The results reported in table 8.1 reveal that a standard-deviation increase in the proportion of constituents from the lowest-income group (roughly .053 or 5 percent; the mean is .142) results in about a .014 point move for Republicans in the liberal direction on the DW-NOMINATE scale, when we control for the size of the highest-income group. The effect of a commensurate one-standard-deviation increase in the highest-income group is practically identical, except in the conservative direction (the standard deviation is .056, the mean .074). With the House parties of today polarized, an interpretation of these findings reveals that an increase in the percentage of highest-income or lowest-income households in a district from zero to 100 (there is, of course, nothing approaching a real-life example) generates an effect on a member's ideology that would still only get them less than halfway from one party's median to the other. The impact of parties on member responsiveness is significantly greater than the size of income groups within their constituencies (Grossmann et al. 2021; Lax et al. 2019).

INEQUALITY

I referred obliquely to inequality above in the discussion of non-Southern urban districts represented by Democrats. I turn now more directly to the topic. What about the district-level effects on individual-member responsiveness to representing relatively large numbers of both wealthy and poor constituents? In a recent study of dyadic representation, Ladewig (2021) shows that the more unequal a district, the more liberal its representative. Given the different shades denoting non-Southern Democrats in the bottom left-hand corners of the panels in figure 8.2, my analysis would appear, at first glance, consistent with this finding. Among those representing a district in the twenty most unequal districts of the 111th Congress (2009–2010), for example, were Elijah Cummings (D-MD), Charlie Rangel (D-NY), Adam Schiff (D-CA), Niki Tsongas (D-MA), and Henry Waxman (D-CA).

Ladewig's is a minority view, however. In their examination of aggregate, as opposed to district-level, representation, several other scholars have provided evidence revealing inequality to be a determinant of the congressional parties' ideological divergence (Duca and Saving 2016; Garand 2010; Iversen and Soskice 2015; Kelly 2019; McCarty et al. 2006). They tend to argue that polarization is asymmetric and that Republicans have, when compared to Democrats, moved away from the center further and at a more rapid pace as the nation's inequality has grown (Bonica et al. 2015; Grossmann and Hopkins 2016; Hacker and Pierson 2005; Mann and Ornstein 2016; Pierson and Schickler 2020; Skocpol and Hertel-Fernandez 2016; Theriault 2008).[9] The precise causal mechanism differs but it is reasonable to suggest from the literature that what happens approximates either a replacement or an influence model. In the first, voters become supportive of Republicans as inequality grows. Kelly (2019) argues racial attitudes condition the effect and whites with negative attitudes of minorities—particularly those of lower socioeconomic status forced into more intense competition for public resources—increasingly vote Republican as inequality intensifies. In the influence model, wealthy Americans prevail on their representatives, particularly but not necessarily exclusively Republicans, to move to the right of the median voter. Low-income and therefore politically ineffective citizens are incapable of countering. Either way, inequality brings about an increase in conservative economic policies that, it is argued, produce even greater inequality.[10]

Figure 8.3 reports the results of the basic model I used in the analysis reported in table 8.1 when I include, in place of income, two indicators of inequality. The first is the Gini coefficient, a statistical measure of dispersion often used to examine income or other kinds of economic inequality. A value of one indicates complete inequality and that one household receives all of the district's income, a zero that each household makes an equal amount of money. The Bureau of the Census's American Community Survey (ACS) has made Gini coefficients available for household income in every congressional

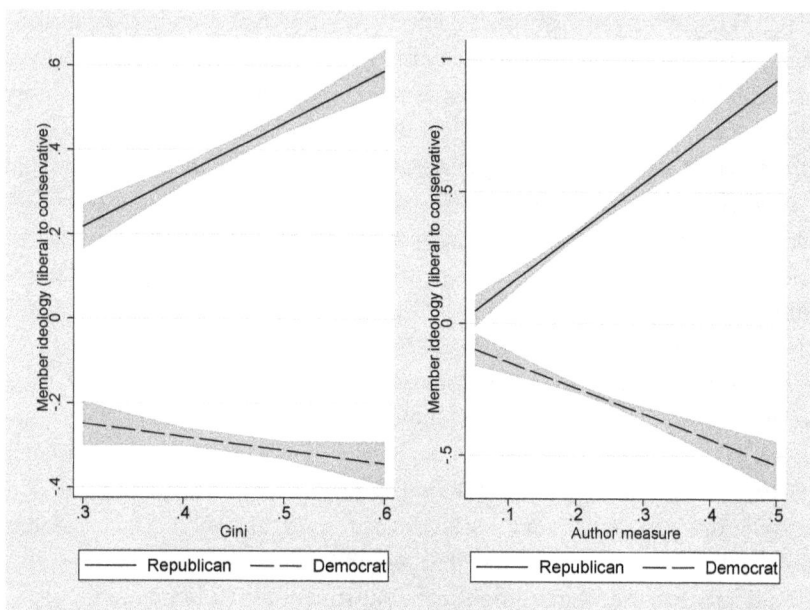

FIGURE 8.3. Effects of district inequality on House member ideology when conditioned by party, 2003–2016
Shaded areas denote 95 percent confidence interval. Income data are from the census.

district since 2009. Not least to extend the analysis backward, I construct a measure of inequality based on my highest and lowest-income group indicators (results are unchanged if I use the broader higher and lower- income groups). I add the proportion of a district's households in each group and divide the sum by the proportion in the smallest group subtracted from one.[11] Larger numbers denote greater inequality, and scores potentially range from 0 to 2.[12]

More precisely, Figure 8.3 presents effects of interactions of the measures of inequality with party when I control for constituency ideology and region. Given my findings above regarding the independent effects of the proportion of high and low-income households, it is unsurprising the impact of district-level inequality on member behavior polarizes the parties. Republicans clearly move more to the right than Democrats do to the left as the district Gini coefficient increases. Polarization also intensifies as my measure of inequality rises, but it is considerably more symmetrical. Together the findings suggest any aggregated ideological bias attributable to district-level inequality is conservative, although I think it is reasonable to argue it is not as striking as the literature implies.

Why do the two indicators of inequality produce different results? The Gini coefficient—and indeed the alternative indicators used by Ladewig (2021)—take into account the incomes of all households, my measure merely the proportion of district households that are poorest and richest. The Gini can therefore make districts with modest median incomes and sizable middle classes seem quite unequal.[13] Districts like Arkansas's Second that historically contains Little Rock, Mississippi's Third that envelopes Jackson's suburbs, central Illinois's rural Thirteenth that includes the university towns of Bloomington and Springfield, and eastern Kansas's Second containing Topeka, Lawrence, and miles of wheat fields have few residents who are rich in a national sense but high Gini coefficients. Here the poor are indeed poor—although the cost of living is low—but wealthy people are professionals or own small businesses or farmland. Places like these—and many throughout the South and Midwest— are conservative but not what Americans generally think of as unequal.[14] It is, instead, the cities of the coasts with their sparkling financial areas as well as duplexes, public housing complexes, and tent villages in parks and under overpasses. These urban and coastal districts score high on my author measure of inequality, especially relative to their Gini coefficient.[15]

We can see the measures' varied effects in a regional analysis. We might expect inequality to be particularly impactful on Southern members. The region makes up a growing and significant proportion of the House Republican conference (Bullock 2014; McKee 2010) and Southern Republicans are especially conservative (Black and Black 2002). The South's population is less affluent and, although potentially quite liberal, lacks resources to self-activate. Union membership is low (Bucci 2018; Francia 2012) and minorities tend to have less political influence than elsewhere in the country (Hutchings et al. 2004). Indeed, the congressional literature often casts Southern Republicans as the "villains" of the polarization narrative, legislators insensitive to the interests of their often numerous poor and Black and Latino constituents and unusually beholden to the wealthy in their community (Bartels 2016; Ellis 2017; McCarty et al. 2006; Rhodes and Schaffner 2017). Greater inequality in the South should therefore result in the election of members, generally Republicans, willing to generate voting records that are to the right of constituent opinion and move economic policy in a conservative direction. Across non-Southern districts, if growing inequality contributes to polarization it is likely to be more symmetrical—especially as Democrats are pressured by a large cadre of lower-income supporters who are often organized and capable of checking the influence of wealthy constituents.

Figure 8.4 tests the proposition regional variance is a hallmark of the country's inequality-driven asymmetric polarization. Here, replicating the analysis in Figure 8.3, I separate cases further, into four groups by party and region. The results provide two important takeaways. First, they cast doubt

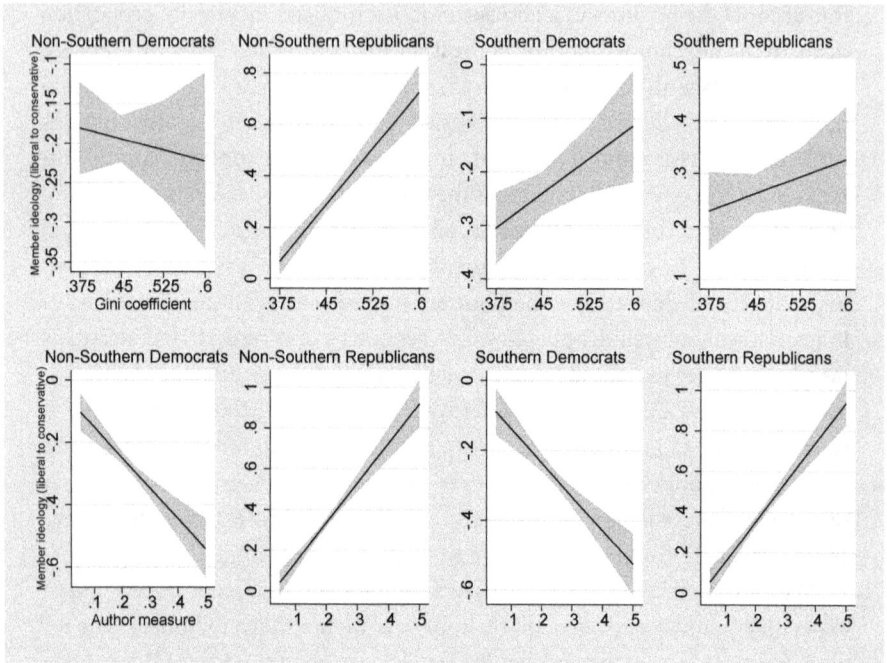

FIGURE 8.4. Effects by region of district inequality on House member ideology when conditioned by party, 2003–2016
Inequality is measured on the X-axis, member DW-NOMINATE score on the Y-axis. Shaded areas denote 95 percent confidence intervals. Income data are from the census.

on the hypothesis. Republicans from outside the South appear as sensitive to inequality—by moving to the right at the same pace—as their Southern co-partisans. Like Jones, Theriault, and Whyman (2019, 205–7), I suggest Southerners are less of a driving force for congressional Republicans' supposed conservative lurch away from public opinion than generally thought. Second, whereas the Gini coefficient shows inequality results in general rightward drift, the author measure produces findings consistent with a narrative in which inequality results in significant but more symmetrical national partisan polarization. Regardless of where they reside, Democrats move to the left as inequality grows and Republicans to the right, although perhaps to a slightly greater degree.

ADDITIONAL ANALYSES OF HOUSE MEMBERS

To this point, I have made standard inferences about the economic policy interests of citizens from different income cohorts. Higher-income Americans want conservative policy, their lower-income compatriots want liberal policy. But what of expressed preferences? As I demonstrate in chapter 4 and chapter 5, at the individual level lower-income Americans do not take unambiguously progressive positions on economic policy. Does this finding extend to the level of congressional districts? The constituency opinion data used above permit an assessment of poorer districts' ideological profiles. We should expect those with significant proportions of low-income households to have distinguishable progressive views if their representatives are to receive clear direction to move economic policy in a leftward direction. Figure 8.5 shows districts distributed by region and income cohort—the data points are only those districts in the top tertiles for both the highest-income group and lowest-income group. The two dimensions capture important distinctions within congressional districts. Along the x-axis is constituency opinion or ideology used above and along the y-axis I have plotted a new measure to my analysis, Tausanovitch and Warshaw's (2013) heterogeneity scores for the measure.[16]

Two important observations present themselves. First, districts with a large proportion of lowest-income households (denoted by filled markers)

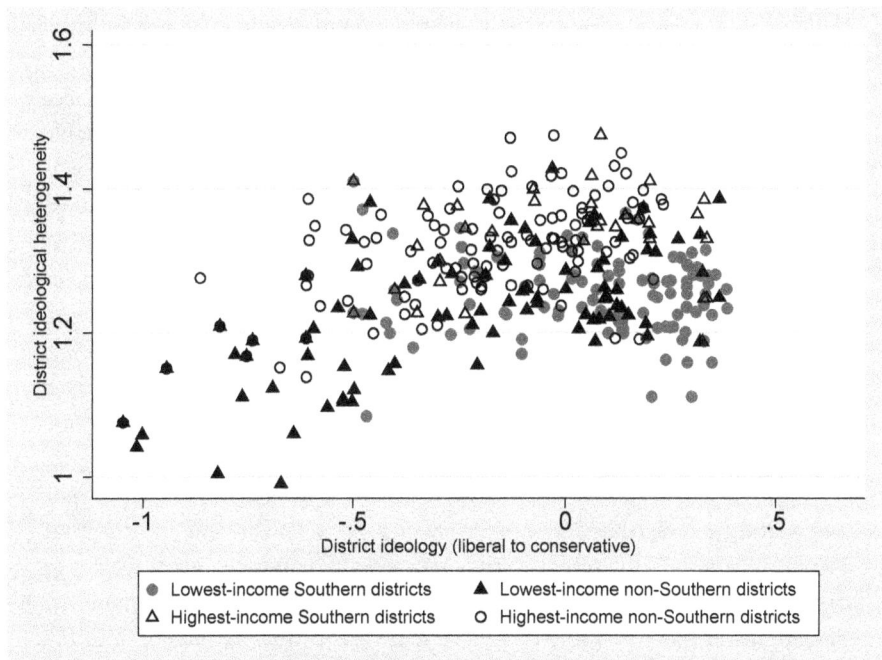

FIGURE 8.5. Ideology and ideological heterogeneity of richest and poorest congressional districts categorized by region, 2003–2016
Income data are from the census.

tend to be lower down on the vertical axis. They are actually more homogeneous in their views—the correlation between the proportion of lowest-
income households and the ideological heterogeneity of a district is −.559
($p < .01$). Second, districts with large proportions of the lowest-income households tend to be extreme in their political opinions; they stretch further and
more evenly along the horizontal axis. Low-income Southern districts con-
gregate toward the conservative end of the spectrum.

Both observations demonstrate low-income congressional districts are
an ideologically diverse bunch, but individually they can be relatively cohesive and presumably capable of providing lucid signals about their collective
policy preferences. Many are progressive and elect very liberal Democratic
representation, particularly in the urban Northeast and Midwest and where
minorities make up a significant proportion of constituents—in recent years
members like Jose Serrano (D-NY) from the Bronx and Carolyn Kirkpatrick
(D-MI) from Detroit, although there are some of them from the South, Bennie Thompson (D-MS) from rural western Mississippi being a good example.
Many districts with a similar socioeconomic profile, however, are solidly conservative and elect Republicans. Rodney Alexander (R-LA), Harold Rogers
(R-KY), and Morgan Griffith (R-VA), for instance, have at one time or another
in the past two decades represented districts in northeastern Louisiana, rural
Appalachian Kentucky, and southwestern Virginia, respectively.

What happens if we make no assumptions as to the ideological preferences
of rich and poor citizens' economic policy preferences? This is a reasonable
approach, especially given my earlier findings. If the distance a legislator is
from constituency opinion conveys an income cohort's capacity to pull legislators toward its views, we might interpret a material difference in the performance of the high and low-income group measures in the analysis below as
indicative of legislator bias toward wealthier citizens. Given their advantages
in political resources, knowledge, and attentiveness, we should expect affluent constituents to be particularly capable of pulling lawmakers toward their
views, regardless of content. Table 8.2, however, suggests the two income
groups are equally proficient at shaping the behavior of members. It reports
the result of a model in which the dependent variable is the absolute distance
between the standardized (z-score) versions of the constituent and member
ideology scores for the 108th–114th Congresses. I deploy the usual measures
of income-group size and two controls in addition to party and region, the
percentage of the vote received by the member in the last election and the
number of terms they have served.[17]

The two income groups have a similar effect on members' responsiveness
to their constituents' opinions. Given the greater range and higher mean of the

TABLE 8.2. Constituent income and absolute distance between constituent and House member ideology, 2003–2016

	Outermost	Broader	Outermost	Broader
Higher-income group	1.48 (.446)*	1.22 (.335)*	1.08 (.472)*	.892 (.351)*
Lower-income group	2.08 (.467)*	1.71 (.376)*	1.78 (.490)*	1.40 (.388)*
Democrat			.153 (.032)*	.158 (.032)*
South			.017 (.033)	.017 (.033)
Vote percentage			−.005 (.001)*	−.005 (.001)*
Seniority			.009 (.004)*	.009 (.004)*
Constant	.180 (.089)*	−.075 (.149)	.459 (.111)*	.262 (.164)
Adjusted R^2	.038	.037	.087	.087

Notes: $N = 3,083$. OLS estimation with robust standard errors clustered by member in parentheses. Congress fixed effects calculated but not reported. "Outermost" refers to very highest- and lowest-income cohorts, "broader" to my more relaxed definition of the cohorts. $*p < .05$.

data for the lower-income groups, I think it is fair to say legislators move away from general constituency opinion at approximately the same rate as both high and low-income sub-constituency groups grow. On a per-household basis, less affluent Americans do not seem to have discernibly less (or more) capacity to move or to restrain their representatives in the House if we make no assumption about the preferred ideological direction of the effort.

As an aside, note the performances of three control variables. Democrats are materially less responsive to constituents. This is suggestive of a liberal bias in policymaking. One explanation of the distortive effects of the parties' polarization at the elite level is its asymmetry discussed earlier (Bonica et al. 2015; Grossmann and Hopkins 2016; Hacker and Pierson 2005; Mann and Ornstein 2016; Pierson and Schickler 2020; Skocpol and Hertel-Fernandez 2016; Theriault 2008). Republicans are moving to the right more than Democrats are to the left, creating aggregated conservative bias relative to the preferences of the national median. An alternative explanation is that partisan uniformity in Washington generates policy that is more progressive than the median American wants since, as figure 8.2 and the Tausanovitch and Warshaw (2013; Tausanovitch 2016) data show, Democrats are more likely to represent districts that are to the right of the center of their congressional party than Republicans are to represent districts that are to the left of theirs. Put another way, compared to the national average, conservative districts are more likely to elect Democrats than liberal districts are to elect Republicans.

As expected, senior members are emboldened to move further away from their constituents' preferences. Contrary to the "marginality hypothesis" and the proposition that electorally insecure members are necessarily more attentive to constituency opinion (Fiorina 1973; Froman 1963; Griffin 2006b), however, as vote share goes down the distance between district attitudes and legislator behavior actually increases. One plausible explanation is that lawmakers who win election narrowly tend to represent moderate districts, but the House's organizationally strong and polarized parties set the floor agenda. This forces legislators to take the more extreme positions of co-partisans (Cox and McCubbins 1993).

SENATORS

Interestingly, Bartels (2016, 242–47) and Tausanovitch (2016) reveal that the gap between the responsiveness of members to high- and low-income constituents is even greater in the Senate. By examining individual issues, Maks-Solomon and Rigby (2020) demonstrate that Republican senators are particularly responsive to affluent constituents on economic issues like tax cuts and the minimum wage.[18] Lax, Phillips, and Zelizer (2019), on the other hand, suggest that there is no difference in the Senate's responsiveness to the wealthy and its responsiveness to the working class. My analysis, replicating the approach for the House described and deployed in table 8.1 above, is more consistent with this contrarian assessment. Table 8.3 reveals that the proportion of constituents in the low-income cohorts has a greater effect on senator behavior, so long as we control for party and region. As that proportion increases, so senators become more liberal. In no specification does the measure of the proportion of a state's households in the higher-income groups reach levels of statistical significance.

As with the House, however, the substantive effect of lower-income cohort size is not large. In the specification containing all variables, a nine-percentage-point increase in the proportion of households in the very lowest-income group moves a senator leftward about the same as the distance between Amy

TABLE 8.3. Constituent income and senator ideology, 2003–2016

	Outermost	Broader	Outermost	Broader
Higher-income group	.301 (.975)	.138 (.808)	−.273 (.420)	−.238 (.333)
Lower-income group	−.384 (.835)	−.211 (.770)	−1.02 (.368)*	−.607 (.325)*
Constituency opinion	1.45 (.131)*	1.45 (.133)*	.437 (.075)*	.445 (.077)*
Democrat			−.620 (.020)*	−.622 (.020)*
South			.092 (.023)*	.081 (.023)*
Constant	.039 (.162)	.036 (.308)	.480 (.068)*	.512 (.125)*
Adjusted R^2	.435	.435	.915	.914

Notes: $N = 721$. OLS estimation with robust standard errors clustered by member in parentheses. Congress fixed effects calculated but not reported. "Outermost" refers to very highest- and lowest-income cohorts, "broader" to my more relaxed definition of the cohorts. *$p < .05$.

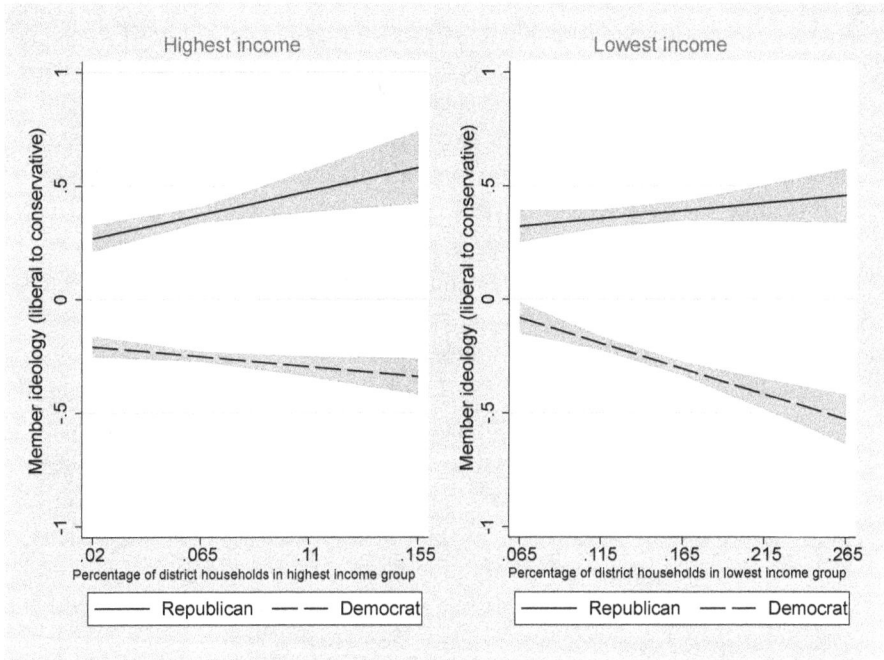

F I G U R E 8.6. Effects of highest- and lowest-income group constituents on senator ideology when conditioned by party, 2003–2016
Shaded areas denote 95 percent confidence intervals. Income data are from the census.

Klobuchar (D-MN) and Patrick Leahy (D-VT) or Mitch McConnell (R-KY) and John Cornyn (R-TX). The manipulation is roughly the difference between a state at the 10th percentile and one at the 90th percentile, but the effect constitutes only a little more than half the distance from Susan Collins (R-ME) to Joe Manchin (D-WV). In other words, not far.

Figure 8.6 reveals the effects of the proportion of state households that are in the highest- and lowest-income groups, when interacted with party in the model specification including all controls. The stronger pull of poorer constituents is on display. Whereas Republicans become more conservative and Democrats slightly more liberal when the proportion of the highest-income households in a state increases, growth in the proportion of lowest-income households has no material effect on Republicans but leads to a noticeable move in the leftward direction among Democrats. This result is distinct from the findings in the House analysis and is indicative of the greater influence that lower-income households appear to have on lawmakers in the Senate.

These findings regarding the upper body take issue with Bartels (2016, 245), who claims that senators are not as responsive to the interests and opinions of low-income constituents as are their House colleagues because they need a great deal of money to win elections. But we might just as easily argue that they must raise money from a more pluralistic and broader group of contributors. Their larger constituencies, more numerous committee assignments, greater attention to matters of foreign policy, and unique constitutional obligations to confirm presidential nominees thrust them into competitive and ideologically diverse national-level interest group politics. It is true that labor groups give more of their money to House than Senate candidates. National left-of-center and deep-pocketed unconnected PACs and super PACs, however, are more prominent in Senate races where significant amounts of "dark money" flow outside traditional party networks (Obklobdzija 2024). Groups like EMILY's List, the League of Conservation Voters, Planned Parenthood, NextGen Climate Action, and several unions, especially in the public sector, have invested heavily in Senate contests in recent cycles, collectively often matching or exceeding the dollars spent by corporate and conservative interests.[19] Senators also receive a greater proportion of their campaign war chests from individuals. Research shows that a large and diverse collection of strategic and ideological Americans give to both Democratic and Republican Senate candidates (Barber et al. 2017).

Moreover, as a category, states are not as heterogeneous as congressional districts. There is less variance in their median incomes and in their proportion of high- and low-income households. When compared to their House equivalents, the generally statistically insignificant coefficients for key variables in table 8.3 and flatter lines of figure 8.6 suggest that, with the possible exception of Democrats representing constituencies with many low-income households, most senators do not think of their states as distinctly rich or poor. They are therefore not especially attentive to the policy interests of sub-constituencies at the socioeconomic extremes.

Conclusion

This analysis of dyadic representation in Congress takes an approach different from that generally pursued in the political science literature on economic inequality. Rather than use measures of constituents' expressed policy preferences, I make conventional assumptions about the economic-policy preferences of low- and high-income Americans and assess legislators' sensitivity to the relative size of these groups within their districts or states. I think it is fair to say that my analysis shows that the influence poorer Americans have on the behavior of their representation is greater than that presented by the scholarly consensus. As they grow in number, lower-income constituents push House members in a liberal direction as, or nearly as, effectively as high-income voters move theirs in a conservative direction. Low-income Americans are more successful than their counterparts when it comes to shifting senators. Any impact made by either income group pales into comparison to that made by party, however. If low-income Americans want leftist economic policy, they should vote individually or as a bloc for Democratic candidates—a point made clear in other recent work (Grossmann, Mahmood, and Isaac 2021; Lax et al. 2019; Tausanovitch 2016). Congressional districts with very large numbers of high-income or low-income households cannot move members away from broader constituency opinion to an extent that remotely approaches the force of the parties.

Rising inequality does move House Republicans rightward, but it has a compensatory effect on Democrats and results in a polarization that is not as asymmetric as many believe. Moreover, there appears no regional element to this development, and Southerners are not as culpable as advertised. There are various measures of district inequality, but I think it is still fair to say that Southern members behave like their non-Southern co-partisans as such inequality increases.

House districts with large proportions of low-income households also constitute a diverse collection. Certainly many of them are liberal, but numerous others are cohesive and conservative. Often these poorer right-of-center districts elect conservative Republicans who go to Washington and vote for conservative economic policies.

9

The Descriptive Representation of Affluence

Do Less Affluent Americans Care?

Descriptive representation—the idea that collectively elected officials should reflect the politically relevant demographic features of their constituents—has been of interest to scholars of Congress for some time. Using conventional standards, Blacks have always been underrepresented in the House and, especially, the Senate. Only in recent years has the percentage of House members who are Black approached thirteen, the proportion of the nation's population that is from that group. A similar observation can be made of women; by the first decade of the 2000s barely one in five members was female, and even after the elections of 2022 the figure was only 29 percent in the House.

The literature in legislative studies considers a lack of descriptive representation problematic. It asserts that the male, white, Christian, and older legislators who dominate Congress and state assemblies are less responsive to the interests of citizens who do not share their characteristics. This is the case for matters like policy, constituency service, and the allocation of government resources.[1] Additionally, research on Congress suggests that women, Blacks, and Latinos feel more efficacious when represented by lawmakers who share their demographic attributes (English et al. 2019; Lowande et al. 2019; West 2017). These effects extend to member traits unrelated to race and gender, including generation, religion, and veteran status (Cormack 2018; Curry and Haydon 2018; Lowande et al. 2019; Mathew 2018).

Unlike their race and gender, the wealth of members and congressional candidates is not often discernible to the public. What is more, legislators clearly do not reflect the socioeconomic makeup of the general population. The estimated median net worth of a member of the House in the early 2020s was roughly $1.1 million, well in excess of the approximately $200,000 for all Americans over forty-five years old.[2] Lawmakers tend to come from an unrepresentative and narrow set of class and occupational backgrounds. As a group, they are white collar. Pre-tenure careers in the fields of law, politics, business, and banking are a distinct feature of contemporary members of Congress.[3]

Still, a literature on the subject of the descriptive representation of affluence in Congress is emerging. The work of Nicholas Carnes (2012, 2013, 2018; Carnes and Sadin 2015; Carnes and Lupu 2016) has been particularly influential. Carnes argues that with few blue-collar legislators, Congress advances the interests of the wealthy, pushing economic policy to the right. This outcome arises because lawmakers tend to introduce and vote for legislation in a manner consistent with their class backgrounds (Carnes 2013). Grumbach (2015) extends the reasoning, finding that the social class of lawmakers' parents has a sizable effect on the voting behavior of Democratic members, with those coming from blue-collar homes more likely to vote for policies consistent with the interests of working people. Barnes, Beall, and Holman (2021) report that American state budget allocations on social services and education are higher when there is a greater proportion of "pink-collar" or working-class female legislators. Miler (2018) argues that a principal reason that issues related to poverty occupy such a small part of the congressional agenda is that there are so few poor, female, and minority lawmakers.

There is also some work on the effect of legislators' personal economic situation on their behavior. Witko and Friedman (2008) show that members with business backgrounds are materially more likely to receive disproportionate funds from corporate PACs and to vote consistently with business interests than congressional colleagues. Researchers report that members' wealth had a direct and material impact on their support for measures reducing or repealing the estate tax (Griffin and Anewalt-Remsburg 2013) and responding to the shock caused by the federal debt–limit crisis in 2011 (Grose 2013). Peterson and Grose (2021) reveal that lawmakers' actions are consistent with efforts to further the interests of companies in which they hold stock. Less affluent members, on the other hand, have fewer financial resources and prominent associations with firms.

This growing research provides the starting point for my analysis in this and the following chapter. In the next chapter, I focus on member behavior and the argument that less affluent representatives are important to progressive federal economic policy because they are more willing and no less capable of advancing the interests of less affluent Americans. In this chapter, I look at individual voter, candidate, member, and district characteristics to see whether there exist relationships between the socioeconomic status of Americans and the people whom they elect to represent them in Congress. I am uninterested in isolating the precise causal mechanism. As noted, the literature on race and gender cited above suggests that voters believe those who share their socioeconomic characteristics serve them better, granting them a feeling of efficacy.[4]

The goal is to discern whether less affluent Americans behave in a way that suggests they would like a Congress that has more members who share, or at least better approximate, their class background. The literature proposes that the general public wants more "ordinary people" to hold elected office. Using surveys fielded in Latin America, Britain, and the United States, researchers demonstrate that citizens are perfectly willing to support blue-collar candidates (Barnes et al. 2023; Campbell and Cowley 2014; Carnes and Lupu 2016). In fact, if there is bias against candidates based upon their class background, the wealthy are its object. Experiments conducted by Griffin, Newman, and Buhr (2020) reveal that American participants view candidates with high incomes as more "intelligent" but less "honest" and "caring" and prefer those with lower incomes to represent them. Piston's (2018) comprehensive analysis of Americans' attitudes about the rich and poor repeatedly detects significant resentment of wealthy compatriots and sympathy toward those who are less well-off.[5]

More specifically, I ask two questions I then endeavor to answer. The first is: Do less affluent members of Congress represent poorer districts? Of course, to become members, individuals first have to be candidates. Candidate emergence and nomination are as much a function of supply and of the limited number of individuals willing and able to run for office as they are of voter demand for candidates of particular types (Maestas et al. 2006; Maisel and Stone 1997). Past decisions by the electorate also send signals to prospective candidates as to whom they are willing to support, and researchers believe these signals suggest that working-class citizens should not run (Carnes 2018; Carnes and Lupu 2016).

Still, the geographic distribution of members by their socioeconomic characteristics can tell us something about the kind of legislator that voters in a district or state want. It is therefore useful to examine whether, within the universe of members, the relatively less affluent, less educated, and blue-collar represent less affluent, less educated, and blue-collar districts. We can see if longitudinal cross-sectional analyses of House members reveal a sort of "matching" of members to jurisdictions. After all, such a dynamic convinces scholars that Blacks and Latinos desire descriptive representation (Bowen and Clark 2014; Grose 2011; Hicks et al. 2018). Majority- and plurality-Black and Latino jurisdictions are considerably more likely to elect a Black or Latino member than districts with a majority or plurality white population.[6]

From this research we conclude that, all other things being equal, relatively Black districts prefer Black representatives, relatively Latino districts Latino representatives, and white districts white representatives.

The second question is: Do less affluent Americans prefer the less affluent candidate when presented with a choice? To date the literature, as noted above, speculates that the answer is often "yes" (Carnes and Lupu 2016; Griffin et al. 2020; Kevins 2021). That Congress is so descriptively unrepresentative of wealth appears to be a function of an inadequate supply of lower-income and working-class candidates, not of voter preference (Treul and Hansen 2023). Carnes (2018, 158–208) offers political "training" and financial support as a corrective. So does the American Academy of Arts and Sciences' Commission on Reimagining Our Economy.[7] But these studies use survey data. I am interested in behavior. Less affluent candidates may not get on the congressional general-election ballot very often, but Americans frequently get to choose between individuals with discernibly different financial situations. New data permit us to see whether the less affluent candidate is elected from a less affluent district or generally voted for by less affluent citizens.

An Analysis of Members

To answer the first question, I look at House and Senate membership over the past several decades. I am interested in three different legislator characteristics. These are net worth, occupation, and education. I look at these indicators because a direct comparison between constituent and legislator income is not worthwhile. With the exception of those in leadership positions, legislators are paid the same amount, and there is no variation in their salaries.[8] Their congressional pay also makes them appear considerably less affluent than they really are. Together, net worth, occupation, and education constitute what we commonly think of as class but are clearly related to members' general financial circumstances.

NET WORTH

I begin with an analysis of members' finances. Researchers have compiled comprehensive data on the net worth of lawmakers, and I use two measures derived from this work. The first is from the Center for Responsive Politics (CFRP). It has collected and calculated House member net-worth data from financial-disclosure documents since 2005.[9] I use the figures in the first year of a Congress for all Congresses from the 108th to 114th (2003–2004 to 2015–2016). In order to extend the data series backward, I use an original measure of net worth that I have constructed from the financial-disclosure documents that members are required to submit by order of the Ethics in Government Act. I calculate members' annual income, excluding congressional salary, add it to their assets or "holdings," and then subtract the product from their total liabilities. The result is divided by one million and expressed in constant 2010 dollars and is for the reporting period in the second year of the Congress from the 98th Congress (1983–1984) through the 111th (2009–2010), the last Congress before the passage of the Stop Trading on Congressional Knowledge or STOCK Act, which altered rules governing legislators' disclosures. My measure is therefore similar but not identical to that derived from the CFRP data.[10]

Of course, as noted above, the net worth of members tends to be much greater than that of the broader population. Still, there is considerable variance across legislators. Between the 109th and 114th Congresses (2005–2015), CFRP calculates the average net worth of a House member to be $5.96 million. The median was $763,000, however, and 6.7 percent of members during those Congresses had no net worth or liabilities that exceeded assets.

Table 9.1 reveals the results of analyses using the two different measures of members' net worth as dependent variables and the indicators of district income that I have employed previously—the median household income and the proportion of households in the highest- and lowest-income groups.[11] I use a battery of intuitive controls that are readily available and account for constituency and member attributes. There is some evidence of a positive relationship between constituent income—and indeed constituent education— and member net worth.[12] Districts with larger proportions of high-income households do seem to have wealthier legislators. Moreover, as household median income increases in the CFRP and author analysis, so representatives' net worth rises. In the CFRP analysis, an increase of $14,000 in the household median income of a district (about one standard deviation and the effect of going from about the 25th to 75th percentile) raises a member's net worth by about $2.67 million when we do not use the constituent-education measure (which is highly correlated with income) as a control. Adding six percentage points to the proportion of households in the highest-income cohort (roughly the standard deviation and median) elevates a member's net worth by approximately $3.5 million under the same conditions.

Certain personal features seem to explain member net worth better than do constituency characteristics like household income, however. The wealthiest legislators are whiter and older in most of the analyses, differences we would observe within the general population. Every year a House member gets older, it increases their net worth by about $60,000 in the longer author

TABLE 9.1. Constituent income and House member net worth, CFRP and author data 1983–2016

Measure(s) of constituency income used	CFRP data				Author data	
	Median	Highest/lowest	Median	Highest/lowest	Median	Highest/lowest
Median income	.189 (.074)*		.036 (.075)		.063 (.032)*	
Highest-income group		58.06 (21.63)*		35.22 (30.34)		12.20 (11.98)
Lowest-income group		-8.63 (18.97)		-6.41 (18.60)		-6.44 (7.48)
Constituent education			.364 (.191)*	.223 (.223)		
Constituent urban	.066 (.049)	.036 (.040)	.045 (.051)	.028 (.044)	.015 (.010)	.010 (.010)
District in the South	.865 (2.21)	.643 (2.19)	.368 (2.25)	.568 (2.18)	.377 (.478)	.397 (.446)
Member Democrat	-2.13 (3.32)	-2.20 (3.15)	-2.62 (3.27)	-2.37 (3.07)	-.613 (.631)	-.493 (.608)
Member female	.746 (2.70)	.518 (2.68)	.519 (2.73)	.471 (2.70)	.991 (1.51)	.909 (1.44)
Member Black	-3.90 (2.03)*	-3.26 (2.32)	-3.98 (2.05)*	-3.21 (2.33)	-1.73 (.621)*	-1.47 (.617)*
Member Latino	.604 (5.34)	1.39 (5.79)	1.65 (5.43)	2.07 (5.74)	-1.70 (.615)*	-1.53 (.527)*
Member age	.076 (1.07)	.071 (.105)	.076 (.105)	.071 (.104)	.059 (.024)*	.059 (.023)*
Member seniority	-.144 (.080)*	-.152 (.079)*	-.150 (.078)*	-.151 (.078)*	-.065 (.035)*	-.065 (.034)*
Adjusted R^2	.013	.017	.017	.018	.027	.027
N	2,602	2,602	2,602	2,602	6,077	6,077

Notes: Method is OLS regression. Dependent variable is net worth in dollars divided by one million. Controls: Constituent urban is percentage of the district classed as urban; member seniority is service in years. Congress dummies used but not reported. CFRP data are from https://www.opensecrets.org. Standard errors clustered by member in parentheses. * $p < .05$.

dataset. Being Black or Latino "costs" House members roughly just short of $2 million in the author data, about $3.5 million in the CFRP data. The dearth of Latino members—as well as their rising net worth—may explain why that variable does not generate a statistically significant coefficient in the analysis of the more up-to-date CFRP data. Seniority is frequently important, and senior members are not as wealthy, as each year of service in recent Congresses costs around $150,000. A long congressional career does not seem directly enriching, therefore, although the literature on lobbying and revolving-door politics suggests that it becomes so for many lawmakers upon their departure from office (Dabros 2017; Lazarus et al. 2016; Makse 2017; Vidal et al. 2012).[13]

OCCUPATION

I next analyze occupation or profession, a characteristic of members that is as, and possibly more, visible to the public than net worth. I again deploy two different indicators. The first is collected from the *Almanac of American Politics* (various years) and is dichotomous with members coded "1" if they had a business or legal career prior to entering elected office.[14] These careers are what we might consider "white-collar" occupational backgrounds. These author data are from the 103rd (1993–1994) through 114th (2105–2016) Congresses. The second measure is from Carnes's (2013) CLASS database. Carnes collects data on the pre-tenure occupations of all members in his time series, including the proportion of time spent in each position. His occupation data extend from the 110th Congress (2007–2008) back to the 106th Congress (1999–2000), so they are richer but occupy a shorter period than mine. I take the proportion of their career each House member spent in several occupation types to create five dependent variables: (1) worker, (2) politics and the law, (3) professional, (4) private sector, and (5) business owner.[15] "Worker" refers specifically to "manual laborers, service industry workers, farm laborers, and union officials," and its average is .015, or 1.5 percent of a member's pre-tenure career. The figure is very small compared to the other categories, confirming a central element of Carnes's argument.[16]

I present the most important results in figures 9.1 and 9.2. Figure 9.1 reveals the analysis of the author data, figure 9.2 the coefficients of the different measures of income from the CLASS data.[17] In the analyses of both datasets, I use the same controls as in the section on net worth.[18] Constituent income and the size of the high- and low-income groups in a district have little impact on the pre-tenure occupations of House members.[19] The variables of greatest interest seldom produce statistically significant coefficients and, when they do, the findings seem contradictory. Figure 9.1 suggests that

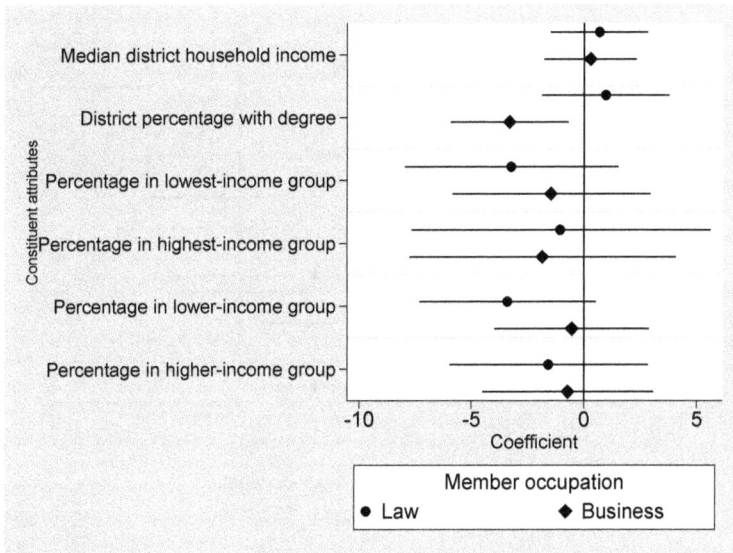

FIGURE 9.1. Constituent socioeconomic status and House member occupation, author data 1993–2016
Bars show 95 percent confidence intervals.

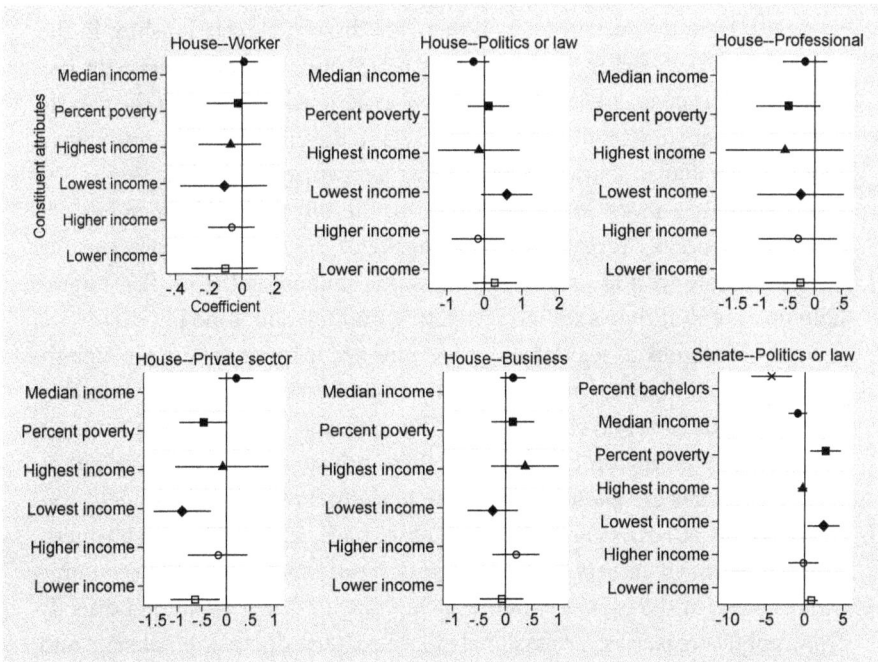

FIGURE 9.2. Constituent income and House member occupation, Carnes CLASS data 1999–2008
Bars show 95 percent confidence intervals. Data are from Carnes (2013).

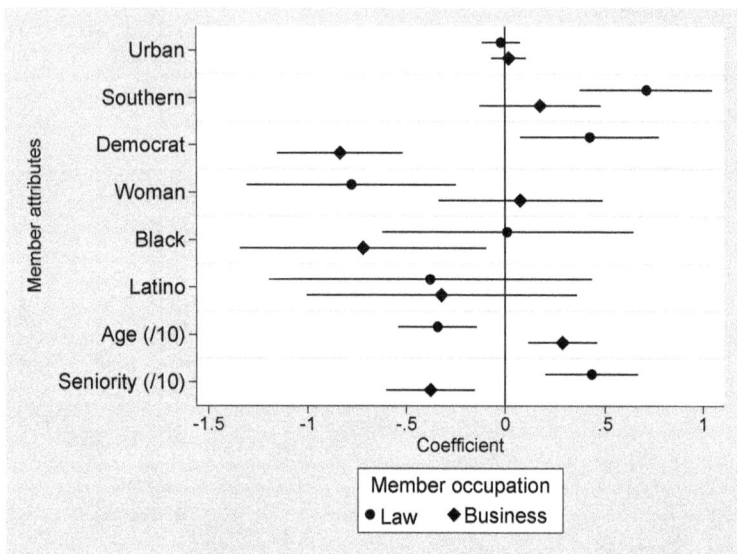

FIGURE 9.3. Other determinants of House member occupation, author data 1993–2016
Bars show 95 percent confidence intervals.

districts where residents are less educated are more likely to select representatives with business backgrounds. If there are discernible relationships in the
CLASS data analyzed in figure 9.2, it is really only that members with less
affluent constituents are less likely to have experienced careers in the private
sector. Neither workers nor business owners in the House disproportionately
represent particular districts characterized by constituent income.[20]

To provide a more complete picture of the forces shaping member occupation, figure 9.3 reveals the performance of the control variables in the
analyses (these are author-data specifications containing the median household income).[21] It shows several interesting findings about the importance of
member attributes to legislators' pre-tenure occupations. There are significant partisan differences, for example. Democratic members are considerably
more likely to have had careers in law. Republicans tend to have spent their
time before Washington in business and the private sector. Using the author
data, Democrats are about a third more likely to have had legal careers; Republicans are about 65 percent more likely to have held positions in business.
These patterns in careers before Congress are consistent with the economic
philosophies of the parties. Often deriving much of their livelihood directly
from public treasuries, professionals like teachers, doctors, engineers, and
lawyers should be less averse to increases in taxes because they perceive
some tangible personal return as a result. They are presumably supportive of

government regulation since they make livings from fields where barriers to entry are high. Businesspeople, particularly if they are wealthy, are likely to have opposite views on taxes and regulation. I shall revisit this argument in greater detail in chapter 11.

There are important racial and gender differences in members' pre-tenure occupations, as well. Black legislators are less likely to have spent time in business before coming to Congress. In fact, whites are about 55 percent more likely than Blacks to have enjoyed a pre-tenure business career. This result mirrors patterns in broader society, where leaders of Black organizations have traditionally come out of law, teaching, and religion. Male lawmakers are about 70 percent more likely than female colleagues to have had a legal career.[22]

Geography furnishes another important part of this story, as figure 9.4 also shows. It reports the performance of control variables in two of Carnes's occupational categories, worker and private sector. Members outside the South are appreciably more likely to have spent time as workers, an observation that might say something about the Democratic machine politics of the urban Northeast and Midwest that provided opportunities for men with blue-collar backgrounds to become political leaders (Rauch 2015). Notice, however, that members with backgrounds in the private sector are disproportionately from the South. The congressional delegations of the Northeast, West Coast, and big cities of the industrial Midwest are replete with Democrats—and indeed

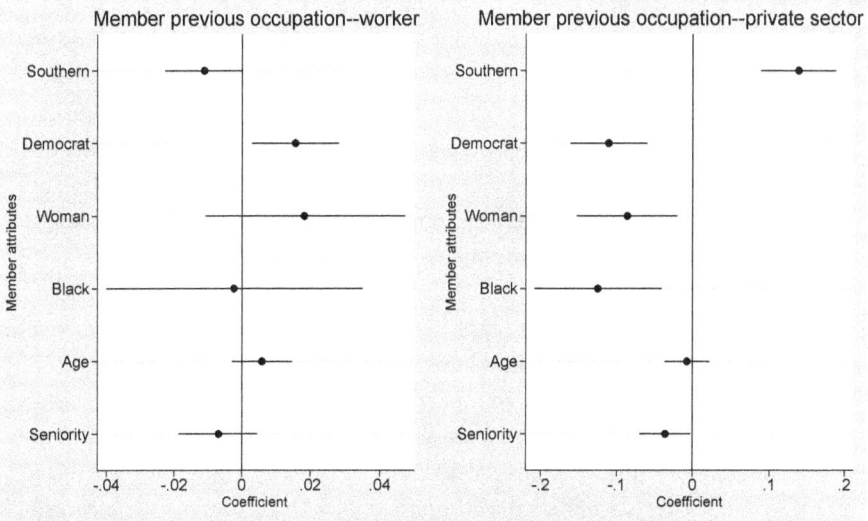

FIGURE 9.4. Other determinants of House member occupation, Carnes CLASS data 1999–2008
Bars show 95 percent confidence intervals. Data are from Carnes (2013).

Republicans—who have backgrounds as teachers, administrators for unions and nonprofits, and political aides to members of Congress and gubernatorial administrations. Legislators from the South, plains, and much of small-town America tend to have spent considerable time in local business, real estate, insurance, banking, and their own law practices. The author data in figure 9.3 report that Southerners were more likely to have been lawyers than were their colleagues from other regions, presumably working in small practices rather than large urban firms or as district attorneys or judges.[23]

The occupations of the Illinois and Pennsylvania delegations in the 108th Congress (2003–2004) provide a dramatic, if not perhaps always typical, example. Among the members from Chicago—all Democrats—were two civil rights activists, two city aldermen, a teacher and social worker, a leader of a progressive advocacy group, and an official from a presidential administration. Democrats also controlled central Philadelphia. Among these lawmakers were a union leader (who had been both a carpenter and realtor), a city housing officer, a political aide, and a couple of attorneys. As Republicans became more prominent in the suburbs of the two cities, there were more large-firm attorneys and teachers as well as, outside of Philadelphia, a social worker and chain restaurateur. More rural areas, dominated by Republicans, counted among their number hometown-practicing lawyers, a car wash owner, an owner of a nursery and landscaping business, two insurance agents, and two auto dealers. The further outside Chicago and Philadelphia a member's district was, the more likely she was to have had military service or be in the reserves.

Or take the Georgia delegation in the more recent 114th Congress (2015–2017). Among the Republicans were small-business owners, a surgeon, a pharmacist, a former congressional aide, and two pastors—one of whom was a talk-radio host as well. The Democrats, all Black, were in law, with the exception of civil rights leader John Lewis and David Scott, a businessman often labeled the Congressional Black Caucus's most conservative member. The legislators representing central and suburban Atlanta tended to have professional degrees, those outside the state's metropolis only baccalaureates.

This little-observed reality of congressional life seems cultural and geographic rather than driven by biases emanating from constituents' affluence or class. Pre-tenure experiences that recommend free-market economic policies to Southern conservative members from all types of districts are consistent with time owning small businesses, not as especially wealthy financiers, owners of large firms, or managers in multinational corporations. Northern and west-coast legislators, on the other hand, often have professional degrees. Even those liberal Democrats without advanced credentials do not seem to have made their livings prior to arrival in Washington "getting their hands dirty" in blue-collar jobs. The "Squad" of minority progressive House members who captured the nation's attention in the early 2020s provide a good example. Of them—Cori Bush (D-MO), Jamaal Bowman (D-NY), Ilhan Omar (D-MN), Alexandria Ocasio-Cortez (D-NY), Ayanna Pressley (D-MA), and Rashida Tlaib (D-MI)—only Bush, who does not have a college degree, and Ocasio-Cortez had anything remotely like traditional blue-collar pre-tenure careers.[24] Today the road to political prominence, particularly for members from traditionally blue-collar urban liberal Democratic districts, runs not through traditional trades or the factory floor but through a big law firm or an administrative position in a congressional office, nonprofit, labor union, or community group advocating progressive politics.[25]

Age and seniority also generate interesting results. Figure 9.3 shows that more senior and younger members tend to have pre-tenure careers in politics and law, suggesting that such careers are still a preferred entryway to Congress, perhaps because they seem to contribute to a lengthy and presumably successful tenure. Older and junior members are more likely to have significant private-sector experience, constructing careers unrelated to politics. Democrats tend to take the first route, Republicans the second. It is Republicans, then, who have provided much of the increased occupational diversity that we have witnessed since the mid-1990s and that proponents of greater descriptive representation in Congress suggest is healthy.

The bottom right-hand panel of figure 9.2 shows the only findings of interest in the CLASS-data models of senators' pre-tenure occupations. Overall, the Senate analysis reveals that the measures derived from constituency income have no real effect, with the exception of the proportion of a member's career spent in politics or the law. As a state becomes increasingly blue-collar—whether measured by education or by income—its senators are more likely to have spent much of their pre-tenure careers in the white-collar world of politics and the law.

EDUCATION

The third set of analyses is of House members' formal education. I code the dependent variables in the author data "1" if a member obtained an undergraduate degree and if they got a professional or graduate degree. I present the results in figure 9.5. Constituent income does not behave in the hypothesized manner, and the data show that a district's affluence has no material effect on the education of its House members.[26]

The measure of constituent education, however, performs more robustly. Increasing the proportion of constituents with a college degree from

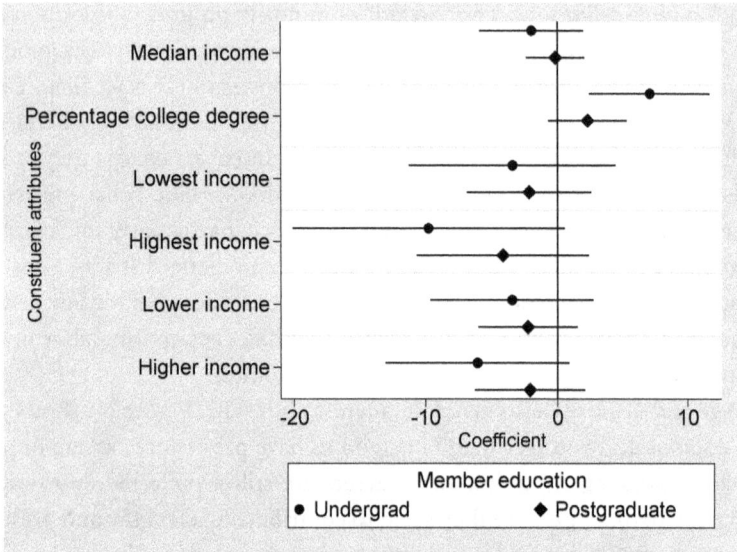

FIGURE 9.5. Constituent socioeconomic status and House member education, author data 1993–2016
Bars show 95 percent confidence intervals.

10 percent to 30 percent (or roughly one standard deviation below the mean to one standard deviation above), elevates the probability of a member having such a degree from roughly 55 percent to about 70 percent. Educated citizens seem to like having educated representatives. To the extent that education is a measure of social class, moreover, we might say that blue-collar districts quite like blue-collar members.

Figure 9.6 and the coefficients of the controls in the author data analysis reveal that other constituent and member characteristics are important, particularly party. Here a Democrat has about a 95 percent chance of having an undergraduate degree, a Republican member approximately 88 percent.[27] For postgraduate degrees, these figures are 71 percent and 58 percent, respectively. Democratic members are more educated and are, of course, more likely to support left-of-center economic policies. Hunt's (2022) data show that over the period from 1944 to 2020, about 95 percent of both Democratic and Republican members had an undergraduate degree, but whereas 61 percent of Democrats had a postgraduate degree, only 52.6 percent of Republicans had obtained one. More anecdotally, of the sixty freshmen in the 117th Congress (2021–2022), only seven did not have college degrees—five of whom were Republicans, including conservatives Lauren Boebert (R-CO) and Madison Cawthorn (R-NC). Volden, Wai, and Wiseman (2020) reveal that whereas the proportion of congressional Democrats educated at an "elite" or "top 20" school (based on SAT scores) has remained steady since the early 1970s, the same cannot be said of Republicans. In both the House and Senate, these numbers have dropped dramatically. Today about half of Senate Democrats and one-third of House Democrats received this kind of higher-level education. The proportions are roughly double those of Republican counterparts.

I do not show findings for the Senate. In no instance does a measure of constituents' income, poverty levels, or education generate a statistically significant coefficient in Carnes's (2013) CLASS data on senators' educational accomplishments. Unreported results show that Democratic and male senators have higher levels of education. The finding about party again suggests that Americans with lower incomes can realize left-of-center policy goals with legislators who have backgrounds very different from their own.

SUMMARY

Cross-district variation in the financial means, occupations, and education credentials of legislators bears little resemblance to these patterns among congressional districts. Other personal attributes explain lawmakers' socio-economic characteristics better than do constituency traits. The wealthiest members tend to be old and white. Members with white-collar backgrounds, particularly in politics and professions like the law, are disproportionately

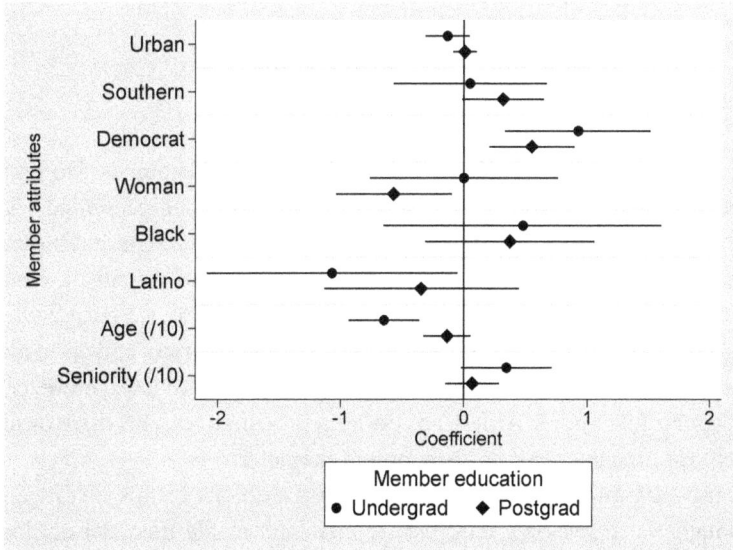

FIGURE 9.6. Other determinants of House member education, author data 1993–2016
Bars show 95 percent confidence intervals.

senior and Democratic. Legislators with higher levels of formal education are often male, young, and Democratic.

This analysis reveals a certain amount of socioeconomic descriptive representation, however. Constituent education shapes members' class characteristics somewhat, with districts containing relatively high numbers of residents with relatively low levels of education disproportionately represented by legislators who have had neither professional careers nor advanced formal educations. Districts with a large proportion of high-income households tend to elect the wealthiest members.

But party mitigates any effect this tendency might produce in economic policy outcomes. If anything, it is Democratic members—who belong to the party with left-of-center economic policy preferences generally attributed to low-income Americans—who more frequently hold the credentials of the American socioeconomic elite. They tend to have professional backgrounds and higher levels of education than do Republicans. Senate Democrats are wealthier than their partisan foes. It is true that Democrats in the House are more likely to have had blue-collar backgrounds and not to have owned businesses. Compared to Republican colleagues, however, they are also more likely to have spent considerable time in white-collar fields like politics and the law before arriving in Washington.

Geography also plays a role. Patterns in member occupation are regional as much as they are determined by constituent affluence. Legislators from the South, for example, are more likely to have enjoyed pre-tenure careers in business and the private sector but not as workers.

An Analysis of Candidates

The second question posed at the beginning of the chapter is: Do less affluent Americans prefer the less affluent candidate when presented with a clear choice? To answer it, I analyze the selections that districts and individuals make at the ballot box. If, at the district level or individually, income is not correlated with the vote for the wealthier candidate, we have evidence congruent with a negative answer. If less affluent districts and individuals disproportionately support the least well-off of two candidates, however, we can suggest that poorer Americans desire representatives who share or more closely approximate their socioeconomic character.

I use data on candidate wealth in House elections in this investigation. Although the House has required its members to file financial-disclosure documents for some time, there was no such compulsion for candidates until recently. Beginning with the 2014 electoral cycle, all candidates who raised or spent $5,000 were required to complete and submit the same financial-disclosure form as sitting lawmakers. The Clerk of the US House of Representatives collects these data and maintains them on the office's website.[28]

These data permit comparisons of the relative financial status of competing candidates. I contrast the net worth of the two major-party candidates in a general election.[29] The differences are coded as "0" (less than $500,000 using my calculations and therefore considered to be no discernible difference) and "1" (in excess of $500,000).[30] The $500,000 "buffer" constitutes an attempt to account for the likelihood that voters are only capable of distinguishing between competitors when differences in their net worth are sizable.[31] In cases where the loser was the wealthier, I code the value of the dependent variable as negative.

Interestingly, the dependent variable suggests that there are fewer differences in the financial status of competing House candidates than we might think and certainly fewer than implied by Griffin, Newman, and Buhr (2020). Their study seeks to understand contrasts in the perceptions respondents have of a candidate with $3 million and one with $75,000. Of the races in the 2014, 2016, and 2018 House elections where both major-party candidates disclosed their finances, the differences in net worth was less than $500,000 in 48.9 percent of them (440 of 899). Indeed, there would be an even greater percentage of districts in those three cycles without any discernible difference in the wealth of the major-party candidates if a larger number of relatively low-net-worth, unchallenged incumbents from safe rural or inner-city districts ran opposed by individuals forced to file—many of these candidates were surely also of modest means. The average district median household income was about $4,000 lower where only the incumbent or, in open seats, at most one candidate filed financial-disclosure documents than in districts where both submitted the information.

When there is what I consider a perceptible difference in the net worth of the two major-party general-election candidates, the wealthier tends to win. This is the case for 338 of the 899 cases (or 37.6 percent) where both candidates filed financial-disclosure forms. The least wealthy candidate won in 121 cases (or 13.5 percent).[32] The results are consistent with Treul and Hansen (2023), who show that candidates with working-class occupations win an appreciably smaller share of the vote in primary elections than do white-collar candidates.

We require multivariate analysis to tell us more, however. Here I look to see whether the less wealthy candidates win disproportionately in less affluent districts. Such a finding would be consistent with the argument that Americans care about the descriptive representation of wealth. I use controls

TABLE 9.2. District socioeconomic characteristics and the election of the wealthier or less wealthy candidate, 2014–2018

	Wealthier win?	Less wealthy win?	Wealthier win?	Less wealthy win?
Median income	−.010 (.011)	−.019 (.013)		
Highest-income group			−4.59 (3.16)	−2.48 (3.39)
Lowest-income group			−4.01 (3.78)	.422 (4.04)
Constituent education	.038 (.017)*	.037 (.022)*	.040 (.019)*	.029 (.024)
Constituent urban	−.005 (.006)	.000 (.007)	−.003 (.006)	.001 (.007)
District in the South	.486 (.210)*	−.297 (.269)	.563 (.208)*	−.232 (.274)
Competitive district	−.012 (.011)	−.043 (.017)*	−.007 (.012)	−.041 (.017)*
Open seat	.070 (.207)	.599 (.279)*	.049 (.210)	.586 (.280)*
Incumbent lost	−.473 (.364)	.333 (.380)	−.456 (.361)	.323 (.380)
Quality challenger	.285 (.237)	.353 (.298)	.279 (.237)	.352 (.298)
Spending advantage of winner	.009 (.005)*	.008 (.006)	.009 (.005)*	.007 (.006)
2016 election	−.039 (.148)	.286 (.258)	−.038 (.148)	.287 (.257)
2018 election	−.259 (.159)	.163 (.264)	−.275 (.160)*	.160 (.266)
Constant	−.422 (.566)	−1.18 (.673)*	−.316 (.760)	−1.89 (.964)*
McFadden's pseudo R^2	.030		.031	
Wald χ^2	49.36*		50.37*	

Notes: Method is multinomial logit. $N = 899$. The dependent variable for the candidate net-worth data uses cases where there is no difference as the reference category. Standard errors clustered by district. $*p < .05$.

I have above in addition to others intuitively important to this model. "Party of Winner" is dichotomous with Republicans coded "1." One variable denotes whether or not the incumbent lost the election. "District Competition" is the absolute difference, in percentage points, of the vote for the Democratic candidate for president in the last election in the district and nationally. Larger numbers therefore indicate less competitive districts. "Quality Challenger" denotes whether or not a challenger to an incumbent had held elected office previously, and "Spending Advantage of Winner" is the margin, divided by $100,000, by which the winner outspent the loser or, when negative, the loser outspent the winner.[33]

Table 9.2 reveals the results of various specifications run on data that include only those districts where both candidates reported their net worth. I use a multinomial logit with no difference in the relative net worth of the candidates as the base outcome. The results suggest that lower-net worth candidates are most likely to win in naturally competitive districts or those where the seat is open. These are contests, in other words, where conditions are most favorable to an "underdog" victory. It is interesting to note that the wealthier candidate is considerably more likely to win in the South. In the region that is poorest but most Republican, this likelihood might be explained by a paucity of viable wealthy Democratic challengers.

More importantly, indicators of income reveal that district characteristics have no effect on the likelihood of either the wealthier or less wealthy candidate winning. The measure of education does produce a statistically significant coefficient, demonstrating that a more highly educated population results in a greater likelihood of the wealthier candidate winning, but the same is also true for the less wealthy candidate. These results do very little to suggest that there is demand for descriptive representation of wealth or that lower socioeconomic districts elect the less affluent candidate.[34]

I turn next to a model of individuals' votes. Here I take CES data from the 2014, 2016, and 2018 House elections and examine the candidate choice of respondents who lived in districts for which I have data on the net worth of both major-party candidates and determined that one candidate was discernibly wealthier.[35] Because only 459 contests during the period have financial data on candidates that permit us to distinguish between them, this set is not a representative sample of CES participants.[36] Still, it is a large number of individuals, over forty-three thousand if we exclude those who did not report their personal income. It also permits observations of individual Americans' choosing between high-profile candidates of markedly different financial status in actual federal elections.

Table 9.3 reports the results of a logit model in which the dependent variable is whether the respondent preferred the wealthier (coded "1") or less wealthy (coded "0") of the two candidates in races where the differences in their net worth was discernible. The demographic variables are indicators of survey participant characteristics. Education and income are ordinal

TABLE 9.3. Income, education, and the individual's decision to vote for the wealthier candidate, 2014–2018

Median income	.001 (.003)		.005 (.004)
Constituent education		−.019 (.007)*	−.021 (.008)*
Shares party ID with wealthier candidate	1.11 (.023)*	1.09 (.022)*	1.11 (.023)*
Party ID	.038 (.013)*	.035 (.012)*	.037 (.013)*
Party of winning candidate	−.141 (.022)*	−.117 (.021)*	−.145 (.022)*
Female	−.055 (.022)*	−.065 (.020)*	−.057 (.022)*
Black	−.121 (.038)*	−.143 (.037)*	−.119 (.038)*
Latino	−.070 (.061)	−.084 (.058)	−.068 (.061)
District in the South	.112 (.024)*	.117 (.023)*	.114 (.024)*
2016 election	−.114 (.027)*	−.103 (.025)*	−.121 (.027)*
2018 election	−.107 (.062)	−.102 (.060)	−.122 (.063)
Constant	−.059 (.038)*	.025 (.039)	−.006 (.044)
McFadden's Pseudo R^2	.050	.047	.050
$LR\ \chi^2$	2628.94*	2812.12	2636.56*
N	38,511	43,100	38,511

Notes: Method is logit. *$p < .05$.

variables.[37] I control for the participants' state of residency ("0" for outside the South, "1" for South), party identification (coded "0–2," with "Democrat" and "Republican" at the poles and "independent" in the middle), and whether or not (coded "1" and "0") they shared party identification with the contest's wealthier candidate ("independents," by definition, could not). I also include measures of the party of the winning candidate ("0" for Democrat, "1" for Republican) and indicators of respondent race, ethnicity, and gender as coded by CES.

It is clear that voter income has no direct effect on the selection of the wealthier or less wealthy candidate. Education generates a statistically significant and counterintuitive negative coefficient, with respondents with only a high school education or less having a 1.4 percentage-point greater probability of voting for the wealthier candidate than respondents who graduated from a four-year college in the specification controlling for income. Interestingly, although income does not exert direct influence on the vote choice, Blacks and women are more likely to vote for the less wealthy candidate, even after accounting for the effect of party, region, and outcome. For the specification including education and income, non-Blacks have a 2.8 percentage-point (54.5 percent to 51.7 percent for Blacks) and men a 1.3 percentage-point (54.9 percent to 53.6 percent for women) greater probability of voting for the wealthier candidate, possibly because wealthier candidates tend to be male and white. The differences are statistically significant. This finding is a matter for future research and plausibly hints again at the greater importance of race and gender in our understanding of descriptive representation in Congress.

There are some insightful partisan findings. Democrats are more likely to vote for the less wealthy candidate even when I control for the respondent sharing party identification with the wealthier candidate. Respondents are, however, more likely to vote for the wealthier candidate in races won by Democrats, regardless of their party affiliation. Perhaps more striking, figure 9.7 demonstrates the effect of income on the choice to vote for the wealthier candidate when it is interacted with party identification. Family income has little to no effect on the vote of Republicans, but high-income Democrats are materially more likely to vote for the wealthier candidate than are lower-income Democrats. Moreover, party only affects vote choice at lower levels of income. When respondents make less than $70,000 a year, Democrats are likelier than Republicans to support the less affluent candidate, but the probability they will vote for this candidate is still under 50 percent.

This finding provides some consolatory evidence consistent with a demand-side argument that Americans want greater descriptive representation of class. At least when class is measured using income, blue-collar Dem-

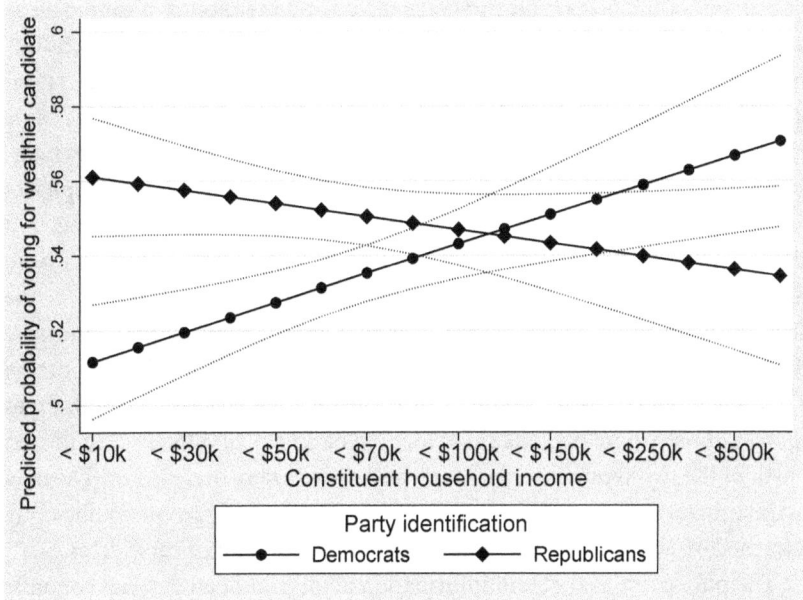

FIGURE 9.7. Income, party identification, and the choice to vote for the wealthier candidate, CES 2014–2018
Dotted lines represent 95 percent confidence intervals. CES data can be found at https://cces.gov.harvard .edu/.

ocrats are more likely to vote for the less affluent candidate than are wealthier co-partisans. Given the increasing number of white-collar and well-off professionals in the Democratic Party, however, this trend is not particularly good news to those who believe that, to achieve progressive economic policies, Democrats need to nominate and elect working-class candidates. We should note, moreover, that blue-collar Republicans are no more likely to vote for these candidates than are rich Republicans.

I should note that the assumption that Americans make a conscious choice to vote for the more or less wealthy of two candidates is based upon the observation that they perceive material differences in office seekers' financial situations. It is possible, however, that many citizens are unaware of the distinction, even when it exists. Given what little basic knowledge the public has about House elections, many citizens may need more than ambient information to distinguish candidates by their socioeconomic status.[38]

To investigate the extent to which House candidates advertise their own class attributes relative to their opponents', I examine all ads related to House elections that aired on television in 2014 and 2016. The data are from the Wesleyan Media Project (WMP) (Fowler et al. 2017, 2019).[39] In 2014, only

0.9 percent of the 625,227 ad showings included a mention of a candidate as working class; 2.4 percent of the ads included a mention of a candidate as upper class. These figures in 2016 were 1.0 percent and 2.4 percent of 621,556 ad broadcasts, respectively. For comparison, this percentage is roughly the same proportion of ads that were produced in Spanish or in which candidates mentioned "China" and many fewer than those that touched upon the topics of "veterans" or "abortion"—these two terms appear in between 5 and 10 percent of ads broadcasted. In other words, very few races involved candidates whose advertising presented their personal wealth as discernibly different—for the Congresses in this analysis, campaigns bought ads highlighting candidate class distinctions in just 3.7 percent of contests. Interestingly, the proportion is practically the same—and not statistically distinguishable—for both types of races, those where my data show there to be an actual difference in the net worth of the two reporting candidates and those where there is not. The data suggest that voters, regardless of economic background, are not sufficiently informed of, and are possibly uninterested in, the wealth of candidates.

The public can also obtain information about candidates' socioeconomic status from media reports. An analysis of media coverage of the elections of 2014, 2016, and 2018 generates similarly sparse findings, however. Using data gathered from Google News searches, I find that news outlets describe 14.9 percent of the 1,284 nonincumbent major-party general-election candidates as wealthy or upper class, 3.6 percent as working class.[40] Moreover, it seems to me that reporters often make these references in passing, as if for stylistic reasons they require adjectives to prevent repeated identification of the candidate by name. The figures, where the threshold for a candidate to be included is just one mention in one story, suggest that the media rarely refer to candidates' socioeconomic backgrounds, perhaps because they do not think the quality is interesting and the American public does not care. My finding is similar to that of Carnes (2023, 170), whose study of local newspaper articles about thirty-two members of the 110th Congress (2007–2008) and their electoral opponents concluded by saying that journalists "haven't typically assigned much importance to economic background information" about candidates.

Conclusion

In terms of wealth and class, Congress is not descriptively representative of America. It is full of affluent, white-collar, and highly educated citizens. This point is not in dispute. The fact is also a key element of political science's explanation for the system's contribution to conservative economic policy and the plausibly related inequality of the current era. Less well-off, blue-collar representatives, many researchers believe, would bring about more progressive policies and a fairer society. Because they share aspirations and preferences with working people, they best know how to deliver the policies these citizens want and the country presumably needs (Carnes 2013, 2018; Miler 2018).

I explore this argument addressing two questions. The first concerns whether members of Congress are similar to their districts. I look at legislator net worth, occupation, and education and find little in the way of a relationship between constituency income and education and members' socioeconomic characteristics. If we deploy the same type of "matching" logic that political scientists use to explain minorities' desire for greater descriptive representation of race and ethnicity, the results suggest that working-class Americans do not care particularly for a Congress that is descriptively representative of affluence.

I also examine the selections that districts and individual voters make when presented with two candidates of perceptibly different net worth. The results show that neither district nor individual voter income has a meaningful effect on the choice. The district analysis is susceptible to ecological fallacy, although my theoretical approach is to conceptualize jurisdictions' general socioeconomic profile. The individual-voter findings leave little doubt. Party might condition the effect of a person's financial status on her choice between two candidates of different means, and poorer Democrats might prefer the less well-off candidate more than do Republicans and richer co-partisans. But, in the aggregate, citizen affluence plays no meaningful role in the decision. Less affluent Americans, in general, do not prefer the less affluent of two candidates.

Unlike much existing survey research on the topic, I find no hard evidence that less affluent Americans care to have more working-class and less well-off legislators—people like themselves—in Congress. In the next chapter, I continue the analysis of the descriptive representation of affluence. I am primarily interested in plausible explanations for my null findings in this chapter. I look to see whether we might attribute citizen indifference to the descriptive representation of affluence to members' legislative behavior.

The Descriptive Representation of Affluence

Are Less Affluent Legislators Liberal and Effective?

Less affluent Americans' indifference toward their descriptive representation in Congress is puzzling if we assume that legislators' behavior and accomplishments are a function of their wealth, occupation, and education. The related literature treats member demographic and socioeconomic attributes as important determinants of legislative behavior like bill sponsorship and roll-call voting. It also implies that these qualities have no bearing on the capacity of a legislator to serve her constituents effectively. In this chapter, I explore whether less affluent lawmakers are more likely to promote and secure progressive economic policy. If they do not hold distinctly left-of-center policy preferences and are less able to achieve policy outcomes, it makes little sense for blue-collar and low-income citizens and districts to elect them.

Do Less Affluent Legislators Promote Liberal Economic Policy?

I begin by examining whether member net worth, occupation, and education shape legislator behavior on economic policy. Figure 10.1 presents specifications of a basic model of member ideology measured by first-dimension DW-NOMINATE scores (with higher scores denoting member conservatism) using the CFRP, author, Carnes CLASS, and Hunt data on net worth, occupation, and education examined in chapter 9.[1] I present a representative selection of important results. Some of the variables measuring the characteristics of interest have material effects in the hypothesized direction. The author data—extended over a longer time series than the CFRP data—suggest that wealthier members are marginally more conservative. This finding is consistent with recent work that looks at members' net worth and their congressional voting (Eggers and

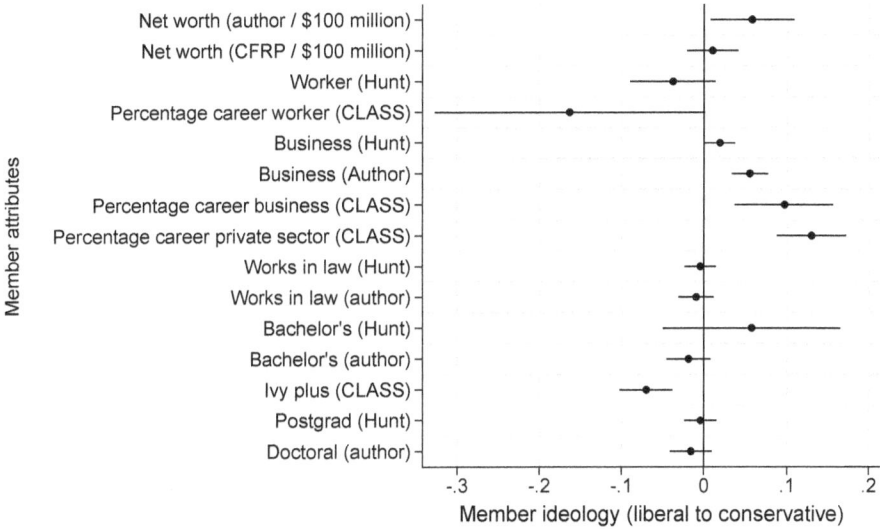

FIGURE 10.1. House members' ideology and their net worth, occupation, and education, 1983–2016
Bars represent 95 percent confidence intervals. Author data variables cover the 103rd–110th Congresses; CLASS data (Carnes 2013) covers the 106th–110th Congresses; CFRP data (https://www.opensecrets.org) covers the 108th–113th Congresses; and Hunt (2022) data covers the 96th–111th Congresses.

Klašnja 2019). Business owners and legislators who spent more of their pre-tenure career in the private sector are clearly more conservative.[2]

However, notice how small many of the substantive effects are. According to the analysis of the author data, in the twenty-first century it takes an increase of around $500 million in a member's net worth just to move them from approximately the chamber median to their party median when they are in the majority. This amount is far in excess of the wealth of all but one House member during the period.[3] In the analysis of the CLASS data, for a member in the Congresses of the current century to go from having spent none of their pre-Washington career as a worker to having spent all of it in that field (remember, the mean is very low—1.5 percent, to be exact) would only move them in the liberal direction roughly a third of the distance between the median Republican and median Democrat.[4] The direction and magnitude of the coefficient of the equivalent variable in the Hunt data is similar, although it does not quite reach conventional levels of statistical significance. Still, given that party—and to a lesser extent race, gender, and ethnicity—explains so much of the variance in member ideology, net worth and working-class and business occupations constitute minor but appreciable intraparty ideological differences in our era of polarization and tribalism.

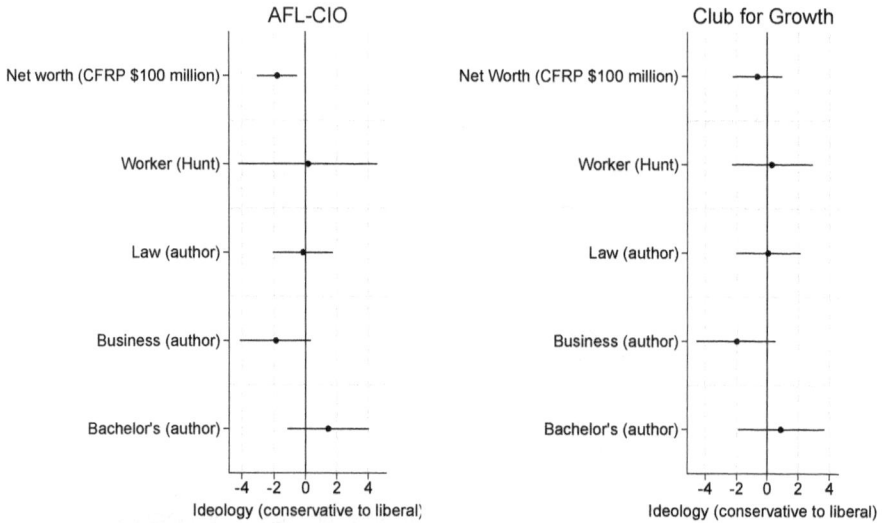

FIGURE 10.2. House members' net worth, occupation, and education and their AFL-CIO and Club for Growth scores, 2009–2014

Bars represent 95 percent confidence intervals. AFL-CIO data can be found at https://aflcio.org/scorecard. Club for Growth scores can be found at https://www.clubforgrowth.org/scorecards/. CFRP data can be found at opensecrets.org; Hunt data is from Hunt 2022.

Not all results are consistent with expectations, though. There are significant null effects, and it does seem as though a prestigious undergraduate education may contribute to greater liberalism. I think it is fair to say that in their aggregate these results do not contradict the proposition that less affluent members are more liberal in their legislative behavior, but they are hardly a ringing endorsement of it. In fact, if low-income Americans want left-of-center economic policy, they could do a lot worse than vote for Harvard-educated lawyers like, from recent Congresses, senators Chuck Schumer (D-NY) and Elizabeth Warren (D-MA) or representatives Katie Porter (D-CA), Jamie Raskin (D-MD), and Adam Schiff (D-CA).[5]

I deploy two additional measures of members' economic-policy preferences based upon their voting records. These are the member scores generated from a sample of roll-call votes and compiled each Congress from the 111th (2009–2010) to 114th (2015–2016) by the American Federation of Labor and Congress of Industrial Organizations (AFL-CIO), the country's largest labor union, and the Club for Growth, a business-oriented group supporting conservative policy. The strategy is similar to that of Carnes (2013, 32–41).[6] Figure 10.2 reports the coefficients of a sample of variables of interest in the author and Hunt datasets in specifications of a regression model in which the group scores are the dependent variables and I use the controls deployed in the analysis of DW-NOMINATE scores above. For consistency of ideological direction when reading the results, I subtract the Club for Growth's scores from 100—and therefore higher scores denote greater liberalism.

Only one variable of interest produces a statistically significant coefficient at the $p < .05$ level.[7] Consistent with the conventional thinking, members with greater net worth, as measured by the CFRP data, receive lower scores from the AFL-CIO, demonstrating their conservative economic-policy voting records. The business variable is statistically significant at the $p < .1$ level in the labor union's model. These findings are therefore also mildly consistent with a conclusion that less affluent members are a bit more liberal than their colleagues.[8] The lion's share of legislator ideology is, however, explained by party.

The findings in this section mask an observation that progressive and Democratic House members and candidates are frequently among the most affluent of all. Within the recent House membership are many wealthy liberal Democrats we do not typically think of as rich but rather as champions of low-income Americans. The San Francisco and New York City–area delegations of recent years (such as Nancy Pelosi and Jackie Speier from the former and Rosa DeLauro, Carolyn Maloney, and Nita Lowey from the latter) provide particularly good examples, but they also include "heartland" liberals like Jim Cooper of Tennessee and Lloyd Doggett of Texas. As the parties polarize and the Democrats become more progressive, they are paradoxically attracting and recruiting increasingly affluent candidates to promote their message. In the 2014–2020 cycles, the party recruited deep-pocketed candidates from many areas of American life. Among others, they found entrepreneurs and financiers like John Delaney (Maryland), Sean Casten (Illinois), and David Trone (Maryland, succeeding Delaney); leaders in large technology and multinational corporations like Suzan Delbene (Washington), Angie Craig (Minnesota), and Josh Gottheimer (New Jersey); local and regional business owners like Don Beyer (Virginia), Dean Phillips (Minnesota), and Bradley Schneider (Illinois); scions of elite economic and political families such as Sara Jacobs (California) and Jake Auchincloss (Massachusetts, ironically succeeding a Kennedy); and lottery winner Gil Cisneros (California).

The scant historical data we have do not help the case that less affluent lawmakers enact policy consistent with the apparent left-of-center interests of less affluent Americans. To be sure, there have been times when Congress enacted significant economic legislation that we can reasonably consider progressive. Established in the frenetic 1930s and 1960s, the historically important New Deal and Great Society programs redistributed wealth and regulated the economy. The Congresses of those decades did not seem to count among their memberships an appreciably larger proportion of less affluent

Americans, however. Using data going back to the start of the twentieth century, Carnes (2012) reveals the occupational composition of the House to be surprisingly stable.

Indeed, influential congressional Democrats who pushed through FDR's New Deal were almost universally lawyers. Members like Ways and Means chair "Farmer Bob" Doughton from North Carolina and David Lewis from Maryland, both of whom played pivotal roles in securing House passage of the Social Security Act, were two of the very few with genuine working-class credentials.[9] In his discussion of Miller and Stokes's "American Representation Study" from 1958, Carnes (2013, 92–95) makes the case that, in terms of the composition of their members' occupations, the Congresses of the 1950s were not materially different from those dominated by conservative Republicans early in the first decade of the 2000s. In a later book, he shows the proportion of workers in Congress to have been quite stable since the early 1960s, with a small if perceptible drop from the mid-1980s through about 2000 and an uptick since then (Carnes 2018, 6–7). Thompson et al. (2019) use deanonymized census data to show that future members of Congress who turned eighteen in 1940 came from families that were twice as wealthy as the average. Many of these individuals then served during the period of progressive economic policymaking of the mid-1960s through the 1970s. Ornstein et al. (2014) report that the proportion of House members who were bankers increased greatly through the liberal 1960s, while the number of educators in the body was at its highest during the considerably more conservative 2000s.

Cross-sectional data from other legislatures is not discernibly consistent with a "yes" answer to the question posed in the title of this section, either. Although the subject is largely unexplored, there is a relationship between member occupation and institutional professionalism in American state legislatures.[10] According to Carnes and Hansen's (2022) state legislator data, professional bodies—those with high pay, lengthy sessions, and significant staff support—tend to contain higher proportions of lawyers and political professionals. These states, California, Illinois, Massachusetts, New Jersey, New York, and Pennsylvania, for example, are among the most liberal in their politics.[11] There are more businesspeople in the less professionalized legislatures of rural and conservative states, but there are often more—presumably less affluent— educators and retirees as well. It is clear that many part-time legislatures of the conservative South and Plains have few blue-collar members. Carnes and Hansen (2022) find that among bodies without a single working-class lawmaker in 2021–2022 were conservative Florida, Mississippi, North Carolina, South Carolina, and Texas. But progressive California, Colorado, New Mexico, and

Oregon did not have any blue-collar members either. Among the states with the most working-class legislators—but still generally below 3 percent of their totals—were blue and red states such as Alaska, Maine, Minnesota, Missouri, New Hampshire, Rhode Island, and West Virginia.

Analysis of the meager data we have from other advanced industrialized democracies points to a similar conclusion. Lawmakers in such countries often enjoy lengthy pre-tenure careers in politics—on town councils, on party committees, and, in places such as France and Israel, even attending institutions, such as professional schools and the military, that consider the preparation of national legislators central to their mission. These legislators are, in many ways, more professionalized than members of Congress, but their parliaments generally produce more progressive policy. Moreover, although lawmakers elsewhere tend not to be as wealthy as their American counterparts, they are more highly educated and considerably more likely to have white-collar occupations than their countries' populations (Best 2007). Even in egalitarian places like Denmark, the Netherlands, Norway, and Sweden, politicians have more education than the general population, and fewer than 5 percent of national legislators came out of blue-collar careers in the 1990s (Dal Bo et al. 2017).[12] A more recent analysis puts the proportion of legislators with working-class occupations in Scandinavian bodies higher, but still a great deal less than their countries' overall population and more than other countries with progressive economic policies like Canada, France, and the Netherlands (Carnes and Lupu 2023). With another new, comprehensive dataset, Gerring et al. (2019) reveal the proportion of global national political leaders with blue-collar occupational backgrounds to be around 2 percent, and only 4 percent in "liberal" Europe.

This body of work all suggests that the occupations, education, and financial means of legislators are largely immaterial. The descriptive representation of affluence does not seem to be important for its substantive representation. It is true that blue-collar House members are a bit more liberal, even if they are few in number. So are those with relatively low net worth. But if lower-income Americans want left-of-center economic policy, they would be advised to vote for Democrats. Not only is an effective scouring of candidate resumes challenging, party affiliation explains considerably more of the difference in members' voting behavior than does variance in their personal attributes—and race, ethnicity, and gender explain more than wealth, occupation, and education. The Democrats, however, are also the party of professionals, Ivy League graduates, and many of the wealthiest members of Congress.

Are Less Affluent Legislators Less Effective?

Americans, regardless of their financial means and class status, presumably desire effective legislators—those who can turn constituent preferences into policy outputs. If legislators with certain socioeconomic characteristics do this more proficiently, then their constituents should want representatives who have these features, even if they are different from these constituents' own. I discussed legislative effectiveness in some detail in chapter 7. I replicate the analysis in table 7.1 using additional independent variables to measure the influence of member net worth, occupation, and education on Volden and Wiseman's (2014) legislative-effectiveness scores.[13] Figure 10.3 reports the coefficients when I add key CFRP, author, CLASS, and Hunt measures of net worth, occupation, and education separately to the model of legislative effectiveness.[14] Again, results are reported for all Congresses in which the critical independent variables are available.

Very few of these important variables generate statistically significant coefficients. If there are patterns, they show that greater education and net worth result in enhanced legislative effectiveness, while careers in business and the private sector tend to be associated with less effective members. Coming out

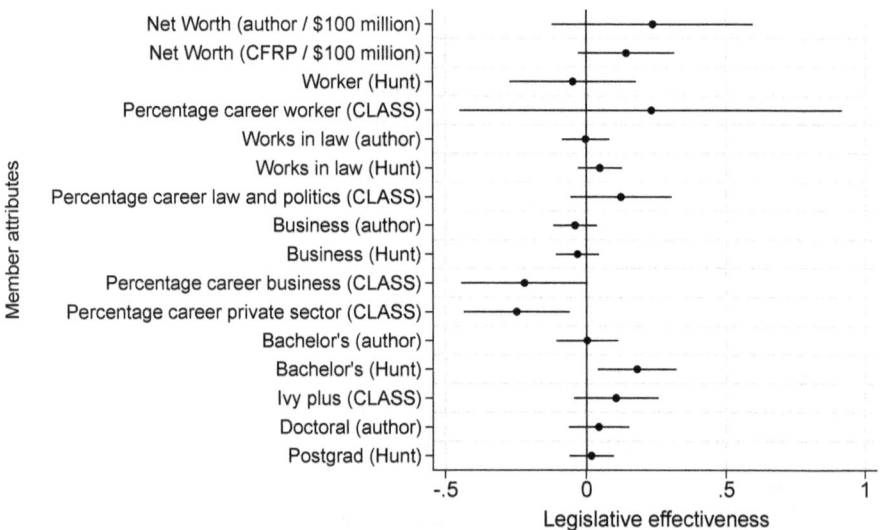

FIGURE 10.3. House members' legislative effectiveness and their net worth, occupation, and education, 1973–2014

Bars represent 95 percent confidence intervals. Author data variables cover the 103rd–110th Congresses; CLASS data (Carnes 2013) covers the 106th–110th Congresses; CFRP data (opensecrets.org) covers the 108th–113th Congresses; and Hunt (2022) data covers the 96th–111th Congresses.

of a working-class occupation has no material effect. These findings are interesting, particularly in light of some research that suggests that wealthier legislators with professional occupations are appreciably more effective (Stacy 2021).[15] It does not appear to make much difference whom less affluent Americans elect if they want an effective legislator to represent them in Congress. If they were forced to choose, however, they might be better off with lawmakers who are wealthier and better educated than most members.

A deeper dive into the legislative-effectiveness data provides further evidence to bolster the guidance, suggested by my findings, that Americans with lower incomes not vote for less affluent, blue-collar, and less educated candidates. Recall from chapter 7 that I dissected the legislative-effectiveness data to examine the capacity of House members to get the bills they sponsor through various hurdles in the legislative process. I replicate that analysis here with key measures of member net worth, occupation, and educational attainment added to Volden and Wiseman's (2014) work. The dependent variables are the number and percentage of a member's total bills and substantive and significant bills that traverse the stages of the legislative process examined in chapter 7—that is, "introduction," "action in committee," "action beyond committee," "passed House," and "became law." As I noted in the previous chapter, we should consider the successful navigation of the legislative process, particularly for important bills, evidence of legislative competency. Such action presumably requires persuading and organizing colleagues, as well as possibly other high-level strategizing—and therefore cognitive abilities and experience in white-collar fields.

Table 10.1 shows when the key independent variables generate statistically significant coefficients in the usual models of legislative effectiveness. The columns denote the models of the various stages of the legislative process, the rows the type of bills. The top panel of the table shows negative binomial regressions where the dependent variable is the number of bills, the bottom panel ordinary least squares (OLS) regressions where the dependent variable is the percentage of introduced bills. The signs describe the direction of the relationship between net worth, occupation, or education and the particular measure of effectiveness. I report only coefficients that reach $p < .05$ levels of statistical significance. I italicize findings consistent with the hypothesis that lower net worth and less educated legislators with pre-tenure careers that we might consider blue-collar are less effective.

Members with undergraduate degrees—although interestingly not doctoral degrees, which appear counterproductive—push more bills through the legislative process. Although a background in law does not seem to help members turn their legislation into public policy, such lawmakers are capable

TABLE 10.1. House members' net worth, occupation, and education and the success of their bills, 1983–2014

Number of bills introduced by a member in the category

	Introduced	Action in committee	Action beyond committee	Passed House	Became law
All bills	Business (Auth & CLASS) – Private sect. (CLASS) – Pols/law (CLASS) + Postgrad (Hunt) –	Bachelors (Hunt) +	Private sect. (CLASS) – Bachelors (Hunt) +	Private sect. (CLASS) – Bachelors (Hunt) +	Bachelors (Hunt) +
Substantive and significant bills	Business (Auth & CLASS) – Private sect. (CLASS) – Pols/law (CLASS) +	Private sect. (CLASS) – Pols/law (CLASS) + Bachelors (Hunt) +	Private sect. (CLASS) – Pols/law (CLASS) + Business (Hunt) –	Business (Auth) – Pols/law (CLASS) + Worker (CLASS) –	Worker (CLASS) –

Percentage of bills introduced by a member in the category

	Introduced	Action in committee	Action beyond committee	Passed House	Became law
All bills		Postgrad (Hunt) –	Postgrad (Auth & Hunt) –	Net worth (Auth) + Law (Auth) – Postgrad (Hunt) –	Postgrad (Auth & Hunt) – Business (CLASS) – Pols/law (CLASS) + Worker (Hunt) –
Substantive and significant bills		Business (Auth & Hunt) – Law (Auth) + Pols/law (CLASS) + Worker (CLASS) – Postgrad (Hunt) –	Business (Auth & Hunt) – Law (Auth & Hunt) + Pols/law (CLASS) + Worker (CLASS) –	Business (Hunt) – Worker (CLASS) –	

Notes: Cell entries in the first part of the table are coefficients from negative binomial regression analyses using the control variables in the model specifications reported in table 7.1, but here the dependent variables are the number of a member's bills in a Congress that traversed the various hurdles in the legislative process, and the lagged measure of legislative effectiveness has been omitted. Cell entries in the second part of the table are coefficients from OLS regression analyses using the same independent variables, but here the dependent variables are the percentage of all bills in the category introduced by the member that traversed the various hurdles in the legislative process. Author data variables cover the 103rd–110th Congresses; CLASS data (Carnes 2013) covers the 106th–110th Congresses; CFRP data (https://www.opensecrets.org) covers the 108th–113th Congresses; and Hunt (2022) data covers the 96th–111th Congresses. I report key independent variables that reach $p < .05$ levels of statistical significance in the models of legislative effectiveness using the usual variables. The sign represents the direction of the relationship between independent and dependent variable. Italicized entries denote those where the relationship was expressed in the hypothesized direction.

of passing bills further along than colleagues with other pre-tenure occupations.[16] We might speculate that these lawmakers have garnered the experience and skills necessary to craft appealing legislation, persuade colleagues, build coalitions, and advance their proposals. Careers in the private sector or business are detrimental to success, perhaps because the competencies acquired in those fields are different and unsuited to success in the legislative process. Private-sector careers can also encompass what we might consider blue-collar and lower-paid jobs (although I do not italicize these findings since this is not obviously the case). We should note that the effect of a member's net worth is not particularly important, but wealthy legislators are more likely to see their bills pass the House in the measure that is the proportion of bills sponsored.

Carnes (2013, 69–82) has argued that members with pre-tenure careers as workers seemed less effective because they had a smaller proportion of their bills enacted. He did not use the Volden and Wiseman data, but the observation is consistent with my findings. The CLASS and Hunt measures of a member's pre-tenure career as a worker produce robust negative coefficients. Workers perform poorly on both the number and percentage of bills metrics, especially on substantive and significant bills. They have less of an effect on bills that move far through the policy process, including those enacted into law, than colleagues without blue-collar backgrounds. Carnes uses such evidence to argue that members with blue-collar backgrounds are unfairly disadvantaged in some way, mainly because they lack access to the networks of likeminded colleagues that are the currency of winning legislative coalitions. Regardless, the results I present suggest that it is wealthy lawyers with lengthy political resumes and not plumbers and other private-sector employees without college degrees who are most likely to turn their own bills into public policy.

I am also interested in members' capacity to secure federal resources for their constituents—that is, their performance in distributive politics. This capacity can be viewed as a form of effectiveness. We saw in chapter 6 that low-income Americans believe their representatives should focus a great deal of attention on securing federal largesse for their constituents. We also learned that lawmakers from lower-income districts seem to do this, because they direct a disproportionately large amount of government spending to their constituents. I add separately the measures of member net worth, occupation, and education I use above and analyze the same indicators of federal resources spent in lawmakers' districts that I deployed in table 6.7—that is, the log of both all programs and so-called high-variance programs (Dynes and Huber 2015). I also use the same controls, including median district household income. There are no specifications where any variable measuring a member's personal socioeconomic characteristics generates a statistically significant coefficient. The results show that although less affluent districts receive more in the way of this type of federal spending, less wealthy, blue-collar, and less educated members are no more (or less) effective than colleagues at securing government funds for constituents.

Given the findings in this chapter, it is hard to claim that blue-collar, less affluent legislators with lower levels of formal education are more willing and capable of securing the progressive economic-policy outcomes lower-income Americans supposedly desire. They are not more liberal than colleagues, but as members of a minority group, they may lack access to the relationships required to build coalitions for their legislative agenda (Carnes 2013; Miler 2018). Lawmakers with less education and pre-tenure careers outside politics, the law, and the boardroom may also have fewer of the cognitive skills and less of the decision-making experience necessary to push their proposals through the legislative process. If the least affluent and educated of members of Congress are demonstrably less effective—and I think I have shown this claim is exaggerated a little by the literature—it is unclear how this point helps the argument that there ought to be more blue-collar legislators in Washington. When considered in light of my analysis, I interpret the view held by Carnes, Miler, and others another way. Should not Americans, including the less affluent, want their representatives to be effective? Should not they want them, therefore, to be wealthy, white-collar, and educated?

How Would We Increase the Number of Less Affluent Legislators?

We have seen that less affluent Americans do not seem to care to elect blue-collar representatives with fewer financial resources and less formal education. I have suggested this indifference makes some sense. Let us suppose, however, that it is desirable for working-class Americans to live under a Congress full of legislators who share or at least better approximate their socioeconomic characteristics. How could we bring about such a Congress?

The most obvious way would be to mandate candidate or member quotas. Governments and parties in many different parts of the world have reserved spots on ballots or seats in parliaments for women. Research suggests that these actions have material effects on the number of female candidates (Barnes and Holman 2020) and public-policy outcomes—including improved health care, decreased military spending, liberalized work-family regulations, and even reductions in tariffs on women's clothing (Betz et al. 2021; Clayton and Zetterberg 2018; Weeks 2022). But there is no apparent appetite in either party to adopt even aspirational or soft targets for the recruitment of blue-collar and low-income candidates in the United States. One obstacle is the obvious difficulty in establishing clear and defensible distinctions among candidates and legislators based upon concepts like wealth, occupation, or education. Another is the current penchant for greater gender and racial diversity in organizations across American public life. What is more, and as I have demonstrated, the progressives who are likely to be the idea's most committed advocates should have little confidence regarding the policy effects of a "working-class" or "low-income" quota.

Policymakers could incentivize low-income Americans to run for office. A simple inducement is to increase pay for elected officials. A study of American state legislators and candidates reveals, however, that salary hikes make the job of lawmaker more attractive to people from all walks of life. In fact, Carnes and Hansen (2016) find that the proportion of state legislators primarily employed in working-class jobs is actually smaller in bodies with generous compensation. Alternatively, Congress could cut members' pay to raise the opportunity costs of running for and holding office, especially on the wealthy. But this approach might also backfire. State legislatures that do not remunerate their members well attract the independently wealthy and retired, not the working class (Carnes and Hansen 2016). What is more, members generally realize the bulk of their financial rewards for congressional service upon departure, diminishing the importance of salary. This is most obviously the case for the many legislators who end up as lobbyists (Dabros 2017; Lazarus et al. 2016; Makse 2017; Vidal et al. 2012).

According to Carnes (2018, 81–87), time is an especially important resource for the less affluent. Working-class Americans often hold multiple jobs and must juggle significant family responsibilities. The prospect of campaigning, a potentially boundless activity with no guarantee of success, is off-putting. Alleviating its burdens ought to be appealing to the less affluent considering a run for Congress. Yet the proportion of lawmakers who are working class is no higher in states with publicly financed legislative elections (Carnes 2018, 178–89). Other possible reforms limiting the need to campaign, such as doing away with primaries or loosening finance restrictions to permit candidates to raise money in larger chunks, might well undermine the independence of legislators, potentially negating any plausible policy benefits brought about by the greater descriptive representation of wealth. Besides, perhaps time is not as much of a barrier to blue-collar congressional candidacies as claimed. The 2021 American Time Use Survey fielded by the Bureau of Labor Statistics reveals that people who make more money work longer hours and devote less of their day to leisure activities, presumably making it harder for them to carve out time to run for political office.[17]

Two other reforms might have more effect. Carnes (2013, 147–51; 2018, 189–206) and the American Academy of Arts and Sciences' Commission on Reimagining Our Economy outline a sort of training program for blue-collar citizens with an interest in and potential aptitude for politics. The goal is to identify and nurture promising working-class individuals. To this end, several progressive groups have created scholarship or training programs. Folke and Rickne (2023), in their study of Swedish legislators, suggest that much of this work should be done within left-of-center parties. Carnes (2018, 189–206) argues that the initial signs in the United States are positive. He points to the success of a labor candidates' "school" in getting blue-collar candidates elected to the New Jersey state legislature.

A second proposal is one rarely offered as a way of enhancing socioeconomic diversity in Congress. Increasing the membership of the House would presumably reduce the costs of winning a single seat. Carnes (2018, 129–36) shows that blue-collar candidates are more successful in contests to represent smaller districts. It is an idea many liberals have proposed.[18] Although expanding the House might increase the number of working-class legislators, however, I suspect it would not do much, if anything, to raise their proportion.

Such is life. Congress will continue to skew toward wealthy professionals and business types with college and postgraduate degrees. Carnes and others may well be correct when they suggest that the reason is discriminatory, likely a function of voters' attitudes and systemic to American elections. I have provided some evidence of inferior legislative performance by members with less formal education, net worth, and experience in white-collar fields, but it is hardly damning. Still, the socioeconomic makeup of Congress is quite understandable. The act of electing members to the House and Senate involves the evaluation of candidates for a highly competitive position that has become increasingly professionalized and appears to require significant cognitive skills demonstrated by education credentials. Asking the "average" American why there are so few poor or middle-class compatriots in Congress is like asking them why there are very few blue-collar people at the top of any business or profession. Working-class citizens have the education and training appropriate to the lower tiers of most fields—as Carnes (2018, 6–7; Carnes and Hansen 2016) has noted, there are more, although in an absolute sense still few, blue-collar lower-income lawmakers in state capitals than there are in Washington. For all the talk of Americans' anti-intellectualism and disregard of experts, we embrace technocratic principles and still believe that formal education, training, and experience are the best indicators of someone's ability to run an organization and make important decisions. Surveys repeatedly show that Americans trust scientists, educators, doctors, engineers, and others in fields that require lengthy training and high levels of education.[19] They view intensive preparation as critical to advancement and success in their own careers, whatever they do.[20] It makes sense that they would look for the same qualities in members of Congress, the people at the top of American politics.

I concur then with Donald Matthews (1954), whose book on the occupation, education, and wealth of politicians across the world included a chapter that constitutes probably the first systematic look at the subject with regard to American legislators. He wrote, "It seems understandable in a society with an accepted stratification system for the electorate to choose men with high social status to represent them in the decision-making process" (Matthews 1954, 32).

Conclusion

It is clear that wealthy Americans with impressive education credentials and reputable white-collar careers dominate Congress. The work of scholars like Carnes (2013; 2018), Grumbach (2015), and Miler (2018) suggest this demographic pattern is an important reason why the preferences of less affluent Americans do not become federal economic policy. They may be correct on certain issues and pieces of legislation. I argue, however, that descriptive underrepresentation does not explain why federal policymakers ignore the working class. I show that the interests—as they are commonly understood—and policy preferences—to the extent that they are distinct—of less affluent Americans can be and frequently are accurately and competently represented by members of Congress with advanced degrees, white-collar careers, and large bank accounts. Often these members are Democrats with liberal policy positions. Constituent attitudes shape their legislative behavior more than do personal traits. Members with blue-collar experiences, less formal education, and fewer financial means are also, if anything, a little less effective in the legislative process. Electing people like themselves to Congress might make less affluent Americans feel politically efficacious, but it could result in less competent representation.

Working-class Americans might experience marginal financial benefits if a larger number of members of Congress were like them, but that is only because Democrats would probably have a few more seats and therefore, especially in an age of partisan parity, would more likely constitute a majority. The socioeconomic composition of Congress's membership is unlikely to change much, however. No matter. Lower-income citizens do not seem to care about the demographic characteristics of their representatives. Even if we assume they want progressive economic-policy outcomes, they are justified in their insouciance. Wealthy members from professional backgrounds often hold left-of-center views, and states and districts will continue to send to Washington wealthy, white-collar, and educated individuals with the experience and skills suited to turning their constituents' wishes, whatever they are, into policy outcomes.

Counterbalance?

The Economic Policy Views of Educated and Professional Democrats

The transformation of the relationships between income and education on one hand and ideology and partisanship on the other is one of the most important and interesting recent developments in American politics. With the end of the Democrats' dominance of the South, socioeconomic status and partisanship became increasingly correlated at the national level in the 1980s and 1990s (Bartels 2008; Brooks and Brady 1999; Franko and Witko 2023b; Gelman 2009; Lewis-Beck et al. 2008, 334–48; McCarty et al. 2006; Stonecash 2006).[1] But, as we moved into the first decade of the 2000s, the connection loosened considerably (Auslen and Phillips 2024; Zacher 2024b). According to exit polls, in 2012 Democrat Barack Obama received a marginally larger proportion of the vote of those who earned between $200,000 and $250,000 than he did those who made between $50,000 and $100,000. In 2020, Joe Biden won a larger share of the vote among those who made $50,000 to $100,000 than he did those who made less than $30,000. Donald Trump captured a slightly larger percentage of the vote of those who made less than $30,000 than those who made over $200,000. He did so again in 2024. The relationship between education and partisanship has not been attenuated, it has been upended (Grossmann and Hopkins 2024; Zingher 2022a). Biden's biggest supporters in 2020 were those with an advanced degree; Trump performed best among those who had "never attended college" in all three elections in which he ran.

For the past twenty years, the proportion of Democrats and liberals we might consider "upper" class—college and often Ivy League–educated, wealthy white-collar professionals and executives—has grown considerably (Brint et al. 2022; Cavaillé 2023; Grossmann and Hopkins 2024; Zingher 2022a). With all the political advantages their economic situation and social status bring, these Americans should be in a position to provide an effective ideological counterbalance to the right's efforts to promote markets, reduce government regulations, and dilute efforts at redistribution. We know that the affluent are politically active, effectively organized, and generous donors to candidates and parties. Democratic candidates and by extension progressive economic policy should benefit from the development.

In this chapter, I examine whether these affluent Americans support left-of-center economic policies. I first test the proposition that educated liberals and Democrats take progressive positions on redistributive policy. This question is particularly interesting because for them to do so would be for them to appear to take a stance against apparent self-interest in favor of the less well-off. Second, I explore interesting differences in the attitudes of the affluent across economic policy types. Here I use a theory based upon occupation and test the hypothesis that, compared to other groups, affluent Democratic and liberal professionals take more progressive positions on economic policies of direct personal interest than they do matters likely to elevate the financial circumstances of blue-collar and low-income Americans—or, to put it differently, other people.

If affluent Democrats, a group that is largely white by race, white-collar by occupation, and coastal by residence, express preferences consistent with the interests of the working class, we might expect federal economic policy to become more liberal. We might also be in possession of evidence that American democracy is not working as it should. With champions like these, economic policy, at least in the twenty-first century, should surely be moving in a leftward direction more robustly than it is.

Do Educated Democrats Have Progressive Attitudes Toward Redistribution?

In chapter 4, I tested the proposition that less affluent Americans had liberal attitudes on economic policy. The theory, built by a sizable literature, was simple and intuitive. Redistributive policy actualized by progressive taxation and transfer payments to the poor is consistent with the material self-interest of blue-collar citizens. They are, in turn, at odds with the material self-interest of the affluent (Franko et al. 2013; Weeden and Kurzban 2017).

Recently, however, political scientists have developed theories consistent with the proposition that the affluent can support redistribution and progressive economic policy more generally. Some of these arguments rest on altruistic, patriotic, religious, or moral attitudes. Gilens and Thal (2018) show that high-income Americans can be altruistic and supportive of redistribution—

values they believe explain much of the realignment of the group to the Democratic Party. Scheve and Stasavage (2016) argue that temporal and cultural variance in the concept of fairness helps explain progressive attitudes toward taxing the wealthy. Hansen (2023) shows that support for taxing the rich is largely a function of an individual's understanding of members of the class as greedy or generous. In an echo of Inglehart's (1997) famous argument, Enke, Polborn, and Wu (2022) describe "morals" as voters' luxury goods. Only the wealthy can afford to have concern for others or broader society affect their choices; the middle and working classes must focus more practically on self-interest. Williamson (2017) shows that many Americans feel a moral imperative to pay their taxes.

Other scholars suggest support for redistribution can be consistent with the financial self-interest of the relatively well-off. Lupu and Pontusson (2011) posit that the opposition of upper- and middle-class citizens to redistribution attenuates as the gap between their incomes and those of the poor narrows. It becomes harder for them to distinguish their own material self-interest from that of others. To the contrary, MacDonald (2020a, 2020b) argues that the rich will become increasingly supportive of redistribution as inequality grows, so long as they enjoy high levels of political knowledge or trust in government—in other words, so long as they have advanced educations. Dimick, Rueda, and Stegmueller (2018) concur, finding that the rich in unequal American states support redistribution more than do those residing in more egalitarian places. The wealthy's "other-regarding" sensibilities—honed by education—also make them care about the broader macro-economy (Cavaillé 2023). They understand that the public good will improve under redistribution since an additional dollar given to a poor person has greater impact on the recipient's situation than one given to a rich person (Kuziemko et al. 2023). Cansunar (2021) proposes that affluent individuals endorse progressive tax rates when they believe others will pay disproportionately. This occurs more frequently than we might expect. Income group identification is subjective and based upon comparisons made with geographically proximate individuals. An objectively wealthy person might consider themselves middle class compared to neighbors and approve of progressive tax hikes—and even transfer payments—as a way of elevating their own financial situation within the immediate community.[2]

Regardless of explanations, recent empirical work shows that Democrats of high socioeconomic status indeed support redistributive policy quite robustly (Kuziemko et al. 2023).[3] Aviña and Blaise (2021) report that high-income Democrats, together with their less well-off co-partisans, opposed the 2017 Tax Cuts and Jobs Acts passed under Trump. Bartels (2018) deployed a poll taken shortly after Trump took office in 2017 to show that Democrats are markedly more cohesive on issues related to the nature of activist government than are Republicans. Maks-Solomon and Rigby (2020) use Americans' views on congressional roll-call votes from 2006 to 2014 to demonstrate that Democrats are unified across income groups in their progressivism on economic issues like tax cuts and the minimum wage—although quite divided on cultural and social matters such as abortion and same-sex marriage. In a similar vein, Lupton, Myers, and Thornton (2022) show that more affluent and educated Democrats demonstrate broad support for the principle of equality in several realms of policy, including the economic kind.

I focus on the effect education specifically has on the support of Democrats for redistribution in this first part of the chapter. The objective is to explore whether an advanced education shapes an individual's economic policy preferences so that they support redistribution more than their financial situation implies. As such, I am developing the observation made by several political scientists that in the twenty-first century, education drives the polarization of policy attitudes more so than does income, even after accounting for other obvious causes like party identification (Grossmann and Hopkins 2024; Zingher 2022a). The hypotheses are that highly educated Democrats are as or more progressive than other Democrats and take positions on redistribution far from their Republican equivalents.[4] As in chapter 4, the dependent variable is the ANES question asked from 1992 to 2016—"Should federal spending on welfare programs be increased, decreased, or kept about the same?" I designate supporters of increased spending with the lowest values and supporters of decreased spending with the highest values. I run a specification interacting education with party, deploying the exact same control variables I did in chapter 4.[5]

Figure 11.1 reveals the predicted probabilities of support for reducing welfare spending. When education conditions party identification, there is a clear and growing difference at the upper end of the continuum. There is little partisan distinction within the cohort of Americans with few educational credentials, but educationally accomplished Democrats are more opposed to cuts in welfare spending than all other groups. In fact, relative to other survey participants, Democrats with high levels of education are now more opposed to cuts in welfare spending than they were during the 1990s. Income, as we saw in chapter 4, tends to exert more of a direct effect on welfare-spending policy preferences.[6]

Figure 11.2 reveals the results of interactions between education and party on the same diverse CES tax questions I use in chapter 4. Higher values of the dependent variable denote support for tax cuts or opposition to tax increases.

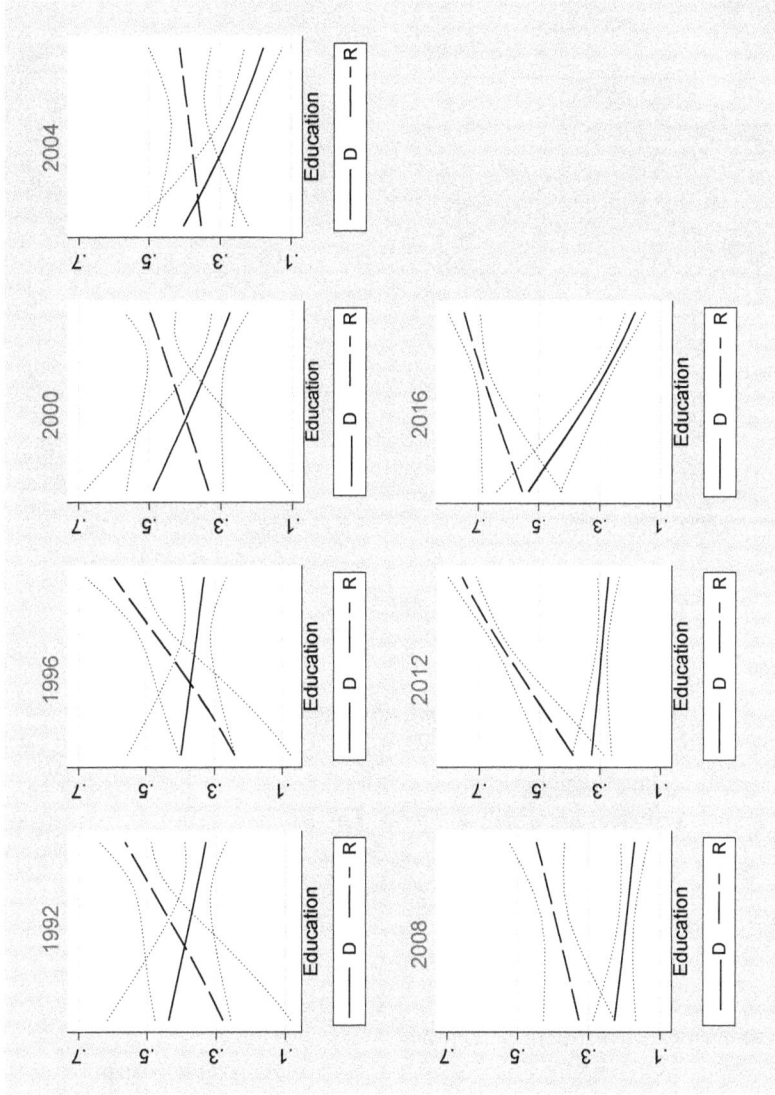

FIGURE 11.1. Effect of education when conditioned by party on attitudes regarding welfare spending, ANES 1992–2016

Higher values on the vertical axis represent predicted probability of support for decreasing welfare spending. D = Democrats, R = Republicans. Dotted lines denote 95 percent confidence intervals. ANES data can be found at https://electionstudies.org/.

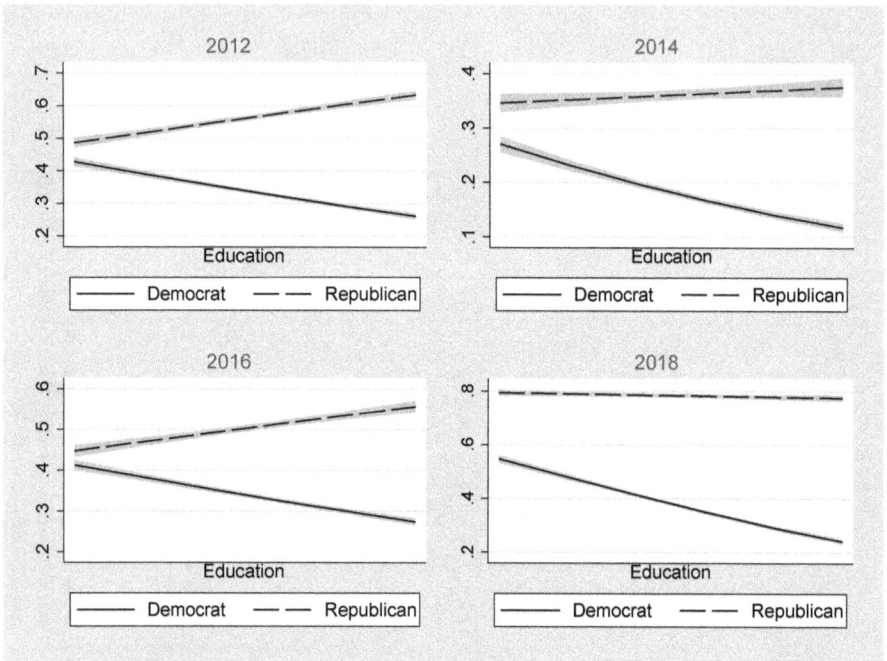

FIGURE 11.2. Effect of education when conditioned by party on attitudes regarding tax policy, CES 2012–2018

Higher values represent support for decreasing taxes. Shaded areas denote 95 percent confidence intervals. CES data can be found at https://cces.gov.harvard.edu/.

The results, showing predicted probabilities of support in an ordered logit for the most "conservative" answer to the question, confirm the basic story. Party does most to explain tax policy preferences, but education exerts indirect and weak, but nevertheless identifiable, effects. The results reveal much greater polarization at the educated end of the spectrum, with well-educated Republicans generally the most conservative group on tax policy and well-educated Democrats the most liberal. The steeper slopes for Democrats also suggest that regardless of partisanship, less educated Americans—and lower-income Americans if we recall the findings from chapter 4—take comparatively more conservative positions on taxes than they do social welfare.

These findings bring into view a broad picture of the politics surrounding redistribution in twenty-first-century America. Party and—because the two are now highly correlated—ideology increasingly determine policy preferences, and the direct effect of indicators of socioeconomic status like income and education is attenuating. The cleavage is no longer so much between classes but parties. It is wealthier Americans with the highest educational accomplishments who are most divided on these issues, and they split deeply along partisan and ideological lines. Democrats of high socioeconomic status have quite progressive views of redistribution. In fact, they appear to be to the left of co-partisans. Less affluent Democrats, in turn, have attitudes closer to those of less affluent Republicans. From my analysis, well-off Democrats could be driving much of the modest recent uptick in public support for more spending on social welfare detected by Soroka and Wlezien (2021). They may have provided a critical defense of the social-welfare status quo against assaults made by conservatives and supported by broader national opinion over the past forty years. If government is disproportionately responsive to the attitudes of affluent educated Americans, these are hopeful signs for those who wish to see progressive economic policy.[7]

But if the well-off determine American redistributive outcomes, we would expect recent decades to have provided us with sudden and dramatic changes in the direction of federal policy as the parties exchanged control of government. By contrast, working-class Americans prefer centrist positions, presumably closer to the status quo—or at least to what is implied as the status quo in the wording of survey questions—namely, in the ANES, that welfare spending should be "kept about the same" and, in the CES, that taxes should be left alone or cuts prioritized over spending hikes.[8] My analysis in chapter 2 and chapter 3 suggests that we experienced zigzags in economic policy outcomes during the first decade of the 2000s. Unlike the general leftward character of policy in the 1960s and 1970s and more conservative 1980s, however, the cumulative ideological effect since the mid-1990s has been minimal. The content of redistributive tax and, especially, social-welfare policy is today largely as it was at the turn of the millennium. On occasion there have been modest moves to the left—the raising of the rate of individual income tax on the highest bracket under Clinton and, with the ACA, Obama—and plausibly less modest darts to the right—as with the Bush tax cuts and their multiple extensions (which lowered marginal rates for nearly all taxpayers) and Trump's Tax Cut and Jobs Act (which mainly reduced corporate rates). The federal government has left social-welfare policy essentially untouched, however. The counter-majoritarian features of the policymaking process in Washington have no doubt disarmed several reform efforts, but the relatively moderate and consensual views of lower-income, less educated Americans of both parties are consistent with stasis. It is the attitudes of blue-collar citizens and not their upper-class compatriots that most closely track the trajectory of federal redistributive policy over the past several decades.

The Particular Economic Policy Preferences of Professionals

THEORY

In this section, I attempt to ascertain the economic issues on which Americans in the professions take the most progressive stances. My goal is to place the support for redistribution of an affluent and important group of Democrats in context. My theoretical approach is to think of occupation as contributing directly and independently to policy preferences. I have provided evidence that partisanship and ideology are key drivers of the left-of-center positions of upscale Democrats and liberals. Here and in chapter 4, I have also shown that income and education continue to have direct effects on economic policy preferences, even if they are increasingly attenuated. Education, particularly, conditions those exerted by party.

Professional work, Leicht (2013, 709) asserts, "involves the application of theoretical and scientific knowledge to tasks tied to core societal values; commands considerable autonomy and freedom from oversight, except from peers in the same profession; and claims to have exclusive or nearly exclusive control over a task domain linked to the application of the knowledge imparted to professionals as part of their training." Doctors, professors, lawyers, and many engineers are therefore professionals. Professionals tend to be affluent. In the CES surveys of tens of thousands of subjects that I deploy below, individuals I code as professionals have statistically significantly higher incomes than those I do not.[9] For the three surveys of 2014, 2016, and 2018, they score a mean of 7.16 on the income indicator (placing them on average in the $60,000–$70,000 group) compared to nonprofessionals' score of 6.30 (which places them in the $50,000–$60,000 group). If we use just the 2012 data when professionals inhabit a single designated occupational category, the gap in income scores is two points and places professionals in the $70,000–$80,000 cohort. A disproportionate number of professionals also work for government or nonprofits. In the 2012 CES data (the only year the survey asked about "employer category"), 53.1 percent of professionals worked in the public sector compared to 25.2 percent of nonprofessionals.

Professionals tend to be Democratic—44.7 percent compared to 38.9 percent of nonprofessionals in the CES data. Well-off Republicans and conservatives, on the other hand, are considerably more likely to be in business and the private and for-profit sectors—58.2 percent of Republicans with above-average incomes in the 2012 survey worked in the private sector, 46.5 percent of the equivalent Democrats. Regarding ideology, on a five-point scale 30.6 percent of professionals considered themselves "very conservative" or "conservative," but 35.8 percent of nonprofessionals characterized themselves this way.

Indeed, professionals constitute an increasingly powerful wing of the Democratic Party. I discussed how they dominate the congressional party in chapter 9. Engstrom and Huckfeldt (2020, 133–9) estimate the proportion of the white Democratic presidential vote that comes from Americans in what they regard as the "professional and managerial" class has increased considerably since the mid-1980s, from about 30 percent to roughly 45 percent today. Unsurprisingly, professionals are now important financial contributors to the party. According to data from Opensecrets.org, in the 1991–1992 election cycle, organized labor provided 14.6 percent of financial donations to Democratic candidates and their party. By 2019–2020, the proportion attributable to labor had collapsed so that a little less than one in fifty dollars received by the Democrats came from unions. At the same time, health care workers and lawyers/lobbyists are giving relatively more to Democrats and less to Republicans. In 1991–1992, people in the medical field gave 51.7 percent of their donations to Democrats, lawyers and lobbyists 71.9 percent. In 2019–2020, the figures were 63 percent and 77.7 percent, respectively.

It is plausible that an occupational identity—whether developed through informal networks of colleagues or formal professional associations—may push professionals to support Democratic candidates and liberal policies. As the literature cited earlier suggests, their education, moral sensibilities, and engagement with public life may generate a concern for the financial situation of those less affluent. There is also reason to believe, however, that, as a result of their occupation, professionals' personal economic interests lead them to prefer certain liberal economic policies more than others. Often deriving much of their livelihood directly from public treasuries, either through salary or by providing contractual services to or receiving grants from government, professionals like professors, doctors, engineers, and lawyers should be less averse to tax increases, including on themselves, because they perceive some tangible personal return as a result. They should be indifferent to the taxes that private-sector corporations pay. Professionals are presumably supportive of government regulation of economic activity since they make livings from fields where barriers to entry are high because of significant formal-education requirements, licensing provisions, and employment protection practices. Regulation tends to shield rather than threaten them.[10] Business leaders, except possibly those of the very largest enterprises, see government interference in markets and economic affairs as bad for commerce and profits (Broockman et al. 2019). Professionals are largely immune from government policy inhospitable to the growth of the private sector.[11]

I argue, however, that the effect of professional occupation on policy attitudes will not be as pronounced regarding some economic issues, making
employment type theoretically distinct from income, education, and other
determinants of economic-policy preferences like party and ideology. As a
function of their occupation, professionals, like wealthy business owners and
executives, will not take especially progressive positions on matters that do
little to affect them materially. Such issues include redistribution in the form
of social-welfare benefits and targeted and Keynesian tax cuts, and varie-
ties of regulatory and distributive policy designed to advance working-class
interests such as elevating the minimum wage and protecting organized labor. Other regulatory and distributive policies, on the other hand, are consistent with professionals' economic self-interest. Much regulation protects
their traditional independence from outside interference and immunity from
economic cycles. Its enforcement provides employment opportunities. Government spending on education, infrastructure, and scientific research are
critical to their livelihoods. My analysis of ANES data in the previous section
suggests that highly educated Democrats—many of whom are professionals—
take positions on social-welfare policy much closer to, and often to the left
of, those of lower-income Americans. Here I compare attitudes on different
policies and hypothesize that professionals will take more progressive positions on matters of regulatory and distributive policy of direct interest to
them than they will on economic policy that appears to promote the interests
of blue-collar Americans, including redistribution.

I am not the first to examine the influence of professional occupation on
political attitudes and behavior. Much of this research recognizes the liberal
policy preferences of professionals. Brint (1984) uncovered a growing professional class's left-wing attitudes, shaped by political socialization experienced in higher education. The work of Brooks and Manza (1997a, 1997b;
Manza and Brooks 1999) confirmed the basic finding. In a recent study, Brint,
Curran, and Mahutga (2022) reveal increasing progressivism among affluent
Democratic professionals on the economy, including redistributive policies
such as those I analyze earlier in the chapter.

SOME TESTS

Recall that I am interested in the variance within the set of economic policies
of the attitudes of professionals and posit that these views will be more liberal
on most regulatory and distributive policies than they will on issues, like labor unions, the minimum wage, expanded employment opportunities, and tax
cuts, that are presumably of lesser personal interest to them but often of greater

interest to less affluent Americans outside the professions. To push my analysis back into the Obama years, in addition to the CES occupation data referred to above I coded information about survey participants' employment provided by the ANES in 2008 and the American Panel Survey (TAPS) in 2012.[12]

In 2008, ANES collected qualitative data about occupation from open-ended questions asked of subjects. Occupations I code as professional are what the 1980 Census Occupational Category considered "professional specialty occupations"—a category that includes engineers, dentists, physicians, scientists, teachers, clergy, lawyers, etc. TAPS used twenty-eight different occupational types. Deploying the same basic principles to classify occupations as the ANES data, I code subjects in each of the categories as professional or not.[13] My study of the ANES data has a little under 1,500 cases, the TAPS data nearly a thousand cases.

The ANES survey asked respondents to provide their views of various groups of Americans by stating their position on a 100-degree "feeling thermometer," with zero denoting a "very cold or unfavorable feeling" and 100 a "very warm or favorable feeling." Theoretical work on the social construction of target populations suggests that those groups viewed as deserving by the public tend to enjoy more favorable policy outputs (Schneider and Ingram 1993; Smith and Kreitzer 2024). I posit that the more favorable professionals are toward a group, the more likely they are to support government action to advance the group's interests. Figure 11.3 reports a coefficient plot of the measure of professionals in multivariate regression models of attitudes toward a series of groups in which I control for factors such as party identification, household income, gender, and race.[14] Professionals clearly have "warm" feelings about gays, feminists, and environmentalists—to the tune of about 4–8 points more than do nonprofessionals. The results suggest approval of policies protecting the environment and promoting the rights of women and LGBT individuals—such as equal-pay requirements and anti-discrimination mandates. These kinds of regulatory policies have been central to the Democratic Party agenda and, indeed, to legislative, judicial, and executive action at the state and federal levels since the 1980s. Law no longer prohibits same-sex marriage, for example, and the federal government and many blue states enacted progressive legislation regarding emissions and other environmental issues, especially in the 1990s (Kraft 2021). However, professionals' attitudes toward Blacks, people on welfare, and labor unions are indistinguishable in statistical terms from those of nonprofessionals and their own views of big business, rich people, and, narrowly, Christian fundamentalists. The findings are consistent with the contention that professionals prefer policymakers to focus on environmental and civil rights regulations rather than on redistributive matters and labor interests.

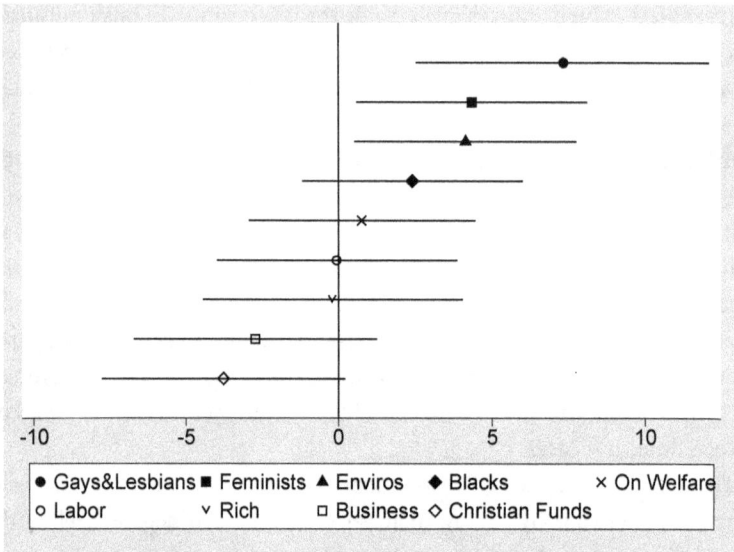

FIGURE 11.3. Professionals' attitudes toward different groups, ANES 2008
Data are regression coefficients for the professional dummy variable. Bars are 95 percent confidence intervals. ANES data can be found at https://electionstudies.org/.

I use the TAPS data to examine attitudes about seven policies. The responses form ordinal dependent variables in which higher values denote increasingly conservative attitudes. Negative coefficients in the results I report in figure 11.4 therefore signify that professionals have more progressive attitudes about the policy in question than do nonprofessionals. The policies are: reducing government spending on scientific research, reducing spending on education, reducing government regulation of business, increasing efforts by government to reduce income inequality, providing a federal guarantee of a higher minimum wage, reducing funding for programs that help lower-income Americans, and raising income taxes for those who make over $250,000 annually.[15] I deploy the same controls as in the ANES analysis.

The occupation variable generates a statistically significant coefficient for only three policies. Professionals are appreciably more liberal when it comes to regulation of business and the distributive policies of spending on education and scientific research. They "disapprove" more than do nonprofessionals of efforts to dilute government regulation of business by a margin of 37.6 percent to 28.6 percent; they disapprove more of reducing funding for education by a margin of 68.7 percent to 58.3 percent; and they disapprove more of reducing scientific-research funding by a margin of 41.4 percent to 38.3 percent. On all other policies, professionals' attitudes are indistinguishable from those of nonprofessionals, including government efforts to lessen inequality, raise the minimum wage, and increase spending to help lower-income Americans. The results are consistent with the proposition that professionals take liberal positions on distributive and regulatory policy but not redistribution and, in turn, with an argument their elevated position of importance within the Democratic Party has resulted in a diminished focus on the economic interests of the working class.

I turn now to the more recent and larger dataset, the CES. CES began asking questions about occupation in 2012. That year, it asked respondents to place themselves in one of fourteen occupational categories, including "professional (lawyer, doctor, teacher, engineer)." It also asked people about the kind of place they worked, to which, of nine categories in total, respondents could respond "private firm—for profit," "private firm—nonprofit," or "government."[16] From 2014–2018, CES asked only about occupation and used twenty-three categories.[17] In these surveys, I code as professional "professional and technical services," "education services," and "health care and social assistance." I subject the CES data to a series of tests of the hypotheses that professionals take more liberal positions on some economic policies, particularly certain distributive and regulatory matters, than their fellow Americans, but that their position on

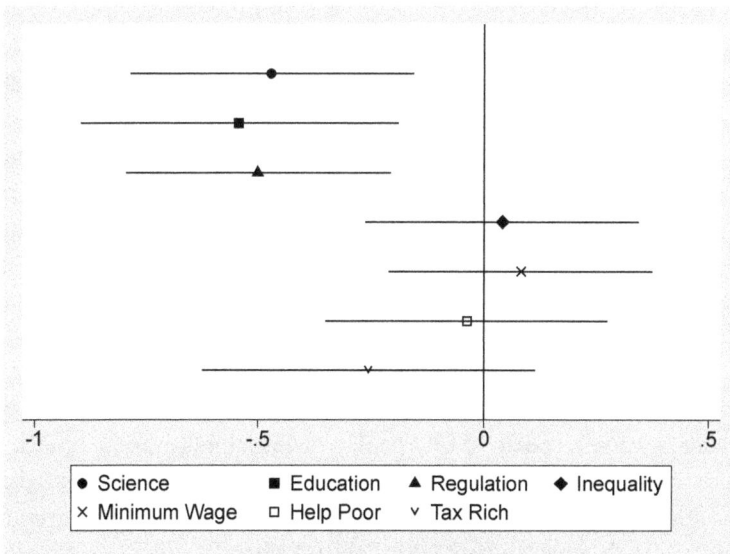

FIGURE 11.4. Professionals' attitudes toward different policies, TAPS 2012
Data are regression coefficients for the professional dummy variable. Higher values denote conservative responses. Bars are 95 percent confidence intervals. TAPS data can be found at https://wc.wustl.edu /taps-data-archive.

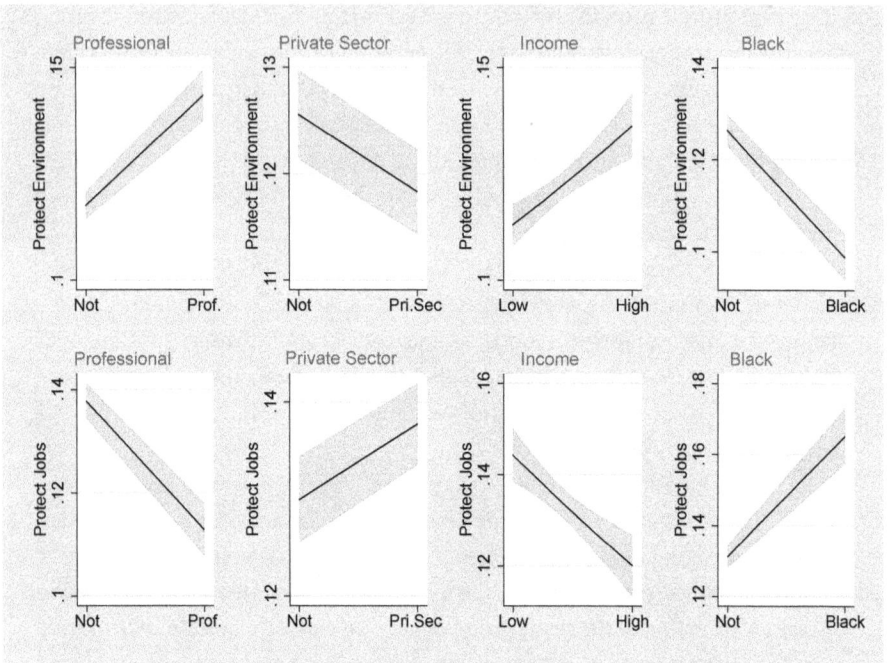

FIGURE 11.5. Group attitudes toward policies to protect the environment and jobs, CES 2012
Data are predicted probabilities. The predicted probability of the groups' members wishing to protect the environment is reported in the upper panel, to protect jobs in the lower panel. Shaded areas are 95 percent confidence intervals. CES data can be found at https://cces.gov.harvard.edu/.

issues directly related to the economic interests of blue-collar citizens, including redistributive policy, is no different from others'.

I first examine the effect of professional occupation on answers to an interesting question about the trade-off between environmental protection and jobs—a question that CES presented to its subjects in 2012. The question asked respondents if they thought it was "much more important to protect the environment even if we lose jobs and get a lower standard of living" (coded "1"), "the environment is somewhat more important (than jobs)," the two are "about the same" in importance, "the economy is somewhat more important," or it is "much more important to protect jobs, even if the environment is worse" (coded "5").[18] I deploy my usual multivariate model, this time as an ordinal logit, and, in figure 11.5, report the changes in predicted probabilities of providing the responses that it is "much more important" to protect either the environment (1) or jobs (5) when I manipulate the professional occupation, place of employment, income, and race variables.

It is quite clear that professionals' views are different from those of private-sector workers and low-income and Black Americans. The effect of profession is also greater in magnitude than the effects of the other three variables. Roughly one in nine professionals assigned the greatest value to protecting jobs, while about one in seven nonprofessionals did. These figures compare to approximately one in eight Blacks as opposed to one in ten whites, and one in seven respondents with a family income between $30,000 and $40,000 as opposed to one in eight receiving between $200,000 and $250,000. Whereas Blacks and low-income Americans place greater emphasis on protecting jobs, professionals are markedly more concerned with environmental protection. Here is evidence of a clear distinction between the policy views of professionals and the expressed preferences of less affluent Americans.

An analysis of a 2016 CES question about the minimum wage reveals similar differences in the economic policy preferences of professionals and others. Asked whether, if they were a member of Congress, they would favor or oppose an increase in the minimum wage to $12 an hour by 2020, a significant majority of respondents supported the idea.[19] Using the same variables in the multivariate analysis undertaken above, however, a logit model generates for professionals a statistically insignificant coefficient—revealing them to be indifferent regarding the policy change. Figure 11.6 suggests that the direct effect of income

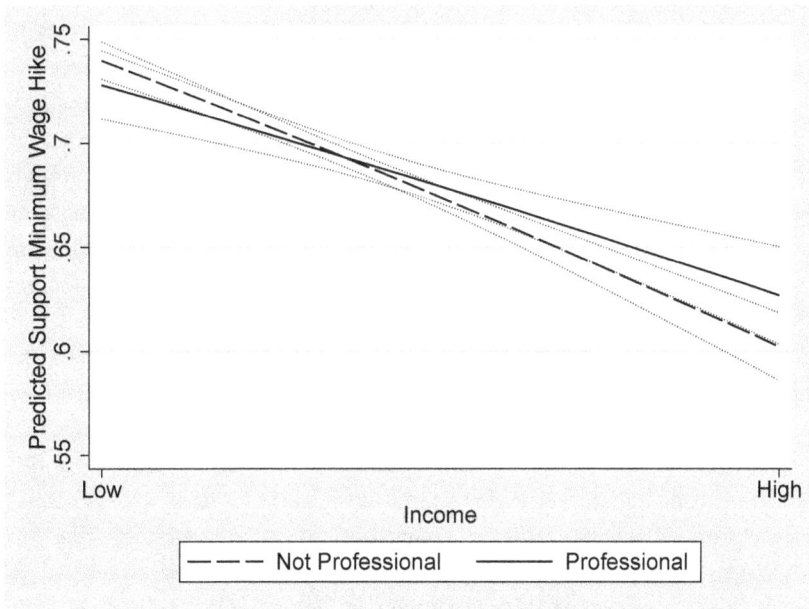

FIGURE 11.6. Conditioning effect of professional occupation on income and attitudes toward a minimum-wage increase, CES 2016
Data are predicted probabilities. Dotted lines are 95 percent confidence intervals. CES data can be found at https://cces.gov.harvard.edu/.

has a greater effect on preferences than professional occupation does. When income and professional occupation are interacted, the results show that there is no value of the income variable for which a professional prefers a minimum wage hike more than a nonprofessional does. Participants with incomes below $60,000 (categories 1–6), on the other hand, support the proposed increase markedly more than do those with incomes above $100,000 (categories 10–16). Women, Blacks, Latinos, single people, and individuals in union families also disproportionately support increasing the minimum wage. Like low-income citizens, they are all considered core Democratic constituencies. Professionals are distinctly at odds with them on this important economic issue.

Finally, I look at support for federal spending on several types of policies using the 2016 and 2018 CES surveys. Again, I expect professionals to take more progressive positions than nonprofessionals on most issues, but their support for increased spending on matters of direct interest to less affluent Americans to be subdued relative to both other policies and support from nonprofessionals. CES asked, "State legislatures must make choices when making spending decisions on important state programs. Would you like your legislature to increase or decrease spending on the five areas below?" The "areas" are "welfare," "healthcare," "education," "law enforcement," and "transportation/infrastructure." Figure 11.7 reveals the percentage of professionals (who collectively amounted to between 13,106 and 13,122 subjects in 2016 and 13,416 to 13,433 in 2018, depending on the question) who wanted to "greatly" or "slightly" decrease spending in the area, subtracted from the percentage who wanted to "greatly" or "slightly" increase spending. Bars above the line denote a general preference for a spending increase. Professionals would most prefer to invest in the three policy areas where they dominate employment—or are at least the highest paid: education, infrastructure (on which many engineers work), and health care. There is less appetite to spend state government dollars on law enforcement and particularly welfare.

Figure 11.8 reports, for both 2016 and 2018, the differences between the predicted probabilities of professionals and nonprofessionals stating that they supported greatly or slightly increasing state government spending on these five issues. I use the same basic multivariate model I have previously in this section. Professionals' preferences are only materially different from those of nonprofessionals on health and education, where they are more likely to want greater state spending. These are two fields with a large presence of professionals, more so than law enforcement, where spending is likely to go to police departments and certainly not to their private clients, and possibly more so than infrastructure, where construction companies and their blue-collar employees seem as likely to experience gains as are engineers. Note

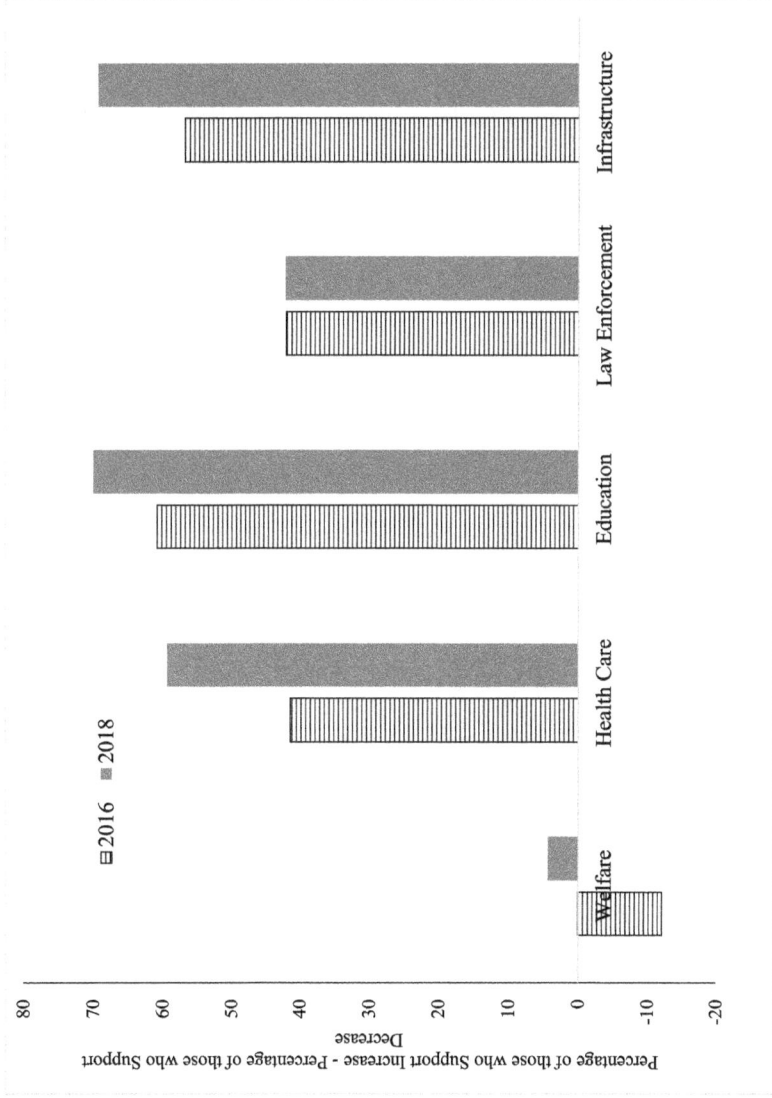

FIGURE 11.7. Professionals' attitudes toward state spending increases and decreases on five policies, CES 2016–2018 Figures are the proportion of professionals who want to decrease spending subtracted from the proportion who want to increase spending. CES data can be found at https://cces.gov.harvard.edu/.

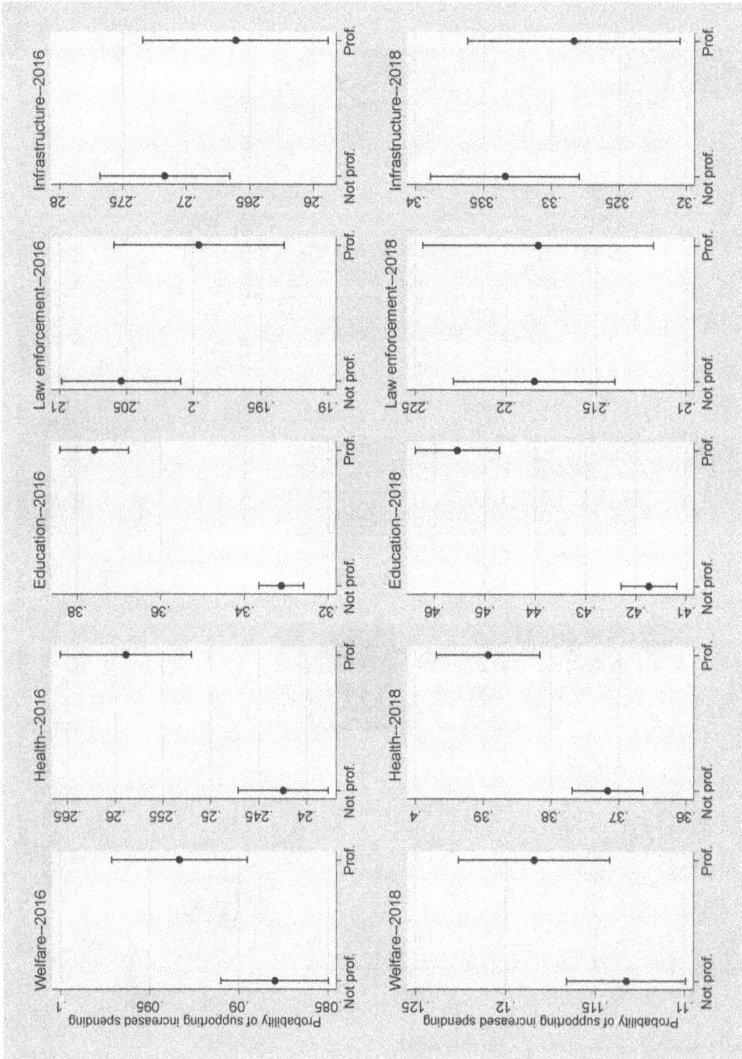

FIGURE 11.8. Professionals' views of increased state government spending on five policy areas, CES 2016–2018

Data are predicted probabilities of respondents wanting to "greatly" or "slightly" increase state spending. Prediction for professionals is on the right, for nonprofessionals on the left. Bars are 95 percent confidence intervals. CES data can be found at https://cces.gov.harvard.edu/.

that professionals are no more likely than nonprofessionals to desire that state governments greatly increase spending on social welfare. Any recent growth in support from affluent Democrats for more progressive social-welfare policy does not seem to be a function of occupation and professionals' expanding importance within the party.

Several important news stories of the time may also have affected respondents' attitudes toward government spending on law enforcement. The high-profile deaths of Black men at the hands of white officers contributed to widespread public support for the Black Lives Matter movement and related calls to "defund," or at least rein in, police forces. Even with the issue racialized in the late 2010s, professionals' indistinguishable views of spending on law enforcement appeared out of step with those of Black Americans, another important component of today's Democratic Party coalition. Black respondents were materially more likely to want states to increase spending on law enforcement in both years—by 4.5 percentage points over whites in 2018.

Conclusion

Rudimentary glances at American political statistics—exit polls, surveys of attitudes, election returns—reveal a clear shift in the ideology and partisanship of many Americans of high socioeconomic status. They have become increasingly liberal and Democratic—a process that has accelerated in the Trump era. Many affluent and educated progressive Democrats are professionals and work as doctors, lawyers, professors and teachers, or engineers. Their ideology and partisanship suggest that they desire left-of-center economic policy. Like other well-off Americans, they vote habitually, give significant amounts to candidates and parties, and are politically active. They should have considerable influence over the Democratic Party and policy outputs. That economic inequality continues and that the federal government has left untouched many of the conservative policies of the 1980s and 1990s are likely signs that American democracy ignores this large and influential group of liberals.

Educated and professional Democrats are the subject of this chapter. I show that higher levels of education actually make Democrats increasingly supportive of social-welfare spending, especially in recent years. The same liberalism is seen on taxes, although to a lesser degree. Moreover, less educated Americans take more moderate positions on welfare and taxes than Americans with significant education credentials do, and partisanship does less to shape their economic policy preferences. The stasis on social-welfare policy and slight rightward drift on taxes over the past thirty years seem as much in keeping with the views of less affluent Americans as they do the wealthy.

Much of the chapter focuses on a specific group of generally well-off Democrats and reputed progressives, those in professional occupations. I hypothesize that their liberal economic policy views are conspicuous on matters of direct interest to their personal circumstances and occupation. Policy advancing the apparent interests of the less affluent—such as unemployment insurance, the minimum wage, and the rights of organized labor—are of lesser concern, evoking views that are, at least compared to those of nonprofessionals, more ideologically moderate. A comprehensive review of professionals' political and policy attitudes over the past decade or so confirms the expectations. Professionals have favorable views of regulations that promote the environment and civil rights and government spending on health care and education. They are no more mindful than the general population, however, of policies raising the minimum wage, creating jobs, and advancing the interests of labor unions.

Political Science, American Democracy, and the Future of Inequality

Concluding Thoughts

Since the turn of the millennium, scholars have produced a great deal of research on the political causes of the economic inequality that is a central feature of modern American life. The outline of a model extends from it. The affluent—those who enjoy high incomes and net worth, own homes, work in white-collar occupations, and have advanced education credentials—donate more to campaigns, are politically active and organized, and turn out to vote in significant numbers. Their kind populate positions of power in Washington. As a result, they are fully equipped to exert disproportionate and possibly unfair influence over elections and elected officials. Legislation promoting their economic interests advances through the legislative process and becomes public policy.

The political system's formal institutions, several of which have countermajoritarian features, facilitate this process. Political inequality begets economic inequality and, as the well-off get richer, so the system amplifies their advantages and the rest of America gets, at least in relative terms, poorer. This trend is evidence—which we can add to such things as gerrymandering, institutionalized racism, and eroding voting rights—of what has come to be known as our "backsliding" democracy and "new political economy."

I challenge the veracity of this account. I think my analysis shows that it is an exaggeration to claim that the American economy reflects a malfunctioning and unjust political system. The views of the public and the workings of representative democracy have largely provided us with the economy most of us want, or at the very least the one we profess we want.

My approach inevitably omits examination of certain important elements of the full model. Institutions are sometimes absent. I do not analyze important constitutional features like federalism and the separation of powers or procedures like the many veto points in the lawmaking process. I do not really look at interest group politics—such as the lobbying and campaign finance activity that appears important to economic-policy outcomes (Becher and Stegmueller 2023). There is discussion but little treatment of political behavior outside voting. There is no significant exploration of executive agencies and the courts, both of which contribute to the making of federal economic policy. State and local governments are not the subject of much examination either—and recent research suggests that they do not represent their publics well and contribute to economic inequality (Franko and Witko 2018; Grumbach 2022; Grumbach et al. 2022; Hertel-Fernandez 2019; Schaffner et al. 2020). I do look at race, ethnicity, and gender, but they are in the background.

I do not, therefore, construct a coherent competing model. I present a general defense of American democracy. I am concerned with whether economic policy, in the behavior of elected officials and the content of rules and laws, reflects mass attitudes and particularly the views of less affluent Americans. In chapters 2 and 3, I show this policy to be reasonably responsive to public opinion during the postwar era. This is the case in aggregate, for particular programmatic approaches, and for important individual policies. In chapters 4 and 5, I reveal less affluent Americans to have economic policy preferences that are not always clear and consistent, but also more like those of their better-off compatriots than political science tends to believe. In chapter 6, I argue that poorer Americans are particularly interested in distributive policy. Chapters 7 and 8 focus on the substantive representation of what we customarily understand as less affluent Americans' progressive economic-policy interests. I demonstrate that households with lower incomes are neither gerrymandered nor malapportioned. The least effective legislators do not represent them. Lawmakers from poorer districts do not especially ignore their constituents. The focus of chapters 9 and 10 is descriptive representation. Here I show that less affluent Americans do not seem to care much that members of Congress are not like them. Their indifference may be because the few blue-collar legislators there are do not have appreciably liberal voting records and are, if anything, less effective than their colleagues. Chapter 11 looks at the economic-policy attitudes of educated Democrats within the electorate, especially those with professional occupations. I show them to be more liberal than less affluent co-partisans on some issues but comparatively uninterested in policy designed to advance the interests of the working class.

I do address several specific assertions and implications of the research used to build the established model, however. I deploy different data and take different theoretical approaches to come to the conclusion the substantive representation of less affluent Americans is stronger than the literature implies, for example. In other places, I merely emphasize a point that existing research has quietly or indirectly made; I do so, I believe, most notably in chapter 6, where I show less affluent Americans and their representatives to be particularly interested in distributive policy, and in chapter 4, where I reveal working-class Americans to have ideologically inconsistent and incoherent economic-policy attitudes. I also bring new topics of discussion to the debate. This is the case with my examination of the policy attitudes of professionals, the views of working-class Americans regarding the relative net worth of candidates, and the occupational backgrounds of members of Congress.

I am not alone in doubting the consensus. I have cited the work of a number of political scientists who have presented evidence inconsistent with the model throughout the book (Branham et al. 2017; Enns 2015; Grossmann et al. 2021; Ura and Ellis 2008; Soroka and Wlezien 2008, 2011). The scholarship has not synthesized the critique into a broad response, however. This account is my contribution. Parts of the dominant argument are evidently accurate, but its conclusions are often simplistic, and its tone exaggerates and distorts.

My contention begs the question: If the consensus is a misrepresentation, how did this model of the relationship between American politics and economic inequality become so influential? I suggest two principal reasons. The first concerns the way we think about public opinion. Policy preferences can be difficult to discern, and researchers often derive them from an understanding of interests. With regard to economic policy, personal material gain makes an intuitively appealing substitute for unobserved policy attitudes. Political science often assumes that less affluent Americans have progressive views of the economy, even when opinions are unrevealed.

I think this approach is simplistic, at best. Researchers frequently explain less affluent Americans' unanticipated moderate or conservative expressed economic policy preferences as a kind of cognitive deficiency that ranges from an unhealthy obsession with cultural matters (Frank 2004; Gest 2016) to an intuitive rather than rational approach to politics (Oliver and Wood 2018). Alternatively, it is the consequence of the undue influence of powerful socioeconomic groups assisted by a conservative media machine (Jacobs et al. 2021; Kimmel and Rader 2021). In many ways, this explanation of the derivation of less affluent Americans' economic policy views is all somewhat beside the point. When policymakers respond to expressed preferences, they are acting in a manner consistent with representative democracy.

What is more, I have shown differences of opinion between socioeconomic groups on matters of distributive policy and suggest that the less affluent may consider such issues to be equally as important as policy characterized as redistributive. I have revealed that differences in attitudes across groups on many economic issues are often quite small. Many political scientists argue that working- and middle-class Americans are in reality liberal on economic policy; they just like to think of themselves as conservatives. They are "symbolically conservative" but "operationally liberal" (Ellis and Stimson 2012). I am not sure that assessment is entirely accurate. Americans, regardless of their personal financial circumstances, do not support inequality, but they do not seem to think much about it either. They focus on economic issues separately. They agree that government should address macroeconomic conditions like high unemployment and inflation but feel that it should do so with a delicate touch. They dislike taxes. They do not like spending on many government programs, particularly those we might call social welfare, but they wish to invest in public goods like education, transportation, and scientific research, especially in their own communities. They are sometimes willing to endorse efforts to enact progressive policies on energy, the environment, and health care, albeit within a regulatory framework using subsidies and tax incentives to encourage private action rather than as fully public enterprises.

Second, academic culture and institutions play a role. In a recent book, Grossmann (2021) argues that social science is continually improving, not least because of new methods, huge datasets, and generations of superbly trained scholars. The social scientists surveyed for his project, however, voiced concerns that their disciplines reward narrow, technical, and inaccessible empirical work prepared for an academic publishing industry geared to short, disparate articles rather than to broader efforts to synthesize information, reconcile competing models, and address fundamental questions (Grossmann 2021, 193–208, 244–50). As areas of inquiry fragment into autonomous and highly specialized subfields, researchers are motivated to discover significant effects consistent with established theories rather than break new ground (Fanelli 2012; Grossmann 2021). The problem of confirmation bias deepens as academics, particularly the risk averse at the beginning of their careers, seek affirmation from the close community of peers in their subfield (Grossmann 2021). Once the political science model of economic inequality gained momentum, therefore, scholars in this emerging subject of study were content to pile on.

Political scientists have other prejudices. I suspect the field draws many young people because they believe that politics matters and they can deliver positive results. Although their academic work is unlikely to have material impact, a reality regretted by Hersh (2020), they often go about it diligently. They view societal problems as pervasive and largely the product of certain groups' powerlessness. They look for political solutions in the form of more democracy, the antidote not only to gerrymandering, voter identification laws, the Electoral College, and the Senate filibuster, but ostensibly also to nonpolitical phenomena such as economic inequality. To observers with traditional liberal views, a democratic economy is rights-based and largely detached from politics and free of government interference. To many of today's social scientists, a democratic economy is organized by the state on behalf of popular majorities.

The Consortium on the American Political Economy (CAPE) is a project in this vein.[1] Its affiliates' approach in a recent edited volume, *The American Political Economy*, is to identify key economic problems of the United States' twenty-first-century market economy such as racial polarization, the concentration of corporate wealth, and demoralized labor unions (Hacker et al. 2022a). They then propose broad political solutions—including congressional reform, election of progressive candidates, and mobilization of blue-collar, Black, and Latino Americans. These solutions make sense for a country that considers itself democratic but that operates what the authors claim is a self-evidently undemocratic economy.

Political scientists are Democrats with a capital D as well. The American Political Science Association (APSA), the discipline's preeminent professional organization, does not provide data on the political affiliations, behavior, and views of its members. Research suggests that a significant majority of professors and other researchers in the field are liberal by ideology and Democratic by partisanship, however (Atkeson and Taylor 2019; Shields and Dunn 2018). Just like the other human beings whom political scientists study, their personal biases presumably affect their work. They are likely to view economic inequality as undesirable and manufactured. Questions and findings consistent with their political views attract them.

A sizable academic community has, as a result, built up around the proposition that politics are culpable for economic inequality and that more democracy is the appropriate response. In 2004, APSA convened a task force of fifteen highly regarded professors to examine "Inequality and American Democracy." The group recommended policies designed to end the wealthy's purported monopoly on political power and facilitate participation of low-income and minority Americans in the country's politics. Its report generated a library of research on the theme, including contributions from a number of the task force's most prominent members such as Larry Bartels, Benjamin Page, and Theda Skocpol, as well as recent bestsellers written for popular audiences by academics such as Barbara Walter (2022) and Steven Levitsky and Daniel Ziblatt (2018, 2023). The Russell Sage Foundation's program on "Social, Political, and Economic Inequality" and the William and Flora Hewlett

Foundation's "Economy and Society" initiative fund much of this work. Organizations like CAPE, Stanford University's Center for a New Moral Political Economy, the City University of New York's Stone Center on Socio-Economic Inequality, and the looser network of scholars at the History and Political Economy Project promote it. The prestigious American Academy of Arts and Sciences' Commission on Reimagining Our Economy issued a report in 2023 calling for political solutions to the problem of economic inequality. APSA has a section on "Class and Inequality" that arranges teaching and research conferences on the relationship between American politics and the American economy. Political-science departments have begun hiring people to work specifically on matters related to inequality, including its economic manifestation. They have recently launched programs of study on the politics and policy of "inequality" or "poverty." Some "activist" scholars have integrated inequality into broad and cohesive curricula and research agendas alongside election administration, climate change, and criminal-justice policy—even though it is unclear whether poorer Americans will see material gains from such reforms. It is not surprising that questioning the literature's core claims is unappealing to political scientists interested in professional advancement.

Trump, Biden, Trump, and the Future of Inequality

I have in effect argued that Americans want and have a market-like economy characterized by low tax rates and moderate regulation. It is distributive rather than redistributive in nature, with few government expenditures on social welfare but significant sums directed toward public goods such as education, transportation, and defense.

The past several years have seen challenges to both public attitudes and this economic model, however. In 2016, Americans elected Donald Trump as president. Several of his economic ideas challenged Republican orthodoxy, particularly on immigration and trade. Trump quite clearly opposed the free flow of goods and people across the country's borders. He also gave up on revocation of the ACA, perhaps with a nod to Americans' growing belief that government should provide more health care, and he was clearly not tempted to reprise Republican George W. Bush's aborted semi-privatization of Social Security.

The 2018 and 2020 elections were better for Democrats, and federal economic policy shifted to the left. Bipartisan coalitions enacted several rounds of COVID-19 relief under both Trump and his successor, Joe Biden. Congress approved about $5.5 trillion in spending outside the regular appropriations process from the beginning of the pandemic until the 2022 midterms. But the president and legislative Democrats wanted to go further than stimulus checks, unemployment relief, tax breaks for low-income citizens, small-business loans, and the roughly $1.1 trillion bipartisan infrastructure bill—designed to modernize roads, rail transportation, and broadband—passed in 2021. Progressives, energized by a young class of left-of-center lawmakers and encouraged by Sen. Bernie Sanders's two presidential campaigns, continued to push for the "Green New Deal," a sprawling plan to provide free college, a single-payer healthcare system (or "Medicare for All"), and 100 percent clean energy by 2030. With greater unity, Democrats proposed the more modest $3.5 trillion Build Back Better (BBB) Act. The plan had many components, including projects to combat climate change, finance apprenticeships, provide universal preschool, build over a million units of affordable housing, support four weeks of medical and family leave, and expand benefits for social care. Higher corporate levies and a new surtax on the very wealthy would pay for it. According to many surveys, the public appeared supportive. Most polls through the winter of 2021–2022 showed a plurality of Americans favoring BBB. Stimson's policy mood, first discussed in chapter 2, registered its most liberal score ever in 2020.

In many ways, however, things have not changed. In late 2017, Trump forced though package of sizable tax cuts, particularly for corporations. Spending on public goods like education, transportation, and scientific research undertaken by agencies like the National Science Foundation and NASA remained roughly constant through his first term in office. Trump worked hard to reduce regulations, particularly through reversals of Obama-era edicts, aggressive use of the Congressional Review Act, and the promulgation of an executive order requiring the rescission of two rules for every new one issued.

Biden's BBB, moreover, did not call for significant increases to social-welfare benefits but for assistance to working parents of all income groups. It proposed capital investments and targeted subsidies to specific parts of the economy, such as alternative energy and electric vehicles. In addition to the surtax on the wealthy and a slight increase in corporate tax rates, the legislation sought to increase child tax care credits and the state and local tax deductions to individual federal income tax, a change that would benefit affluent residents of high-tax blue states like California and New York. And, with Republican opposition solid, pivotal Democrats wavering, and President Biden's approval ratings dropping precipitously in the face of the highest inflation rate in four decades, BBB languished. Democrats reinvented it as the IRA and passed the bill in August 2022 with significant investments in health care and clean energy and other strategies to combat climate change. As an accompaniment to Trump's protectionist trade policies, the legislation formed what many observers called a new American industrial policy—a term also attached to the CHIPS and Science Act, which allocated $280 billion for research and manufacturing in semiconductors. Still, at $485 billion, the IRA spent around $300 billion less in nominal dollars than the ARRA enacted thirteen years before had, and, reflecting centrist impulses, it was more than paid for—with many of the offsets, such as plans to allow Medicare to negotiate directly with drug companies and the IRS to invigorate enforcement, manifest as savings rather than revenue enhancements. When congressional Republicans took a swipe at "Bidenomics" in their 2023 debt-ceiling deal, the Democrats were able to protect the climate and energy provisions of the IRA but could not exempt some social-welfare programs from mandatory work requirements.

Critics of the postwar American economic consensus took comfort in the nominations of Trump and Vice President Kamala Harris as the parties' presidential candidates in 2024. Trump said he would seek further cuts to the corporate tax rate, but he also doubled down on his first-term trade policies. Harris, who by measures of ideology derived from congressional roll-call votes used throughout this book was one of the most liberal senators during her time in the upper body, offered, among a laundry list of proposals, policies to control rent, food, energy, and drug prices, provide down-payment assistance to first-time homebuyers, and eliminate medical debt. Republicans inevitably called her ideas radical, but, for the most part, they were quite popular, at least when first announced.[2] Still, Harris consciously avoided advocating moves to redistribute wealth or meaningfully alter important features of the economy. She also lost, and many Black, Latino, and low-income voters appeared to defect from the Democratic coalition. As he embarked on a second term, Trump led a regime forged by an electorate with little appetite for meaningful economic change, at least not in a leftward direction.

To be sure, polls suggest that Americans, particularly millennials and Gen Z, are increasingly hostile to capitalism and supportive of progressive policies. A *Wall Street Journal*/NORC survey fielded in the fall of 2023 reported that 36 percent of respondents felt the American Dream—of working hard and getting ahead—"still holds true," nine percentage points fewer than the respondents who determined that "it once held true but not anymore."[3] Organized labor, moreover, appears to have a pulse. Approximately half a million American workers walked off their jobs in 2023. Yet despite a tight labor market, the broader union movement is feeble, and membership remains at historic lows. The economy's general state, including its tenacious inequality, continues to worry many experts, especially those on the left. They believe that our electoral and governmental institutions have calcified and perpetuate the political and therefore economic advantages enjoyed by the affluent.

American public opinion can be fluid, as significant changes in citizens' attitudes toward issues such as same-sex marriage, marijuana legalization, and the death penalty over the past two decades attest. But on the economy, mass views have yielded little since turning to the right somewhat in the 1970s, despite occasional liberal and conservative interludes. Americans, particularly the less affluent, often express ambiguous and contradictory views on individual economic issues as well as abstract economic objectives. There is little evidence that they wish to change the contours of our postwar economy, one characterized by low taxes, moderate regulation, often-generous support of public goods, and, despite an increasing tolerance for government debt, relatively little redistribution, at least when compared to the country's European peers. For the most part, the working class accept the economy's central features. Progressives should understand that it is the views of the public, and not our electoral and governmental institutions, that constitute the biggest, quite possibly insurmountable, obstacle to their efforts to overhaul the American economy.

Notes

Chapter 1

1. See, for example, his remarks on economic mobility to the Center for American Progress on December 4, 2013, in Washington, DC, released by the White House Office of the Press Secretary and archived at https://obamawhitehouse.archives.gov/the-press-office/2013/12/04/remarks-president-economic-mobility.

2. It is impossible to cite even a representative sample of the social science literature on modern American inequality. Some books on the topic that have influenced elite and popular opinion on the topic include Atkinson (2015), Bartels (2008, 2016), DiMaggio (2021), Gilens (2012), Hacker and Pierson (2010, 2020), Noah (2012), Page and Gilens (2017), Reich (2020), Schlozman et al. (2018), Stewart (2021), and Stiglitz (2012). I will discuss many of these works throughout my book. I think it is fair to say the consensus is that politics, if they did not create inequality, surely exacerbate it tremendously.

3. Most prominent among the literature consistent with this basic model of America's politics and economy are works by Franko et al. (2016), Gilens (2012), Grumbach et al. (2022), Hacker and Pierson (2010, 2016, 2020), Hasen (2016), Noah (2012), Mayer (2016), Peterson and Grose (2020), Stewart (2021), and Verba et al. (1995).

4. Many scholars have observed this fact of American political life, including Brady et al. (1995), Campbell et al. (1960), Ellis (2017, 35–56), Franko et al. (2016), Hall and Yoder (2022), Leighley and Nagler (2014), Ojeda (2018), Schlozman et al. (2012, 2018), Soss and Jacobs (2009), and Verba and Nie (1972). It also played a prominent role in an important report on democracy and inequality published by the American Political Science Association in 2004 (Task Force on Inequality and American Democracy 2004).

5. This point is also uncontroversial. See Barber (2022), Barber et al. (2017), Broockman and Malhotra (2020), Bartels (2016), Bonica et al. (2013), Bonica (2014), Canes-Wrone and Miller (2022), Crosson et al. (2020), Gimpel et al. (2008), Kalla and Broockman (2016), Larcinese and Parmigiani (2023), Magleby et al. (2018), Page et al. (2018), Schlozman et al. (2012, 2018), and Selling (2023).

6. On this topic, we can again point to a large literature. Influential examples include Becher and Stegmueller (2023), Broockman and Skovron (2018), Dalton (2017), Gilens (2012), and Schlozman et al. (2012, 2018).

7. Some research suggests the ultra-wealthy are especially effective at shaping policy (Broockman et al. 2019; Burris 2000; Page et al. 2013; Page et al. 2018; Winters and Page 2009).

8. The Dēmos report, published in February 2013, is *Stacked Deck: How the Dominance of Politics by the Affluent and Business Undermines Economic Mobility in America*, by David Callahan and J. Mijin Cha, https://www.demos.org/sites/default/files/publications/StackedDeck_1.pdf.

9. Kelly and Enns (2010) present a cyclical model in which income disparities move public opinion to the right, therefore generating less pressure for redistribution. There are others, however, who argue that inequality moves public opinion to the left (Johnston and Newman 2016; Newman 2020).

Chapter 2

1. Analysis at this highly aggregated level has its faults. As Page and Shapiro (1992) note, perhaps the most important is that measurement errors may not be randomly distributed across the population and time. The use of reputable and widely used indicators, many different surveys, and some analysis at the individual-issue level should assuage readers who have this concern about my approach in this chapter.

2. For a detailed explanation of how Stimson conceives of public mood, see Stimson 2015, 23–57. See Stimson 2015 (58–95) for how he uses survey questions to measure it over time.

3. Gray and Jenkins (2017) and Howell et al. (2000) use the same approach, explaining the two different time series captured by sweeps one and two make them difficult to compare.

4. The effect is therefore to apply Ellis and Stimson's approach to ideology to both mood and legislative output. Erikson, MacKuen, and Stimson (2002, 325–80) code Mayhew's (2005) laws as liberal or conservative, but they venture beyond strictly economic policy, and their time series ends in 1996. If anything, they argue that policy output is more liberal than I present it as being. Only eight of the 124 laws are coded "conservative."

5. Grossmann (2019, 51–82) makes a similar observation about economic policymaking in the states where he sees a general growth in the scope and size of government through the 1990s and the first decade of the 2000s, regardless of party control.

6. Much of the liberal policy produced in the 1960s and 1970s is considered the "Great Broadening" of the policy agenda and driven as much by social movements as general opinion (Jones et al. 2019, 112–30).

7. Erikson et al. (2002, 340–42) find an even stronger relationship when they use a mood measure observed two Congresses prior to Mayhew's.

8. DW-NOMINATE uses members' roll-call votes to place them on a single ideological dimension in a Congress. Scores range from +1 at the conservative pole to -1 at the liberal pole. The first—and primary—dimension is what Poole and Rosenthal (1997) call "liberal-to-conservative" or "economic."

9. The Congressional Bills Project can be found at http://www.congressionalbills.org/. The bills used are those that become public law and are deemed important—Adler and Wilkerson, the project's principal investigators, filter out legislation that does things of minor consequence, such as the naming of buildings. To identify bills as economic in nature, I use those that are given the following policy "major topic" codes: 1, macroeconomics; 3, health; 5, labor; 6, education; 7, environment; 8, energy; 10, transportation; 13, social welfare; 14, housing; and 15, domestic commerce.

10. The data are from the Regulatory Studies Center (RSC) at George Washington University: https://regulatorystudies.columbian.gwu.edu/. The RSC argues that the Code of Federal

Regulations is a better gauge of aggregate regulation of economic activity than the Federal Register—which also includes rules that are deregulatory in nature—is.

11. Others have drawn similar conclusions. Using data from 1981 to 2002, Gilens (2012, 70–77) shows there is a strong relationship between the proportion of Americans favoring policy change on an issue and whether or not change occurs.

12. The data can be found via the Comparative Agendas Project, accessed November 11, 2024, https://www.comparativeagendas.net. See also Atkinson et al. (2021, 16–22).

13. Stimson organizes the surveys he uses to construct the policy-specific mood variables deploying exactly the same categories.

14. These bills all make Mayhew's dataset: the Surface Transportation and Uniform Relocation Assistance Act of 1987, Intermodal Surface Transportation Efficiency Act (ISTEA) of 1991, the Transportation Equity Act for the 21st Century (TEA-21) of 1998, the Safe, Accountable, Flexible, Efficient Transportation Equity Act: A Legacy for Users (SAFETEA-LU) of 2005, and Fixing America's Surface Transportation Act (FAST) of 2015.

15. Most notably, these laws include important air-pollution legislation in 1967 and 1969 and clean-water legislation in 1965 and 1972.

16. Some argue that Americans' conservatism on many of these policies is driven by racial attitudes and the belief that African Americans benefit undeservingly from them (Gilens 1999).

17. The data are available via the Comparative Agendas Project, "United States," accessed November 11, 2024, at https://comparativeagendas.net/us. The survey asks subjects what they believe is the "most important problem facing the United States." Responses are open-ended.

18. For a brief history of the reconciliation procedure, see Oleszek et al. (2019, 65–87).

19. This assertion challenges some important work on mass attitudes and economic policy. Ellis and Stimson (2012) and Grossman and Hopkins (2016) argue that Americans are "symbolically" conservative in that they prefer the ideological label to that of liberal and, in the abstract, give support to right-of-center economic policies. They are, however, "operationally" liberal in that they prefer government to administer left-of-center economic policies if they must live under them.

Chapter 3

1. See "Taxes," Gallup, Inc., 2024, https://news.gallup.com/poll/1714/taxes.aspx.

2. See "The ANES Guide to Public Opinion and Electoral Behavior," American National Election Studies, accessed November 13, 2024, https://electionstudies.org/resources/anes-guide /top-tables/?id=35.

3. For more on what polls revealed about public opinion of Reagan's economic policy in his first term, see Auxier (2010).

4. At 15.8 percent of respondents, the "federal budget deficit" beat by some distance all other issues offered by interviewers to the question: "Were any of the following very important to you in deciding how to vote for candidates today?"

5. The legislation raised individual income tax on high earners and larger corporations and increased taxes on Social Security and fuel. The spending cuts amounted to around $200 billion over five years according to some estimates (CQ Almanac 1993; Kennedy 1993), as much as $250 billion according to others (Quirk and Cunion 2000; Quirk and Hinchcliffe 1996). Many of them were attributable to the "peace dividend" generated in the defense budget by the end of the Cold War, but there were material cuts in the growth of Medicare, Medicaid, and social-welfare programs and the existing budgets of many discretionary items.

6. These were terms frequently used to describe Clinton's approach to politics and policy. An emphasis on fiscal discipline was a central feature of proponents' efforts to move the Democratic Party to the center on economic issues.

7. For an insightful treatment of the passage of TARP, see McCarty, Poole, and Rosenthal (2013, 214–26).

8. ARRA contained about $330 billion in spending on education, health care, and support for low-income Americans; $105 billion on many different forms of infrastructure including $48 billion for transportation; about $27 billion on energy efficiency; and roughly $30 billion on other items. Nearly $300 billion worth of individual and corporate tax incentives, mainly in the form of credits, was also passed.

9. The full formal name of the legislation is The Dodd–Frank Wall Street Reform and Consumer Protection Act. The law was an effort to increase regulation of financial services, most notably by charging the Fed to make sure banks and the banking system could cope with certain contingencies, instituting the Volcker Rule to prevent banks making certain investments, reforming mortgage lending, and creating a number of oversight agencies like the Consumer Financial Protection Bureau. Polls repeatedly showed that more Americans blamed the banks for the financial crisis than blamed the government.

10. Indeed, critics believe Trump's effort had little material impact, not least because the courts often intervened before initiatives could take effect (Rampell 2019). For more, see Raso (2018).

11. For the entire period of nearly sixty-five years over which Gallup has asked such a question, less than 5 percent of respondents have argued they pay "too little" in taxes.

12. Heffington, Park, and Williams (2017) aggregate responses to Gallup, ANES, and other polls about the most important problem into years and issue areas using three different forms of issue categorization. The data here are from their use of Singer's (2011) conceptualization of issue areas. The "wages" variable is singer5_perc. The data can be found at https://ropercenter .cornell.edu/ipoll/study/31094159.

13. The "inflation" variable is singer3_perc.

14. Third Way characterizes itself as a "center-left" think tank. For more on its poll, see *Third Way Nationwide Registered Voter Project*, Anzalone Liszt Grove Research, December 2015, https://thirdway.imgix.net/downloads/december-2015-national-poll-of-registered-voters/De cember_2015_National_Poll_of_Registered_Voters.pdf. The position of the minimum wage in the policy interests of Democrats may have changed since then, however. The Nationscape project that looked at the priorities of voters in 2019 did show that increasing the minimum wage to $15 was of quite high importance to Democrats.

15. See "Low Wage Workforce Tracker," Economic Policy Institute, 2024, https://www.epi .org/low-wage-workforce/.

16. Zacher (2024a) argues that Americans' support for redistribution increases when they believe the cost of the policy will be borne by a small, finite group like the very wealthy.

17. A *The Hill*-Harris poll fielded three months earlier showed that a majority of respondents supported Ocasio-Cortez's proposal.

18. For more on the survey, see "Americans Are Dissatisfied with the Government's Spending Priorities," AP-NORC Center and GSS staff, accessed November 13, 2024, https://apnorc.org /projects/americans-are-dissatisfied-with-the-governments-spending-priorities.

19. The data can be found at *General Social Survey Final Report: Trends in National Spending Priorities, 1973–2014* (NORC at the University of Chicago, March 2015), https://www.norc.org /PDFs/GSS%20Reports/GSS_Trends%20in%20Spending_1973-2014.pdf.

20. The figure for state and local spending was about $115 billion in 2017, according to the Urban Institute (Auxier 2020).

21. Since 1984, GSS has asked participants about spending on "assistance to the poor." A much greater proportion say "too little" is spent on this. How respondents see "assistance to the poor" as different from "welfare" I am not sure, but clearly the choice of language is critical. GSS dropped the category "welfare" after 2014.

22. It is important to note, however, that since the passage of the ACA even some Republican states have expanded Medicaid coverage.

23. For more on TANF and how it overhauled AFDC, see Gilens (1999, 11–20).

24. They were Mary Jo Bane, Peter B. Edelman, and Wendell E. Primus. All three served at the assistant-secretary level in the Department of Health and Human Services.

25. Research has suggested that Americans' view of the deservingness of Medicaid recipients is a function not so much of whether beneficiaries work but more by whether they have a health condition for which they are personally responsible (Wu 2021).

26. Gilens (1999) argues that racial prejudice contributes greatly to Americans' views of welfare policy.

27. Kuziemko et al. (2023) argue that less educated, working-class Americans tend to support "pre-distribution" policies such as the minimum wage more than they support "redistribution" policies like welfare.

Chapter 4

1. Rehm et al. (2012) argue that economic security—as opposed to income—drives policy preferences. The "insecure" or those who feel their job or other sources of income are precarious are more likely to hold liberal views than the "secure."

2. Gilens (2012) imputes the positions of the 10th, 50th, and 90th percentiles from the surveys by assigning respondents income scores and preferences. He explains the method precisely on pages 61–62. The survey questions were fielded between 1981 and 2002. Following Gilens (2012), I collapse the values into groupings rather than using the calculated percentages in favor. See Gilens (2012, 118) for these figures, but—essentially—income groups receive scores ranging from –5 (when less than 15 percent support policy change on the issue) through to 5 (when more than 85 percent support change), with a middle of 0 (if the percentage endorsing policy change is between 45 and 55 percent). The data can be found at Martin Gilens, "Economic Inequality and Political Representation," Russell Sage Foundation, accessed November 13, 2024, https://www.russellsage.org/datasets/economic-inequality-and-political-representation.

3. For explanations of the questions considered to be on economic and social-welfare policy, see Gilens (2012, 113–21).

4. Several years ago, Carnes (2016) wrote an essay titled "Who Votes for Inequality?" I would argue that few, if any, Americans do. Inequality is a condition—the consequences, often unintended, of government policies and many other factors. Even those who support policies with potential to increase inequality view the economic condition as a regrettable cost to improve social outcomes in other ways.

5. For more on ANES, see https://electionstudies.org.

6. This research is primarily the work of economists John Early and Robert Ekelund and former Senator Phil Gramm, Republican, of Texas. They argue that redistributive policies reduce the Gini coefficient, measuring income distribution from about 0.48 to around 0.35 for the

decade of the 2010s. Auten and Splinter (2024) published a paper making a similar case using new analyses of pre-tax income and transfer payment data.

7. See Newport (2019).

8. Heffington, Park, and Williams (2017) code responses to Gallup, ANES, and a few other polls about the most important problem into issue areas using three different forms of categorization. The data here are from their use of Singer's (2011) conceptualization of issue areas. The "poverty/inequality" variable is singer7_perc. The data can be found at https://ropercenter .cornell.edu/ipoll/study/31094159.

9. The variable is singer30_perc.

10. See "4. Important Issues in the 2020 Election," Pew Research Center, August 13, 2020, https://www.pewresearch.org/politics/2020/08/13/important-issues-in-the-2020-election/.

11. See "American Trends Panel Wave 54," Pew Research Center, field dates September 16–29, 2019, https://www.pewresearch.org/social-trends/dataset/american-trends-panel -wave-54/.

12. See Rainie et al. (2019).

13. For more on the Harvard CAPS–Harris poll, see https://harvardharrispoll.com/.

14. For the purposes of this survey, Pew calculated low-income respondents as having family incomes below $40,100 in 2018.

15. See Newport (2011). In 2011, 52 percent of respondents described the situation as an "acceptable part of the economic system."

16. Pew calculates the income strata from income and place of residence.

17. This assessment uses the Singer (2011) classification of policy types.

18. See "Chapter 4. The Casualties: Faith in Hard Work and Capitalism," Pew Research Center, July 12, 2012, https://www.pewresearch.org/global/2012/07/12/chapter-4-the-casualties-faith-in -hard-work-and-capitalism/.

19. See "3. Views of the Economic System and Social Safety Net," December 17, 2019, https://www .pewresearch.org/politics/2019/12/17/views-of-the-economic-system-and-social-safety-net/.

20. See Mitchell (2019).

21. See Ekins (2015).

22. By comparison, 42 percent of respondents said, "Capitalism and free markets are not working well in the U.S." or "Capitalism and free markets are broken in the U.S." See Cannon and Bevan (2019).

23. See Younis (2019).

24. I think a good example of this phenomenon is their significant and enduring support for Social Security but propensity for private investment. Various sources give different figures, but there seems to be a consensus that whereas only about one in eight Europeans has investments in the stock market, about 60 percent of Americans do.

25. The variables are V923726 in 1992, V960497 in 1996, V000676 in 2000, V043169 in 2004, V083145 in 2008, fedspend_welfare in 2012, and V161209 in 2016. ANES reports a small number of respondents who volunteered that welfare spending should be "cut out entirely." I code these cases as "decreased."

26. The independent variables are indicators of gender, race (Black or not), Latino ethnicity (excluded in 1992 because of small numbers), marital status, region of residence (South or not), age, religiosity (whether religion is an important part of the respondent's life), union membership (whether you or anyone in the household belongs to a union), ideology (from liberal to conservative with a moderate midpoint), and party identification (Democrat, independent, or

Republican). I measure income using over twenty categories (that change over time), and education is measured using seven categories (eighth grade or less to advanced degree).

27. The distribution of responses varies considerably across years. For whatever reason, the proportion of "keep about the same" respondents was less than 10 percent in 1996. It was 45 percent in 2004.

28. See "Taxes," Gallup, Inc., 2024, https://news.gallup.com/poll/1714/taxes.aspx.

29. See McCarthy (2015).

30. The questions are as follows: (1) "Would you support or oppose an increase in taxes that would be used to reduce the federal budget deficit?" (1992, variable V900484, responses "support," "depends," "oppose"); (2) "Do you favor increases in taxes paid by ordinary Americans in order to cut the budget deficit?" (1996, V961228, responses "favor" or "don't favor"); (3) "Some people have proposed that most of the expected federal budget surplus should be used to cut taxes. Do you approve or disapprove of this proposal? Do you approve of this proposal strongly or not strongly? Do you disapprove of this proposal strongly or not strongly?" (2000, V000690, responses "disapprove strongly," "disapprove not strongly," "approve not strongly," "approve strongly"); (4) "Do you favor cuts in spending on domestic programs like Medicare, education, and highways to cut the taxes paid by ordinary Americans?" (2004, VV45098, responses "don't favor" or "favor"); and (5) "Do you favor an increase in the federal budget deficit in order to cut the taxes paid by ordinary Americans?" (2004, VV45097, responses "don't favor" or "favor").

31. In each year I study, ANES asks a similar question with the subject being spending on "aid to the poor" rather than "welfare." Perhaps not surprisingly, fewer respondents want to decrease and more want to increase spending for the poor than on welfare. However, use of these questions generates identical findings regarding the effect of income and class—as well as race and ethnicity that I discuss later in the chapter—on Americans' attitudes about spending on these kinds of programs.

32. For more on CES, see https://cces.gov.harvard.edu. Harvard University hosts and the PIs are Stephen Ansolabehere, Brian F. Schaffner, and Samantha Luks. CES recruits large numbers of subjects (in excess of fifty thousand since 2010) and asks them a battery of questions about their political knowledge, policy attitudes, voting behavior, and demographic characteristics.

I use the same independent variables, although CES measures them a little differently on occasion. Income, for example, is by family rather than household (a small difference) and has only sixteen categories.

33. The questions are as follows: (1) "The federal budget deficit is approximately $1 trillion this year. If the Congress were to balance the budget it would have to consider cutting defense spending, cutting domestic spending (such as Medicare and Social Security), or raising taxes to cover the deficit. What would you most/least prefer that Congress do? Cut domestic spending, cut defense spending, or raise taxes?" (2012, cc328 and cc329, responses are coded "1" if "raising taxes" is most preferred and "3" if "raising taxes" is least preferred); (2) "Do you support or oppose the Tax Hike Prevention Act that would extend all Bush-era tax cuts regardless of income and increase the budget deficit by $405 billion?" (2014, CC14_325_4, responses "oppose," "support"); (3) "The federal budget deficit is approximately 1 trillion this year. If the Congress were to balance the budget it would have to consider cutting defense spending, cutting domestic spending (such as Medicare and Social Security), or raising taxes to cover the deficit. Please rank the options below from what would you most prefer that Congress do to what you would least prefer they do" (2016, CC16_337_1, CC16_337_2, CC16_337_3, responses "raise taxes" most prefer, second choice, least prefer); and (4) Would you support or oppose a tax bill that does all

of the following? Cuts the Corporate Income Tax rate from 39 percent to 21 percent. Reduces the mortgage interest deduction from $1 million to $500,000. Caps the amount of state and local tax that can be deducted to $10,000 (previously there was no limit). Increases the standard deduction from $12,000 to $25,000. Cuts income tax rates for all income groups by 3 percent (2018 [the 2017 TCJA], CC18_326, responses "oppose," "support").

34. Following Gilens (2012)—and as noted earlier—I collapse the values into groupings rather than use the calculated percentages in favor. Income groups receive scores ranging from –5 (when less than 15 percent support policy change on the issue) through to 5 (when more than 85 percent support change), with a middle of 0 (if the percentage endorsing policy change is between 45 and 55 percent).

35. This finding is consistent with Gilens's (2012, 99, 117–22) observation that relative to the other issues he analyzes, Americans are least supportive of change on social-welfare policy.

36. Gilens (2012; Gilens and Page 2014) uses the number of years to passage and gives an extra 0.5 of a point for a policy change that was only partially realized. The minimum is 2; the maximum is 4.5. The mean for the economic policy items is 2.25; for the social-welfare items, it is 2.26.

37. The limited number of cases and the clustering of change at two years (the length of a Congress) reduces the likelihood of discovering material differences.

Chapter 5

1. The Almond-Lippmann consensus, named after Gabriel Almond and Walter Lippmann, was a dominant view in political science during much of the twentieth century. A central feature was the assertion that public opinion was incoherent and lacked any organizing principle.

2. There is no president's ideology data for 2008; CES asked respondents to place President Bush on an ideological thermometer scale from 0–100, with no opportunity to state "not sure."

The figures are the percentage of the category who responded "not sure" to the following questions: (1) "Thinking about politics these days, how would you describe your own political viewpoint?/In general, how would you describe your own political viewpoint?"; and (2) "How would you rate each of the following individuals and groups? . . . President Obama (for 2010–16)/ Trump (for 2018 and 2020)." It does seem unlikely that a respondent would have a fully formed ideology but feel the options did not sufficiently describe it. Each year, subjects were presented with a five-point scale ranging from "very liberal" to "very conservative."

3. The controls are the same for all three years: gender (male or female), race (Black or not Black), ethnicity (Latino or not Latino), age, education, religious (or not), married (or not), and place of residence (in the South or not).

4. The descriptive statistics are as follows: (1) 2010—three questions on immigration, maximum = 1, mean = .450, standard deviation = .498; (2) 2012—six questions on immigration, maximum = 3, mean = 1.19, standard deviation = 1.02; (3) 2014—five questions on immigration, maximum = 2, mean = .927, standard deviation = .815, and four questions on environment, maximum = 2, mean = .608, standard deviation = .744; (4) 2016—four questions on immigration, maximum = 2, mean = .772, standard deviation = .734, and four questions on the environment, maximum = 2, mean = .566, standard deviation = .728; (5) 2018—six questions on immigration, maximum = 3, mean = 1.47, standard deviation = –.862, five questions on the environment, maximum = 2, mean = .950, standard deviation = .622, and six questions on taxes, maximum = 3, mean = 1.89, standard deviation = .851; (6) 2020—five questions on immigration, maximum = 2, mean = 1.73,

standard deviation = .498, four questions on the environment, maximum = 2, mean = .480, standard deviation = .689, and four questions on health care, maximum = 2, mean = .779, standard deviation = .728.

5. Recent research has rehabilitated the American moderate somewhat, suggesting that they take comprehensible policy positions and vote logically—including for centrist candidates—by a considerably greater amount than do ideologues (Fowler et al. 2023). The fact that candidates disregard them, therefore, is a mistake.

6. To be sure, there is overlap between self-described "moderates" and "independents," but researchers have shown that this overlap is not as great as we might think (Drutman 2019; Klar and Krupnikov 2016).

7. These variables—in addition to those mentioned—are gender, race (Black or white), Latino (yes or no), age, education, married, religiosity, from the South, belonging to a union family, and belonging to a military family.

8. Respondents in midterm election years were asked whom they voted for in the immediately previous presidential election.

9. For more on the Democracy Fund Voter Study Group survey methodology, see https://www.voterstudygroup.org/data.

10. DW-NOMINATE generates cut-points from votes that permits it to predict how members will vote on other measures.

11. It is also interesting to note that conservatives tend to generate more errors and therefore create a less ideologically coherent voting record than liberals.

12. The "most important issue" questions were asked to a subsample of CES respondents—approximately two thousand to five thousand in each income cohort.

13. In the CES survey, all cohorts—perhaps in a sign of Trump's appeal as an outsider in the election that year—thought that government corruption was important.

14. Infrastructure effectively replaces poverty in the top twelve issues for wealthier respondents. This is interesting given my argument about distributive policy in the next chapter. Lower-income respondents may downplay "infrastructure" because the term is nebulous and they do not differentiate between a national program and projects in their local communities.

Chapter 6

1. Research shows that both Black members of Congress and citizens are more supportive of the allocation of federal resources to the districts they represent and live in than their white counterparts are (Grose 2011, 134–66; Tate 2003).

2. A 2016 Pew Research survey showed that higher-income and college-educated Blacks were considerably more likely than their working-class counterparts to "feel connected to a broader Black community in the United States." The study can be found at "2. Views of Race Relations," Pew Research Center, July 27, 2016, https://www.pewsocialtrends.org/2016/06/27/2-views-of-race-relations/#roughly-a-third-of-blacks-say-they-feel-very-connected-to-a-broader-black-community.

3. For example, higher-income Americans are much more likely to travel by taking a vacation across the country or overseas. They are also more likely to use social media—although the gap is narrowing.

4. Literally meaning "yellow vests"—after the reflective bibs worn by workers—the movement organized a series of protests in 2018 and 2019 designed to persuade the French government

to, among other things, decrease fuel prices, reintroduce a wealth tax, and increase the minimum wage. It was widely characterized as "populist," and its supporters were largely working-class.

5. Trump did not quite replicate his earlier feat in 2020. His vote share among middle-income earners was down, while the proportion of the vote he received from those in the higher-income brackets (above $100,000) in the exit polls increased.

6. There is another interpretation of the rise of populism, of course. This is the cultural backlash thesis, which proposes that the cleavages driven into their societies by Trump's presidential candidacy and Brexit divided rather than unified working-class citizens. Racial resentment and anti-immigration attitudes were particularly important here (Sides et al. 2018; Sobolewska and Ford 2020, 218–49).

7. Hunt does not have much data on challengers in the 2020 elections.

8. I measure this effect using Jacobson and Carson's (2020) "candidate quality" variable.

9. This result emerged despite the fact that in their analysis of distributive politics at the state level, Gamm and Kousser (2023) find that districts with higher proportions of Black and Latino constituents have historically received less spending for services like schools, hospitals, and transportation.

10. Harden (2016, 78–82) shows that less affluent (and particularly unemployed) and racial-minority respondents tend to believe that allocation is the most important job a state legislator can undertake. He also reveals that poorer respondents are more supportive of legislators who describe their successes in distributive policymaking as maximizing the district's allocation rather than securing a "fair share" for their constituents (Harden 2016, 59–66).

11. Bernhard and Sulkin (2018, 73–81) only present an explanatory model of district advocates for freshmen. They do not include measures of district income, wealth, or education in that model.

12. The Bureau of the Census only started collecting household data for the various income groupings beginning in 1980. It started collecting these data annually from 2005 in the American Community Survey (ACS). Since then, it has provided annual estimates of the median household income for a district for every year to the present. From 2005, I report the district median household income using the ACS for the first year of the Congress, rather than using the figure for the immediately preceding full census. I use these data in much of the analysis in the remainder of the book.

The groupings used are as follows. The lowest- and highest-income household groups: 1980 and 1990—under $5,000 and over $100,000; 2000—under $15,000 and over $150,000; and 2010—under $15,000 and over $150,000. For the larger groups of low-income and high-income: 1980 and 1990—under $10,000 and over $75,000; 2000—under $25,000 and over $100,000; and 2010—under $35,000 and over $100,000. I shifted categories in an effort to maintain roughly the same proportion of households in each group across the four decades.

Unfortunately, however, the equivalent lower- and higher-income groups are unavoidably different in size. The mean percentages of households in each district in each decade in each group are: lowest-income 13.2 (1980), 6.0 (1990), 14.9 (2000), 12.6 (2010); highest-income 4.5 (1980), 4.3 (1990), 6.2 (2000), 10.4 (2010); low-income 21.2 (1980), 15.5 (1990), 26.9 (2000), 45.8 (2010); high-income 13.2 (1980), 9.4 (1990), 16.4 (2000), 34.0 (2010). Dividing census categories in other potentially defensible ways would not have produced more-consistently-proportioned groups.

13. Districts that are more than 75 percent urban are 30 percent wealthier than all other

districts and roughly 45 percent wealthier than districts that are less than 50 percent urban. The coefficient of variation of the median household income for these districts is .459 (meaning they are the most heterogeneous by income; for those that are less than 75 percent but more than 50 percent urban it is .423, and for those that are less than 50 percent urban it is .340.

14. A "local-topic" post specifically mentioned "a place, group, individual(s), or event in the politician's district." Such topics included such things as a "discussion of government programs, facilities, or commemorative events," "town-hall meetings or other community events," "references to practices that primarily apply to a particular state, district, city, or community," and "local or state places, organizations, and events."

15. Data on membership to Appropriations are from Charles Stewart's website, "Charles Stewart's Congressional Data Page," accessed November 17, 2024, http://web.mit.edu/17.251 /www/data_page.html.

16. Frisch and Kelly's (2006) request data go back to the 86th Congress for both parties. They gathered request data for 2,480 members over the period.

17. There are ninety member-Congress cases where Appropriations is requested but not as the individual's first choice.

18. High-variance programs are identified by how much they vary across time. For more on the programs in the dataset and how the authors categorize them, see Dynes and Huber (2015) and the January 2015 online appendix to their article at http://adamdynes.com /documents/0PUB_2015_APSR_dynes-huber_partisanship-federal-spending_appendix.pdf.

Chapter 7

1. The 1982 amendment to section 2 of the Voting Rights Act generated an avalanche of litigation and US Department of Justice pressure that, in turn, culminated with many Southern states drawing congressional districts in which a majority of residents were of the minority race or ethnicity. During the 1990s, the Supreme Court issued several rulings effectively ending the practice (Bullock et al. 2016, 25–32).

2. In a study of congressional trade politics, Schiller (1995) shows that the interests of industries located in less populated states are better represented than those that reside in states with large populations.

3. Oregon moved back above the national median in 2020.

4. Ellis (2017, 77–78) borrows freely from the work done in sociology and psychology about intergroup contact. A summary of much of this work can be found in Pettigrew and Tropp (2006).

5. This capacity is sometimes called "hit rate"; measures of the proportion of a member's bills passed by the body have been used by a number of scholars (Anderson et al. 2003; Cox and Terry 2008; Hasecke and Mycoff 2007; Jeydel and Taylor 2003).

6. Greater detail about how these scores were calculated can be found in Volden and Wiseman (2014, 19–28).

7. Volden and Wiseman provide more recent data on their website, https://thelawmakers .org. The up-to-date state legislative professionalization score is from Squire (2014, 308–9) and the state legislative experience score from the National Conference of State Legislatures website (https://www.ncsl.org).

8. There is no appreciable difference in results when I use measures of the proportion of households in either of the low-income groups.

Chapter 8

1. For exceptions, see Bhatti and Erikson (2011), Brunner et al. (2013), Lax et al. (2019), and Tausanovitch (2016). Mathisen (2024) argues that gender disparities in wealth explain why American public policy is more responsive to the policy views of men than it is to those of women.

2. In recent research, Becher and Stegmueller (2021) have shown that union membership can have a material effect on the responsiveness of House members. As a district's union membership grows, so its representative becomes considerably more responsive to the views of lower-income constituents.

3. Bartels (2016, 239–42) derives his measure of constituency opinion from the 2010 and 2012 CES surveys.

4. By combining responses from a variety of reputable surveys, the indicator takes account of the attitudes of high- and low-income residents as part of broader district opinion. I am interested in seeing whether members of high- and low-income households exert influence by dint of their numbers, independent of their expressed views as incorporated in this measure.

5. I define the South as comprising the eleven states of the old Confederacy in addition to Kentucky and Oklahoma. This usage is conventional. In some places, where I state that I have used proprietary data graciously supplied by colleagues, the "South" label may refer to a slightly different group of states—that is, it might exclude Kentucky and Oklahoma or add Maryland.

6. Franko and Witko (2023b) show that less affluent Democrats place greater emphasis on economic issues than do less affluent Republicans. Their work appears consistent with my finding that Democratic and Republican members who represent poorer districts are particularly polarized.

7. Hersh and Nall (2015) might explain these members' behavior as a response as much to the racial as socioeconomic composition of their districts. They find that the most loyal low-income Democratic voters are in moderately conservative Southern jurisdictions with many minority residents.

8. A good example of this phenomenon might be Speaker Nancy Pelosi's (D-CA) effort to roll back the limit on the amount of state and local tax payments Americans can deduct from their federal taxes during the debates over COVID recovery legislation in 2020. The so-called SALT policy was part of the tax bill that passed in late 2017. Many affluent residents in high-tax states—like Pelosi's constituents in San Francisco—found the provision particularly onerous.

9. For a contrarian view, see Dettrey and Campbell (2013) and Campbell (2016, chapter 7).

10. A body of work also examines inequality's direct effect on public opinion. Here, levels of inequality result in a commensurate reduction in pressures for redistributive fiscal policy and a general increase in the conservatism of mass attitudes (Kelly 2009, 2019; Kelly and Enns 2010; Luttig 2013; McCarty et al. 2006, 115–38; O'Brian 2019; Voorheis et al. 2015). Several researchers have challenged this position recently, however (Johnston and Newman 2016; Ladewig 2021; Newman and Kane 2017; Newman 2020).

11. That is: proportion highest + proportion lowest / 1 - (proportion smallest of highest/lowest).

12. The measure's one weakness is that it considers districts with very high levels of concentration in one of the groups as unequal. As a practical matter, however, there are not districts like this anywhere in the time series. The largest difference between the two groups in a district is .41.

13. Ladewig (2021) uses two measures of inequality: the mean household income as a proportion of the median household income and the percent difference between the mean and the

median (mean - median / mean + median). Like the Gini coefficient, these measures are good at conveying the concept of inequality within a district but not so much across districts. Absolute differences in the incomes of households are ignored. For example, hypothetical district A, with three households receiving incomes of $50,000, $30,000, and $10,000 has the same Gini coefficient and Ladewig scores as district B, with three households making $100,000, $60,000, and $20,000 (Gini = .296, Ladewig measures = 1 and 0). The wealthiest household in A has an income that is less than B's median. The distance between the highest and lowest incomes is twice as great in district B. I do not think most Americans would consider the districts equally unequal.

14. According to an Economic Policy Institute survey, in 2015 an annual income of $200,000 would put you in the top 1 percent of the most affluent households in all but ninety-two of the 916 American metro areas. These are places like Bucyrus, Ohio; Deming, New Mexico; Eagle Pass, Texas; Henderson, North Carolina; Malvern, Arkansas; and Peru, Indiana. See Sommeiller and Price 2018.

15. For the time period I analyze, Southern districts' median household income is negatively correlated with the Gini coefficient ($-.30$, $p < .05$) and the author measure ($-.22$, $p < .05$), but for non-Southern districts the correlations are positive for the author measure ($.17$, $p < .05$) but insignificant for the Gini ($-.02$, $p > .05$).

16. Tausanovitch and Warshaw (2013) provide heterogeneity scores only for the districts drawn in 2000—that is, the data for 2003–2012. These scores are calculated from estimates of preferences of quantiles other than the district's median subject.

17. I include a measure of the competitiveness of the district because of my agnosticism about the direction in which the income groups pull member ideology away from constituency attitudes. We should expect legislators who won tight races to hew close to district opinion. It is unclear how district competiveness should affect a member's ideology, and so I omit such a measure from the House and Senate analyses below.

18. Democrats overrepresent the rich on noneconomic matters (Maks-Solomon and Rigby 2020).

19. For data and more details on the campaign finance habits of interest groups and individuals, see the Federal Elections Commission website (https://www.fec.gov) or Campaign Finance Institute's website (https://www.cfinst.org).

Chapter 9

1. The work on descriptive representation and Congress is vast and growing rapidly. Important recent contributions that confirm this general proposition include Bowen and Clark (2014), Broockman (2013), Butler and Broockman (2011), Gonzalez Juenke and Preuhs (2012), Griffin and Newman (2008), Griffin et al. (2012), Grose (2011), Hansen and Treul (2015), Lowande et al. (2019), Martin (2019), Mendez and Grose (2018), Reingold and Harrell (2010), Schildkraut (2016), Sanbonmatsu (2020), and Swers and Rouse (2011).

2. Moreover, the gap appears to be growing. Klick (2017) estimates the average annual increase in member net worth in real dollars between 2004 and 2014 to be about 3.6 percent.

3. It is almost a cliché that Americans complain of there being too many lawyers in Congress. Bonica (2020) argues that this state of affairs has not come about because voters are drawn to candidates from the occupation but because such candidates benefit from low opportunity costs when running for office and from the fundraising networks the legal profession provides.

4. Barnes and Saxton (2019) have shown that Latin American voters feel more positively toward government when their representatives have similar socioeconomic backgrounds to themselves.

5. Carnes and Sadin (2015), Grumbach (2015), and Vivyan et al. (2020) examine what the latter call "class roots" as well as "class markers." I do not examine the family backgrounds of legislators and candidates, including their parents' occupations and class status, only their personal socioeconomic attributes.

6. For example, of the thirty-one House districts with at least 40 percent black population in the 117th Congress (2021–2022), only one had a non-Black representative: Michigan's Sixth District, represented by Rashida Tlaib. Of the thirty-six majority-Hispanic districts, only six had non-Latino members. Only one of the top 150 districts by white population had a Black member—Lauren Underwood from the northern and western Chicago exurbs—although there were a number of Hispanic and Asian-American representatives in this group.

7. See American Academy of Arts and Sciences (2023).

8. All members of the House and Senate receive annual salaries of $174,000. Floor leaders and those occupying Congress's constitutionally mandated positions get additional compensation.

9. CFRP reports its methodology on its website; see "Personal Finances: About the Personal Finances Data & OpenSecrets' Methodology," OpenSecrets, accessed November 17, 2024, https://www.opensecrets.org/personal-finances/methodology. As CFRP notes, the 2012 STOCK Act made collecting these data easier. The legislation also required more frequent and complete reporting by members, compelling them, for instance, to report mortgages.

10. The data can be found at "Financial Disclosure Reports," Clerk of the US House of Representatives, accessed November 17, 2024, https://clerk.house.gov/FinancialDisclosure. Calculating members' net worth from the disclosure documents so that data are directly comparable across time and legislators is challenging. Stipulations have changed over time, and requirements have provided members with varying degrees of discretion over what to report and how to document it. Rules were particularly liberal in the early years. Some members, for example, felt a need to report the net worth of spouses and minor children; a majority did not. Most members use the broad categories provided to report amounts, in which case for purposes of arithmetic simplicity I calculated figures to be roughly the midpoint for that category—for example, if a member could report a holding as being worth "C," or between $15,000 and $50,000, I have assumed its value to be $30,000. Other members give actual and precise dollar amounts. Again, especially in the early years, many departing members did not report and, where possible, I imputed the amount submitted in the immediately preceding period. Sometimes members' net worth changes dramatically. In these cases, it is sometimes hard to determine whether the variance is real or explained by a change in the member's approach to reporting. Regardless, I always took the report at face value. I calculate net worth as liabilities subtracted from assets and income.

11. The most important results—that is, the performance of the constituent income variables—are identical if we use the more relaxed measures of high- and low-income groups.

12. I do not report the author data with the constituent education variable included. None of the important variables generates statistically significant coefficients in these specifications.

13. I refer to Carnes's (2013) CLASS data, which spans the 108th–110th Congresses (2003–2008), later in the chapter, but it is worth noting here that he does have a measure of net worth. If we subject his data to the same analysis I use in table 9.1, we get few substantive differences, and constituent income does not affect member net worth. However, Carnes's (2013) CLASS data

show that Democrats can be considered wealthier than Republicans in the upper body—the median net worth for Republicans is, at just shy of $2 million, over $300,000 greater than that for Democrats, but the mean for Democrats is about $23.5 million, while for Republicans it is only $7.4 million. Most of the senators with the lowest net worth are Democrats, but the wealthiest ones are as well—in the CLASS data, these include Jon Corzine (D-NJ), John Kerry (D-MA), Herb Kohl (D-WI), and Jay Rockefeller (D-WV).

14. Research assistants coded the data from members' biographies in the almanac. Occupation and education data are readily available in summary form at the beginning of these biographies. I consider members to have had legal careers if they become attorneys and/or judges after receiving a JD. A business career is one outside of farming, government service, and the professions—law, teaching, medicine, clergy, engineering etc. Accountants, engineers, and scientists are considered to have business backgrounds if their biographical summaries denote an affiliation with a company.

15. Carnes (2013) categorizes members into ten occupational categories. "Politics and the law" includes members' time spent as "politicians/staffer" and/or "lawyer." "Professionals" are those employed in his three categories of lawyer, technical professional, and service-based professional. Those in the "private sector" are business owners, business employees, and farm owners/managers. Business owners also include Carnes's "farm owners/managers." For more detail on Carnes's occupational types, see the online appendix for Carnes (2013), https://www.press.uchicago.edu/sites/carnes/carnes_Appendix_Ch1.pdf.

16. Data collected by Carnes and Lupu (2023) reveal that roughly 2 percent of members of Congress who served from 2016–2018 were primarily employed in working-class occupations before they went to Washington. This figure is below the OECD average of 3 percent.

17. I use a logit model for the author data and OLS regression for the Carnes data. I deploy Congress fixed effects and cluster standard errors by member.

18. The controls in the Hunt analysis are whether the member was a Democrat, a woman, non-white, or a Southerner; the percentage of the district that was urban; and the incumbent's age and number of terms served. The education coefficient in the author and Carnes data is from the specification using median income.

19. Carnes also uses a measure of the proportion of a district's households in poverty. I include it here.

20. The Hunt (2022) data I examined in chapter 6 contain a measure of blue-collar worker. A multivariate regression using intuitive controls and measures of constituency income and education finds that district socioeconomic characteristics have no material effect on whether or not a member had a pre-tenure blue-collar career. Consistent with Carnes's findings that very few legislators have had such careers, Hunt's data show that of 2,980 members in his dataset, 5.7 percent had pre-tenure careers that he determines to constitute prior blue-collar experience.

21. The control variables perform similarly in the models of the CLASS data.

22. The unreported analysis of the Hunt data produces practically identical findings.

23. Not all the findings are consistent with this rather precise interpretation. The urban variable's coefficient does not reach levels of statistical significance in figure 9.3.

24. Ocasio-Cortez's job as a bartender was a side gig, as she ran a community book publisher and worked for a nonprofit.

25. The media have also become interested in the idea of electing working-class Democrats as an antidote to Republican populism. In the summer of 2024, for example, *The New York Times* profiled Representative Marie Gluesenkamp Perez of Washington (Zengerle 2024). But she has

a degree from a prestigious liberal arts college and opened a business with her husband. This background more closely resembles those of the many small-town Republican business owners who have entered Congress since the 1990s.

26. This claim is true of an analysis of the Hunt data. Hunt (2022) codes members as either having a college degree or not and having any postgraduate degree or not.

27. This finding is interesting since Carnes and Lupu (2023) show that between 2016 and 2018, roughly twice as many working-class members of Congress were Democratic than Republican.

28. The data can be found at "Financial Disclosure Reports," Clerk of the US House of Representatives. The approach is identical to that I used when calculating members' net worth earlier, except that I compared the opposing candidates' statements and canceled out commonalities when I could. I then took the remainder and generated estimates using the earlier approach that I could then compare with one another.

29. These candidates can be two Democrats or two Republicans in states that have a jungle primary.

30. These numbers are naturally approximations of the actual figures because, as noted above, both candidates use broad categories to describe assets and liabilities. If one candidate's assets or liabilities tend to be toward the top of categories and the other's toward the bottom, their actual net worths may be narrower than I indicate, or vice versa. See note 10 for further explanation of data collection.

31. This determination is inevitably arbitrary. I also ran identical analyses using a $1 million "buffer." Doing so had no material effects on my findings, although it did increase the number of races where I considered the candidates' net worth effectively equal by 58 percent (to 695 cases).

32. This finding suggests that wealthier candidates have, for whatever reason, an advantage.

33. Gary Jacobson provided these data.

34. The measures of income do not have a material effect when the district education variable is dropped.

35. I glean House vote choice from respondents in the pre-election wave when they were asked whom they "preferred." Doing so increases the number of observations and is highly correlated with the question about whom they voted for in the post-election wave.

36. In the individual-level analysis, I do not analyze survey respondents from districts where there is no discernible difference between candidates because I am interested merely in the vote choice citizens make between candidates when they can plausibly perceive a difference in net worth.

37. CES provides sixteen values for income: less than $10,000; $10,000 to $19,999; $20,000 to $29,999; $30,000 to $39,999; $40,000 to $49,999; $50,000 to $59,999; $60,000 to $69,999; $70,000 to $79,999; $80,000 to $99,999; $100,000 to $119,999; $120,000 to $149,999; $150,000 to $199,999; $200,000 to $249,999; $250,000 to $349,999; $350,000 to $499,999; and $500,000 or more.

Education is ordinal as well. It is coded, 1 through 6, as "no high school," "high school diploma," "some college," "two-year college degree," "four-year college degree," and "postgraduate degree." Because a sizeable number of respondents do not report their income, the specification excluding the income variable has more cases.

38. Voters may be especially in need of extra information in the case of challengers. Generally, fewer than two-thirds of voters are capable of recognizing the names of these candidates (Jacobson and Carson 2020, 172–78).

39. Each case in the WMP data is the airing of an ad in a House election. Most ads air multiple times. To attribute mentions of relative wealth or financial status of House candidates, I included

only ads where coders considered the focus "personal characteristics" or both "policy matters and personal characteristics" (variable "per_ply"). Of these, an observation was only included if the "favored" candidate and/or "opposing" candidate were mentioned (variables "f_mention" and "o_mention"). I then identified the target of the ad by taking its tone. WMP divides ads into "contrast," "promote," or "attack" (variable "ad_tone"). I attributed ads promoting the favored candidate as attacking the opposing candidate. I divided contrast ads based upon whether they were coded "more promote than attack" or "more attack than promote" (variable "cnt_prp"). I dropped other types of contrast ads because I could not clearly identify the target candidate.

Finally, I attributed target candidates as being "wealthy" or "poor" based upon whether there was a mention of a candidate as "working class" (variable "mentionwc") or "upper class/rich/wealthy" (variable "mentionuc"). Doing so created four different observations that were included in the data I analyze, where the target candidate or other candidate were considered "wealthy" or "poor." Unsurprisingly, a large majority of "poorer" ads promote the candidate (and are therefore considered ads by candidates about themselves). An even greater proportion of "wealthy" ads attack a candidate (and I therefore consider them to be ads about the candidate's opponent).

The figures for mentions of issues to which I compare the use of candidate class are taken directly from variables in the WMP data.

40. I took all nonincumbent, major-party general-election candidates from the 2014, 2016, and 2018 House elections. From January 1 to November 1 of the election year, I searched Google News using each candidate's name, their state, and the word "election." I took the first twenty stories (if there were that many) about the candidate and searched for any reference to their class. I coded the reference as "working class" if a story used one or more of the following terms when describing the candidate: "working class," "blue collar," "poor," "low-income," "public housing," "immigrant," "single mother," "union job," "factory worker," "student." I coded the reference as "upper class" if a story used one or more of the following terms when describing the candidate: "upper class," "wealthy," "businessman/woman," "business owner," "rich," "millionaire," "billionaire," "entrepreneur," "banker," "executive," "lottery winner."

Chapter 10

1. The model includes controls for a member's gender, race, Latino ethnicity, age, seniority, geographic region (South), and party used previously. For the Hunt data, I use his measure denoting whether a member is white or not in place of race and Latino ethnicity. I use Congress fixed effects and cluster standard errors by member. Each key independent variable is deployed in a separate model. The number of Congresses in each analysis spans the entire range of the particular dataset used.

The independent variable using CLASS data "Ivy Plus" denotes whether a member received a bachelor's degree from an elite institution—here defined as one of the eight Ivy League schools or California-Berkeley, Chicago, MIT, or Stanford.

2. This finding appears consistent with Kirkland's (2021) research showing that city mayors with experience as business executives prefer to direct public investment to transportation infrastructure rather than to more progressive housing and community-development policy.

3. The legislator is Darrell Issa (R-CA), who made his fortune in the car alarm business.

4. The "proportion of career spent as a worker" variable is statistically significant at the $p < .05$ level if we take just the right-hand side of the distribution. This result confirms a finding of

Carnes (2013, 32–41), who creates different measures of ideology from votes only on economic policy.

Carnes (2013, 32–41) argues that the substantive effects he finds are impressive. But he thinks of them in terms of members who have never been workers and those who spent their entire careers prior to entering Congress as workers. As I have noted, members of the latter group are exceedingly rare—actually not one of the legislators in Carnes's study qualified. There are clearly detectable effects of past labor experience, and as a legislator spent more of their time as a worker they were likely to be more progressive, particularly on economic policy. But these effects have no real-world meaning, since 90 percent of members in Carnes's sample were never workers, and 95 percent of members spent less than 9 percent of their time in the occupation.

5. I should note that prominent conservatives like Sen. Tom Cotton (R-AR) and Ted Cruz (R-TX) also graduated from Harvard Law.

6. Carnes uses AFL-CIO and Chamber of Commerce scores over his earlier time series.

7. No other measures of member net worth, occupation, and education produce statistically significant coefficients.

8. Using the same controls, I added measures of member net worth, occupation, and education from all datasets to models of individual roll-call votes on key economic legislation of the past couple decades: original passage of the 1996 welfare reform bill, the 2001 Bush tax cuts, and the 2009 ACA. Not one key measure of member net worth, occupation, or education produced a statistically significant coefficient.

9. Sen. Robert Wagner (D-NY)—who gave his name to the Social Security Act—had a working-class background but was a lawyer. All three of FDR's Speakers were lawyers—Jo Byrns (D-TN), William Bankhead (D-AL), and Sam Rayburn (D-TX). So were his two Senate majority leaders, Joseph Taylor Robinson (D-AR) and Alben W. Barkley (D-KY). If anything, congressional leaders in the 1930s tended to have backgrounds similar to those of many conservative Republican lawyers in the modern Congress; that is, they often attended law school in their home states and worked in small practices.

10. There is a significant amount of work on the professionalization of state legislatures (Malhotra 2006; Squire and Hamm 2005; Squire 2014, 266–316). The work generally thinks of Congress as highly professionalized and measures professionalization on several continua with dimensions like pay, time in session, and the number of institutional and personal staff. Professionalized legislatures have more "career" politicians and lawyers among their members.

11. Squire (2014, 311–12) surveys a literature that argues that professionalization increases the likelihood that a legislature will produce liberal policy.

12. The 5 percent figure comes from Borchert and Zeiss (2003). Their edited volume analyzes what they call the "political class" in twenty advanced industrialized countries.

13. Again, I refer the reader to Volden and Wiseman (2014, 19–28).

14. I include the measure of lagged legislative effectiveness.

15. Stacy (2021) uses data from Eggers and Klašnja (2019) to show that the top 20 percent of members by wealth are perceptibly more effective than the bottom 80 percent.

16. This particular finding is consistent with Makse's (2022) study of state legislators.

17. See "American Time Use Survey—2023 Results," Bureau of Labor Statistics news release, June 27, 2024, https://www.bls.gov/news.release/pdf/atus.pdf. This finding does not quite hold true for occupation and education, however. For example, individuals who work in blue-collar manufacturing positions work relatively long hours.

18. During 2018, the left-of-center media were awash with opinion pieces advocating an expansion of the House's membership. See, for example, Drutman et al. (2021); "America Needs a Bigger House" 2018.

19. See, for example, Ipsos-Mori's annual "Trust in the Professions" survey. The November 7, 2018, version is at https://www.slideshare.net/IpsosMORI/ipsos-mori-veracity-index-2018 -trust-in-professions.

20. See, for example, the Pew Research Center's *The State of American Jobs* October 6, 2016 survey, at http://www.pewsocialtrends.org/2016/10/06/4-skills-and-training-needed-to-com pete-in-todays-economy/.

Chapter 11

1. A great deal of literature questioned the magnitude of any direct effect that individuals' financial status had on their voting behavior in the 1960s and 1970s. Some of this literature spoke to growing affluence and the diversion of citizens' attention to "post-industrial" matters (Bell 1962; Inglehart 1977). Some of it described how race constituted a cross-cutting force, especially for poorer whites (Carmines and Stimson 1989; Huckfeldt and Kohfeld 1989).

2. Condon and Wichowsky (2020) also argue that Americans rely on subjective analyses of income-group affiliation. They claim, however, that Americans tend to "look down" and compare themselves to less affluent citizens. This tendency results in the adoption of policy preferences that we tend to attribute to wealthier individuals.

3. Kuziemko et al. (2023) use numerous surveys to show that Democrats with more years of schooling have generally preferred higher tax rates and more spending on social welfare than co-partisans with less formal education, presumably because they can more readily discern the redistributive benefits of policies that affect general economic well-being and do not show up simply as gross personal pay.

4. The results are practically identical when we condition the effects of education by ideology in place of party identification.

5. In some years ANES measures education as level attained and in others as the number of years of schooling.

6. This finding is somewhat consistent with a recent comprehensive study of numerous countries that shows that whereas higher-educated citizens are increasingly voting for left-of-center parties, those with higher incomes tend still to vote for right-of-center parties (Gethin et al. 2021).

7. Kuziemko et al. (2023) argue that Democrats with greater education credentials have been more supportive of redistribution than their less schooled co-partisans for over half a century.

8. The response "kept about the same" to the ANES question about welfare spending is the modal category in every survey from 2000 on with the exceptions of 2012 and 2016, when "decreased" was the modal category. In every presidential election year in that period except 2016, at least 40 percent of respondents wished existing spending levels to be maintained.

9. CES labels one of its occupational categories (variable "occupationcat") "professional-lawyer, doctor, teacher, engineer" in 2012. It altered its coding for 2014–2018. I count professionals as those in the "industry classification" variable considered to qualify as "professional, scientific, and technical," "education services," or "health care and social assistance."

10. Brint et al. (2022), on the other hand, suggest that the employment security affluent professionals enjoy permits them to shift their economic focus away from themselves.

11. Individuals' ideology or partisanship can vary by occupation even within narrowly de-fined professional fields. For example, a survey of the large Catalist dataset shows that over twice the proportion of surgeons identify as Republicans as do pediatricians (Sanger-Katz 2016).

12. This is Washington University in St. Louis Weidenbaum Center's American Panel Survey (Smith 2014). Because it contains questions I am particularly interested in, I use the November 2012 panel. See https://wc.wustl.edu/taps-data-archive.

13. The questions about occupation are, for ANES, "What is your main occupation?" (V083234) and, for TAPS, "In your main job, what kind of work do you do?" (EMPL9S12). The professional occupations I use come from the 2010 Census Occupational Category codes and are: architects, surveyors, and cartographers; engineers; life scientists; physical scientists; social scientists and related workers; religious workers; lawyers, judges, and related workers; post-secondary teachers; preschool, primary, secondary, and special education school teachers; other teachers and instructors; librarians, curators, and archivists; and health diagnosing and treating practitioners. In the entire ANES dataset, 150 (or 10.1 percent of those who gave an occupation) were professionals. For the TAPS data, it was 304 (or 30.9 percent). The difference is reasonably large, with ANES producing an amount below the proportion of professionals in the national workforce and TAPS producing one above. The discrepancy is presumably a function of the surveys' different samples and treatment of responses to the occupation question.

14. These variables are age in years, education (measured as years completed (for ANES) or stage completed (for TAPS)), race, gender, marital status, Hispanic ethnicity, union mem-bership (household for ANES, personal for TAPS), whether or not the respondent lived in the South, household income, and a three-point party identification measure with an independent midpoint.

15. The prompts and responses are: Government should reduce federal funding for on sci-entific research (DEF12512), "disapprove," "neither approve nor disapprove," "approve"; Govern-ment should reduce federal funding for education (DEF3512), "disapprove," "neither approve nor disapprove," "approve"; Are you in favor of less government regulation of business? (SFFK358), "strongly against," "against," "neither favor nor against," "favor," "strongly favor"; Do you think it should be government's responsibility to reduce income differences between the rich and the poor? (SFFK1758), "definitely should," "probably should," "don't know," "probably should not," "definitely should not"; The federal government should guarantee a higher minimum wage for workers (IMINWGS13), "strongly agree," "agree," "neither agree not disagree," "disagree," "strongly disagree"; Government should reduce federal funding for programs that help lower income Americans (DEF1512), "disapprove," "neither approve nor disapprove," "approve"; Gov-ernment should raise taxes on incomes over $250,000 (DEF11512), "disapprove," "neither approve nor disapprove," "approve."

16. The variable is "employercat." I just use these three of the nine possible answers.

17. The variable is "industryclass."

18. The variable is CC325.

19. The variable is CC16_351K. For a defense of why Congress did not increase the minimum wage, see chapter 3.

Chapter 12

1. For more on the Consortium on the American Political Economy, see https://www.ameri canpoliticaleconomy.org/.

2. A YouGov poll revealed significant support among the American public. See Orth (2024).

3. For more on the poll, see *WSJ/NORC Poll October 2023*, NORC at the University of Chicago, October 2023, https://s.wsj.net/public/resources/documents/WSJ_NORC_Partial_Oct _2023.pdf. This view should not be exaggerated. An April 2024 Pew Research Center poll reported that the proportion of respondents who believed the "American Dream is still possible" exceeded the proportion who believed it "was once possible" or "was never possible" by 6 percentage points. See Borelli (2024).

References

Abernathy, Scott Franklin. 2007. *No Child Left Behind and the Public Schools: Why NCLB Will Fail to Close the Achievement Gap—and What We Can Do About It.* University of Michigan Press.

Abramowitz, Alan I. 2010. *The Disappearing Center: Engaged Citizens, Polarization and American Democracy.* Yale University Press.

Achen, Christopher H., and Larry M. Bartels. 2016. *Democracy for Realists: Why Elections Do Not Produce Responsive Government.* Princeton University Press.

Adler, E. Scott. 2002. *Why Congressional Reforms Fail: Reelection and the House Committee System.* University of Chicago Press.

Adler, E. Scott, and John S. Lapinski. 1997. "Demand-Side Theory and Congressional Committee Composition: A Constituency Characteristics Approach." *American Journal of Political Science* 41: 895–918.

Agnew, John A. 1987. *Place and Politics: The Geographical Mediation of State and Society.* Routledge.

Ahler, Douglas J., and David E. Broockman. 2018. "The Delegate Paradox: Why Polarized Politicians Can Represent Citizens Best." *Journal of Politics* 80: 1117–33.

Albouy, David. 2013. "Partisan Representation in Congress and the Geographic Distribution of Federal Funds." *Review of Economics and Statistics* 95: 127–41.

Almanac of American Politics. Various years. National Journal.

Althaus, Scott. 2003. *Collective Preferences in Democratic Politics: Opinion Surveys and the Will of the People.* Cambridge University Press.

"America Needs a Bigger House." 2018. *New York Times,* November 9.

American Academy of Arts and Sciences. 2023. *Advancing a People-First Economy.* American Academy of Arts and Sciences. https://www.amacad.org/sites/default/files/publication/downloads/2023_CORE_People-First-Economy.pdf.

Anderson, William, Janet M. Box-Steffensmeier, and Valeria N. Sinclair. 2003. "The Keys to Legislative Success in the U.S. House of Representatives." *Legislative Studies Quarterly* 28: 357–86.

Ansolabehere, Stephen, James M. Snyder, and Michael Ting. 2003. "Bargaining in Bicameral Legislatures." *American Political Science Review* 97: 471–81.

Atkeson, Lonna Rae, and Andrew J. Taylor. 2019. "Partisan Affiliation in Political Science: Insights from Florida and North Carolina." *PS: Political Science and Politics* 52: 706–10.

Atkinson, Anthony B. 2015. *Inequality: What Can Be Done?* Harvard University Press.

Atkinson, Mary Layton, K. Elizabeth Coggins, James A. Stimson, and Frank R. Baumgartner. 2021. *The Dynamics of Public Opinion.* Cambridge University Press.

Auslen, Michael, and Justin H. Phillips. 2024. "Divided by Income? Policy Preferences of the Rich and Poor Within the Democratic and Republican Parties." *Political Behavior* 46: 2473–95. https://doi.org/10.1007/s11109-024-09927-9.

Auten, Gerald, and David Splinter. 2024. "Income Inequality in the U.S.: Using Tax Data to Measure Long-Term Trends." *Journal of Political Economy* 132, no. 7: 2179–227. https://doi .org/10.1086/728741.

Auxier, Richard C. 2010. *Reagan's Recession.* Pew Research Center, December 14. https://www .pewresearch.org/2010/12/14/reagans-recession/.

Auxier, Richard C. 2020. "What Police Spending Data Can (and Cannot) Explain Amid Calls to Defund the Police." Urban Institute, June 9. https://www.urban.org/urban-wire /what-police-spending-data-can-and-cannot-explain-amid-calls-defund-police.

Avery, James M., and Jeffrey A. Fine. 2012. "Racial Composition, White Racial Attitudes, and Black Representation: Testing the Racial Threat Hypothesis in the United States Senate." *Political Behavior* 34: 391–410.

Aviña, Marco Mendoza, and Andre Blaise. 2021. "Are Tax Cuts Supporters Self-Interested and/ or Partisan? The Case of the Tax Cuts and Jobs Act." *American Politics Research* 50: 416–27.

Bacon, Perry, Jr., and Massimo Calabresi. 2006. "America's Ten Best Senators: Those Who Make a Difference in the U.S. Senate—and Five Who Fall Short." *Time*, April 24: 24–36.

Badger, Emily, and Quoctrong Bui. 2018. "Americans Say Their Politics Don't Define Them, but It's Complicated." *New York Times*, October 12. https://www.nytimes.com/interactive /2018/10/12/upshot/us-politics-identity.html.

Bafumi, Joseph, and Michael Herron. 2010. "Leapfrog Representation and Extremism: A Study of American Voters and Their Members of Congress." *American Political Science Review* 104: 519–42.

Bailey, Michael. 2001. "Quiet Influence: The Representation of Diffuse Interests on Trade Policy, 1983–94." *Legislative Studies Quarterly* 26: 45–80.

Baldassarri, Delia, and Andrew Gelman. 2008. "Partisans Without Constraint: Political Polarization and Trends in American Public Opinion." *American Journal of Sociology* 114: 408–46.

Balla, Steven J., Eric D. Lawrence, Forrest Maltzman, and Lee Sigelman. 2002. "Partisanship, Blame Avoidance, and the Distribution of Legislative Pork." *American Journal of Political Science* 46: 515–25.

Ballard-Rosa, Cameron, Lucy Martin, and Kenneth Scheve. 2017. "The Structure of American Income Tax Policy Preferences." *Journal of Politics* 79: 1–16.

Balz, Dan. 2017. "Can Salesmanship About the Tax Bill Change the GOP's Midterm Fortunes?" December 23, *Washington Post.* https://www.washingtonpost.com/politics/can-salesmanship -about-the-tax-bill-change-the-gops-midterms-fortunes/2017/12/23/f2ab3b60-e74f-11e7 -833f-155031558ff4_story.html.

Barber, Michael. J. 2022. "Comparing Campaign Finance and Vote-Based Measures of Ideology." *Journal of Politics*: 84: 613–19.

Barber, Michael J., Brandice Canes-Wrone, and Sharece Thrower. 2017. "Ideologically Sophisticated Donors: Which Candidates Do Individual Contributors Finance?" *American Journal of Political Science* 61: 271–88.

Barber, Michael J., and Jeremy C. Pope. 2018. "Who is Ideological? Measuring Ideological Responses to Policy Questions in the American Public." *Forum* 16: 97–122.

Barber, Michael J., and Jeremy C. Pope. 2019. "Does Party Trump Ideology? Disentangling Party and Ideology in America." *American Political Science Review* 113: 38–54.

Barnes, Tiffany D., Victoria D. Beall, and Mirya R. Holman. 2021. "Pink-Collar Representation and Budgetary Outcomes in the United States." *Legislative Studies Quarterly* 46: 119–54.

Barnes, Tiffany D., and Mirya Holman. 2020. "The Effect of Gender Quotas on Legislative Diversity." *Journal of Politics* 82: 1271–86.

Barnes, Tiffany D., Yana P. Kereval, and Gregory W. Saxton. 2023. *Working Class Inclusion: Evaluations of Democratic Institutions in Latin America.* Cambridge University Press.

Barnes, Tiffany, and Gregory W. Saxton. 2019. "Working-Class Legislators and Perceptions of Representation in Latin America." *Political Research Quarterly* 72: 910–28.

Bartels, Larry M. 2008. *Unequal Democracy: The Political Economy of the New Gilded Age.* Russell Sage Foundation and Princeton University Press.

Bartels, Larry M. 2016. *Unequal Democracy: The Political Economy of the New Gilded Age.* 2nd ed. Russell Sage Foundation and Princeton University Press.

Bartels, Larry M. 2018. "Partisanship in the Trump Era." *Journal of Politics* 80: 1483–94.

Bartels, Larry M., Joshua D. Clinton, and John G. Geer. 2016. "Representation." In *Oxford Handbook of American Development*, edited by Richard Valelly, Suzanne Metler, and Robert Lieberman, 399–426. Oxford University Press.

Bartlett, Bruce. 2009. *The New American Economy: The Failure of Reaganomics and a New Way Forward.* St. Martin's Press.

Baumgartner, Frank R., and Beth L. Leech. 1998. *Basic Interests: The Importance of Groups in Politics and Political Science.* Princeton University Press.

Becher, Michael, and Daniel Stegmueller. 2021. "Reducing Unequal Representation: The Impact of Labor Unions on Legislative Responsiveness in the U.S. Congress." *Perspectives on Politics* 19: 92–109.

Becher, Michael, and Daniel Stegmueller. 2023. "Organized Interests and Mechanisms Behind Unequal Representation in Legislatures." In *Unequal Democracies: Public Policy, Responsiveness, and Redistribution in an Era of Rising Economic Inequality*, edited by Noam Lupu and Jonas Pontusson, 133–55. Cambridge University Press.

Bell, Daniel. 1962. *The End of Ideology.* Harvard University Press.

Beramendi, Pablo, and Phillip Rehm. 2016. "Who Gives, Who Gains? Progressivity and Preferences." *Comparative Political Studies* 49: 529–63.

Berinsky, Adam J. 2004. "Can We Talk? Self-Presentation and the Survey Response." *Political Psychology* 25: 643–59.

Bernhard, William, and Tracy Sulkin. 2018. *Legislative Style.* University of Chicago Press.

Berry, Christopher R., Barry C. Burden, and William G. Howell. 2010. "The President and the Distribution of Federal Spending." *American Political Science Review* 104: 783–99.

Berry, Christopher R., and Anthony Fowler. 2016. "Cardinals or Clerics: Congressional Committees and the Distribution of Pork." *American Journal of Political Science* 60: 692–708.

Best, Heinrich. 2007. "New Challenges, New Elites? Changes in the Recruitment and Career Patterns of European Representative Elites." *Comparative Sociology* 6: 85–113.

Betz, Timm, David Fortunato, and Diana Z. O'Brien. 2021. " "Women's Descriptive Representation and Gendered Import Tax Discrimination." *American Political Science Review* 115: 307–15.

Bhatti, Yosef, and Robert S. Erikson. 2011. "How Poorly Are the Poor Represented in the U.S. Senate?" In *Who Gets Represented?*, edited by Peter K. Enns and Christopher Wlezien, 223–46. Russell Sage Foundation.

Bickers, Kenneth N., and Robert M. Stein. 1996. "The Electoral Dynamics of the Federal Pork Barrel." *American Journal of Political Science* 40: 1300–26.

Binder, Sarah A., and Mark Spindel. 2017. *The Myth of Independence: How Congress Governs the Federal Reserve*. Princeton University Press.

Bishin, Benjamin G. 2000. "Constituency Influence in Congress: Does Subconstituency Matter?" *Legislative Studies Quarterly* 25: 389–415.

Bishin, Benjamin G. 2009. *Tyranny of the Minority: The Subconstituency Politics Theory of Representation*. Temple University Press.

Black, Earl, and Merle E. Black. 2002. *The Rise of the Southern Republicans*. Belknap Press.

Bonica, Adam. 2014. "Mapping the Ideological Marketplace." *American Journal of Political Science* 58: 367–86.

Bonica, Adam. 2020. "Why Are There So Many Lawyers in Congress?" *Legislative Studies Quarterly* 45: 253–89.

Bonica, Adam, Nolan McCarty, Keith T. Poole, and Howard Rosenthal. 2013. "Why Hasn't Democracy Slowed Rising Inequality?" *Journal of Economic Perspectives* 27: 103–24.

Bonica, Adam, Nolan McCarty, Keith T. Poole, and Howard Rosenthal. 2015. "Congressional Polarization and Its Connection to Income Inequality." In *American Gridlock: The Sources, Character, and Impact of Political Polarization*, edited by James A. Thurber and Antoine Yoshinaka, 357–77. Cambridge University Press.

Borchert, Jens, and Jurgen Zeiss, eds. 2003. *The Political Class in Advanced Democracies: A Comparative Handbook*. Oxford University Press.

Bovitz, Gregory, and Jamie Carson. 2006. "Position Taking and Electoral Accountability in the U.S. House of Representatives." *Political Research Quarterly* 59: 297–312.

Bowen, Daniel C., and Christopher J. Clark. 2014. "Revisiting Descriptive Representation in Congress: Assessing the Effect of Race on the Constituent–Legislator Relationship." *Political Research Quarterly* 67: 695–707.

Bower-Bir, Jacob S. 2022. "Desert and Redistribution: Justice as a Remedy for, and Cause of, Economic Inequality." *Policy Studies Journal* 50: 757–95.

Bowman, Jarron. 2020. "Do the Affluent Override Average Americans? Measuring Policy Disagreement and Unequal Influence." *Social Science Quarterly* 101: 1018–37.

Borelli, Gabriel. 2024. "Americans Are Split over the State of the American Dream." Pew Research Center, July 2. https://www.pewresearch.org/short-reads/2024/07/02/americans-are-split-over-the-state-of-the-american-dream/.

Box-Steffensmeier, Janet M., Laura W. Arnold, and Christopher J. W. Zorn. 1997. "The Strategic Timing of Position Taking in Congress: A Study of the North American Free Trade Agreement." *American Political Science Review* 91: 324–38.

Brady, Henry, Sidney Verba, and Kay Lehman Schlozman. 1995. "Beyond SES: A Resource Model of Political Participation." *American Political Science Review* 89: 271–94.

Branham, J. Alexander, Stuart N. Soroka, and Christopher Wlezien. 2017. "When Do the Rich Win?" *Political Science Quarterly* 132: 43–62.

Brint, Steven. 1984. "'New Class' and Cumulative Trend Explanations of the Liberal Political Attitudes of Professionals." *American Journal of Sociology* 90: 30–70.

Brint, Steven, Michaela Curran, and Matthew C. Mahutga. 2022. "Are U.S. Professionals and

Managers More Left Than Blue-Collar Workers? An Analysis of the General Social Survey, 1974 to 2018." *Socius* 8. https://doi.org/10.1177/23780231211068654.

Broockman, David E. 2013. "Black Politicians Are More Intrinsically Motivated to Advance Blacks' Interests: A Field Experiment Manipulating Political Incentives." *American Journal of Political Science* 57: 521–36.

Broockman, David E. 2016. "Approaches to Studying Policy Representation." *Legislative Studies Quarterly* 41: 181–215.

Broockman, David E., Gregory Ferenstein, and Neil Malhotra. 2019. "Predispositions and the Political Behavior of American Economic Elites: Evidence from Technology Entrepreneurs." *American Journal of Political Science* 63: 212–33.

Broockman, David E., and Neil Malhotra. 2020. "What Do Partisan Donors Want?" *Public Opinion Quarterly* 84: 104–18.

Broockman, David E., and Christopher Skovron. 2018. "Bias in Perceptions of Public Opinion Among Political Elites." *American Political Science Review* 112: 542–63.

Brooks, Clem, and David Brady. 1999. "Income, Economic Voting, and Long-Term Political Change in the U.S., 1952–1996." *Social Forces* 77: 1339–75.

Brooks, Clem, and Jeff Manza. 1997a. "The Social and Ideological Bases of Middle Class Political Alignments in the United States, 1972–92." *American Sociological Review* 62: 191–208.

Brooks, Clem, and Jeff Manza. 1997b. "Class Politics and Political Change in the United States, 1952–1992." *Social Forces* 76: 379–409.

Brunner, Eric, Stephen L. Ross, and Ebonya Washington. 2013. "Does Less Income Mean Less Representation?" *American Economic Journal: Economic Policy* 5: 53–76.

Bucci, Laura C. 2018. "Organized Labor's Check on Economic Inequality." *State Politics and Policy Quarterly* 18: 148–73.

Bullock, Charles, III. 2014. "Politics in the South: Out of Step with the Nation Once Again." In *The New Politics of the Old South an Introduction to Southern Politics*, 5th ed., edited by Charles S. Bullock III and Mark J. Rozell, 1–25. Rowman and Littlefield.

Bullock, Charles, III, Ronald Keith Gaddie, and Justin J. Wert. 2016. *The Rise and Fall of the Voting Rights Act*. University of Oklahoma Press.

Burns, John W., and Andrew J. Taylor. 2000. "The Mythical Causes of the Republican Supply-Side Economics Revolution." *Party Politics* 6: 419–40.

Burris, Val. 2000. "The Myth of Old Money Liberalism: The Politics of the 'Forbes' 400 Richest Americans." *Social Forces* 47: 360–78.

Burstein, Paul. 2014. *American Public Opinion, Advocacy, and Policy in Congress: What the Public Wants and What It Gets*. Cambridge University Press.

Butler, Daniel M., and David E. Broockman. 2011. "Do Politicians Racially Discriminate Against Their Constituents? A Field Experiment on State Legislators." *American Journal of Political Science* 55: 463–77.

Butler, Daniel M., and Adam M. Dynes. 2016. "How Politicians Discount the Opinions of Constituents with Whom They Disagree." *American Journal of Political Science* 60: 975–89.

Byers, Jason S., and Laine P. Shay. 2023. "What Explains a Representative's Staffing 'Style'? Exploring the Relationship Between Congressional Staffing Decisions and Electoral Considerations." *American Politics Research* 51: 749–62.

Cain, Bruce, John Ferejohn, and Morris Fiorina. 1987. *The Personal Vote: Constituency Service and Electoral Independence*. Harvard University Press.

Campbell, Andrea Louise. 2002. "Self-Interest, Social Security, and the Distinctive Participation Patterns of Senior Citizens." *American Political Science Review* 96: 565–74.

Campbell, Angus, Philip E. Converse, Warren E. Miller, and Donald Stokes. 1960. *The American Voter*. Wiley.

Campbell, James E. 2016. *Polarized: Making Sense of a Divided America*. Princeton University Press.

Campbell, Rosie, and Philip Cowley. 2014. "What Voters Want: Reactions to Candidate Characteristics in a Survey Experiment." *Political Studies* 62: 745–65.

Canes-Wrone, Brandice. 2006. *Who Leads Whom? Presidents, Policy, and the Public*. University of Chicago Press.

Canes-Wrone, Brandice. 2015. "From Mass Preferences to Policy." *Annual Review of Political Science* 18: 147–65.

Canes-Wrone, Brandice, and Kenneth M. Miller. 2022. "Out-of-District Donors and Representation in the U.S. House." *Legislative Studies Quarterly* 47: 361–95.

Cann, Damon. 2008. *Sharing the Wealth: Member Contributions and the Exchange Theory of Party Influence in the U.S. House of Representatives*. SUNY Press.

Cann, Damon M., and Andrew H. Sidman. 2011. "Exchange Theory, Political Parties, and the Allocation of Federal Distributive Benefits in the House of Representatives." *Journal of Politics* 73: 1128–41.

Cannon, Carl, and Tom Bevan. 2019. "The American Dream—Not Dead Yet." RealClear Opinion Research, March 6. https://www.realclearpolitics.com/real_clear_opinion_research /sweeping_new_poll_reveals_american_attitudes_toward_the_american_dream_and _capitalism.html.

Cansunar, Asli. 2021. "Who Is High Income, Anyway? Social Comparison, Subjective Group Identification, and Preferences over Progressive Taxation." *Journal of Politics* 83: 1292–306.

Carmines, Edward G., and James A. Stimson. 1989. *Issue Evolution: Race and the Transformation of American Politics*. Princeton University Press.

Carnes, Nicholas. 2012. "Does the Numerical Underrepresentation of the Working Class in Congress Matter?" *Legislative Studies Quarterly* 37: 5–34.

Carnes, Nicholas. 2013. *White-Collar Government: The Hidden Role of Class in Economic Policymaking*. University of Chicago Press.

Carnes, Nicholas. 2016. "Who Votes for Inequality?" In *Congress and Policy Making in the 21st Century*, edited by Jeffrey A. Jenkins and Eric M. Patashnik, 106–34. Cambridge University Press.

Carnes, Nicholas. 2018. *The Cash Ceiling: Why Only the Rich Run for Office—and What We Can Do About It*. Princeton University Press.

Carnes, Nicholas. 2023. "Inequality, or Invisibility and Inaccuracy? How Local Newspapers Cover the Occupational Backgrounds of Congressional Incumbents and Challengers." In *Accountability Reconsidered: Voters, Interests, and Information in U.S. Policymaking*, edited by Charles M. Cameron, Brandice Canes-Wrone, Sanford C. Gordon, and Gregory A. Huber, 150–72. Cambridge University Press.

Carnes, Nicholas, and Eric R. Hansen. 2016. "Does Paying Politicians More Promote Economic Diversity in Legislatures?" *American Political Science Review* 110: 699–716.

Carnes, Nicholas, and Eric R. Hansen. 2022. *The 2021–2 State Legislators Dataset*, version 1.5 [computer file]. Duke University https://people.duke.edu/~nwc8/stateleg.html.

Carnes, Nicholas, and Noam Lupu. 2016. "Do Voters Dislike Working Class Candidates? Voter Biases and the Descriptive Underrepresentation of the Working Class." *American Political Science Review* 110: 832–44.

Carnes, Nicholas, and Noam Lupu. 2023. "Working-Class Officeholding in the OECD." In *Unequal Democracies: Public Policy, Responsiveness, and Redistribution in an Era of Rising Economic Inequality*, edited by Noam Lupu and Jonas Pontusson, 177–95. Cambridge University Press.

Carnes, Nicholas, and Meredith L. Sadin. 2015. "The 'Mill Worker's Son' Heuristic: How Voters Perceive Politicians from Working-Class Families—and How They Really Behave in Office." *Journal of Politics* 77: 285–98.

Carroll, Royce, and Henry A. Kim. 2010. "Party Government and 'the Cohesive Power of Public Plunder.'" *American Journal of Political Science* 54: 34–44.

Carsey, Thomas M., and Barry Rundquist. 1999. "Party and Committee in Distributive Politics: Evidence from Defense Spending." *Journal of Politics* 61: 1156–69.

Cavaillé, Charlotte. 2023. *Fair Enough? Support for Redistribution in the Age of Inequality.* Cambridge University Press.

Cayton, Adam, and Ryan Dawkins. 2020. "Incongruent Voting or Symbolic Representation? Asymmetrical Representation in Congress, 2008–2014." *Perspectives on Politics* 20: 916–30.

Chase, Kerry A. 2015. "Domestic Geography and Policy Pressures." In *The Oxford Handbook of the Political Economy of International Trade*, edited by Lisa L. Martin, 316–34. Oxford University Press.

Chetty, Raj, David Grusky, Maximilian Hell, Nathaniel Hendren, Robert Manduca, and Jimmy Narang. 2017. "The Fading American Dream: Trends in Absolute Income Mobility Since 1940." *Science* 356: 398–406.

Chetty, Raj, Matthew O. Jackson, Theresa Kuchler, Johannes Stroebel, Nathaniel Hendren, Robert B. Fluegge, et al. 2022. "Social Capital I: Measurement and Associations with Economic Mobility." *Nature* 608: 108–21.

Claassen, Christopher, Patrick Tucker, and Steven S. Smith. 2015. "Ideological Labels in America." *Political Behavior* 37: 253–78.

Clarke, Harold D., Matthew Goodwin, and Paul Whiteley. 2017. *Brexit: Why Britain Voted to Leave the European Union.* Cambridge University Press.

Clayton, Amanda, and Par Zetterberg. 2018. "Quota Shocks: The Budgetary Implications of Electoral Gender Quotas Worldwide." *Journal of Politics* 80: 916–32.

Clemens, Austin C., Michael H. Crespin, and Charles J. Finocchiaro. 2015. "The Political Geography of Distributive Politics." *Legislative Studies Quarterly* 40: 111–36.

Clinton, Joshua D. 2006. "Representation in Congress: Constituents and Roll Calls in the 106th House." *Journal of Politics* 68: 397–409.

Cohen, Geoffrey L. 2003. "Party over Policy: The Dominating Impact of Group Influence on Political Beliefs." *Journal of Personality and Social Psychology* 85: 808–22.

Cohn, Alain, Lasse J. Jessen, Marko Klašnja, and Paul Smeets. 2023. "Wealthy Americans and Redistribution: The Role of Fairness Principles." *Journal of Public Economics* 225 (September): 104977. https://doi.org/10.1016/j.jpubeco.2023.104977.

Condon, Meghan, and Amber Wichowsky. 2020. *The Economic Other: Inequality in the American Political Imagination.* University of Chicago Press.

Converse, Phillip. 1964. "The Nature of Belief Systems in Mass Publics." In *Ideology and Its Discontent*, edited by D. E. Apter, 206–61. Free Press of Glencoe.

Cook, Fay Lomax, and Edith Barrett. 1992. *Support for the American Welfare State.* Columbia University Press.

Cooper, Christopher A., and H. Gibbs Knotts. 2017. *The Resilience of Southern Identity.* University of North Carolina Press.

Cormack, Lindsey. 2018. *Congress and U.S. Veterans: From the GI Bill to the VA Crisis.* Praeger.

Cox, Gary W., and Mathew D. McCubbins. 1993. *Legislative Leviathan: Party Government in the House.* University of California Press.

Cox, Gary W., and Mathew D. McCubbins. 2005. *Setting the Agenda: Responsible Party Government in the U.S. House of Representatives.* Cambridge University Press.

Cox, Gary, and William C. Terry. 2008. "Legislative Productivity in the 93d–105th Congresses." *Legislative Studies Quarterly* 33: 603–18.

CQ Almanac. 1993. *The 49th Annual CQ Almanac, 103rd Congress, 1st Session.* CQ Press.

Cramer, Katherine J. 2016. *The Politics of Resentment: Rural Consciousness in Wisconsin and the Rise of Scott Walker.* University of Chicago Press.

Crosson, Jesse, Alexander C. Furnas, and Geoffrey Lorenz. 2020. "Polarized Pluralism: Organizational Preferences and Biases in the American Pressure System." *American Political Science Review* 114: 1117–37.

Curry, James M., and Christopher P. Donnelly. 2021. "State Congressional Delegations and the Distribution of Federal Funds." *Political Research Quarterly* 74: 756–71.

Curry, James M., and Matthew R. Haydon. 2018. "Lawmaker Age, Issue Salience, and Senior Representation in Congress." *American Politics Research* 46: 567–95.

Dabros, Matthew S. 2017. *Careers After Congress: Do Jobseeking Legislators Shortchange Constituents?* Praeger.

Dahl, Robert. 1956. *A Preface to Democratic Theory.* University of Chicago Press.

Dal Bo, Ernesto, Frederico Finan, Olle Folke, Torsten Perrson, and Johanna Rickne. 2017. "Who Becomes a Politician?" *Quarterly Journal of Economics* 132: 1877–914.

Dalton, Russell J. 2017. *The Participation Gap: Social Status and Political Inequality.* Oxford University Press.

Dawkins, Ryan, Zoe Nemerever, B. Kal Munis, and Francesca Verville. 2023. "Place, Race, and the Geographic Politics of White Grievance." *Political Behavior* 46: 1813–35. https://doi.org/10.1007/s11109-023-09897-4.

Deering, Christopher, and Steven S. Smith. 1997. *Committees in Congress.* 3rd ed. Congressional Quarterly Press.

Delli Carpini, Michael X., and Scott Keeter. 1996. *What Americans Know About Politics and Why it Matters.* Yale University Press.

Den Hartog, Chris, and Nathan Monroe. 2011. *Agenda Setting in the U.S. Senate.* Cambridge University Press.

Dettrey, Bryan J., and James E. Campbell. 2013. "Has Growing Income Inequality Polarized the American Electorate? Class, Party, and Ideological Polarization." *Social Science Quarterly* 94: 1062–83.

DiMaggio, Anthony R. 2021. *Unequal America: Class Consciousness, Mass Media, and Political Beliefs in an Era of Record Inequality.* Routledge.

Dimick, Matthew, David Rueda, and Daniel Stegmueller. 2018. "Models of Other-Regarding Preferences, Inequality, and Redistribution." *Annual Review of Political Science* 21, no. 1 (May): 441–60.

Dixit, Avinash, and John Londregan. 1996. "The Determinants of Success of Special Interests in Redistributive Politics." *Journal of Politics* 58: 1132–55.

Donovan, Todd, and Shaun Bowler. 2022. "Who Wants to Raise Taxes?" *Political Research Quarterly* 75: 35–46.

Downs, Anthony. 1957. *An Economic Theory of Democracy.* Harper.

Drew, Elizabeth. 1994. *On the Edge: The Clinton Presidency.* Simon and Schuster.

Drutman, Lee. 2019. "The Moderate Middle Is a Myth." *FiveThirtyEight*, September 24. https://fivethirtyeight.com/features/the-moderate-middle-is-a-myth/.

Drutman, Lee, Jonathan D. Cohen, Yuval Levin, and Norman J. Ornstein. 2021. *The Case for Enlarging the House of Representatives.* Academy of Arts and Sciences.

Duca, John V., and Jason L. Saving. 2016. "Income Inequality and Political Polarization: Time Series Evidence over Nine Decades." *Review of Income and Wealth* 62: 445–66.

Dynes, Adam M., and Gregory A. Huber. 2015. "Partisanship and the Allocation of Federal Spending: Do Same-Party Legislators or Voters Benefit from Shared Party Affiliation with the President and the House Majority?" *American Political Science Review* 109: 172–86.

Early, John F. 2018. "Reassessing the Facts about Inequality, Poverty, and Redistribution." Policy analysis no. 839. Cato Institute, April 24. https://www.cato.org/policy-analysis/reassessing-facts-about-inequality-poverty-redistribution.

Edwards, George C. III. 2021. *Changing Their Minds? Donald Trump and Presidential Leadership.* University of Chicago Press.

Eggers, Andrew, and Marko Klašnja. 2019. "Wealth, Fundraising, and Voting in the U.S. Congress." Working paper, Georgetown University. Presented at the 8th Annual Conference of the European Political Science Association, Vienna, Austria, June 21–23, 2018.

Ekins, Emily. 2015. "Poll: Americans Like Free Markets More Than Capitalism and Socialism More Than a Govt Managed Economy." *Reason*, February 12. https://reason.com/2015/02/12/poll-americans-like-free-markets-more-th/.

Elder, Elizabeth Mitchell, and Neil A. O'Brian. 2022. "Social Groups as the Source of Political Belief Systems: Fresh Evidence on an Old Theory." *American Political Science Review* 116: 1407–24.

Elkjaer, Mads Andreas, and Torben Iversen. 2023. "The Democratic State and Redistribution: Whose Interests Are Served?" *American Political Science Review* 117: 391–406.

Elkjaer, Mads Andreas, and Michael Baggesen Klitgaard. 2024. "Economic Inequality and Political Responsiveness: A Systematic Review." *Perspectives on Politics* 22: 318–37.

Ellis, Christopher. 2012. "Understanding Economic Biases in Representation: Income, Resources, and Policy Representation in the 110th House." *Political Research Quarterly* 65: 938–51.

Ellis, Christopher. 2013. "Social Context and Economic Biases in Representation." *Journal of Politics* 75: 773–86.

Ellis, Christopher. 2017. *Putting Inequality in Context: Class, Public Opinion, and Representation in the United States.* University of Michigan Press.

Ellis, Christopher, and Christopher Faricy. 2021. *The Other Side of the Coin: Public Opinion Toward Social Tax Expenditures.* Russell Sage Foundation.

Ellis, Christopher, and James A. Stimson. 2012. *Ideology in America* Cambridge University Press.

Ellis, Christopher, and Joseph Daniel Ura. 2011. "United We Divide? Education, Income, and Heterogeneity in Mass Partisan Polarization." In *Who Gets Represented?*, edited by Peter K. Enns and Christopher Wlezien, 61–92. Russell Sage Foundation.

English, Ashley, Kathryn Pearson, and Dara Z. Strolovitch. 2019. "Who Represents Me? Race, Gender, Partisan Congruence, and Representational Alternatives in a Polarized America." *Political Research Quarterly* 72: 785–804.

Engstrom, Erik J., and Robert Huckfeldt. 2020. *Race, Class, and Social Welfare: American Populism Since the New Deal.* Cambridge University Press.

Engstrom, Erik J., and Georg Vanberg. 2010. "Assessing the Allocation of Pork: Evidence from Congressional Earmarks." *American Politics Research* 38: 959–85.

Enke, Benjamin, Mattias K. Polborn, and Alex Wu. 2022. "Morals as Luxury Goods and Political Polarization." Working paper. September 30. https://benjamin-enke.com/pdf/Morals_po larization.pdf.

Enns, Peter K. 2015. "Relative Policy Support and Coincidental Representation." *Perspectives on Politics* 13: 1053–64.

Enns, Peter K. 2022. "Reconsidering Representation: How the Same Data Can Produce Divergent Conclusions About the Quality of Democratic Responsiveness in the United States." In *Contested Representation: Challenges, Shortcomings, and Reforms*, edited by Claudia Landwehr, Thomas Saalfeld, and Armin Schafer, 103–28. Cambridge University Press.

Enns, Peter K., and Paul M. Kellstedt. 2008. "Policy Mood and Political Sophistication: Why Everybody Moves Mood." *British Journal of Political Science* 38: 433–54.

Enns, Peter K., Nathan J. Kelly, Jana Morgan, Thomas Volscho, and Christopher Witko. 2014. "Conditional Status Quo Bias and Top Income Shares: How U.S. Political Institutions Have Benefited the Rich." *Journal of Politics* 76: 289–303.

Enns, Peter K., and Christopher Wlezien. 2011. "Group Opinion and the Study of Representation." In *Who Gets Represented?*, edited by Peter K. Enns and Christopher Wlezien, 1–25. Russell Sage Foundation.

Enos, Ryan D. 2016. "What the Demolition of Public Housing Teaches Us About the Impact of Racial Threat on Political Behavior." *American Journal of Political Science* 60: 123–42.

Enten, Harry. 2017. "The GOP Tax Cuts Are Even More Unpopular Than Past Tax Hikes." *FiveThirtyEight*, November 29. https://fivethirtyeight.com/features/the-gop-tax-cuts-are -even-more-unpopular-than-past-tax-hikes/.

Erikson, Robert S., Michael B. MacKuen, and James A. Stimson. 2002. *The Macro Polity.* Cambridge University Press.

Erikson, Robert S., Gerald C. Wright, and John P. McIver. 1993. *Statehouse Democracy: Public Opinion and Policy in the American States.* Cambridge University Press.

Essig, Joseph, Ping Xu, James C. Garand, and Ceren Keser. 2021. "The 'Trump' Effect: Political Elite and Support for Free Trade in America." *American Politics Research* 49: 328–48.

Esterling, Kevin M. 2007. "Buying Expertise: Campaign Contributions and Attention to Policy Analysis in Congressional Committees." *American Political Science Review* 101: 93–109.

Evans, C. Lawrence. 2024. "Senate Countermajoritarianism." *American Political Science Review*: 1–18. https://doi.org/10.1017/S0003055424000510.

Evans, Diana. 2004. *Greasing the Wheels: Using Pork Barrel Projects to Build Majority Coalitions in Congress.* Cambridge University Press.

Fanelli, Daniele. 2012. "Negative Results Are Disappearing from Most Disciplines and Countries." *Scientometrics* 90: 891–904.

Faricy, Christopher. 2015. *Welfare for the Wealthy: Parties, Social Spending, and Inequality in the United States.* Cambridge University Press.

Fenno, Richard F., Jr. 1978. *Home Style: House Members in Their Districts.* Little, Brown.

Ferejohn, John A. 1974. *Pork Barrel Politics: Rivers and Harbors Legislation, 1947–1968.* Stanford University Press.

Fine, Jeffrey A., and James M. Avery. 2014. "Do Senators Respond to Minority Voters? Latino Turnout and Representation." *Social Science Quarterly* 95: 1172–88.

Fiorina, Morris P. 1973. "Electoral Margins, Constituency Influence and Policy Moderation: A Critical Assessment." *American Politics Quarterly* 1: 479–98.

Fiorina, Morris P. 1977. *Congress: Keystone of the Washington Establishment*. Yale University Press.

Fiorina, Morris P. 1981. *Retrospective Voting in American Elections*. Yale University Press.

Flavin, Patrick. 2018. "Labor Union Strength and the Equality of Political Representation." *British Journal of Political Science* 48: 1075–91.

Folke, Olle, and Johanna Rickne. 2023. "The Class Ceiling in Politics." *American Political Science Review*: 1–18. https://doi.org/10.1017/S0003055424001011.

Fowler, Anthony, Seth J. Hill, Jeffrey B. Lewis, Chris Tausanovitch, Lynn Vavreck, and Christopher Warshaw. 2023. "Moderates." *American Political Science Review* 173: 643–60.

Fowler, Erika Franklin, Michael Franz, and Travis N. Ridout. 2017. "Political Advertising in 2014." Version 1.0 [dataset]. Wesleyan Media Project, Department of Government at Wesleyan University. https://mediaproject.wesleyan.edu/.

Fowler, Erika Franklin, Michael M. Franz, Travis N. Ridout, and Laura M. Baum. 2019. "Political Advertising in 2016." Version 1.0 [dataset]. Wesleyan Media Project, Department of Government at Wesleyan University. https://mediaproject.wesleyan.edu/.

Francia, Peter. L. 2006. *The Future of Organized Labor in American Politics*. Columbia University Press.

Francia, Peter. L. 2012. "Do Unions Still Matter in U.S. Elections? Assessing Labor's Political Power and Significance." *Forum* 10, no. 1: article 3.

Frank, Thomas. 2004. *What's the Matter with Kansas? How Conservatives Won the Heart of America*. Holt.

Franko, William, Nathan J. Kelly, and Christopher Witko. 2016. "Class Bias in Voter Turnout, Representation, and Income Inequality." *Perspectives on Politics* 14: 351–68.

Franko, William, Caroline Tolbert, and Christopher Witko. 2013. "Inequality, Self-Interest, and Public Support for 'Robin Hood' Tax Policies." *Political Research Quarterly* 66: 923–37.

Franko, William W., and Christopher Witko. 2018. *The New Economic Populism: How States Respond to Economic Inequality*. Oxford University Press.

Franko, William W., and Christopher Witko. 2023a. "Unions, Class Identification, and Policy Attitudes." *Journal of Politics* 85: 553–67.

Franko, William W., and Christopher Witko. 2023b. "Class, Policy Attitudes, and U.S. Presidential Voting in the Post-Industrial Era: The Importance of Issue Salience." *Political Research Quarterly* 76, no. 2: 882–98.

Frankovic, Kathleen A. 1993. "Public Opinion in the 1992 Campaign." In *The Election of 1992*, edited by Gerald M. Pomper, 110–31. Chatham House.

Frisch, Scott A., and Sean Q. Kelly. 2006. *Committee Assignment Politics in the U.S. House*. University of Oklahoma Press.

Froman, Lewis A. 1963. *Congressmen and Their Constituencies*. Rand, McNally.

Gailmard, Sean, and Jeffrey A. Jenkins. 2007. "Negative Agenda Control in the Senate and House: Fingerprints of Majority Party Power." *Journal of Politics* 69: 689–700.

Gamm, Gerald, and Thad Kousser. 2023. "The Last Shall be the Last: Ethnic, Racial, and Nativist Bias in Distributive Politics." *Legislative Studies Quarterly* 48: 765–96.

Ganz, Scott, and Alex Brill. 2020. "Progressivity, Redistribution, and Inequality." *National Affairs* 53 (Fall): 74–86.

Garand, James C. 2010. "Income Inequality, Party Polarization, and Roll-Call Voting in the U.S. Senate." *Journal of Politics* 72: 1109–28.

Gelman, Andrew. 2009. *Red State, Blue State, Rich State, Poor State*. Princeton University Press.

Gerring, John, Erzen Oncel, Kevin Morrison, and Daniel Pemstein. 2019. "Who Rules the World? A Portrait of the Global Leadership Class." *Perspectives on Politics* 17: 1079–97.

Gest, Justin. 2016. *The New Minority: White Working Class Politics in an Age of Immigration and Inequality*. Oxford University Press.

Gethin, Amory, Clara Martinez-Toledano, and Thomas Piketty, eds. 2021. *Political Cleavages and Social Inequalities: A Study of Fifty Democracies, 1948–2020*. Harvard University Press.

Gilens, Martin. 1999. *Why Americans Hate Welfare: Race, Media, and the Politics of Anti-Poverty Policy*. University of Chicago Press.

Gilens, Martin. 2012. *Affluence and Influence: Economic Inequality and Political Power in America*. Russell Sage Foundation and Princeton University Press.

Gilens, Martin, and Benjamin I. Page. 2014. "Testing Theories of American Politics: Elites, Interest Groups, and Average Citizens." *Perspectives on Politics* 12: 564–81.

Gilens, Martin, and Adam Thal. 2018. "Doing Well and Doing Good? How Concern for Others Shapes Policy Preferences and Partisanship Among Affluent Americans." *Public Opinion Quarterly* 82: 209–30.

Gimpel, James G., Frances E. Lee, and Shanna Pearson-Merkowitz. 2008. "The Check Is in the Mail: Inter-District Funding Flows in Congressional Elections." *American Journal of Political Science* 52: 373–94.

Gonzalez Juenke, Eric, and Robert R. Preuhs. 2012. "Irreplaceable Legislators? Rethinking Minority Representatives in the New Century." *American Journal of Political Science* 56: 705–15.

Goodhart, David. 2017. *The Road to Somewhere: The Populist Revolt and the Future of Politics*. Hurst.

Gordon, Sanford C., and Hannah K. Simpson. 2018. "The Birth of Pork: Local Appropriations in America's First Century." *American Political Science Review* 112: 564–79.

Goren, Lilly. 2003. *The Politics of Military Base Closings: Not in My District*. Peter Lang.

Graetz, Michael J., and Ian Shapiro. 2005. *Death by a Thousand Cuts: The Fight over Taxing Inherited Wealth*. Princeton University Press.

Gramm, Phil, Robert Ekelund, and John Early. 2022. *The Myth of American Inequality: How Government Biases Policy Debate*. Rowman Littlefield.

Gray, Thomas R., and Jeffery A. Jenkins. 2017. "Unpacking Pivotal Politics: Exploring the Differential Effects of the Filibuster and Veto Pivots." *Public Choice* 172: 359–76.

Green, Donald, Bradley Palmquist, and Eric Schickler. 2002. *Partisan Hearts and Minds: Political Parties and the Social Identities of Voters*. Yale University Press.

Greene, Steven. 1999. "Understanding Party Identification: A Social Identity Approach." *Political Psychology* 20: 393–403.

Griffin, John D. 2006a. "Senate Apportionment as a Source of Political Inequality." *Legislative Studies Quarterly* 31: 405–32.

Griffin, John D. 2006b. "Electoral Competition and Democratic Responsiveness: A Defense of the Marginality Hypothesis." *Journal of Politics* 68: 909–19.

Griffin, John D., and Claudia Anewalt-Remsburg. 2013. "Legislator Wealth and the Effort to Repeal the Estate Tax." *American Politics Research* 41: 599–622.

Griffin, John D., and Patrick Flavin. 2011. "How Citizens and Their Legislators Prioritize Spheres of Representation." *Political Research Quarterly* 64: 520–33.

Griffin, John D., and Brian Newman. 2008. *Minority Report: Evaluating Political Equality in America*. University of Chicago Press.

Griffin, John D., and Brian Newman. 2013. "Voting Power, Policy Representation, and Disparities in Voting's Rewards." *Journal of Politics* 75: 52–64.

Griffin, John D., Brian Newman, and Patrick Buhr. 2020. "Class War in the Voting Booth: Bias Against High-Income Congressional Candidates." *Legislative Studies Quarterly* 45: 131–45.

Griffin, John D., Brian Newman, and Christina Wolbrecht. 2012. "A Gender Gap in Policy Representation in the U.S. Congress." *Legislative Studies Quarterly* 37: 35–66.

Grimmer, Justin, Solomon Messing, and Sean J. Westwood. 2012. "How Words and Money Cultivate a Personal Vote: The Effect of Legislator Credit Claiming on Constituent Credit Allocation." *American Political Science Review* 106: 703–19.

Grimmer, Justin, Sean J. Westwood, and Solomon Messing. 2014. *The Impression of Influence: Legislator Communication, Representation, and Democratic Accountability*. Princeton University Press.

Grose, Christian R. 2011. *Congress in Black and White: Race and Representation in Washington and at Home*. Cambridge University Press.

Grose, Christian R. 2013. "Risk and Roll Calls: How Legislators' Personal Finances Shape Congressional Decisions." USC CLASS research paper no. CLASS13-7; USC Law legal studies paper no. 13-20. *Social Science Research Network*, December 10. https://ssrn.com/abstract=2220524 or http://dx.doi.org/10.2139/ssrn.2220524.

Groseclose, Tim, and James Snyder. 1996. "Buying Supermajorities." *American Political Science Review* 90: 303–15.

Groseclose, Tim, and Charles Stewart, III. 1998. "The Value of Committee Seats in the House, 1947–91." *American Journal of Political Science* 42: 453–74.

Grossmann, Matt. 2019. *Red State Blues: How the Conservative Revolution Stalled in the States*. Cambridge University Press.

Grossmann, Matt. 2021. *How Social Science Got Better: Overcoming Bias with More Evidence, Diversity, and Self-Reflection*. Oxford University Press.

Grossmann, Matt, and David A. Hopkins. 2016. *Asymmetric Politics: Ideological Republicans and Interest Group Democrats*. Oxford University Press.

Grossmann, Matt, and David A. Hopkins. 2024. *Polarized by Degrees: How the Diploma Divide and Culture War Transformed American Politics*. Cambridge University Press.

Grossmann, Matt, Zuhaib Mahmood, and William Isaac. 2021. "Political Parties, Interest Groups, and Unequal Class Influence in American Policy." *Journal of Politics* 83: 1706–20.

Grossmann, Matt, and Kurt Pyle. 2013. "Lobbying and Congressional Bill Advancement." *Interest Groups and Advocacy* 2: 91–111.

Grossmann, Matt, and Christopher Wlezien. 2024. "A Thermostatic Model of Congressional Elections." *American Politics Research* 52: 355–66.

Grumbach, Jacob M. 2015. "Does the American Dream Matter for Members of Congress? Social Class Backgrounds and Roll-Call Votes." *Political Research Quarterly* 68: 306–23.

Grumbach, Jacob M. 2022. *Laboratories Against Democracy: How National Parties Transformed State Politics*. Princeton University Press.

Grumbach, Jacob M., Jacob S. Hacker, and Paul Pierson. 2022. "The Political Economies of Red States." In *The American Political Economy: Politics, Markets, and Power*, edited by Jacob S. Hacker, Alexander Hertel-Fernandez, Paul Pierson, and Kathleen Thelen, 209–43. Cambridge University Press.

Hacker, Jacob S. 2002. *The Divided Welfare State: The Battle over Public and Private Social Benefits in the United States*. Cambridge University Press.

Hacker, Jacob S., Alexander Hertel-Fernandez, Paul Pierson, and Kathleen Thelen, eds. 2022a. *The American Political Economy: Politics, Markets, and Power*. Cambridge University Press.

Hacker, Jacob S., Alexander Hertel-Fernandez, Paul Pierson, and Kathleen Thelen, eds. 2022b. "Introduction: The American Political Economy: A Framework and Agenda for Research." In *The American Political Economy: Politics, Markets, and Power*, edited by Jacob S. Hacker, Alexander Hertel-Fernandez, Paul Pierson, and Kathleen Thelen, 1–48. Cambridge University Press.

Hacker, Jacob S., and Paul Pierson. 2005. *Off-Center: The Republican Revolution and the Erosion of American Democracy*. Yale University Press.

Hacker, Jacob S., and Paul Pierson. 2010. *Winner-Take-All Politics*. Simon and Schuster.

Hacker, Jacob S., and Paul Pierson. 2016. *American Amnesia: How the War on Government Led Us to Forget What Made America Prosper*. Simon and Schuster.

Hacker, Jacob S., and Paul Pierson. 2020. *Let Them Eat Tweets: How the Right Rules in an Age of Extreme Inequality*. Simon and Schuster.

Haider-Markel, Donald P. 2010. *Out and Running: Gay and Lesbian Candidates, Elections, and Policy Representation*. Georgetown University Press.

Hajnal, Zoltan. 2020. *Dangerously Divided: How Race and Class Shape Winning and Losing in American Politics*. Cambridge University Press.

Hall, Andrew B., and Jesse Yoder. 2022. "Does Homeownership Influence Political Behavior? Evidence from Administrative Data." *Journal of Politics* 84: 351–66.

Halliez, Adrien A., and Judd R. Thornton. 2021. "Examining Trends in Ideological Identification: 1972–2016." *American Politics Research* 49: 259–68.

Hansen, Eric R., and Sarah A. Treul. 2015. "The Symbolic and Substantive Representation of LGB Americans in the U.S. House." *Journal of Politics* 77: 955–67.

Hansen, Kristina Jessen. 2023. "Greed, Envy, and Admiration: The Distinct Nature of Public Opinion About Redistribution from the Rich." *American Political Science Review* 117: 217–34.

Harden, Jeffrey J. 2016. *Multidimensional Democracy: A Supply and Demand Theory of Representation in American Legislatures*. Cambridge University Press.

Hare, Christopher. 2022. "Constrained Citizens? Ideological Structure and Conflict Extension in the U.S. Electorate, 1980–2016." *British Journal of Political Science* 52: 1602–21.

Harris, John F. 2005. *The Survivor: Bill Clinton in the White House*. Random House.

Hartz, Louis. 1955. *The Liberal Tradition in America*. Harcourt Brace.

Harvey, David. 2005. *A Brief History of Neoliberalism*. Oxford University Press.

Hasecke, Edward B., and Jason D. Mycoff. 2007. "Party Loyalty and Legislative Success: Are Loyal Majority Party Members More Successful in the U.S. House of Representatives?" *Political Research Quarterly* 60: 607–17.

Hasen, Richard L. 2016. *Plutocrats United: Campaign Money, the Supreme Court, and the Distortion of American Elections*. Yale University Press.

Hauk, William R., Jr., and Roman Wacziarg. 2007. "Small States, Big Pork." *Quarterly Journal of Political Science* 2: 95–106.

Hayes, Thomas J. 2013. "Responsiveness in an Era of Inequality: The Case of the U.S. Senate." *Political Research Quarterly* 66: 585–99.

Hayes, Thomas J., and Benjamin G. Bishin. 2012. "Issue Salience, Subconstituency Politics, and Legislative Representation." *Congress and the Presidency* 39: 133–59.

Hays, R. Allen. 1995. *The Federal Government and Urban Housing: Ideology and Change in Public Policy*. State University of New York Press.

Heberlig, Eric S., and Bruce A. Larson. 2012. *Congressional Parties, Institutional Ambition, and the Financing of Majority Control*. University of Michigan Press.

Heffington, Colton, Brandon Beomseob Park, and Laron K. Williams. 2017. "The 'Most Important Problem' Dataset (MIPD): A New Dataset on American Issue Importance." *Conflict Management and Peace Science* 36: 312–35.

Herrera, Richard, and Michael Yawn. 1999. "The Emergence of the Personal Vote." *Journal of Politics* 61: 136–50.

Hersh, Eitan D. 2020. *Politics Is for Power: How to Move Beyond Political Hobbyism, Take Action, and Make Real Change*. Scribner.

Hersh, Eitan D., and Clayton Nall. 2015. "The Primacy of Race in the Geography of Income-Based Voting: New Evidence from Public Voting Records." *American Journal of Political Science* 60: 289–303.

Hertel-Fernandez, Alexander. 2019. *State Capture: How Conservative Activists, Big Businesses and Wealthy Donors Reshaped the American States—and the Nation*. Oxford University Press.

Hertel-Fernandez, Alexander. 2022. "Collective Action, Law, and the Fragmented Development of the American Labor Movement." In *The American Political Economy: Politics, Markets, and Power*, edited by Jacob S. Hacker, Alexander Hertel-Fernandez, Paul Pierson, and Kathleen Thelen, 103–29. Cambridge University Press.

Hibbs, Douglas A., Jr. 1977. "Political Parties and Macroeconomic Policy." *American Political Science Review* 71: 1467–87.

Hicks, William D., Carl E. Klarner, Seth C. McKee, and Daniel A. Smith. 2018. "Revisiting Majority-Minority Districts and Black Representation." *Political Research Quarterly* 71: 408–23.

Higgs, Robert, and Anthony Kilduff. 1994. "Public Opinion: A Powerful Predictor of U.S. Defense Spending?" *Defense Economics* 5: 255–8.

Hillygus, D. Sunshine, and Todd A. Shields. 2008. *The Persuadable Voter: Wedge Issues in Presidential Campaigns*. Princeton University Press.

Hochschild, Jennifer L. 1981. *What's Fair: American Beliefs About Distributive Justice*. Harvard University Press.

Holian, David B., Timothy B. Krebs, and Michael H. Walsh. 1997. "Constituency Opinion, Ross Perot, and Roll-Call Behavior in the U.S. House: The Case of NAFTA." *Legislative Studies Quarterly* 22: 369–92.

Hopkins, Daniel J. 2018. *The Increasingly United States: How and Why American Political Behavior Nationalized*. University of Chicago Press.

Hopkins, Daniel J. 2023. *Stable Condition: Elites' Limited Influence on Health Care Attitudes*. Russell Sage Foundation.

Howard, Christopher. 1997. *The Hidden Welfare State: Tax Expenditures and Social Policy in the United States*. Princeton University Press.

Howard, Christopher. 2007. *The Welfare State Nobody Knows: Debunking Myths About U.S. Social Policy*. Princeton University Press.

Howell, William, Scott Adler, Charles Cameron, and Charles Riemann. 2000. "Divided Government and the Legislative Productivity of Congress, 1945–94." *Legislative Studies Quarterly* 25: 285–312.

Hoy, Christopher, and Franziska Mager. 2021. "Why Are Relatively Poor People Not More Supportive of Redistribution? Evidence from a Randomized Survey Experiment Across Ten Countries." *American Economic Journal: Economic Policy* 13: 299–328.

Huckfeldt, Robert, and Carol Weitzel Kohfeld. 1989. *Race and the Decline of Class in American Politics*. University of Illinois Press.

Huddy, Leonie, Lilliana Mason, and Lene Aaroe. 2015. "Expressive Partisanship: Campaign Involvement, Political Emotion, and Partisan Identity." *American Political Science Review* 109: 1–17.

Hunt, Charles. 2022. *Home Field Advantage: Roots, Reelection, and Representation in the Modern Congress*. University of Michigan Press.

Hutchings, Vincent L., Harwood K. McClerking, and Guy-Uriel Charles. 2004. "Congressional Representation of Black Interests: Recognizing the Importance of Stability." *Journal of Politics* 66: 450–68.

Inglehart, Ronald. 1977. *The Silent Revolution: Changing Values and Political Styles Among Western Publics*. Princeton University Press.

Irwin, Douglas A. 2017. *Clashing over Commerce: A History of U.S. Trade Policy*. University of Chicago Press.

Iversen, Torben, and David Soskice. 2015. "Information, Inequality, and Mass Polarization: Ideology in Advanced Democracies." *Comparative Political Studies* 48: 1781–813.

Jacobs, Alan M., J. Scott Matthews, Timothy Hicks, and Eric Merkley. 2021. "Whose News? Class-Based Economic Reporting in the United States." *American Political Science Review* 115: 1016–33.

Jacobs, Nicholas F., and B. Kal Munis. 2019. "Place-Based Imagery and Voter Evaluations: Experimental Evidence on the Politics of Place." *Political Research Quarterly* 72: 263–77.

Jacobs, Nicholas F., and B. Kal Munis. 2023. "Place-Based Resentment in Contemporary U.S. Elections: The Individual Sources of America's Urban-Rural Divide." *Political Research Quarterly* 76: 1102–18.

Jacobs, Nicholas F., and Daniel M. Shea. 2024. *The Rural Voter: The Politics of Place and the Disuniting of America*. Columbia University Press.

Jacobson, Gary C., and Jamie L. Carson. 2020. *The Politics of Congressional Elections*. 10th ed. Rowman and Littlefield.

Jacoby, William G. 1994. "Public Attitudes Toward Government Spending." *American Journal of Political Science* 38: 336–61.

Jacoby, William G. 1995. "The Structure of Ideological Thinking in the American Electorate." *American Journal of Political Science* 39: 314–35.

Jaeger, Jillian, 2019. "Sub-Constituencies and Legislative Responsiveness: Evidence from the States." *Political Research Quarterly* 72: 473–87.

Jessee, Stephen J. 2017. "'Don't Know' Responses, Personality, and the Measurement of Political Knowledge." *Political Science Research and Methods* 5: 711–31.

Jewitt, Caitlin E., and Paul Goren. 2016. "Ideological Structure and Consistency in the Age of Polarization." *American Politics Research* 44: 81–105.

Jeydel, Alana, and Andrew J. Taylor. 2003. "Are Women Effective Legislators? Evidence from the 103rd–105th Congresses." *Political Research Quarterly* 56: 19–27.

Jochim, Ashley E., and Bryan D. Jones. 2013. "Issue Politics in a Polarized Congress." *Political Research Quarterly* 66: 352–69.

Johnson, Richard, and Lisa L. Miller. 2023. "The Conservative Policy Bias of U.S. Senate Malapportionment." *PS: Political Science and Politics* 56: 10–17.

Johnston, Christopher D., and Benjamin J. Newman. 2016. "Economic Inequality and U.S. Public Policy Mood Across Time and Space." *American Politics Research* 44: 164–91.

Jones, Bryan D., and Frank R. Baumgartner. 2004. "Representation and Agenda Setting." *Policy Studies Journal* 32: 1–24.

Jones, Bryan D., Sean M. Theriault, and Michelle Whyman. 2019. *The Great Broadening: How the Vast Expansion of the Policymaking Agenda Transformed American Politics.* University of Chicago Press.

Jones, Bryan D., Frank R. Baumgartner, Sean M. Theriault, Derek A. Epp, Cheyenne Lee, Miranda E. Sullivan. 2023. Policy Agendas Project: Most Important Problem. https://www .comparativeagendas.net/datasets_codebooks.

Kalla, Joshua L., and David Broockman. 2016. "Campaign Contributions Facilitate Access to Congressional Officials: A Randomized Field Experiment." *American Journal of Political Science* 60: 545–58.

Kalmoe, Nathan P. 2020. "Uses and Abuses of Ideology in Political Psychology." *Political Psychology* 41: 771–93.

Kalt, Joseph P., and Mark A. Zupan. 1984. "Capture and Ideology in the Economic Theory of Politics." *American Economic Review* 74: 279–300.

Kam, Cindy D. 2005. "Who Toes the Party Line? Cues, Values, and Individual Differences." *Political Behavior* 27: 163–82.

Kaslovsky, Jaclyn. 2022. "Senators at Home: Local Attentiveness and Policy Representation in Congress." *American Political Science Review* 116: 645–61.

Katz, Michael B. 1989. *The Undeserving Poor: From the War on Poverty to the War on Welfare.* Pantheon.

Kelly, Nathan J. 2009. *The Politics of Income Inequality in the United States.* Cambridge University Press.

Kelly, Nathan J. 2019. *America's Inequality Trap.* University of Chicago Press.

Kelly, Nathan J., and Peter K. Enns. 2010. "Inequality and the Dynamics of Public Opinion: The Self-Reinforcing Link Between Economic Inequality and Mass Preferences." *American Journal of Political Science* 54: 855–70.

Kelly, Nathan J., and Jana Morgan. 2022. "Hurdles to Shared Prosperity: Congress, Parties, and the National Policy Process in an Era of Inequality." In *The American Political Economy: Politics, Markets, and Power,* edited by Jacob S. Hacker, Alexander Hertel-Fernandez, Paul Pierson, and Kathleen Thelen, 51–75. Cambridge University Press.

Kennedy, Joseph V. 1993. *The Omnibus Budget Reconciliation Act of 1993: Will It Reduce the Deficit?* MAPI Policy Review, August. https://www.thenewatlantis.com/wp-content/uploads /legacy-pdfs/20120213_TheOmnibusBudgetReconciliationActof1993.pdf.

Kenworthy, Lane, and Leslie McCall. 2008. "Inequality, Public Opinion, and Redistribution." *Socio-Economic Review* 6: 35–68.

Kevins, Anthony. 2021. "Race, Class or Both? Responses to Candidate Characteristics in Canada, the UK, and the US." *Politics, Groups, and Identities* 9: 699–720.

Kim, Eunji. 2023. "Entertaining Beliefs in Economic Mobility." *American Journal of Political Science* 67: 39–54.

Kinder, Donald R., and Nathan P. Kalmoe. 2017. *Neither Liberal nor Conservative: Ideological Innocence in the American Public.* University of Chicago Press.

Kingdon, John W. 1989. *Congressmen's Voting Decisions.* University of Michigan Press.

Kirkland, Patricia. 2021. "Business Owners and Executives as Politicians: The Effect on Public Policy." *Journal of Politics* 83: 1652–68.

Klar, Samara, and Yanna Krupnikov. 2016. *Independent Politics: How American Disdain for Politics Leads to Political Inaction*. Cambridge University Press.

Klick, Jonathan. 2017. "The Wealth of Congress." *Harvard Journal of Law and Public Policy* 40: 603–38.

Koger, Gregory. 2010. *Filibustering: A Political History of Obstruction in the House and Senate*. University of Chicago Press.

Kozlowski, Austin C., and James P. Murphy. 2021. "Issue Alignment and Partisanship in the American Public: Revisiting the 'Partisans Without Constraint' Thesis." *Social Science Research* 94: 102498.

Kraft, Michael E. 2021. *Environmental Policy and Politics*. Routledge.

Krimmel, Katherine, and Kelly Rader. 2021. "Racial Fairness and Fiscal Politics." *American Politics Research* 49: 143–56.

Kriner, Douglas L., and Andrew Reeves. 2014. "Responsive Partisanship: Public Support for the Clinton and Obama Health Care Plans." *Journal of Health Politics, Policy, and Law* 39: 717–49.

Kriner, Douglas L., and Andrew Reeves. 2015. *The Particularistic President: Executive Branch Politics and Political Inequality*. Cambridge University Press.

Kuziemko, Ilyana, Michael I. Norton, Emmanuel Saez, and Stefanie Stantchiva. 2015. "How Elastic Are Preferences for Redistribution? Evidence from Randomized Survey Experiments." *American Economic Review* 105: 1478–508.

Kuziemko, Ilyana, Nicolas Longuet-Marx, and Suresh Naidu. 2023. "'Compensate the Losers?' Economic Policy and Partisan Realignment in the U.S." Working paper no. 31794. National Bureau of Economic Research, October. https://www.nber.org/system/files/working_papers/w31794/w31794.pdf.

Ladewig, Jeffrey W. 2021. "Income Inequality and Ideological Positions in the U.S. Congress." *Political Research Quarterly* 74: 599–614.

Lapinski, John, Matt Levendusky, Ken Winneg, and Kathleen Hall Jamieson. 2016. "What Do Citizens Want from Their Member of Congress?" *Political Research Quarterly* 69: 535–45.

Larcinese, Valentino, and Alberto Parmigiani. 2023. "Income Inequality and Campaign Contributions: Evidence from the Reagan Tax Cut." Working paper no. 87, International Inequalities Institute, London School of Economics. https://eprints.lse.ac.uk/118456/1/Larcinese_Parmigiani_III_WP_87.pdf.

Larcinese, Valentino, Leonzio Rizzo, and Cecilia Testa. 2013. "Why Do Small States Receive More Federal Money? U.S. Senate Representation and the Allocation of the Federal Budget." *Economics and Politics* 25: 257–82.

Lau, Richard R., David J. Andersen, and David P. Redlawsk. 2008. "An Exploration of Correct Voting in Recent U.S. Presidential Elections." *American Journal of Political Science* 52: 395–411.

Lau, Richard R., and David P. Redlawsk. 1997. "Voting Correctly." *American Political Science Review* 91: 585–98.

Lax, Jeffrey R., Justin H. Phillips, and Adam Zelizer. 2019. "The Party or the Purse: Unequal Representation in the U.S. Senate." *American Political Science Review* 113: 917–40.

Layman, Geoffrey C., and Thomas M. Carsey. 2002. "Party Polarization and 'Conflict Extension' in the American Electorate." *American Journal of Political Science* 46: 786–802.

Lazarus, Jeffrey. 2009. "Party, Electoral Vulnerability, and Earmarks in the U.S. House of Representatives." *Journal of Politics* 71: 1050–61.

Lazarus, Jeffrey. 2010. "Giving the People What They Want? The Distribution of Earmarks in the U.S. House of Representatives." *American Journal of Political Science* 54: 338–53.

Lazarus, Jeffrey, Amy McKay, and Lindsey Herbel. 2013. "Who Walks Through the 'Revolving Door'? Examining the Lobbying Activity of Former Congress Members and Staffers." *Interest Groups and Advocacy* 6: 82–100.

Lee, Boram, Michael Pomirchy, and Bryan Schonfeld. 2023. "Does the U.S. Congress Respond to Public Opinion on Trade?" *American Politics Research* 51: 731–48.

Lee, Frances E. 2003. "Geographic Politics in the U.S. House of Representatives: Coalition Building and Distribution of Benefits." *American Journal of Political Science* 47: 713–27.

Lee, Frances E. 2004. "Bicameral Institutions and Geographic Politics: Allocating Federal Funds for Transportation in the House and Senate." *Legislative Studies Quarterly* 24: 185–214.

Lee, Frances E. 2023. "Populism, Democracy, and the Post-2020 Republican Party in Congress." *Presidential Studies Quarterly* 53: 169–85.

Lee, Frances E., and Bruce I. Oppenheimer. 1999. *Sizing Up the Senate: The Unequal Consequences of Equal Representation*. University of Chicago Press.

Leicht, Kevin T. 2013. "Professional Work." In *Sociology of Work: An Encyclopedia*, edited by Vicki Smith, 709–13. Sage.

Leighley, Jan E., and Jonathan Nagler. 2014. *Who Votes Now? Demographics, Issues, Inequality, and Turnout in the United States*. Princeton University Press.

Lendway, Paul, and Gregory A. Huber. 2023. "The Effect of Priming Structural Fairness on Inequality Beliefs and Preferences." *American Politics Research* 51: 443–56.

Lenz, Gabriel S. 2012. *Follow the Leader? How Voters Respond to Politicians' Policies and Performance*. University of Chicago Press.

Lerman, Amy E., Meredith L. Sadin, and Samuel Trachtman. 2017. "Policy Uptake as Political Behavior: Evidence from the Affordable Care Act." *American Political Science Review* 111: 755–70.

Levitin, Teresa E., and Warren E. Miller. 1979. "Ideological Interpretations of Presidential Elections." *American Political Science Review* 73: 751–71.

Levitsky, Steven, and Daniel Ziblatt. 2018. *How Democracies Die*. Crown.

Levitsky, Steven, and Daniel Ziblatt. 2023. *Tyranny of the Minority: Why American Democracy Reached the Breaking Point*. Crown.

Lewis, Jeffrey B., Keith Poole, Howard Rosenthal, Adam Boche, Aaron Rudkin, and Luke Sonnet. 2024. *Voteview: Congressional Roll-Call Votes Database*. https://voteview.com/.

Lewis-Beck, Michael S., William G. Jacoby, Helmut Norpoth, and Herbert F. Weisberg. 2008. *The American Voter Revisited*. University of Michigan Press.

Lowande, Kenneth, Melinda Ritchie, and Erinn Lauterbach. 2019. "Descriptive and Substantive Representation in Congress: Evidence from 80,000 Congressional Inquiries." *American Journal of Political Science* 63: 644–59.

Lowi, Theodore J. 1972. "Four Systems of Politics, Policy, and Choice." *Public Administration Review* 32: 298–310.

Lublin, David. 1997. "The Election of African-Americans and Latinos to the U.S. House of Representatives, 1972–1994." *American Politics Research* 25: 269–86.

Lupton, Robert N., William M. Myers, and Judd R. Thornton. 2015. "Political Sophistication and the Dimensionality of Elite and Mass Attitudes, 1980–2004." *Journal of Politics* 77: 363–80.

Lupton, Robert N., William M. Myers, and Judd R. Thornton. 2022. "Carriers of the Creed: Examining Democrats' Commitment to Egalitarianism as Principle and Policy." *Political Behavior* 44: 1025–47.

Lupu, Noam, and Jonas Pontusson. 2011. "The Structure of Inequality and the Politics of Redistribution." *American Political Science Review* 105: 316–36.

Luskin, Robert C., and John G. Bullock. 2011. "'Don't Know' Means 'Don't Know': DK Responses and the Public's Level of Political Knowledge." *Journal of Politics* 73: 547–57.

Luttig, Matthew. 2013. "The Structure of Inequality and Americans' Attitudes Toward Redistribution." *Public Opinion Quarterly* 77: 811–21.

Macdonald, David. 2020a. "Class Attitudes, Political Knowledge, and Support for Redistribution in an Era of Inequality." *Social Science Quarterly* 101: 960–77.

Macdonald, David. 2020b. "Trust in Government and the American Public's Responsiveness to Rising Inequality." *Political Research Quarterly* 73: 790–804.

Maestas, Cherie, Sarah A. Fulton, L. Sandy Maisel, and Walter J. Stone. 2006. "When to Risk it? Institutions, Ambitions, and the Decision to Run for the U.S. House." *American Political Science Review* 100: 195–208.

Magleby, David B., Jay Goodliffe, and Joseph A. Olsen. 2018. *Who Donates in Campaigns? The Importance of Message, Messenger, Medium, and Structure.* Cambridge University Press.

Maisel, L. Sandy, and Walter J. Stone. 1997. "Determinants of Candidate Emergence in U.S. House Elections: An Exploratory Study." *Legislative Studies Quarterly* 22: 79–96.

Maks-Solomon, Cory, and Elizabeth Rigby. 2020. "Are Democrats Really the Party of the Poor? Partisanship, Class, and Representation in the U.S. Senate." *Political Research Quarterly* 73: 848–65.

Makse, Todd. 2017. "A Very Particular Set of Skills: Former Legislator Traits and Revolving Door Lobbying in Congress." *American Politics Research* 45: 866–86.

Makse, Todd. 2022. "Instant Credibility: The Conditional Role of Professional Background in Policymaking Success." *Political Research Quarterly* 75: 118–33.

Malhotra, Neil. 2006. "Government Growth and Professionalism in U.S. State Legislatures." *Legislative Studies Quarterly* 31: 563–84.

Malhotra, Neal, and Connor Raso. 2007. "Racial Representation and U.S. Senate Apportionment." *Social Science Quarterly* 88: 1038–48.

Maltzman, Forrest. 1997. *Competing Principals: Committees, Parties, and the Organization of Congress.* University of Michigan Press.

Mann, Thomas E., and Norman J. Ornstein. 2016. *It's Even Worse Than It Looks: How the American Constitutional System Collided with the New Politics of Extremism.* Basic Books.

Manza, Jeff, and Clem Brooks. 1999. *Social Cleavages and Political Change: Voter Alignments and U.S. Party Coalitions.* Oxford University Press.

Martin, Danielle Joesten. 2019. "Playing the Women's Card: How Women Respond to Female Candidates' Descriptive Versus Substantive Representation." *American Politics Research* 47: 549–81.

Martin, Gregory J., and Ali Yurukoglu. 2017. "Bias in Cable News: Persuasion and Polarization." *American Economic Review* 107: 2565–99.

Mason, Lilliana. 2018. *Uncivil Agreement: How Politics Became Our Identity.* University of Chicago Press.

Mathew, Nicole Asmussen. 2018. "Evangelizing Congress: The Emergence of Evangelical Republicans and Party Polarization in Congress." *Legislative Studies Quarterly* 43: 409–55.

Mathisen, Ruben D. 2024. "The Influence Gap: Unequal Policy Responsiveness to Men and Women." *Journal of Politics* 86, no. 3. http://dx.doi.org/10.1086/729964.

Matthews, Donald. 1954. *The Social Background of Political Decision-Makers.* Random House.

Mayer, Jane. 2016. *Dark Money: The Hidden History of the Billionaires Behind the Rise of the Radical Right.* Anchor Books.

Mayer, William G. 2008. *The Swing Voter in American Politics.* Brookings Institution Press.

Mayhew, David R. 1974. *Congress: The Electoral Connection.* Yale University Press.

Mayhew, David R. 2005. *Divided We Govern: Party Control, Lawmaking and Investigations, 1946–2002.* 2nd ed. Yale University Press.

McCall, Leslie. 2013. *The Underserving Rich: American Beliefs About Inequality, Opportunity, and Redistribution.* Cambridge University Press.

McCall, Leslie, and Lane Kenworthy. 2009. "Americans' Social Policy Preferences in an Era of Rising Inequality." *Perspectives on Politics* 7: 459–84.

McCarthy, Justin. 2015. "More Americans Say Low-Income Earners Pay Too Much in Taxes." Gallup, April 15. https://news.gallup.com/poll/182426/americans-say-low-income-earners -pay-taxes.aspx.

McCarty, Nolan, Keith T. Poole, and Howard Rosenthal. 2006. *Polarized America: The Dance of Ideology and Unequal Riches.* MIT Press.

McCarty, Nolan, Keith T. Poole, and Howard Rosenthal. 2013. *Political Bubbles: Financial Crises and the Failure of American Democracy.* Princeton University Press.

McGann, Anthony J., Charles Anthony Smith, Michael Latner, and Alex Keena. 2016. *Gerrymandering in America: The House of Representatives, the Supreme Court, and the Future of Popular Sovereignty.* Cambridge University Press.

McKee, Seth C. 2010. *Republican Ascendancy in Southern U.S. House Elections.* Routledge.

McKee, Seth C. 2019. *The Dynamics of Southern Politics: Causes and Consequences.* Sage.

Meltzer, Allan H., and Scott F. Richard. 1981. "A Rational Theory of the Size of Government." *Journal of Political Economy* 89: 914–27.

Mendez, Matthew S., and Christian R. Grose. 2018. "Doubling Down: Inequality in Responsiveness and the Policy Preferences of Elected Officials." *Legislative Studies Quarterly* 43: 457–91.

Mettler, Suzanne. 2011. *The Submerged State: How Invisible Government Policies Undermine American Democracy.* University of Chicago Press.

Miler, Kristina C. 2007. "The View from the Hill: Legislative Perceptions of the District." *Legislative Studies Quarterly* 32: 597–628.

Miler, Kristina C. 2010. *Constituency Representation in Congress: The View from Capitol Hill.* Cambridge University Press.

Miler, Kristina C. 2018. *Poor Representation: Congress and the Politics of Poverty in the United States.* Cambridge University Press.

Miller, Warren E., and Donald E. Stokes. 1963. "Constituency Influence in Congress." *American Political Science Review* 57: 45–56.

Mitchell, Matthew D. 2019. "Public Perceptions of Markets, Government, and Favoritism." Policy brief. Mercatus Center, George Mason University, October. https://www.mercatus .org/system/files/mitchell_-_policy_brief_-_public_perception_of_markets_business_and _favoritism_-_v1.pdf.

Mondak, Jeffery J. 2000. "Reconsidering the Measurement of Political Knowledge." *Political Analysis* 8: 57–82.

Monroe, Nathan W., and Gregory Robinson. 2008. "Do Restrictive Rules Produce Non-Median Outcomes? A Theory with Evidence from the 101st–108th Congresses." *Journal of Politics* 70: 217–31.

Morgan, Iwan. 2009. *The Age of Deficits: Presidents and Unbalanced Budgets from Jimmy Carter to George W. Bush.* University Press of Kansas.

Morgan, Kimberly J., and Andrea Louise Campbell. 2011. *The Delegated Welfare State: Medicare, Markets, and the Governance of Social Policy.* Oxford University Press.

Munis, B. Kal. 2020. "Us Versus Them over There . . . Literally: Measuring Place Resentment in American Politics." *Political Behavior* 44: 1057–78.

Newman, Benjamin J. 2020. "Inequality Growth and Economic Policy Liberalism: An Updated Test of a Classic Theory." *Journal of Politics* 82: 765–70.

Newman, Benjamin J., and John V. Kane. 2017. "Economic Inequality and Public Support for Organized Labor." *Political Research Quarterly* 70: 918–32.

Newman, Benjamin J., Tyler T. Reny, and Bea-Sim Ooi. 2022. "The Color of Disparity: Racialized Income Inequality and Support for Liberal Economic Policies." *Journal of Politics* 84: 1818–22.

Newport, Frank. 2011. "Americans Prioritize Economy over Reducing Wealth Gap." Gallup, December 16. https://news.gallup.com/poll/151568/americans-prioritize-growing-economy -reducing-wealth-gap.aspx.

Newport, Frank. 2019. "Inequality as a Voter Concern in 2020." Gallup, July 31. https://news.gal lup.com/opinion/polling-matters/262439/inequality-voter-concern-2020.aspx.

Niou, Emerson M. S., and Peter C. Ordeshook. 1985. "Universalism in Congress." *American Journal of Political Science* 29: 246–58.

Noah, Timothy. 2012. *The Great Divergence: America's Growing Inequality Crisis and What We Can Do About It.* Bloomsbury Press.

Norton, Michael I., and Dan Ariely. 2011. "Building a Better America—One Wealth Quintile at a Time." *Perspectives on Psychological Science* 6: 9–12.

Obklobelzija, Stan. 2024. "Dark Parties: Unveiling Nonparty Committees in American Political Campaigns." *American Political Science Review* 108: 401–22.

O'Brian, Neil A. 2019. "Income Inequality and Congressional Republican Position Taking, 1913–2013." *Journal of Politics* 81: 1533–38.

Ojeda, Christopher. 2018. "The Two-Income Participation Gaps." *American Journal of Political Science* 62: 813–29.

Oleszek, Walter J., Mark J. Oleszek, Elizabeth Rybicki, and Bill Heniff Jr. 2019. *Congressional Procedures and the Policy Process.* 11th ed. CQ Press.

Oliver, J. Eric, and Thomas J. Wood. 2018. *Enchanted America: How Intuition and Reason Divide Our Politics.* University of Chicago Press.

Olson, Mancur. 1965. *The Logic of Collective Action: Public Goods and the Theory of Groups.* Harvard University Press.

Omarova, Saule T. 2013. "The Merchants of Wall Street: Banking, Commerce, and Commodities." *Minnesota Law Review* 98: 265–355.

Organization for Economic Cooperation and Development (OECD). 2021. *Does Inequality Matter? How People Perceive Economic Disparities and Social Mobility.* OECD Publishing. https://doi.org/10.1787/3023ed40-en.

Ornstein, Norman J., Thomas E. Mann, Michael J. Malbin, Andrew Rugg, and Raffaela Wakeman. 2014. *Vital Statistics on Congress.* American Enterprise Institute.

Orth, Taylor. 2024. "Kamala Harris' Economic Platform Resonates Across Party Lines." YouGov, August 23. https://today.yougov.com/politics/articles/50369-kamala-harris-economic-platform -resonates-across-party-lines.

Owen, Erica, and Dennis P. Quinn. 2014. "Does Economic Globalization Influence the U.S. Policy Mood? A Study of U.S. Public Sentiment, 1956–2011." *British Journal of Political Science* 46: 95–125.

Page, Benjamin I., Larry M. Bartels, and Jason Seawright. 2013. "Democracy and the Policy Preferences of Wealthy Americans." *Perspectives on Politics* 11: 51–73.

Page, Benjamin I., and Martin Gilens. 2017. *Democracy in America? What Has Gone Wrong and What We Can Do About It.* University of Chicago Press.

Page, Benjamin I., and Lawrence R. Jacobs. 2009. *Class War? What Americans Really Think About Economic Inequality.* University of Chicago Press.

Page, Benjamin I., Jason Seawright, and Matthew J. Lacombe. 2018. *Billionaires and Stealth Politics.* University of Chicago Press.

Page, Benjamin I., and Robert Y. Shapiro. 1992. *The Rational Public: Fifty Years of Trends in Americans' Policy Preferences.* University of Chicago Press.

Payne, A. Abigail. 2003. "The Effects of Congressional Appropriation Committee Membership on the Distribution of Federal Research Funding to Universities." *Economic Inquiry* 41: 325–45.

Peterson, Jordan Carr, and Christian R. Grose. 2020. "The Private Interests of Public Officials: Financial Regulation in the US Congress." *Legislative Studies Quarterly* 46: 49–84.

Peterson, Paul E., and Mark Rom. 1988. "Lower Taxes, More Spending, and Budget Deficits." In *The Reagan Legacy: Promise and Performance,* edited by Charles O. Jones, 213–40. Chatham House.

Pettigrew, Thomas F., and Linda R. Tropp. 2006. "A Meta-Analytic Test of Intergroup Contact Theory." *Journal of Personality and Social Psychology* 90: 751–83.

Pfeffer, Fabian T., and Nora Waitkus. 2021. "The Wealth Inequality of Nations." *American Sociological Review* 86: 567–602.

Pierson, Paul, and Eric Schickler. 2020. "Madison's Constitution Under Stress: A Developmental Analysis of Political Polarization." *Annual Review of Political Science* 23: 37–58.

Piff, Paul K., Michael W. Kraus, Stephane Cote, Bonnie Hayden Cheng, and Dacher Keltner. 2010. "Having Less, Giving More: The Influence of Social Class on Prosocial Behavior." *Journal of Personality and Social Psychology* 99: 771–84.

Piston, Spencer. 2018. *Class Attitudes in America: Sympathy for the Poor, Resentment of the Rich, and Political Implications.* Cambridge University Press.

Poole, Keith T., and Howard Rosenthal. 1997. *Congress: A Political Economic History of Roll-Call Voting.* Oxford University Press.

Preuhs, Robert R. 2007. "Descriptive Representation as a Mechanism to Mitigate Policy Backlash: Latino Incorporation and Welfare Policy in the American States." *Political Research Quarterly* 60: 277–92.

Quirk, Paul J., and William Cunion. 2000. "Clinton's Domestic Policy: The Lessons of a 'New Democrat.'" In *The Clinton Legacy,* edited by Colin Campbell and Bert A. Rockman, 200–25. Chatham House.

Quirk, Paul J., and Joseph Hinchcliffe. 1996. "Domestic Policy: The Trials of a Centrist Democrat." In *The Clinton Presidency: First Appraisals,* edited by Colin Campbell and Bert A. Rockman, 262–89. Chatham House.

Rahn, Wendy M. 1993. "The Role of Partisan Stereotypes in Information Processing About Political Candidates." *American Journal of Political Science* 37: 472–96.

Rainie, Lee, Scott Keeter, and Andrew Perrin. 2019. *Trust and Distrust in America.* Pew Research Center, July 22. https://www.pewresearch.org/politics/2019/07/22/trust-and-distrust -in-america.

Rampell, Catherine. 2019. "Some Tout Trump's Deregulation: It's Actually Been a Bust." *Washington Post,* October 28. https://www.washingtonpost.com/opinions/the-white-house-touts -trumps-deregulation-its-actually-been-a-bust/2019/10/28/c9fcbdc8-f9c3-11e9-ac8c-8ec ed29ca6ef_story.html.

Raso, Connor. 2018. *How Has Trump's Deregulatory Order Worked in Practice?* Brookings Institution, September 6. https://www.brookings.edu/articles/how-has-trumps-deregulatory -order-worked-in-practice/.

Rauch, Jonathan. 2015. *Political Realism: How Hacks, Machines, Big Money, and Back-Room Deals Can Strengthen American Democracy.* Brookings Institution.

Rehm, Philipp, Jacob Hacker, and Mark Schlesinger. 2012. "Insecure Alliances: Risk, Inequality, and Support for the Welfare State." *American Political Science Review* 106: 386–406.

Reich, Robert B. 2020. *The System: Who Rigged It, How We Fix It.* Vintage.

Reingold, Beth, and Jessica Harrell. 2010. "The Impact of Descriptive Representation on Women's Political Engagement: Does Party Matter?" *Political Research Quarterly* 63: 280–94.

Rhodes, Jesse H., and Brian F. Schaffner. 2017. "Testing Models of Unequal Representation: Democratic Populists and Republican Oligarchs?" *Quarterly Journal of Political Science* 12: 185–204.

Robison, Joshua. 2021. "What's the Value of Partisan Loyalty? Partisan Ambivalence, Motivated Reasoning, and Correct Voting in U.S. Presidential Elections." *Political Psychology* 42: 977–93.

Rodden, Jonathan A. 2019. *Why Cities Lose: The Deep Roots of the Urban-Rural Political Divide.* Basic Books.

Rogowski, Ronald. 1989. *Commerce and Coalitions.* Princeton University Press.

Rohde, David W. 1991. *Parties and Leaders in the Postreform House.* University of Chicago Press.

Romer, Thomas. 1975. "Individual Welfare, Majority Voting, and the Properties of a Linear Income Tax." *Journal of Public Economics* 4: 163–85.

Rueda, David, and Daniel Stegmueller. 2019. *Who Wants What? Redistribution Preferences in Comparative Perspective.* Cambridge University Press.

Sanbonmatsu, Kira. 2020. "Women's Underrepresentation in the U.S. Congress." *Daedalus* 149: 40–55.

Sanger-Katz, Margot. 2016. "Your Surgeon Is Probably a Republican, Your Psychiatrist a Democrat." *New York Times*, October 6.

Schaffner, Brian S., Jesse H. Rhodes, and Raymond J. La Raja. 2020. *Hometown Inequality: Race, Class, and Representation in American Local Politics.* Cambridge University Press.

Schaffner, Brian S., Jesse H. Rhodes, and Raymond J. La Raja. 2022. "The Conservative Bias in America's Local Governments." *Public Opinion Quarterly* 137: 125–54.

Scheve, Kenneth, and David Stasavage. 2016. *Taxing the Rich: A History of Fiscal Fairness in Europe and the United States.* Princeton University Press.

Schiffer, Adam J. 2000. "I'm Not That Liberal: Explaining Conservative Democratic Identification." *Political Behavior* 22: 293–310.

Schildkraut, Deborah J. 2016. "Latino Attitudes About Surrogate Representation." *Social Science Quarterly* 97: 714–28.

Schiller, Wendy. 1995. "Senators as Political Entrepreneurs: Using Bill Sponsorship to Shape Legislative Agendas." *American Journal of Political Science* 39: 186–203.

Schlozman, Kay Lehman, Henry E. Brady, and Sidney Verba. 2018. *Unequal and Unrepresented: Political Inequality and the People's Voice in the New Gilded Age.* Princeton University Press.

Schlozman, Kay Lehman, Sidney Verba, and Henry E. Brady. 2012. *The Unheavenly Chorus: Unequal Political Voice and the Broken Promise of American Democracy.* Princeton University Press.

Schneider, Anne, and Helen Ingram. 1993. "Social Construction of Target Populations: Implications for Politics and Policy." *American Political Science Review* 87: 334–47.

Schradie, Jen. 2019. *The Revolution That Wasn't: How Digital Activism Favors Conservatives.* Harvard University Press.

Selling, Nils. 2023. "Either With Us or Against Us: Business Power and Campaign Contributions in an Age of Hyper-Partisanship." *Political Research Quarterly* 76: 1764–79.

Shaw, Greg M. 2009–2010. "Changes in Public Opinion and the American Welfare State." *Political Science Quarterly* 124: 627–53.

Shayo, Moses. 2009. "A Model of Social Identity with an Application to Political Economy: Nation, Class, and Redistribution." *American Political Science Review* 103: 147–74.

Shepsle, Kenneth A., Robert P. van Houweling, Samuel J. Abrams, and Peter C. Hanson. 2009. "The Senate Electoral Cycle and Bicameral Appropriations Politics." *American Journal of Political Science* 53: 343–59.

Shepsle, Kenneth A., and Barry R. Weingast. 1981. "Political Preferences for the Pork Barrel: A Generalization." *American Journal of Political Science* 26: 86–111.

Shields, Jon A., and Joshua M. Dunn Sr. 2018. *Passing on the Right: Conservative Professors in the Progressive University.* Oxford University Press.

Shotts, Kenneth W. 2002. "Gerrymandering, Legislative Composition, and National Policy Outcomes." *American Journal of Political Science* 46: 398–414.

Shuman, Howard E. 1992. *Politics and the Budget: The Struggle Between the President and the Congress.* Prentice Hall.

Sides, John, Michael Tesler, and Lynn Vavreck. 2018. *Identity Crisis: The 2016 Presidential Campaign and the Battle for the Meaning of America.* Princeton University Press.

Sidman, Andrew H. 2019. *Pork Barrel Politics: How Government Spending Determines Elections in a Polarized Era.* Columbia University Press.

Sinclair, Barbara. 2012. *Unorthodox Lawmaking.* 4th ed. Congressional Quarterly Press.

Singer, Matthew M. 2011. "Who Says 'It's the Economy'? Cross-National and Cross-Individual Variation in the Salience of Economic Performance." *Comparative Political Studies* 44: 284–312.

Skocpol, Theda. 1996. *Boomerang: Clinton's Health Security Effort and the Turn Against Government in U.S. Politics.* W. W. Norton.

Skocpol, Theda, and Alexander Hertel-Fernandez. 2016. "The Koch Network and Republican Party Extremism." *Perspectives on Politics* 14: 681–99.

Skocpol, Theda, and Caroline Tervo, eds. 2020. *Upending American Politics: Polarizing Parties, Ideological Elites, and Citizen Activists from the Tea Party to the Anti-Trump Resistance.* Oxford University Press.

Smidt, Corwin D. 2017. "Polarization and the Decline of the American Floating Voter." *American Journal of Political Science* 61: 365–81.

Smith, Candice Watts, and Rebecca J. Kreitzer. 2024. "Where's the Party in Social Construction Theory? Partisan Mappings of Politically Relevant Target Groups." *Journal of Politics* 86: 624–41.

Smith, Steven S. 2014. *TAPS.* Washington University, St. Louis [producer]; Harvard Dataverse Network [distributor]. https://wc.wustl.edu/american-panel-survey.

Sobolewska, Maria, and Robert Ford. 2020. *Brexitland: Identity, Diversity, and the Reshaping of British Politics.* Cambridge University Press.

Sommeiller, Estelle, and Mark Price. 2018. *The New Gilded Age: Income Inequality in the U.S. by State, Metropolitan Area, and County.* Economic Policy Institute, July 19. https://www.epi.org/publication/the-new-gilded-age-income-inequality-in-the-u-s-by-state-metropolitan-area-and-county/#epi-toc-14.

Soroka, Stuart N., and Christopher Wlezien. 2008. "On the Limits to Inequality in Representation." *PS: Political Science and Politics* 41: 319–27.

Soroka, Stuart N., and Christopher Wlezien. 2010. *Degrees of Democracy: Politics, Public Opinion, and Policy*. Cambridge University Press.

Soroka, Stuart N., and Christopher Wlezien. 2021. "Trends in Public Support for Welfare Spending: How the Economy Matters." *British Journal of Political Science* 51: 163–80.

Soroka, Stuart N., and Christopher Wlezien. 2022. *Information and Democracy: Public Policy in the News*. Cambridge University Press.

Soss, Joe, and Lawrence R. Jacobs. 2009. "The Place of Inequality: Non-Participation in the American Polity." *Political Science Quarterly* 124: 95–125.

Soss, Joe, and Sanford F. Schram. 2007. "A Public Transformed? Welfare Reform as Policy Feedback." *American Political Science Review* 101: 111–27.

Spring, Amy, Elizabeth Ackert, Kyle Crowder, and Scott J. South. 2017. "Influence of Proximity to Kin on Residential Mobility and Destination Choice: Examining Local Movers in Metropolitan Areas." *Demography* 54: 1277–304.

Squire, Peverill. 2014. *The Evolution of American Legislatures: Colonies, Territories, and States, 1619–2009*. University of Michigan Press.

Squire, Peverill, and Keith E. Hamm. 2005. *101 Chambers: Congress, State Legislatures, and the Future of Legislative Studies*. Ohio State University Press.

Stacy, Darrian. 2021. "Wealth and Political Inequality in the U.S. Congress." PhD diss., Vanderbilt University. https://irbe.library.vanderbilt.edu/server/api/core/bitstreams/71406af6-a88c -4bf6-95d7-1df125f8b72c/content.

Stein, Robert M., and Kenneth N. Bickers. 1995. *Perpetuating the Pork Barrel: Policy Subsystems and American Democracy*. Cambridge University Press.

Stephens, Nicole M., Hazel Rose Markus, and L. Taylor Phillips. 2014. "Social Class Culture Cycles: How Three Gateway Contexts Shape Selves and Fuel Inequality." *Annual Review of Psychology* 65: 611–34.

Stewart, Matthew. 2021. *The 9.9 Percent: The New Aristocracy That Is Entrenching Inequality and Warping Our Culture*. Simon and Schuster.

Stiglitz, Joseph E. 2012. *The Price of Inequality: How Today's Divided Society Endangers Our Future*. W. W. Norton.

Stimson, James A. 1998. *Public Opinion in America: Moods, Cycles, and Swings*. Rev. 2nd ed. Westview Press.

Stimson, James A. 2004. *Tides of Consent: How Public Opinion Shapes American Politics*. Cambridge University Press.

Stimson, James A. 2015. *Tides of Consent: How Public Opinion Shapes American Politics*. Rev. 2nd ed. Cambridge University Press.

Stimson, James A., Michael B. MacKuen, and Robert S. Erikson. 1995. "Dynamic Representation." *American Political Science Review* 89: 543–65.

Stimson, James, and Emily Wager. 2020. *Converging on Truth: A Dynamic Perspective on Factual Debates in American Public Opinion*. Cambridge University Press.

Stokes, Susan C., Thad Dunning, Marcelo Nazareno, and Valeria Brusco. 2013. *Brokers, Voters, and Clientelism: The Puzzle of Distributive Politics*. Cambridge University Press.

Stonecash, Jeffrey M. 2006. *Political Parties Matter: Realignment and the Return of Partisan Voting*. Lynne-Rienner.

Strain, Michael R. 2019. "Maybe Inequality Isn't What Is Making People Mad." *Bloomberg Opinion*, July 17. https://www.bloomberg.com/opinion/articles/2019-07-17/income-inequality -isn-t-the-thing-that-s-making-people-mad#xj4y7vzkg.

Sturgis, Patrick, Nick Allum, and Patten Smith. 2008. "An Experiment on the Measurement of Political Knowledge in Surveys." *Public Opinion Quarterly* 85: 90–102.

Suhay, Elizabeth, Marko Klašnja, and Gonzalo Rivero. 2021. "Ideology of Affluence: Explanations for Inequality and Economic Policy Preferences Among Rich Americans." *Journal of Politics* 83: 367–80.

Suhay, Elizabeth, Mark Tenenbaum, and Austin Bartola. 2022. "Explanations for Inequality and Party Polarization in the U.S., 1980–2020." *Forum* 20: 5–36.

Sullivan, John L., James Piereson, and George E. Marcus. 1978. "Ideological Constraint in the Mass Public: A Methodological Critique and Some New Findings." *American Journal of Political Science* 22: 233–49.

Sussman, Barry. 1982. "Poll Finds Most Think Recovery Program Hurts." *Washington Post*, February 5. https://www.washingtonpost.com/archive/politics/1982/02/05/poll-finds-most-think -recovery-program-hurts/bdb13213-7ce3-4bb0-affe-e45e2ad61f2e/.

Swers, Michelle L., and Stella M. Rouse. 2011. "Descriptive Representation: Understanding the Impact of Identity on Substantive Representation of Group Interests." In *Oxford Handbook of the American Congress.*, edited by George C. Edwards III, Frances Lee, and Eric Schickler, 241–71. Oxford University Press.

Task Force on Inequality and American Democracy. 2004. *American Democracy in an Age of Rising Inequality.* American Political Science Association. Archived at https://web.archive .org/web/20240801191710/https://apsanet.org/Portals/54/files/Task%20Force%20Reports /taskforcereport.pdf.

Tate, Katherine. 2003. *Black Faces in the Mirror: African Americans and their Representatives in Congress.* Princeton University Press.

Tausanovitch, Chris. 2016. "Income, Ideology, and Representation." *RSF: The Russell Sage Foundation Journal of the Social Sciences* 2: 33–50.

Tausanovitch, Chris, and Christopher Warshaw. 2013. "Measuring Constituent Policy Preferences in Congress, State Legislatures, and Cities." *Journal of Politics* 75: 330–42.

Taylor, Andrew J. 2008. "The Presidential Pork Barrel and the Conditioning Effect of Term." *Presidential Studies Quarterly* 38: 97–110.

Taylor, Andrew J. 2012. *The Floor in Congressional Life.* University of Michigan Press.

Tesler, Michael. 2012. "The Spillover of Racialization into Health Care: How President Obama Polarized Public Opinion by Racial Attitudes and Race." *American Journal of Political Science* 56: 690–704.

Theriault, Sean M. 2008. *Party Polarization in the U.S. Congress.* Cambridge University Press.

Thompson, Daniel M., James J. Feigenbaum, Andrew B. Hall, and Jesse Yoder. 2019. "Who Becomes a Member of Congress? Evidence from De-Anonymized Census Data." NBER working paper no. 26156. National Bureau of Economic Research, August. https://www.nber.org /papers/w26156.

Thorpe, Rebecca U. 2014. *The American Warfare State: The Domestic Politics of Military Spending.* University of Chicago Press.

Treul, Sarah A., and Eric R. Hansen. 2023. "Primary Barriers to Working Class Representation." *Political Research Quarterly* 76: 1516–28.

Tromborg, Mathias Wessel, and Leslie A. Schwindt-Bayer. 2019. "Constituent Demand and District-Focused Legislative Representation." *Legislative Studies Quarterly* 44: 35–64.

Trounstine, Jessica. 2008. *Political Monopolies in American Cities: The Rise and Fall of Bosses and Reformers*. University of Chicago Press.

Trujillo, Kristin L. 2022. "Rural Identity as a Contributing Factor to Anti-Intellectualism in the U.S." *Political Behavior* 44: 1509–32.

Trujillo, Kristin L., and Zack Crowley. 2022. "Symbolic Versus Material Concerns of Rural Consciousness in the United States." *Political Geography* 96: 102658.

Trump, Kris-Stella. 2018. "Income Inequality Influences Perceptions of Legitimate Income Differences." *British Journal of Political Science* 48: 929–52.

Ura, Joseph Daniel, and Christopher R. Ellis. 2008. "Income, Preferences, and the Dynamics of Policy Responsiveness." *PS: Political Science and Politics* 41: 785–94.

Ura, Joseph Daniel, and Christopher R. Ellis. 2012. "Partisan Moods: Polarization and the Dynamics of Mass Party Preferences." *Journal of Politics* 74: 277–91.

Uslaner, Eric M. 1998. "Trade Winds: NAFTA and the Rational Public." *Political Behavior* 20: 341–60.

Vance, J. D. 2016. *Hillbilly Elegy: A Memoir of a Family and Culture in Crisis*. Harper.

van Kessell, Patrick, Adam Hughes, and Solomon Messing. 2018. *Taking Sides on Facebook: How Congressional Research Changed Under President Trump*. Pew Research Center, July. https://www.pewresearch.org/politics/wp-content/uploads/sites/4/2018/07/TakingSides_FullReport.pdf.

Varela, Julio Ricardo. 2015. "The Latino Vote in Presidential Races: 1980–2012." *Latino USA*, October 29. https://www.latinousa.org/2015/10/29/the-latino-vote-in-presidential-races/.

Verba, Sidney, and Norman H. Nie. 1972. *Participation in America: Political Democracy and Social Equality*. University of Chicago Press.

Verba, Sidney, Kay Lehman Schlozman, and Henry E. Brady. 1995. *Voice and Equality: Civic Voluntarism in American Politics*. Harvard University Press.

Vidal, Jordi Blanes, Mirko Draca, and Christian Fons-Rosen. 2012. "Revolving Door Lobbyists." *American Economic Review* 102: 3731–48.

Vivyan, Nick, Markus Wagner, Konstantin Glinitzer, and Jakob Moritz-Eberl. 2020. "Do Humble Beginnings Help? How Politician Class Roots Shape Voter Evaluations." *Electoral Studies* 63: 102093.

Volden, Craig, Jonathan Wai, and Alan E. Wiseman. 2020. "Elite Education and Legislative Behavior in the US Congress." Working paper. Center for Effective Lawmaking, May. Archived at https://thelawmakers.org/wp-content/uploads/2020/05/Working-Paper-CEL-Elite-Education-and-Legislative-Effectiveness-1.pdf.

Volden, Craig, and Alan E. Wiseman. 2014. *Legislative Effectiveness in Congress*. Cambridge University Press.

Volden, Craig, and Alan E. Wiseman. 2018. "Legislative Effectiveness in the United States Senate." *Journal of Politics* 80: 731–35.

Voorheis, John, Nolan McCarty, and Boris Shor. 2015. "Unequal Incomes, Ideology and Gridlock: How Rising Inequality Increases Political Polarization." *Social Science Research Network*, August 21. https://dx.doi.org/10.2139/ssrn.2649215.

Wager, Emily. 2024. "People Like Us? How Mass Preferences Are Shaped by Economic Inequality and Racial Diversity." *State Politics and Policy Quarterly* 24: 167–206.

Walker, Karen. 1995. "'Always There for Me': Friendship Patterns and Expectations Among Middle and Working-Class Men and Women." *Sociological Forum* 10: 273–96.

Walter, Barbara. 2022. *How Civil Wars Start: And How to Stop Them.* Crown.

Weeden, Jason, and Robert Kurzban. 2017. "Self-Interest Is Often a Major Determinant of Issue Attitudes." *Political Psychology* 38: 67–90.

Weeks, Ana Catalano. 2022. *Making Gender Salient: From Gender Quota Laws to Policy.* Cambridge University Press.

Weingast, Barry R. 1979. "A Rational Choice Perspective on Congressional Norms." *American Journal of Political Science* 24: 245–62.

Weingast, Barry W., and William J. Marshall. 1988. "The Industrial Organization of Congress, or, Why Legislatures, Like Firms, Are Not Organized as Markets." *Journal of Political Economy* 96: 132–63.

West, Emily A. 2017. "Descriptive Representation and Political Efficacy: Evidence from Obama and Clinton." *Journal of Politics* 79: 351–55.

White, Joseph, and Aaron Wildavsky. 1989. *The Deficit and the Public Interest: The Search for Responsible Budgeting in the 1980s.* University of California Press.

Wink, Kenneth, C. Donald Livingston, and James C. Garand. 1996. "Dispositions, Constituencies, and Cross-Pressures: Modeling Roll-Call Voting on the North American Free Trade Agreement in the U.S. House." *Political Research Quarterly* 49: 351–76.

Witko, Christopher, and Sally Friedman. 2008. "Business Backgrounds and Congressional Behavior." *Congress and the Presidency* 35: 71–86.

Witko, Christopher, Jana Morgan, Nathan J. Kelly, and Peter K. Enns. 2021. *Hijacking the Agenda: Economic Power and Political Influence.* Russell Sage Foundation.

Williamson, Vanessa S. 2017. *Read My Lips: Why Americans Are Proud to Pay Taxes.* Princeton University Press.

Winters, Jeffrey A., and Benjamin I. Page. 2009. "Oligarchy in the United States?" *Perspectives on Politics* 7: 731–51.

Wlezien, Christopher. 1995. "The Public as Thermostat." *American Journal of Political Science* 39: 981–1000.

Wlezien, Christopher. 2017. "Public Opinion and Policy Representation: On Conceptualization, Measurement, and Interpretation." *Policy Studies Journal* 45: 561–82.

Wlezien, Christopher, and Stuart Soroka. 2011. "Inequality in Policy Responsiveness?" In *Who Gets Represented?*, edited by Peter K. Enns and Christopher Wlezien, 285–310. Russell Sage Foundation.

Wlezien, Christopher, and Stuart Soroka. 2021. "Trends in Public Support for Welfare Spending: How the Economy Matters." *British Journal of Political Science* 51: 163–80.

Wolak, Jennifer, and David A. M. Peterson. 2020. "The Dynamic American Dream." *American Journal of Political Science* 64: 968–81.

Wong, Cara. 2010. *Boundaries of Obligation in American Politics: Geographic, National, and Racial Communities.* Cambridge University Press.

Wu, Jennifer D. 2021. "Work Requirements and Perceived Deservingness of Medicaid." *American Politics Research* 49: 30–45.

Xu, Ping, and James C. Garand. 2010. "Economic Context and Americans' Perceptions of Income Inequality." *Social Science Quarterly* 91: 1220–41.

Younis, Mohamed. 2019. "Four in 10 Americans Embrace Some Form of Socialism." Gallup, May 20. https://news.gallup.com/poll/257639/four-americans-embrace-form-socialism.aspx.

Zacher, Sam. 2024a. "Polarization of the Rich: The New Democratic Allegiance of Affluent Americans and the Politics of Redistribution." *Perspectives on Politics* 22: 338–56.

Zacher, Sam. 2024b. "What Forms of Redistribution Do Americans Want? Understanding Preferences for Policy Benefit-Cost Tradeoffs." *Political Research Quarterly* 77, no. 4: 1146–63. https://doi.org/10.1177/10659129241260413.

Zaller, John R. 1992. *The Nature and Origins of Mass Opinion*. Cambridge University Press.

Zeleny, Jeff. 2008. "Obama Remarks Called 'Out of Touch.'" *New York Times*, April 12: A15.

Zelizer, Julian E. 2015. *The Fierce Urgency of Now: Lyndon Johnson, Congress, and the Battle for the Great Society*. Penguin Press.

Zengerle, Jason. 2024. "The Blue-Collar Democrats Who Wants to Fix the Party's Other Big Problem." *New York Times*, July 7 (Sunday Magazine): 20.

Zingher, Joshua N. 2018. "Polarization, Demographic Change, and White Flight from the Democratic Party." *Journal of Politics* 80: 860–72.

Zingher, Joshua N. 2022a. "Diploma Divide: Educational Attainment and the Realignment of the American Electorate." *Political Research Quarterly* 75: 263–77.

Zingher, Joshua N. 2022b. *Political Choice in a Polarized America: How Elite Polarization Shapes Mass Behavior*. Oxford University Press.

Zingher, Joshua N. 2023. "How Educational Attainment Moderates the Recursive Relationship Between Policy Orientation and Partisanship." *American Politics Research* 51: 480–91.

Zingher, Joshua N., and Michael E. Flynn. 2019. "Does Polarization Affect Even the Inattentive? Assessing the Relationship between Political Sophistication, Policy Orientations, and Elite Cues." *Electoral Studies* 57: 131–42.

Zumbrun, Josh, Feliz Solomon, and Jeffrey Lewis. 2020. "U.S.-China Trade War Reshaped Global Commerce." *Wall Street Journal*, February 9. https://www.wsj.com/articles/u-s-china -trade-war-reshaped-global-commerce-11581244201.

Index

Page numbers followed by "f" and "t" refer to figures and tables, respectively.

www.ingramcontent.com/pod-product-compliance
Lightning Source LLC
Chambersburg PA
CBHW022138020426
42334CB00015B/948